OXFORD EUROPEAN COMMUNITY LAW SERIES

General Editor: F. G. Jacobs
Advocate-General, The Court of Justice
of the European Communities

EC Tax Law

OXFORD EUROPEAN COMMUNITY LAW SERIES

The aim of this series is to publish important and original studies of the various branches of European Community Law. Each work will provide a clear, concise, and critical exposition of the law in its social, economic, and political context, at a level which will interest the advanced student, the practitioner, the academic, and government and Community officials.

Other Titles in this Series

The European Internal Market and International Trade: A Legal Analysis
P. Eeckhout

The Law of Money and Financial Services in the European Community
J.A. Usher

Legal Aspects of Agriculture in the European Community
J.A. Usher

European Community Sex Equality Law
Evelyn Ellis

European Community Competition Law
Second Edition
Dan Goyder

EC TAX LAW

PAUL FARMER

LL.B., M.Phil., A.C.A.

Legal Secretary, Court of Justice of the European Communities

and

RICHARD LYAL

B.A., LL.B., B.C.L., D.E.S.

Member of the Legal Service, Commission of the European Communities

CLARENDON PRESS · OXFORD

This book has been printed digitally and produced in a standard specification in order to ensure its continuing availability

OXFORD
UNIVERSITY PRESS

Great Clarendon Street, Oxford OX2 6DP

Oxford University Press is a department of the University of Oxford.
It furthers the University's objective of excellence in research, scholarship,
and education by publishing worldwide in

Oxford New York

Auckland Bangkok Buenos Aires Cape Town Chennai
Dar es Salaam Delhi Hong Kong Istanbul Karachi Kolkata
Kuala Lumpur Madrid Melbourne Mexico City Mumbai Nairobi
São Paulo Shanghai Taipei Tokyo Toronto

Oxford is a registered trade mark of Oxford University Press
in the UK and in certain other countries

Published in the United States
by Oxford University Press Inc., New York

Reprinted 2003

ISBN 0-19-825764-3

Preface

The purpose of this book is to give a comprehensive account of EC tax legislation and case law which will be useful to students and practitioners. We have sought to cater for the needs both of Community lawyers who need some knowledge of the specialised field of taxation, and of tax lawyers and accountants who need some knowledge of the Community dimension which is of increasing importance in their work. Accordingly, we have discussed in some detail the relevant Treaty provisions and their application, the legislation on VAT and other indirect taxation, the recent legislation on company taxation, and the case law; we have taken into account material available to us in May 1994. For better understanding of the situation today we have included a chapter on the development of EC tax law. We have, however, omitted any discussion of the provisions on capital duty, partly because it is of limited interest to British and Irish readers and partly because we regard it as a perverse tax which should have been abolished long ago.

Paul Farmer wrote chapters 4 to 9, 11 to 14, and 16, while Richard Lyal wrote chapters 1 to 3, 10 and 15; however, each of us has commented on the other's drafts. It should be self-evident that the views expressed are strictly our own and in no way reflect the position of any Community institution. We have been fairly free in our critical remarks, and some of them will certainly arouse disagreement; we welcome comments from readers.

Our thanks are due to a host of people who commented on early drafts of one or more chapters and pointed us in the right direction: in particular, John Arnold, chartered accountant and VAT consultant; Malcolm Gammie, of Linklaters & Paines; Professor Ben Terra, of Moret, Ernst & Young, Judge David Edward, Vanessa Edwards, Piet Eeckhout and Timothy Millett, of the Court of Justice of the European Communities; Servaas van Thiel, of the Council of the European Union; and Stephen Bill, Michael Bott, Daniel Calleja, Henri Etienne and Dirk Schelpe, of the European Commission. We are also grateful to Kate Elliott for turning our ill-disciplined drafts into a book and especially to Francis Jacobs for his support, guidance and patience.

Paul Farmer
Richard Lyal
July 1994

General Editor's Foreword

The impact of Community law on tax is now an essential concern, and for a variety of reasons. Certain important areas of tax law are of course directly governed by Community law, notably value added tax, excise duty and some areas of company tax; here the EC Treaty, Community legislation, and a substantial body of case-law have to be taken into account. Moreover all taxes on inter-State trade fall within the scope of Community law; the Treaty prohibition of discriminatory taxation is for this purpose broadly construed, and the scope of this prohibition is the subject of a complex body of case-law. But the impact of Community law is potentially far broader, since tax in general, like all other economic activities, is increasingly affected by it, and the whole range of the Treaty may be relevant. In particular—and increasingly in recent years—the fundamental freedoms of the Treaty, and other general provisions of Community law, have been shown to impinge on areas of taxation—including direct taxation—which otherwise would fall within the fiscal sovereignty of the Member States. In all these ways, tax intersects with many aspects of the Treaty. Understanding the impact of Community law on tax therefore requires both the expertise of the tax specialist and a familiarity with the Treaty as a whole, and with the approach by the Court of Justice to its interpretation.

This book succeeds in explaining the subject from those different perspectives, and will meet the needs both of the practitioner and of the student, being both practical and scholarly in its approach. It includes detailed and systematic analysis of the Treaty's tax provisions; clear exposition of the legislation, both on VAT and also in other areas including the recent legislation on company taxation; and careful and original discussion of the developing impact of the Treaty's fundamental freedoms on direct taxation. Constructive discussion of the case-law of the Court of Justice, with close analysis of the reasoning of the judgments and of the Opinions of the Advocates General, gives the reader an exceptionally clear insight into the Court's approach to the texts, showing also how the Court's approach reflects a systematic process of interpretation which not infrequently differs from what a tax specialist might expect. Both the tax specialist and the generalist Community lawyer will thus benefit greatly from the authors' guidance.

By reason of its approach, and its appeal to the scholar and the practitioner, the book is a valuable addition to the Oxford Series on European Community Law. It places its subject squarely in its historical context, paying special attention to the historical development of Community tax law without which the subject cannot be properly understood, while its authors' expertise also succeeds in setting the subject in the relevant economic and fiscal context.

September 1994 — Francis G. Jacobs

Contents

Table of Cases xi

Table of Legislation xx

1. Introduction 1
2. Development of Tax Harmonization in the Community 13

Indirect Taxation and VAT

3. The Tax Provisions of the Treaty: Articles 95 to 99 34
4. Basic Principles and Scope of the Common System of Value Added Tax 85
5. Place of Supply and International Transactions 135
6. Domestic Exemptions 170
7. The Right of Deduction 190
8. Payment of Tax, Rates, and Administration 199
9. Special Schemes and Derogating Measures 214
10. Excise Duties and Similar Taxes 225

Direct Taxation and Company Taxation

11. Introduction to Company Taxation 246
12. The Parent–Subsidiary Directive 254
13. The Merger Directive 277
14. Proposals for Further Legislation on Company Taxation and the Report of the Ruding Committee 293
15. The Arbitration Convention 300
16. The Prohibition of Discrimination and the Fundamental Freedoms: Their Impact in the Sphere of Direct Taxation 309

Conclusion

17. Conclusions and Prospects 336

Further Reading 341

Index 343

Table of Cases from the European Court of Justice and Court of First Instance

Aldo Bozzi *v* Cassa Nazionale di Previdenza a favore degli avvocati e dei 'procuratori legali' (Case C 347/90) [1992] ECR I-2947 133
Amministrazione delle Finanze dello Stato *v* Essevi and Salengo (Joined Cases 142 and 143/80) [1981] ECR 1413 ....35, 46, 70, 71
Amministrazione delle Finanze *v* San Giorgio (Case 199/82) [1983] ECR 3595...76–7
Apple & Pear Development Council *v* Commissioners of Customs and Excise (Case 102/86) [1988] ECR 1443..........................125–6
Apple & Pear Development Council *v* Lewis (Case 222/82) [1983] ECR 4083 ....46, 52
Atlas Marketing *v* Commissioners of Customs and Excise (UK) [1986] 1 CMLR 71...111
Ayuntamiento de Sevilla *v* Recaudadores de las Zonas Primera y Segunda (Case C-202/90) [1991] ECR I-4247 (*pending*) 115, 116

BAZ Bausystem *v* Finanzamt München (Case 222/81) [1982] ECR 2527 ..128
BLP Group plc *v* Commissioners of Customs and Excise (Case C-4/94)....114
Bachmann *v* Belgian State (Case C-204/90) [1992] ECR I-249.....325, 327, 328, 329, 330–3, 336
Balocchi *v* Ministero delle Finanze dello Stato (Case C-10/92) [1993] ECR I-5105...209
Banco de Crédito Industrial *v* Ayuntamiento de Valencia (Case 387/92) [1994] ECR I-877..7
Bauhuis *v* Netherlands (Case 46/76) [1977] ECR 5 ....52, 53
Beaulande *v* Directeur des Services Fiscaux de Nantes (Case 208/91) [1992] ECR I-6709 133
Becker *v* Finanzamt Münster-Innenstadt (Case 8/81) [1982] ECR 53.....173
Bergeres-Becque *v* Service Interrégional des Douanes (Case 39/85) [1986] ECR 259..64
Bergandi *v* Directeur Général des Impôts (Case 252/86) [1988] ECR 1343.......................................42, 47, 70, 73, 132
Berkholz *v* Finanzamt Hamburg (Case 168/84) [1985] ECR 2251 158–60
Biehl *v* Administration des Contributions de Luxembourg (Case 175/88) [1990] ECR I 1779..............................323, 324, 325
Bobie Getränkevertrieb *v* Hauptzollamt Aachen-Nord (Case 127/75) [1976] ECR 1079...70

Bond van Adverteerders *v* Netherlands (Case 352/85) [1988] ECR 2085 326
Boots *v* Commissioners of Customs and Excise (Case C-126/88) [1990] ECR I 1235 121
Boussac *v* Gerstenmeier (Case 22/80) [1980] ECR 3427 313
British Airways plc *v* Commissioners of Customs and Excise (UK) [1990] STC 643 97

Capolongo *v* Maya (Case 77/72) [1973] ECR 611 . . . . . 40, 41, 44, 62
'Cassis de Dijon' see: Rewe-Zentrale *v* Bundesmonopolverwaltung für Branntwein CELBI *v* Fazenda Pùblica (Case C-266/91) [1993] ECR I-4337 . . . . . 41, 45
Chaussures Bally *v* Ministère des Finances (Case C-18/92) [1993] ECR 1 2871 . . . . . 127, 188
Chemial Farmaceutici *v* DAF (Case 140/79) [1981] ECR 1 . . . 36, 74, 75, 233
Claeys (Case 114/91) [1992] ECR I 6599 41
Co-Frutta *v* Amministrazione delle Finanze dello Stato (Case 193/85) [1987] ECR 2085 . . . . . 40, 51, 65
Cogis *v* Amministrazione delle Finanze dello Stato (Case 216/81) [1982] ECR 2701 . . . . . 58–9, 66, 75
Commerz-Credit-Bank AG-Europartner *v* Finanzamt Saarbrücken (Case 50/91) [1992] ECR I-5225 285
Commission *v* Belgium (Case 77/69) [1970] ECR 237 60
Commission *v* Belgium (Case 314/82) [1984] ECR 1543 . . . . . 42, 48
Commission *v* Belgium (Case 324/82) [1984] ECR 1861 . . . . . 120, 223
Commission *v* Belgium (Case 221/85) [1987] ECR 719 311
Commission *v* Belgium (Case 356/85) [1987] ECR 3299 . . . . . 66, 68
Commission *v* Belgium (Case C 153/89) [1991] ECR I-3171 . . . . . 71, 78, 234
Commission *v* Belgium (Case 300/90) [1992] ECR I-305 327
Commission *v* Belgium and Luxembourg ('Pain d'épices') (Joined Cases 2 and 3/62) [1962] ECR 425 . . . . . 38, 48
Commission *v* Denmark (Case 171/78) [1980] ECR 447 . . . . . 27, 36, 57, 58, 67, 68
Commission *v* Denmark (Case 106/84) [1986] ECR 833 . . . . . 59, 66, 73, 75
Commission *v* Denmark (Case 47/88) [1990] ECR I-4509 . . . . . 43, 54
Commission *v* France (Case 168/78) [1980] ECR 347 . . . . . 6, 27, 35, 57, 58, 65, 66, 68
Commission *v* France (Case 90/79) [1981] ECR 283 40
Commission *v* France (Case 270/83) [1986] ECR 273 . . . . . 312, 313–5, 316, 318, 323, 330, 331, 332
Commission *v* France (vins doux naturels) (Case 196/85) [1987] ECR 1597 . . . . . 70, 71, 72, 235
Commission *v* France (Case 50/87) [1988] ECR 4797 . . . . . 110, 190

Commission *v* France (Case C 276/91) [1993] ECR I-4413 . . . . 61, 64
Commission *v* France (Case 68/92) [1993] ECR I-5881 155
Commission *v* Germany (Case 107/84) [1985] ECR 2655 . . . . . 116, 173, 175
Commission *v* Germany (Case 205/84) [1986] ECR 3755 . . . . . 311, 318, 326, 331, 333
Commission *v* Germany (Case C 195/90) [1992] ECR I-3141 . . . . 47, 243
Commission *v* Germany (Case C 74/91) [1992] ECR I-5437 219
Commission *v* Greece (Case 305/87) [1989] ECR 1461 310
Commission *v* Greece (Case C 132/88) [1990] ECR I-1567 73
Commission *v* Greece (Case C 105/91) [1992] ECR I-5871 43
Commission *v* Ireland (Case 55/79) [1980] ECR 481 . . . . 36, 48, 61
Commission *v* Ireland (Case 17/84) [1985] ECR 2375 219
Commission *v* Ireland (Case 415) [1988] ECR 3097 204
Commission *v* Italy (Case 13/63) [1963] ECR 165 67
Commission *v* Italy (Case 45/64) [1965] ECR 857; [1969] ECR 433 . . 47, 74
Commission *v* Italy (Case 7/68) [1968] ECR 423 43
Commission *v* Italy (Case 24/68) [1969] ECR 193 . . . . 38, 39
Commission *v* Italy (Case 7/69) [1970] ECR 111 60
Commission *v* Italy (Case 16/69) [1969] ECR 377 . . . . 18, 60, 75
Commission *v* Italy (Case 28/69) [1970] ECR 187 57
Commission *v* Italy (Case 169/78) [1980] ECR 385 . . . . 27, 57, 58, 68
Commission *v* Italy (Case 21/79) [1980] ECR 1 . . . . 35, 61
Commission *v* Italy (Case 73/79) [1980] ECR 1533 . . . . 41, 45, 62
Commission *v* Italy (Case 319/81) [1983] ECR 601 . . . . 59, 65, 71, 72, 73
Commission *v* Italy (Case 277/83) [1985] ECR 2049 . . . . 68, 73
Commission *v* Italy (Case 278/83) [1985] ECR 2503 . . . . 72, 73
Commission *v* Italy (Case 184/85) [1987] ECR 2013 . . . . 59, 65
Commission *v* Italy (Case 200/85) [1986] ECR 3953 . . . . 67, 70, 73
Commission *v* Italy (Case 3/86) [1988] ECR 3369 216
Commission *v* Italy (Case 104/86) [1988] ECR 1799 77
Commission *v* Italy (Case 257/86) [1988] ECR 3249 61
Commission *v* Italy (Case 323/87) [1989] ECR 2275 . . . . 35, 48, 68, 75
Commission *v* Italy (Case C 3/88) [1989] ECR 4035 313
Commission *v* Luxembourg (Case C-152/89) [1991] ECR I 3141 . . . . 71, 78, 234
Commission *v* Luxembourg (Case 351/90) [1992] ECR I-3945 311
Commission *v* Luxembourg (Case 69/92) [1993] ECR I-5907 155
Commission *v* Netherlands (Case 16/84) [1985] ECR 2355 219
Commission *v* Netherlands (Case 235/85) [1987] ECR 1471 . . . 108, 114, 116
Commission *v* Spain (Case 73/92) [1993] ECR I-5997 155
Commission *v* United Kingdom (Case 170/78) [1980] ECR 417 (interlocutory); [1983] ECR 2265 (final) 27, 57, 58, 59, 65, 66, 67, 68, 72
Commission *v* United Kingdom (Case 353/85) [1988] ECR 817 . . . . 173, 176

Commission *v* United Kingdom (Case 416/85) [1988] ECR 3127........204
Commissioners of Customs and Excise *v* Lord Fisher (UK) [1981] STC 238........111
Compagnie Alitalia (France) [1990] 1 CMLR 248........102
Compagnie Commerciale de l'Ouest *v* Receveur Principal des Douanes (Joined Cases C 78/90 to C 83/90) [1992] ECR I-1847........41, 45
Comune di Carpaneto Piacentino *v* Ufficio Provinciale Imposta sul Valore Aggiunto di Piacenza (Case C 4/89) [1990] ECR I-1869........116, 197
Cucchi *v* Avez (Case 77/76) [1977] ECR 987........41, 44, 45, 62

Daily Mail *see*: Queen (The) *v* HM Treasury and Commissioners of Inland Revenue *ex p.* Daily Mail and General Trust plc
Dansk Denkavit *v* Ministeriet for Skatter og Afgifter (Case 42/83) [1984] ECR 2649........37, 61
Dansk Denkavit *v* Danish Ministry of Agriculture (Case 29/87) [1988] ECR 2965........43, 62
Dansk Denkavit *v* Skatteministeriet (Case C 200/90) [1992] ECR I-2217...133
De Jong *v* Staatssecretaris van Financiën (Case C-20/91) [1992] ECR I-2847........101, 103
Demag *v* Finanzamt Duisburg-Süd (Case 27/74) [1974] ECR 1037........42, 55, 78
Demoor Gilbert en Zonen *v* Belgium (Joined Cases 144 and 145/91) [1992] ECR I-6613........41
Deutschmann *v* Germany (Case 10/65) [1965] ECR 469........38, 46
Deville *v* Administration des Impôts (Case 240/87) [1988] ECR 3513.....76
Direct Cosmetics Ltd *v* Commissioners of Customs and Excise (Case 5/84) [1985] ECR 617........223
Direct Cosmetics Ltd and Laughtons Photographs Ltd *v* Commissioners of Customs and Excise (Joined Cases 138 and 139/86) [1988] ECR 3937........224
Drexl (Case 299/86) [1988] ECR 1213........61

Einberger *v* Hauptzollamt Freiburg ('Einberger I') (Case 240/81) [1982] ECR 3699........130
Einberger *v* Hauptzollamt Freiburg ('Einberger II') (Case 294/82) [1984] ECR 1177........130
Empire Stores *v* Commissioners of Customs and Excise (Case C 33/93) [1994] ECR I-2345........122

FOR *v* VKS (Case 54/72) [1973] ECR 193........61
Feldain *v* Directeur des Services Fiscaux (Case 433/85) [1987] ECR 3521........73, 76
Finanzamt Köln-Altstadt *v* Roland Schumacker (Case C-279/93) (*pending*)...324

Finanzamt Uelzen *v* Armbrecht (Case C-291/92) 102
Fink-Frucht *v* Hauptzollamt München Landesbergerstraße (Case 27/67) [1968] ECR 233 . . . . 40, 43, 57, 65, 66
France *v* Commission (Case 47/69) [1970] ECR 487 46

Geddo *v* Ente Nazionale Risi (Case 2/73) [1973] ECR 865. 74
Giant NV *v* Gemeente Overijse (Case C-109/90) [1991] ECR I 1385 133
Glawe *v* Finanzamt Hamburg-Barmbek-Uhlenhorst (Case C-38/93) [1994] ECR I-1679 189

Halliburton Services BV *v* Staatssecretaris van Financiën (Case C-1/93) [1994] ECR I-1137 . . . . 317–18, 329
Hamann *v* Finanzamt Hamburg-Eimsbüttel (Case 51/88) [1989] ECR 767 156
Hansen *v* Hauptzollamt Flensburg (Case 91/78) [1979] ECR 935 49
Hansen & Balle *v* Hauptzollamt Flensburg (Case 148/77) [1978] ECR 1787 49
Happy Family *v* Inspecteur der Omzetbelasting (Case 289/86) [1988] ECR 3655 131
Hauptzollamt Flensburg *v* Andresen (Case 4/81) [1981] ECR 2835 . . . . 44, 48
Hauptzollamt Flensburg *v* Hansen (Case 38/82) [1983] ECR 1271 71
Hauptzollamt Mainz *v* Kupferberg (Case 104/81) [1982] ECR 3641 . . . 49, 59
Haydon-Baillie *v* Commissioners of Customs and Excise (UK) [1985] VATTR 232 111
Horvath *v* Hauptzollamt Hamburg-Jonas (Case 50/80) [1981] ECR 385 130
Hulst *v* Produktschap voor Siergewassen (Case 51/74) [1975] ECR 79 . . . . 41, 42, 52, 53, 55
Humblot *v* Directeur des Services Fiscaux (Case 112/84) [1985] ECR 1367 . . . . 47, 68, 73, 76

IGAV *v* Ente Nazionale per la Cellulosa e per la Carta (Case 94/74) [1975] ECR 699 . . . . 38, 41
Iannelli & Volpi *v* Meroni (Case 74/76) [1977] ECR 557 . . . . . . 42, 45, 46, 60
Interzuccheri *v* Rezzano e Cavassa (Case 105/76) [1977] ECR 1029 . . . . 41, 45, 46
'Intiem' *see*: Leesportefeuille 'Intiem' CV *v* Staatssecretaris van Financiën

Jeunehomme and Others *v* Belgian State (Joined Cases 123 and 334/87) [1988] ECR 4517 208
John Walker *v* Ministeriet for Skatter og Afgifter (Case 243/84) [1986] ECR 875 73–4

Just v Ministry for Fiscal Affairs (Case 68/79) [1980] ECR 501 .... 51, 73, 77

Keck & Mithouard (Joined Cases C-267 and C-268/91) [1993] ECR I-6097 .... 44, 329
Kerrutt *v* Finanzamt Mönchengladbach-Mitte (Case 73/85) [1986] ECR 2219 133
Knoors *v* Secretary of State for Economic Affairs (Case 115/78) [1979] ECR 399 323
Konstantinidis *v* Stadt Altensteig and Others (Case C-168/91) [1993] ECR I-1191 311
Kraus *v* Land Baden-Württemberg (Case C-19/92) [1993] ECR I-1663 .... 311, 326
Kühne *v* Finanzamt München III (Case 50/88) [1989] ECR 1925 .... 101, 104
Kunstmühle Twoli *v* Hauptzollamt Würtburg (Case 20/67) [1968] ECR 199 40

Lambert *v* Directeur des Services Fiscaux (Joined Cases 317/86, 48, 49, 285 and 363 to 367/87 and 65 and 78 to 80/88) [1989] ECR 787 .... 73, 133
Lange *v* Finanzamt Fürstfeldenbruck (Case 111/92) [1993] ECR I-4677 131
Leesportefeuille 'Intiem' CV *v* Staatssecretaris van Financiën (Case 165/86) [1988] ECR 1471 191
Legros *v* Administration des Douanes (Case C-163/90) [1992] ECR I-4625 39
Lennartz *v* Finanzamt München III (Case C-97/90) [1991] ECR I-3795 .... 102, 103, 112, 194, 197, 223
Lornoy *v* Belgium (Case C-17/91) [1992] ECR I 6523 41
Lubbock Fine *v* Commissioners of Customs and Excise (Case C 63/92) [1993] ECR I-6665 184
Lütticke *v* Commission (Case 4/69) [1971] ECR 325 80
Lütticke *v* Commission (Case 48/65) [1966] ECR 19 80
Lütticke *v* Hauptzollamt Saarlouis (Case 57/65) [1966] ECR 205 .... 36, 39, 40, 79–80

Mander Laundries Ltd [1973] VATTR 136 97
Metalsa (Case C 312/91) [1993] ECR I-3751 49
Michael Jackson Bloodstock Ltd *v* Commissioners of Customs and Excise (UK) (LON 90/650 X (7863) 111
Milch-, Fett- und Eierkontor *v* Hauptzollamt Saarbrücken (Case 25/67) [1968] ECR 207 80
Ministère Public et Direction du Travail et de l'Emploi *v* Levy (Case 158/91) [1993] ECR I-4287 319

Mohsche *v* Finanzamt München III (Case C-193/91) [1993] ECR I-2615 .... 104, 106
Mol *v* Inspecteur der Invoerrechten en Accijnzen (Case 269/86) [1988] ECR 3627 131
Mölkerei Zentrale Westfalen/Lippe *v* Hauptzollamt Paderborn (Case 28/67) [1968] ECR 143 .... 47, 64
Muwi Bouwgroep *v* Staatssecretaris van Financiën (Case C-164/90) [1991] ECR I-6049 284
Muys' en de Winter's Bouw- en Aannemingsbedrijf BV *v* Staatssecretaris van Financiën (Case C-281/91) [1993] ECR I-5405.... 97, 98, 128, 172, 187

Naturally Yours Cosmetics Ltd *v* Commissioners of Customs and Excise (Case 230/87) [1988] ECR 6365........ 122, 123
Nederlandse Ondernemingen *v* Inspecteur der Invoerrechten en Accijnzen (Case 51/76) [1977] ECR 113 196
Nederlandse Spoorwegen *v* Staatssecretaris van Financiën (Case 126/78) [1979] ECR 2041........ 97

ORO Amsterdam Beheer BV and Concerto BV *v* Inspecteur der Omzetbelasting, Amsterdam (Case C-165/88) [1989] ECR 4081.... 191, 219
Office National de l'Emploi *v* Minne (Case C-13/93) [1994] ECR I...... 319
Officier van Justitie *v* Kortmann (Case 32/80) [1981] ECR 251........ 40, 43, 47, 62, 64

Pabst & Richarz *v* Hauptzollamt Oldenburg (Case 17/81) [1982] ECR 1331. 45, 50, 65
Peureux *v* Directeur des Services Fiscaux de la Haute-Saône (Case 86/78) [1979] ECR 897 .... 45, 49
Polydor *v* Harlequin (Case 270/80) [1982] ECR 329 49
Polysar Investments Netherlands BV *v* Inspecteur der Invoerrechten en Accijnzen te Arnhem (Case C-60/90) [1991] ECR I-3111... 99, 110, 112, 113

Queen (The) *v* Inland Revenue Commissioners, *ex parte* Commerzbank (Case C-330/91) [1993] ECR I-4017........ 313, 316
Queen (The) *v* HM Treasury and Commissioners of Inland Revenue *ex parte* Daily Mail and General Trust plc (Case 81/87) [1988] ECR 5483 .... 312, 319, 331

Rewe *v* Hauptzollamt Landau/Pfalz (Case 45/75) [1976] ECR 181........ 44, 48, 57, 58, 60, 61, 65
Rewe-Zentrale *v* Bundesmonopolverwaltung für Branntwein ('Cassis de Dijon') (Case 120/78) [1979] ECR 649........ 42, 43, 70, 74, 310, 326
Rompelman *v* Minister van Financiën (Case 268/83) [1985] ECR 655 ... 112

Rousseau Wilmot SA *v* Organic (Case 295/84) [1985] ECR 3759 ... 132, 134
Rumhaus Hansen *v* Hauptzollamt Flensburg (Case 153/80) [1981] ECR 1165 ... 71

SATAM SA (now 'Sofitam') *v* Ministre chargé du Budget (Case C-333/91) [1993] ECR I 3513 ... 100, 113, 195
SUFA *see*: Stiching Uitvoering Financiële Acties *v* Staatssecretaris van Financiën
Säger *v* Dennemeyer (Case C 76/90) [1991] ECR I-4221 ... 326, 329, 330
Sanders Adour *v* Directeur des Services Fiscaux des Pyrenées Atlantiques (Joined Cases C-149 and C-150/91) [1992] ECR I-3899 ... 41
Scharbatke *v* Germany (Case C-72/92) [1993] ECR I-5509 ... 41, 56, 63
Schloh *v* Auto Contrôle Technique (Case 50/85) [1986] ECR 1855 ... 42, 47
Schneider Import *v* Hauptzollamt Mainz (Case 26/80) [1980] ECR 3469 ... 35, 70, 71
Schöttle *v* Finanzamt Freudenstadt (Case 20/76) [1977] ECR 247 ... 47
Schul *v* Inspecteur der Invoerrechten en Accijnzen ('Schul I') (Case 15/81) [1982] ECR 1409 ... 27, 35, 37, 56, 62–3, 64
'Schul II' *see*: Staatssecretaris van Financiën *v* Gaston Schul Douane-Expediteur
Seguela and Others *v* Administration des Impôts (Joined Cases 76, 86–89 and 149/87) [1988] ECR 2397 ... 76
Simmenthal *v* Minister of Finance (Case 35/76) [1976] ECR 1871 ... 42, 47
Skatteministeriet *v* Henriksen (Case 173/88) [1989] ECR 2763 ... 185
Sociaal Fonds voor de Diamantarbeiders *v* Brachfeld (Joined Cases 2 and 3/69) [1969] ECR 211 ... 38
Sofitam *see*: SATAM SA
Sotgiu *v* Deutsche Bundespost (Case 152/73) [1974] ECR 153 ... 313
Staatssecretaris van Financiën *v* Coöperatieve Aardappelenbewaarplaats (Case 154/80) [1981] ECR 445 ... 120, 121, 125, 179
Staatssecretaris van Financiën *v* Gaston Schul Douane-Expediteur (Case 'Schul II') (Case 47/84) [1985] ECR 1491 ... 64
Staatssecretaris van Financiën *v* Hong Kong Trade Development Council (Case 89/81) [1982] ECR 1277 ... 109, 179
Staatssecretaris van Financiën *v* Shipping and Forwarding Enterprise SAFE BV (Case 320/88) [1990] ECR I-285 ... 90, 93, 100
Statens Kontrol med Ædle Metaller *v* Larsen (Case 142/77) [1978] ECR 1543 ... 37, 52, 59, 63, 74
Steinike and Weinlig *v* Germany (Case 78/76) [1977] ECR 595 ... 39
Stitching Collectieve Anttennevoorziening Gouda *v* Commissariaat voor de Media (Case C-288/89) [1991] ECR I-4007 ... 326
Stitching Uitvoering Financiële Acties *v* Staatssecretaris van Financiën (Case 348/87) [1989] ECR 1737 ... 173, 177

Stier *v* Hauptzollamt Hamburg-Ericus (Case 31/67) [1968] ECR 235 .... 40, 43
Stirling *v* Commissioners of Customs and Excise (UK) [1985] VATTR 232 111

Tolsma *v* Inspecteur der Omzetbelasting Leeuwarden (Case C 16/93) [1994] ECR I-743 126
Trafalgar Tours *v* Commissioners of Customs and Excise [1990] STC 127 119

Ufficio Distrettuale delle Imposte di Fiorenzuola d'Arda *v* Comune di Carpaneto Piacentino (Case 231/87) [1989] ECR 3233 .... 116, 197
United Brands *v* Commission (Case 27/76) [1978] ECR 207 59

Van Binsbergen *v* Bestuur van de Bedrijfsvereniging voor de Metaalnijverheid (Case 33/74) [1974] ECR 1299 311
Van Dijk's Boekhuis *v* Staatssecretaris van Financiën (Case 139/84) [1985] ECR 1405 96
Van Eycke *v* ASPA (Case 267/86) [1988] ECR 4769 48
Van Ginkel BV *v* Inspecteur der Omzetbelasting, Utrecht (Case C 163/91) [1992] ECR I-5723 .... 217, 218
Van Tiem *v* Staatssecretaris van Financiën (Case C-186/89) [1990] ECR I-4363 .... 108, 113
Vinal *v* Orbat (Case 46/80) [1981] ECR 77 .... 36, 74, 75, 233
Vlassopoulou (Case C 340/89) [1991] ECR I-2357 .... 311, 318, 326

Werner *v* Finanzamt Aachen-Innenstadt (Case C-112/91) [1993] ECR I 429 322
Wisselink *v* Staatssecretaris van Financiën (Cases 93 and 94/88) [1989] ECR 2671 133
Witzemann *v* Hauptzollamt München-Mitte (Case C-343/89) [1990] ECR I-4477 .... 130, 131
Wohrmann *v* Hauptzollamt Bad Reichenhall (Case 7/67) [1968] ECR 177 39
Wolf *v* Hauptzollamt Düsseldorf (Case 221/81) [1982] ECR 3688 ... 130, 131

Table of Legislation

EUROPEAN COMMUNITY TREATIES and CONVENTIONS

Act of Accession (UK)
  Article 28 92
Arbitration Convention of 23 July 1990 (OJ 1990 L225/10).... 6, 297, 300–8
EC Treaty (Treaty of Rome) 1, 3, 92, 309–335
  Articles 2 .... 35, 63, 65, 130
  Article 3.......... 35, 63, 65
    (b) 130, 131
  Article 5 319
  Article 6 .... 7, 309, 310–11, 318
  Article 7a 82–3
  Article 8a.......... 82
  Articles 9.......... 35, 38, 50, 52, 161
  Article 10 161
  Article 12.......... 37, 38–42, 43, 51, 55, 78
  Article 13 .... 37, 38–42, 51
  Article 16.......... 52, 54–5
  Article 29 131
  Article 30.......... 35, 37, 42–4, 49, 51, 54, 70, 310, 325, 326, 329
  Article 34.......... 52, 54–5
  Article 36.......... 42, 43
  Article 37.......... 37, 44–5
  Article 40(3) 52
  Article 48 .... 7, 8, 309, 310, 311, 323–9
    (1), (2) 324
  Article 52 .... 7, 8, 266–7, 280, 309, 310, 311–35
  Article 54(3) 283, 284, 320, 322
  Article 58.......... 311, 312, 317, 320, 331
  Article 59 .... 7, 8, 309, 310, 313, 318, 323, 325–9
  Article 67.......... 19, 31
  Article 73b 9, 309, 310, 333–5
    Article c 334
    Article d.......... 8, 333–5
  Article 75.......... 241, 243
  Article 76.......... 7, 243
  Article 85 59
  Article 86 59

Article 92 .... 7, 37, 45–6, 62
Article 93 .... 7, 37, 45–6, 62
Article 95 .... 3, 6, 8, 18, 27, 34–84, 91, 232, 234, 237
Para. 1 .... 56–65, 66
Para. 2 .... 56–7, 58, 65–8
Article 96 .... 3, 6, 34, 47, 54, 55, 77–8, 79–81, 82, 234
Article 97 .... 6, 14, 34, 78, 79–81
Article 98 .... 6, 34, 47, 78, 81–2
Article 99 .... 6, 7, 9, 36, 82–4, 91, 226, 241, 243
Article 100 .... 6, 7, 82, 83, 246, 254, 277, 301–2, 307, 309
Article 100a 7
Article 101 .... 7, 82, 83
Article 115 51
Article 169 .... 38, 80, 118, 307, 319
Article 177 308
Article 220 .... 6, 27, 246, 302, 307, 309, 319, 320
Article 221 7
Article 227 91
(2) 49, 91
(3), (4), (5) 92
Article 234 319
Article 235 8
Annex IV 91, 92
Brussels Convention on jurisdiction and enforcement of judgments .. 302, 308
EEC Treaty (see: EC Treaty) 3, 13
ECSC Treaty 13, 161
Article 7 7
Single European Act 8, 27–8, 82, 238
Treaty on European Union (Maastricht Treaty) 3, 7, 8, 309, 333–4
Treaty of Rome 1

COMMUNITY INSTRUMENTS

Decisions

Decision 30/53 (OJ 1953 109) 13
Decision 65/271 (OJ, English Spec. Ed., 1965–1960, 67) 241
Decision 70/192 (OJ, English Spec. Ed., Second Series, x, 11) 22
Decision 70/243 (OJ, English Spec. Ed., 1970 (I) 224) 86
Article 4 .... 18, 86
Decision 70/549 (OJ, English Spec. Ed., Second Series, I(2), 164)
Article 5(1) 49
Decision 86/283 (OJ 1986 L175/1) 49

Decision 89/466 (OJ 1989 L226/23) 183
Decision 89/659 (OJ 1989 L394/1) 7
Decision 90/127 (OJ 1990 L72/32) 108
Decision 92/510 (OJ 1992 L316/16) 30, 240

Directives

Directive (OJ 1960, 921) (OJ, English Spec. Ed., 1959–1962, 49) 19
Directive (1962, 2214) 81
Directive 63/2 (OJ, English Spec. Ed., 1963–64, 5) 19
Directive 67/227 (OJ, English Spec. Ed., 1967, 14) (1st VAT Directive) 18, 85, 86
  Article 2 .... 85–6, 87, 90, 120, 122, 132, 190
Directive 67/228 (OJ, English Spec. Ed., 1967, 16) (2nd VAT Directive) .. 18, 85, 86, 87, 96, 98, 120
  Article 2 121
  Article 6(2) 86
  Article 10 .... 56, 61
    (3) 86, 170
  Article 14 214
  Article 17 .... 86, 204, 205
    (1) 190
  Annex B 97, 189
Directive 68/221 (OJ, English Spec. Ed., 1968 (I), 114) 81
Directive 68/297 (OJ, English Spec. Ed., 1968 (II), 313) 228
Directive 69/12 (OJ 1969 L10/14) 81
Directive 69/69 (OJ 1969 L52/6) 81
Directive 69/169 (OJ, English Spec. Ed., 1969 (I), 232) 19, 163, 228
Directive 69/335 (OJ, English Spec. Ed., 1969 (II), 412) 19, 285, 287
  Article 7(1) 284–5
Directive 69/463 (OJ, English Spec. Ed., 1969 (II), 551) 85
Directive 71/401 (OJ 1971, L283/41) 85
Directive 72/464 (OJ 1972 L303/1) 230, 231
Directive 72/250 (OJ 1972, L162/18) 85
Directive 74/651 (OJ 1974, L354/57) 19, 163, 228
Directive 76/308 (OJ 1976 L73/18) 24, 228
Directive 77/388 (OJ 1977 L145/1) (6th VAT Directive) . 26, 29, 30, 86–134, 135–169, 220, 256, 333, 337
  Article 2 .... 90–1, 92, 108, 111, 119, 121, 139, 161
  Article 3 .... 148, 161
    (2), (3) 91, 92, 167
    (4) 92
  Article 4 112
    (1) 108–9, 114

(2) . . . 108
(3) . . . 108–9, 182, 183
(4) . . . 108, 113, 114, 115, 117–18, 212
(5) . . . 115–17, 125, 180, 197
Article 5 . . . 92, 99, 141, 147, 273
(1) . . . 92, 96, 100, 103, 141
(2) . . . 95
(3) . . . 94, 95, 96, 99, 186
(4) . . . 94–5, 99, 199
(5) . . . 96–7, 99, 145
(6) . . . 97, 100–1, 103, 105, 107, 124, 127
(7) . . . 97, 99, 106, 127, 183, 184, 190
(8) . . . 97, 107, 108
Article 6 . . . 92, 97
(1) . . . 93, 99
(2) . . . 100–1, 103, 104–5, 106, 127, 209
(3) . . . 99, 106, 127, 190, 212
(4) . . . 95
(5) . . . 107–8
Article 7 . . . 139
(1) . . . 161, 166, 169
(2) . . . 161
(3) . . . 161, 164, 168, 169, 200
Article 8(1) . . . 139, 141–2, 150, 151, 152
(2) . . . 150, 164
Article 9 . . . 154–160, 181, 191
(1) . . . 154, 157, 158, 159, 160
(2) . . 99, 109, 154, 155, 156, 157, 158, 159, 160, 166, 181, 187, 192, 206
Article 10 . . . 199, 209
(1) . . . 199
(2) . . . 199, 205
(3) . . . 130, 164, 169, 200, 205
Article 11 . . . 120–1, 124, 219
(A) . . . 105–7, 119, 121, 126–9, 146, 191, 194, 203, 217
(B) . . . 64, 129, 166, 203
(C) . . . 128, 129, 210
Article 12(1) . . . 203, 205
(3) . . . 202, 203, 220
(4) . . . 201, 202
(5) . . . 205
Article 13 . . . 116, 163, 167, 168, 170–189
(A) . . . 109, 171–3, 175–81
(B) . . . 98, 114, 128, 172, 181–9, 192, 195, 196, 220

(C) 103, 147, 170, 173, 174, 181–4, 187, 192, 196
Article 14 167
(1) 149, 162–7, 191, 193
(2) 162
Article 15 . . . . . . 56, 132, 139, 142, 144, 147, 167–8, 191, 193, 221
(1), (2) 167
(3) 168
(4) 218
Article 16 . . . . . . 170, 191, 193
(1) 161–2, 168, 169, 212
(2) 169, 191, 212
(3) 164
Article 17 . . . . . . 113, 197, 201
(1) 190, 194, 199
(2) 114, 151, 190, 191, 193, 197
(3) 146, 149, 150, 151, 152, 166, 167, 187, 191–3
(4) 149, 150, 192, 193, 216
(5) 194–5
(6) 102, 185, 194
(7) 212
Article 18(1), (2) 197, 198
Article 18(3), (4) 198
Article 19(1) 113, 194, 195
(2) 100, 195
(3) 195
Article 20 . . . . . . 107, 184, 185, 209
(2) 104, 106, 196, 197
(3), (4) 196, 197
(5) 196, 197, 212
Article 21 . . . . . . 108, 109, 136, 153, 158, 159
(1) 193, 205, 206, 207, 210
(2) 163
Article 22 . . . . . . 136, 138, 207, 208, 217
(2) 146, 208
(3) 98, 208
(4) 199, 209, 217
(5) 209
(6) 153, 209, 210
Article 22(7), (8), (9), ... 211
(10) 210
(11) 144, 211
(12) 210
Article 24 . . . . . . 117, 122, 142, 148, 220

(1) 212, 214, 215, 217
(2)–(6) 214
(8) 215
Article 25 .... 142, 215
(2) 215, 216
(3) 216
(4) 217
(5) 216
(6), (8) 216
(9) 217
(10), (12) 217
Article 26 .... 189, 217, 218, 219
Article a 203, 220, 221
Article 27 .... 102, 111, 121, 223
(1) 222, 223, 224
(2), (4) 222
(5) 222, 223
Article 28 .... 116, 136
(1a) 203
(2) 201, 203, 204, 205
(3) 89, 95, 174, 175, 176, 180, 185, 107, 218
(4) 174
Article 28 (a) 90–1, 97, 119, 129, 139–52, 146, 147, 148, 149, 150, 151, 152, 164, 166, 190–1, 207, 210, 216, 221
(b) 139–40, 142, 144, 148, 149, 150, 151, 152, 153, 156, 157, 206, 217, 221
(c) 129, 143, 146, 147, 148, 149, 151, 152, 153, 163, 164, 169, 191, 193, 200, 205, 206, 209, 210, 221
(d) 199, 200
(e) 128, 129, 146
(f) 150, 151, 166, 167, 197
(g) 136, 205
(h) 136, 144, 146, 199, 207
(i) 214
(j) 216, 217
(l) 136, 221
(o) 221, 222
Article 29 .... 106, 196
(1), (2) 212
Article 32 .... 219, 220
Article 33 .... 132–4, 143, 182, 188, 244
(a) 161–2, 169
Article 34 116

Article 36 87
Annex A. 215, 216
Annex B 216
Annex C 217
Annex D 116, 117, 125, 180
Annex E. 174, 176, 180, 183, 218
Annex F 174, 175, 176, 180, 183, 188, 189, 218, 219
Annex G 174, 175, 176, 180
Annex H. 202–4
Annex I. 220
Directive 77/799 (OJ 1977 L336/15) 24, 29, 211, 302, 317
Directive 77/805 (OJ 1977 L338/22) 230
Directive 78/855 (OJ 1978 L295/36) (3rd Company Law Directive)
Articles 3, 4, 24 283
Directive 78/1035 (OJ 1978 L366/34) 19
Directive 79/32 (OJ 1979 L10/8) 230
Directive 79/1070 (OJ 1979 L331/8) 24, 211, 228, 317
Directive 79/1071 (OJ 1979 L331/10) 24, 228
Directive 79/1072 (OJ 1979 L331/11) (8th VAT Directive) 26, 88, 109, 150, 159, 160, 192–3
Article 1 193
Article 2 192
Articles 3 ff. 193
Article 7(1) 193
Directive 80/368 (OJ 1980 L90/41) (11th VAT Directive) 26
Directive 82/891 (OJ 1982 L378/47) (6th Company Law Directive) 284
Directive 83/181 (OJ 1983 L105/38) 89, 163, 165
Directive 83/182 (OJ 1983 L105/59) 163
Directive 83/183 (OJ 1983 105/64) 163, 228
Directive 84/386 (OJ 1984 L208/58) (10th VAT Directive) 26
Directive 85/361 (OJ 1985 L192/18) (20th VAT Directive) 26
Directive 85/362 (OJ 1985 L192/20) (17th VAT Directive) 26, 163, 164
Directive 86/246 (OJ 1986 L164/26) 230
Directive 86/560 (OJ 1986 L326/40) (13th VAT Directive) 26, 89, 109, 150, 159, 160, 192–3
Article 1(2) 181
Article 2(2) 193
Directive 88/361 (OJ 1988 L178/5) 31
Directive 88/663 (OJ 1988 L382/40) 163
Directive 89/219 (OJ 1989 L92/13) 163
Directive 89/465 (OJ 1989 L226/21) (18th VAT Directive) 26, 89, 174, 189
Article 1(1) 174
Article 2 189

Directive 89/604 (OJ 1989 L348/28) 163
Directive 90/434 (OJ 1990 L225/1) ('Merger Directive') 7, 10, 31, 246–7, 270, 277–92, 302, 307, 316, 338
Article 1 .... 279–80, 288
Article 2 280–5
Article 3 .... 279, 280
Article 4 .... 285–7, 289
Article 5 287–8
Article 6 288
Article 7 288–9
Article 8 289–90
Article 9 .... 286, 288
Article 10 .... 280, 286, 290–1
Article 11 .... 260, 291–2
Directive 90/435 (OJ 1990 L225/6) ('Parent–Subsidiary Directive') 7, 10, 31, 246–7, 255–76, 279, 280, 291, 294, 295, 297, 298, 302, 307, 316, 338
Article 1 .... 256–62, 265, 268, 269
Article 2 .... 261, 262–7, 268, 279
Article 3 .... 256, 267–8, 288
Article 4 .... 261, 266, 268–70, 271, 272, 273
Article 5 .... 269, 270–5
Article 6 275
Article 7 .... 274, 275–6
Annex 262, 279
Directive 91/191 (OJ 1991 L94/24) 163
Directive 91/680 (OJ 1991 L376/1) 9, 29, 88, 119, 128, 129, 135, 136, 144, 152, 156, 158, 162, 164, 167, 168, 187, 190, 197, 207, 208, 216, 217
Article 1(1) 91
(2) 139, 161, 164
(3), (5) 150, 164
(6) 199, 200
(8) 166
(11) 163, 166
Articles 1 (12) ff. 167
(14)–(19) 168
(20) 169
(23) 143
(24) 163
Article 2 163
(1) 166
Directive 92/12 (OJ 1992 L76/1) 30, 138, 143, 144, 149, 227, 228, 239, 245, 317

Article 1(12) 149
Article 3(3) 240
Directive 92/77 (OJ 1992 L316/1) 30, 69, 89, 201
Article 1(2), (3) 202
Directives 92/78 to 92/84 30
Directive 92/78 (OJ 1992 L316/5) 231
Directive 92/79 (OJ 1992 L316/8) 231
Directive 92/80 (OJ 1992 L316/10) 231
Directive 92/81 (OJ 1992 L316/12) 30, 228, 239
Article 8(1) 240
(4) 240
Directive 92/82 (OJ) 1992 L316/19) 239, 240
Directive 92/83 (OJ 1992 L316/21) 236
Article 15 237
Directive 92/84 (OJ 1992 L316/29) 237
Directive 92/108 (OJ 1992 L390/124) 30, 143, 228
Directive 92/111 (OJ 1992 L384/47) 9, 29, 88, 92, 119, 135, 153, 158, 162, 163, 164, 168, 202, 207, 208
Article 1(1) 91
(2) 162
(3) 161
(4) 150
(5) 129
(6) 205
(7) 202
(8) 166
(9) 167, 168
(10) 142, 143, 147
(11) 151, 153
(12) 143
(14) 199, 200
(15) 200
(16) 128
(17) 128, 205
(18) 190, 191, 193
(19) 153, 205
(20) 144, 153, 207, 208, 209, 210
(21) 214
(23) 161
Article 2 197
Article 4 135
(2) 153
Directive 93/89 (OJ 1993 L279/32) 243

Directive 94/5 (OJ 1994 L60/16) 29, 129, 145, 203, 205, 220, 221
Article 2 222

Recommendations

Commission Recommendation 76/2 (OJ 1976 L2/13) 23
Commission Recommendation 94/79 (OJ 1994 L39/22) 32, 324

Commission Regulations

Reg. 3046/92 (OJ 1992 L307/27) 211
Reg. 3590/92 (OJ 1992 L364/32) 211

Council Regulations

Reg. 1612/68 (OJ, English Spec. Ed. 1968(II), 475) 7, 32
Article 7 ....32, 324
Reg. 284/72 (OJ L301/166)..50
Reg. 918/83 (OJ 1983 L105/1).......................................165
Reg. 2137/85 (OJ 1985 L199/1) 322
Reg. 2144/87 (OJ 1987 L201/15)
Article 2(2) 131
Reg. 2658/87 (OJ 19897 L256/1)
Annex I...236
Reg. 1553/89 (OJ 1989 L155/9)
Article 2(1) 170
Article 2(2) 174
Reg. 4064/89 (OJ 1989 L395/1) ('Merger Regulation')
Article 3(3) 312
Reg. 3330/91 (OJ 1991 L316/1) 211
Reg. 218/92 (OJ 1992 L24/1)..............................29, 84, 211
Reg. 2913/92 (OJ 1992 L302/1).......................................49
Articles 28–36 129
Articles 91 ff...161
Articles 137 ff..161
Articles 163 ff..161
Articles 185–7 166
Reg. 2551/93 (OJ 1993 L241/1) 236
Reg. 3118/93 (OJ 1993 L279/1) 243

Resolutions

Resolution of 21 Apr. 1970 (OJ 1970 C50/1) 229
Resolution of 22 March 1971 (OJ, English Spec. ED., Second Series, ix, 40) 22
Resolution of 21 Mar. 1972 (OJ, English Spec. ED., Second Series, ix, 65)..23
Resolution of 10 Feb. 1975 (OJ 1975 C35/1) 24

INTERNATIONAL TREATIES, AGREEMENTS and CONVENTIONS

Agreement between the EEC and Portugal of 22 July 1972
  Article 21 50
Agreement between the EEC and Greece
  Article 53(1) 50
Agreement on the European Economic Area (EEA) 8
  Article 1 50
  Article 14 50
General Agreement on Tariffs and Trade 3, 6
  Article III 3, 34, 35, 51, 55
OECD Model Convention 1963 279
OECD Model Double Taxation Convention 301, 302
  Article 7 .... 301, 303
  Article 9 301
OECD Model Income Tax Convention 1977
  Articles 11, 12 294
OECD Model Income Tax Convention 268
  Article 4 263–4
  Article 5 278
  Article 7 278
  Article 9 272
  Article 10 .... 267, 271, 274
  Article 11 272
  Article 23 248
  Article 25 272
United States–Netherlands Treaty
  Article 26 319

DOMESTIC LEGISLATION

Denmark

Act of 18 Dec. 1987 133

France

Code Général des Impôts
  Article 209 .... 259, 314
Livre de Procédures Fiscales
  Article L64 257

Germany

Abgabenordnung
s. 42 257
Kapitalanlagegesellschaftengesetzt 265
Körperschaftsteuergesetz
s. 26(8) 270
Umwandlungsteuergesetz
s. 25(4) 292

Luxembourg

Act of 31 July 1929 265

The Netherlands

Corporation Tax Act 1969
Article 28 265

United Kingdom

Finance Act 1984
ss. 82, 91 259
Finance Act 1988
s. 158 321
Income and Corporation Taxes Act 1988
ss. 770, 773(4) 301
Value Added Tax Act 1983
s. 10(3) 121, 122
Sched. 4 224

1

Introduction

From its inception the European Community has had an impact on tax law. Although the Treaty of Rome itself contained few provisions expressly concerned with tax, and these were directed mainly at the elimination of tax discrimination on the importation and exportation of goods, the Community institutions soon turned their attention to tax harmonization. Today the taxation of goods and services is primarily governed by Community law under the common system of Value Added Tax, and some of the proceeds are attributed to the Community as part of its revenue. The Community itself raises agricultural levies and taxes coal and steel products. Excise duties and transport taxes are harmonized to some extent. Some aspects of company taxation are subject to common rules, while others may entail consultation between tax authorities. There is provision for the exchange of information between the tax authorities of Member States and for co-operation in recovering tax debts.

THE ROLE OF TAX IN THE COMMUNITY FRAMEWORK

The first question which arises in a study of this kind is a fundamental one: why should the Community be involved in matters of taxation in the first place? The power to tax, both as a means of gathering revenue and as an instrument of economic management, is one of the most basic and jealously guarded prerogatives of the state, and it might be expected that the Member States would be reluctant to allow the Community to trespass on their jurisdiction in this area. How a Member State raises the money necessary for the functions of its government is, it might be argued, entirely its own affair. It may of course choose, either unilaterally or by agreement with other states, to limit its right to tax in order to eliminate or reduce double taxation of traders or individuals whose income falls within the tax jurisdiction claimed by two or more states. Similarly, it may, if it so wishes, restrict its indirect taxes to goods which are consumed within its territory by introducing a system of frontier tax adjustments under which goods are exported free of tax. In other respects, however, its system of taxation is no business of other states or of supranational organizations.

That, of course, is at best a simplistic view and, in a community of states whose aim is to create an economic area with the characteristics of an internal market, one which is wholly untenable. In the sphere of direct taxation classical forms of unilateral or bilateral tax relief can address only a few of the tax-induced distortions in cross-border trade and investment, which range from the obvious problems of discriminatory taxation of non-residents, double taxation of cross-border income flows, and failure to extend relief for losses and business reorganizations to cross-border operations, to the more deep-seated distortions arising from the differing returns on cross-border investment in the absence of harmonized tax rates and bases. With respect to indirect taxes, even frontier tax adjustments are made difficult by the cumulative multi-stage taxes on turnover traditionally applied by many states, since accurate calculation of the tax burden on goods at any given commercial stage is impossible. Tax adjustments themselves may be a source of discrimination, and the very existence of tax frontiers presents an obstacle to the free flow of goods. Where tax frontiers are eliminated, differences in tax rates and the tax base may lead to cross-border shopping or relocation of suppliers. Accordingly, it is natural that fiscal measures which impinge on the free movement of goods, services, workers, and capital and equal conditions of competition should be a matter of fundamental Community concern and give rise to a need for accommodation or harmonization.

Tax harmonization is, however, a difficult and sensitive process since it does not relate merely to technical issues. Taxation reflects economic, social, and political conditions and budgetary requirements in the state concerned, and any harmonization which is to be effective is likely to conflict with one or more of those interests in several Member States. This makes it particularly necessary in the field of tax to identify—and explain—clearly the benefits expected to flow from harmonization. Moreover, full harmonization may not always be necessary; in many cases it may be possible to achieve Community goals of free movement and fair competition by less intrusive means. The early success enjoyed by the Community in harmonizing turnover taxes was due mainly to a general awareness of the need for reform and to the convincing case put for the introduction of a common system of value added tax. Member States have yet to find the same compelling need for harmonization of company taxes.

TYPES OF TAXATION

There are probably as many possible kinds of tax as there are government treasuries with fertile imaginations. Leaving aside specific policy considerations, it is generally accepted that a 'good' tax must nevertheless meet three criteria: it should be easy to calculate, cheap to collect, and hard to evade. It should also be perceived as fair by the bulk of the population who are called upon to pay it. Modern taxes are levied on the basis of more or less clearly defined statutory rules and criteria of universal application; 'Morton's fork' is no longer an acceptable method of assessment. Although taxes are very varied in form, it is often thought useful to classify them as 'direct' and 'indirect', and much of the discussion in this book reflects that distinction. The distinction itself is a difficult one. The criterion is most frequently said to be whether or not the burden of the tax in question can be shifted by the taxpayer to someone else. It is not always clear, however, that turnover taxes, the paradigm of indirect taxes, are shifted in their entirety to consumers, and it is arguable that corporation taxes, usually classified as direct taxes, are shifted in both directions, that is to say both to customers and to shareholders. In general, taxes on individuals and corporations—income tax, wealth tax, corporate income tax, capital gains tax, etc.—are regarded as direct taxes, while taxes on goods or transactions—consumption taxes, stamp duties, etc.—are considered indirect.

Within the category of indirect taxes a further important distinction, in the context of international trade, relates to the manner in which sales taxes or other taxes on goods are levied, or more specifically by whom. Here the classical distinction is between origin and destination taxation, that is to say whether goods are taxed by (and at the rates applicable in) the country of exportation or the country of importation. The choice of system has implications not only for the revenue of the states concerned. In an origin system, for example, the goods of a country which charges high rates of tax are placed at a competitive disadvantage in other countries (and vice versa), while the operation of a destination system requires frontier tax adjustments, formalities which may themselves impede trade. As will be seen, initially the Community—like the GATT before it—assumed and provided for the retention of a destination system.[1] However, the simple dichotomy of origin and destination taxation is truly appropriate only in relation to a single-stage tax. In a multi-stage system, especially one operated in common by a number of states, intermediate solutions are conceivable, in particular the taxation by each state of the stages which take place within its territory. This has been referred to as a 'common market' or 'tax union' system.[2]

PRE-EXISTING SYSTEMS

When the EEC Treaty[3] came into force in 1958 each of the original six Member States[4] had a range of direct and indirect taxes. Their systems were broadly similar: all had some form of income tax for individuals, corporation

[1] See Arts. 95 and 96 of the Treaty; cf Art. III of GATT.

[2] See in particular D. Biehl, *Ausfuhrlandprinzip, Einfuhrlandprinzip und Gemeinsamer Markt-Prinzip* (Cologne: Heymanns, 1969).

[3] Now called the EC Treaty, after the entry into force of the Maastricht Treaty on European Union.

[4] Belgium, West Germany, France, Italy, Luxembourg, and the Netherlands.

tax calculated on business profits, gift and succession duties, some form of tax on land and buildings, turnover tax, and other indirect taxes including excise duties.[5] However, there was great diversity in the structures of those taxes and in the distribution of revenue; for example, the Netherlands derived a large proportion of tax revenue from individual income tax, whereas Italy, at the other extreme, relied heavily on a great variety of indirect taxes. Nor were tax structures stable; for example, most Member States had experimented with different types of corporate income tax, and continued to do so.[6] Some of those disparities presented obvious obstacles to trade within the Community, while others had a more subtle distortive effect on conditions of competition.

With regard to indirect taxation, France had a system of Value Added Tax similar to that now in force throughout the Community. It applied only as far as the wholesale stage, largely on the assumption that the accounts of small retailers were not sufficiently sophisticated to permit the application of a tax on monthly sales with a credit for inputs. Retailers (and wholesalers on an optional basis) paid a local turnover tax on total sales. The French system was hailed at the time as 'a model of what a turnover tax should be',[7] mainly because of its neutrality in relation to the organization of production and distribution.

The other Member States had cumulative multi-stage turnover taxes at low rates—that is to say, taxes payable each time goods changed hands, with no repayment of input tax. Even here, however, there was no uniformity. Tax was payable up to the retail stage in some states but not in others. Some states taxed (imaginary) transfers within integrated businesses while others exempted transactions between related businesses (for example the *Organschaft* rule in Germany). Some states taxed all goods and services in a uniform manner while others had separate taxes for goods and services. This 'cascade' system was recognized to be unsatisfactory, above all because it encouraged vertical integration and discouraged economically efficient specialization; the total amount of tax ultimately paid on any product depended on the number of stages through which it had passed. It also made the accurate calculation of frontier tax adjustments impossible. The application of composite rates at a single stage for some products and the existence of a variety of exemptions and different rates merely compounded the problem.

The Member States charged excise duties on differing groups of products, at differing rates and on different bases. All the Member States applied the destination principle to indirect taxes; exports were exempted from excise duty and turnover tax, and tax already paid was refundable, while tax was payable on the importation of goods.

[5] A description of the systems existing at the time may be found in the Neumark Report, discussed in Ch. 2, and in E. B. Nortcliffe, *Common Market Fiscal Systems* (London: Sweet & Maxwell, 1960).

[6] See the introduction to A. J. van den Tempel, *Corporation Tax and Individual Income Tax in the European Communities* (Brussels: E. C. Commission, 1970), referred to in Ch. 2.

[7] Nortcliffe, *Common Market Fiscal Systems*, 47.

In the field of direct taxation, there was not always a clear distinction between company tax and individual income tax, and in some countries different types of income were taxed in different ways. For example, Italy charged schedular taxes at fixed rates on interest income, business profits of individuals and companies, and income from employment. Individuals then paid a progressive surtax on aggregate income (and a household income tax charged by local authorities), and companies paid a combined tax on capital and profits. Similarly, in Belgium there were separate taxes on income from the use of capital and on income from employment or retained business profits (*taxe professionnelle*); again, individuals paid a progressive surtax on all income. Both these countries thus had what was called a 'dual' or 'analytic' system of income taxation; France had applied a similar system until 1948. Some countries had an annual wealth tax on individuals. In relation to company tax there were considerable disparities in arrangements for avoiding economic double taxation of distributed profits, in the taxation of non-residents, and in the treatment of foreign income. Some states had a dual-rate system for distributed and retained profits, while others applied a classical system in which all corporate income was taxed at a uniform rate and distributed profits were then subject to income tax in the hands of shareholders (although France, for example, granted some relief on payments of dividends by subsidiaries to their parent companies). In general the income arising from the permanent establishment of a non-resident was taxed essentially on the same basis as that of a resident, but the treatment of other income varied. Most of the Member States taxed all income of residents from domestic or foreign sources (the main exception being Italy, where the schedular taxes were in general payable only on income from domestic sources), but most provided some form of relief for tax paid in the source country. All the Member States had double taxation treaties with other countries, but there was not a complete 'grid' of such treaties and the treaties that did exist were inconsistent in their attribution of primary tax jurisdiction and the form of relief. The calculation of taxable business profits also varied considerably.

Certain Member States also had tax monopolies, public bodies with the sole right to manufacture or sell specific products (such as tobacco, spirits, and even matches) and collect tax on them. Such monopolies could by their mere existence raise barriers to imports, quite apart from the tax implications.

The addition of new Member States further complicated matters. With the exception of Greece, Portugal, and the United Kingdom, the States which acceded to the Community after the introduction of the common system of Value Added Tax had introduced VAT before accession (the same is true of the four EFTA countries which are due to join the Community in 1995[8]), but the arrival of Denmark, Ireland, and the United Kingdom in 1973

[8] Austria, Finland, Norway, and Sweden.

exacerbated the differences in excise duty rates, if not the range of products on which duty was payable. Similarly, the new Member States had varying approaches to company tax.

TREATY PROVISIONS

The provisions of the EC Treaty which are directly concerned with taxation are restricted in their scope. The main tax provisions are Articles 95 to 99, in Title I (Common rules) of Part Three of the Treaty (Policy of the Community). They deal almost exclusively with indirect taxation, but their position in the Treaty shows that they are directed not solely at the free movement of goods but more generally at the achievement of the Community's objectives as a whole. In particular, the Court of Justice has remarked on their relevance to the objective of free and fair competition among businesses from all Member States.[9] Articles 95 and 96, which reflect the relevant provisions of the GATT, provide for border tax adjustments; Articles 97 and 98 add provisions for the application of those principles. They assume a destination system of taxation (one in which goods are taxed by and in the country in which they are consumed) and seek simply to eliminate discrimination in the taxation of imports and exports. It is through its case law on Article 95 in particular that the Court of Justice has exerted a strong influence on the development of a Community law of taxation.

Article 99 gives the Council the power to adopt legislation for the harmonization of national law on turnover taxes, excise duties, and other forms of indirect taxation. It has been (part of) the legal basis for the existing legislation on VAT and on excise duties and is the proposed legal basis for the draft legislation still under discussion in those fields; it is one of the legal bases for legislation and draft legislation on capital duty and taxation of transfers of securities, on a carbon tax, and on road tax for heavy goods vehicles.

A further Treaty provision which refers directly to tax is Article 220, which requires Member States, in so far as is necessary, to enter into negotiations for the abolition of double taxation. The utility of this provision may be questioned, since measures which result in double taxation within the Community must be presumed to affect the functioning of the common market, so that harmonization measures may be taken under Article 100. The only tax convention adopted under Article 220 is the 1990 Arbitration Convention (Convention on the elimination of double taxation in connection with the adjustment of profits of associated enterprises).[10]

[9] See, e.g., Case 168/78, *Commission* v. *France* [1980] ECR 347.

[10] OJ 1990, L 225/10; discussed in Ch. 15. The Commission's original proposal was for a directive under Art. 100. The Member States have also entered into a series of bilateral double taxation conventions, and some commentators suggest that these at least partly fulfil the Member States' obligation under Art. 220.

The provisions which refer specifically to tax are not, however, the only ones with any bearing on the matter. Many provisions dealing with particular areas of Community concern may have tax implications. Examples are Article 6,[11] which prohibits discrimination on grounds of nationality in matters within the scope of the Treaty, Article 48 on freedom of movement for workers (and the implementing regulation, Regulation No 1612/68),[12] Article 52 on freedom of establishment, Article 59 on freedom to provide services, Article 76 on transport, and Article 221 on equal treatment of foreign investors. The sections of the Treaty on freedom of movement also contain provisions giving legislative powers, as do the sections on transport and on the environment, and they may become the legal basis for measures harmonizing relevant tax legislation.[13] The provisions on state aid in Articles 92 to 94 prevent Member States from granting tax exemptions or concessions as a form of subsidy to national industries.[14]

Furthermore, under Articles 100 and 101 of the Treaty the Council has jurisdiction to adopt directives for the approximation of provisions of national law. Article 100 allows the Council to legislate in relation to provisions which 'directly affect' the establishment or functioning of the common market. This wording is, on the face of it, rather broader than that of Article 99; it may be doubted, though, whether that entails any real difference in the Council's authority. Since Article 99 is concerned only with indirect taxation, it is to Article 100 that the Council has had recourse in adopting legislation on direct taxation such as the Merger and Parent–Subsidiary Directives.[15] Like Article 99, Article 100 requires the Council to act unanimously. Article 100a, introduced by the Single European Act, allows the Council to act by a qualified majority in adopting measures concerning the establishment or functioning of the internal market, but fiscal provisions are expressly excluded from the scope of this procedural relaxation.

Where a difference in provisions of national law distorts conditions of competition, under Article 101 the Council may adopt directives and it or the Commission may take other appropriate measures. Article 101 has never been used as a basis for legislation, although it was mooted as a solution to problems of tax discrimination in the early 1960s and there was again some interest in its possibilities in the early 1980s; one of its attractions is the procedural one that it allows the Council to act by a qualified majority rather than unanimously.

[11] Formerly Art. 7, renumbered by the Maastricht Treaty on European Union.

[12] OJ 1968, L 257/13 (English Spec. Ed. 1968 (II) 475); see in particular Art. 7.

[13] e.g., the recent road tax legislation (see below, Ch. 10) is based on Arts. 75 and 99.

[14] Case C–387/92, *Banco de Crédito Industrial* v. *Ayuntamiento de Valencia* [1994] ECR I–877. See also, e.g., Commission Decision 89/659 (OJ 1989, L394/1), which declared certain aspects of a Greek tax on companies unlawful under Art. 93(2) on the ground that they constituted export aid, since export earnings were exempt from the tax.

[15] Directives 90/434 and 90/435, discussed in Chs. 12 and 13.

Finally, Article 235 should be mentioned, although its use as a legal basis for tax harmonization is perhaps unlikely, since there are more appropriate provisions for most purposes. It is a general provision which gives the Council authority to adopt legislation for which no specific powers are granted elsewhere in the Treaty but which appears necessary in order to achieve one of the objectives of the Community. It has been used, for instance, as (part of) the legal basis for environmental legislation (prior to the insertion of Title VII of Part Three of the Treaty by the Single European Act).

The amendments made to the original Treaty by the Single European Act have already been mentioned in so far as they are relevant. The amendments made by the Maastricht Treaty on European Union also contain provisions concerning tax, some of which are not entirely clear in their scope. In a series of new provisions on the free movement of capital Article 73d(1)(a) reserves the right of the Member States to apply tax provisions which distinguish between taxpayers who are not in the same situation with regard to the place of their residence or with regard to the place where their capital is invested. Article 73d(3) expressly states that such measures may not constitute a means of arbitrary discrimination or a disguised restriction on the free movement of capital and payments. Article 73d(1) also expressly allows Member States to take all necessary measures to prevent tax evasion.

Mention should also be made of the Agreement on the European Economic Area, which extends the operation of the 'four freedoms' and the competition rules to the member countries of EFTA other than Switzerland. It does not alter the position within the Community, but prohibits tax discrimination in relation to imports and exports between EC Member States and the other signatories.

THE PURPOSE OF HARMONIZATION

The need for harmonization, and the nature of the harmonization required, are determined by the aims of the Community. The primary objectives set out in the Treaty are the 'four freedoms': free movement of goods, persons, services, and capital. Linked to these fundamental pillars are a number of common policies, in particular a set of rules on free competition. The ultimate aim is an economic area with the same characteristics as an internal national market. Harmonization therefore seeks to eliminate fiscal obstacles to economic integration. It is necessary on the one hand to enable people, goods, services, and capital to move freely across political frontiers and on the other to put an end to flows of trade and capital which exist only because of tax disparities.

The Treaty provisions themselves go some way in that direction. Article 95 deals with discriminatory taxation of foreign products, and Articles 48, 52, 59, and 73b prohibit discriminatory restrictions on cross-border movement of goods, services, persons, and capital. However, removal of fiscal discrimination, that is to say, the imposition by a state of a higher level of domestic taxation on foreign goods or nationals than on its own goods or nationals, does not provide a complete answer. Obstacles to economic integration also arise from non-discriminatory measures. For example, neither frontier taxes on goods nor withholding taxes on dividends and interest payments necessarily involve discrimination prohibited by the Treaty.

Initially, however, it was the need to eliminate mutual suspicion between Member States of discrimination against imports of goods and of disguised export subsidies that provided much of the motivation for turnover tax harmonization under Article 99 of the Treaty. The introduction by the First and Second Directives[16] on turnover tax of a system of Value Added Tax based on common structures facilitated accurate frontier tax adjustments. That the tax also ensured a higher degree of competitive neutrality in domestic trade than existing turnover taxes provided an additional major incentive for its introduction. Further harmonization of the tax base became a priority when the Council decided, in 1970, to use VAT as a basis for the Community's own resources. This was substantially achieved by the Sixth Directive,[17] adopted in 1977. Only after the 1985 White Paper rekindled the drive for a true single market did the elimination of tax frontiers become a priority. Although the Commission advocated a system based on collection of tax in the country of origin, the Council was unable to reach agreement and adopted transitional arrangements reconciling the removal of frontiers with the continued collection of tax on goods in the country of destination.[18] The removal of the insulating effect of fiscal frontiers required some harmonization of rates in order to avoid significant diversions of trade due to tax-induced price variations. Only limited agreement could be reached on rates of tax, however, and the transitional arrangements contain extensive special rules designed to prevent distortions of trade. Further alignment of rates, particularly rate structures, remains desirable, as does the abolition of the remaining transitional derogations from the VAT base. The Commission must also submit proposals for a definitive system (based on collection of tax in the country of origin) by the end of 1994.

Similar considerations apply to excise duties; harmonization is necessary for the free flow of dutiable goods throughout the Community, although the fact that such goods generally remain under state supervision until the distribution stage makes the problem less acute. Following earlier partial harmonization of tobacco duties, a series of directives adopted in 1992 harmonized structures and rates of duty on the main dutiable products: tobacco, alcoholic drinks, and petroleum products. The harmonization of rates, however, was restricted

[16] See Ch. 4. [17] See Chs. 4 to 9. [18] Directives 91/680 and 92/111; see Ch. 5.

to the minimum considered necessary in order to avoid excessive cross-border shopping.

In the sphere of direct taxation, harmonization is necessary in order to enable businesses to operate freely and raise capital throughout the Community. The obstacles to economic integration arising from national systems of company taxation may be categorized under two main heads:

(*a*) distortion of cross-border investment decisions arising from the differing post-tax returns on investment in the absence of harmonized tax rates and tax base.

(*b*) specific obstacles to cross-border investment resulting from the interaction of national tax systems, in particular double taxation of profits and non-extension of reliefs to cross-border operations. Such obstacles arise, for example, from withholding taxes imposed on cross-border dividends, interest payments and royalties, non-extension of tax relief to cross-border operations and imposition of imputation taxes on foreign income.[19]

While it can scarcely be disputed that from a theoretical viewpoint a single European tax system, involving agreement on tax rates, tax base, and type of system (classical, imputation, or split-rate), would be the best means of remedying both types of obstacle, Member States are naturally reluctant to accept the resultant loss of fiscal sovereignty and budgetary freedom. The Commission has investigated in detail the possibility of full harmonization of the national tax systems, but has had success only with measures designed to remove specific obstacles. In 1991 the Council adopted the Parent–Subsidiary Directive,[20] which abolishes withholding taxes and provides for parent-company relief in respect of cross-border dividends paid by subsidiaries to their parents, and the Merger Directive[21] requiring deferral of taxation in respect of various cross-border grouping and restructuring operations. The Member States also entered into a Convention[22] providing for a mutual agreement procedure in transfer pricing disputes.

The achievement of roughly equal conditions of competition is a step further, and raises difficult questions of priorities for Member States. Both direct and indirect taxes affect the conditions of competition between businesses in different countries, and the degree of harmonization necessary in order to ensure equality is much greater than that necessary for the elimination of tax frontiers. In the absence of harmonization differences in taxation are often viewed more or less explicitly as a means of attracting businesses to a state or region; the result can be *de facto* downward harmonization and a shortfall in revenue that must be made up in other areas.

[19] These problems are discussed further in Chs. 11 to 15.
[20] See Ch. 12. [21] See Ch. 13. [22] See Ch. 15.

TAX AS A POLICY INSTRUMENT

It should be emphasized that the Community's activity in the field is largely restricted to harmonization and to attempts to eliminate or reduce the impact of tax obstacles to economic integration. The Community does not have a fiscal policy in the fullest sense of the term—that is to say, a policy using tax measures as a tool of macro-economic management—and is not likely to have one in any foreseeable future, although considerable harmonization of national macro-economic policies is inevitable if it is desired to move towards economic and monetary union. Indeed, the Community is in the rather anomalous position of having legislative power over taxation without being the recipient of the revenue, except in so far as it receives a portion of Value Added Tax (and ECSC production levies). The mandate given to the Neumark Committee in 1962[23] envisaged a redistributive role for a Community tax (along the lines of the *Finanzausgleich* system in Germany), but that suggestion was not followed up, although the various Community structural funds play a similar role to a limited extent.

Although the Community cannot have a fiscal policy in the full sense of the term, various policy considerations (economic, environmental, transport, energy, and so on) must be taken into account in any initiatives on tax harmonization. Environmental concerns in particular were taken into account, for example, in the proposals for the harmonization of excise duties on mineral oils. Moreover, the absence of a fiscal policy does not prevent the Community from adopting tax measures not solely in order to harmonize national systems but to achieve the objectives laid down in the Treaty. Rather sweeping statements were made in the early 1960s about the use of tax measures as a direct means of achieving policy objectives, and such measures have from time to time been advocated,[24] but it was not until recently that specific measures were proposed by the Commission. For example, as a supplement to its proposals for harmonization of excise duties the Commission submitted a draft directive providing for special treatment for motor fuels produced from agricultural products ('biofuels').[25] That may, however, be regarded simply as an extreme example of the influence of policy considerations in the harmonization process, particularly since provision for favourable treatment for unleaded petrol had already been made in the general proposals on rates of duty on mineral oils. The first proposal applying taxation as a policy tool

[23] See below, Ch. 2.

[24] See, e.g., the 1984 European Parliament resolution on a Community energy tax on the consumption of hydrocarbons and its effects on energy policy, OJ 1984, C127/258; the 1985 draft Council resolution on tax measures in the cultural sector (Economic and Social Committee opinion, OJ 1985, C344/1).

[25] Proposal for a Council Directive on excise duties on motor fuels from agricultural sources; see below, Ch. 10.

in its own right is the draft directive on a Community carbon and energy tax.[26] In addition to its obvious purpose of environmental protection, that proposal is seen as a means of reducing the tax burden on employment by providing an alternative source of revenue; more generally, it has been proposed that tax structures should be reviewed in order to reduce disincentives to employment and enterprise.[27] It has also been suggested that measures intended to favour small businesses should include provisions alleviating tax constraints on their establishment and operations.

[26] Proposal for a Council directive introducing a tax on carbon dioxide emissions and energy, OJ 1992, C196/1; see below, Ch. 10.

[27] Commission White Paper on Growth, Competitiveness and Employment, Bull. Supp. 6/93.

2

Development of Tax Harmonization in the Community

While the purpose of this book is to provide an account of the existing Community law on taxation, it is difficult fully to understand the law without some knowledge of its background. Community measures, in tax as in other fields, are often the fruit of long negotiation and sometimes the final result is quite different from the original proposal—indeed, it may be as useful to know what has not been done as to see what has. In particular, much of the tax legislation enacted as part of the 1992 single market project had been under discussion for twenty years and more. Moreover, the findings and conclusions of many of the studies carried out on behalf of the Commission and other institutions in the early years of the Community are still valid today.

The influence of national tax measures on the establishment and functioning of the common market was recognized at an early stage. Even before the conclusion of the EEC Treaty the obstacles to trade posed by differing systems of indirect taxation were a matter of concern in relation to the products covered by the ECSC Treaty. In 1953 the High Authority appointed a committee of experts (the Tinbergen Committee) to study the existing turnover taxes and exemptions, their effects on prices of domestic products and imports, and the economic consequences for the functioning of the common market in coal and steel of a system of destination or of origin taxation.[1] In its report the committee stated that the existing systems of turnover taxation did not permit a true destination system since it was impossible to calculate the amount of tax on a product at any given stage in the production process. An origin system was not feasible for a single product or range of products. The only practical possibility, said the committee, was a modified destination system under which tax paid at the last production stage was refunded and a corresponding import charge imposed.

The EEC Treaty came into force on 1 January 1958, and from the outset of its activities the Commission devoted considerable attention to fiscal questions. In keeping with the emphasis, in the early stages of the Community's development, on free movement of goods and the establishment of a free trade area, its initial efforts and studies were concentrated on indirect taxation, in particular turnover tax. The harmonization of turnover tax and excise duties was given high priority, because of their immediate effect on prices, the

[1] See Orders 1/53 and 2/53 of the High Authority of 5 March 1953, JO 1953, 33 and 34. For the results of the committee's recommendations, see the notice attached to Decision 30/53 of the High Authority, JO 1953, 109.

diversity of the systems applied by the Member States and the obstacle to the free movement of goods created by the resultant tax frontiers. The dissatisfaction of the Member States other than France with their 'cascade' systems of turnover tax also meant that there was political will for reform at the national level. It was thought that many other fiscal obstacles to the establishment of a common market, in particular those relating to direct taxes, could be dealt with only after certain non-fiscal matters and economic or financial choices had been resolved, but the Commission nevertheless began also to study the economic effect of direct taxation, especially taxes affecting capital movements.

THE FIRST STUDIES

Working groups composed of Commission officials and officials of national tax authorities were established to study the problems posed by the diversity of national tax systems. The working group on indirect taxation defined four main problems: the difficulties inherent in the application of the average rates of turnover tax provided for under Article 97 of the Treaty,[2] the tendency of cumulative 'cascade' systems of turnover tax to promote vertical integration, the barriers to free movement created by the retention of tax frontiers, and the obstacles to international trade created by the multiplicity of tax systems itself. Three subgroups studied various options for the removal of physical inspections at frontiers and harmonized systems of taxation.[3] Subgroup A studied the simple elimination of physical inspections at intra-Community frontiers; subgroup B a single-stage wholesale tax, with an optional retail tax; and subgroup C the alternatives of a common tax at the production stage or a common value added tax, both with an optional retail tax. Subgroup A considered the manner in which frontier tax adjustments could be made in the absence of checks at frontiers, and concluded that the disadvantages of such arrangements would outweigh the benefits so long as rates and exemptions were not harmonized. The problems it identified included the possible non-taxation of imports by individuals, the difficulty of ascertaining customs value after importation, the scope for fraud, and the difficulty of dealing with transactions other than sale.

In a preliminary report subgroups B and C considered the general requirements of a turnover tax: financial rationality and competitive neutrality. By financial rationality they meant the achievement of a high and consistent yield at the lowest possible rate of tax (thus the broadest possible tax base) and the lowest possible cost of collection, both to the state and to the taxpayer (thus

[2] See below, Ch. 3.

[3] Their reports are published in English translation with the Neumark Report as *The EEC Reports on Tax Harmonization* (Amsterdam: IBFD, 1963).

the simplest possible system). Competitive neutrality meant that taxation should have no influence on the price structure of exports and that imports should be taxed in the same way as domestic products. At the internal level there should be no difference in the tax burden according to the number of stages of production, the tax should not distinguish between different types of goods (except where differentiation was justified on economic or social grounds), and it should be easy to pass on.

Subgroup B studied the possibility of a single-stage tax at entry to the retail stage (sale to a retailer or provider of services or to the final consumer). Such a tax would impose the same tax burden on all goods. There would be no incentive to vertical integration and frontier tax adjustments would in most cases be unnecessary. However, the subgroup did not consider a single-stage wholesale tax to be a satisfactory solution, although it would be better than the existing cascade systems.

Subgroup C studied various combinations of single- and multi-stage taxes on production and added value. A value added tax was considered to be the option which best met the desiderata set out in the preliminary report, particularly if it extended to the retail stage (but some delegates regarded taxation of retailers as impractical—there was a widely-held view that retailers were incapable of keeping the necessary accounts). Even if internal tax frontiers were retained in the Community, such a tax would eliminate the other main problems identified by the working group. Moreover, it would permit the elimination of tax frontiers if tax bases and rates were unified; even in the absence of unification, special measures preserving, in effect, the destination principle would make the elimination of frontiers possible if the tax extended to the retail stage.

From the beginning the Commission was concerned not solely with obstacles to the free movement of goods but more generally with the distortion of competition and measures hindering the development of the common market as a whole. In 1960 it therefore convened a committee of fiscal and financial experts under the chairmanship of Professor Fritz Neumark. The committee was instructed to study whether and to what extent the differences in the existing systems of taxation and public finances of the Member States (including regional and local taxation and expenditure) constituted an obstacle to the achievement of a common market with the characteristics of an internal market (free movement not only of goods but also of businesses, capital, and labour) and to what extent it was possible to eliminate the disparities which gave rise to such obstacles. It was to pay particular attention to those aspects which resulted in distortion of competition. It thus had an extremely broad mandate to consider every aspect of direct and indirect taxation and public expenditure.

In its report[4] the Fiscal and Financial Committee began by summarizing

[4] *The EEC Reports on Tax Harmonization* (Amsterdam: IBFD, 1963).

the objectives of the common market and outlining the differences in the overall tax burden in each Member State, the disparities in the composition of public expenditure, and the differences in tax structures. Its attitude was not doctrinaire; it recognized that many policy differences reflected differences in consumption habits or different views on the role of taxation in influencing behaviour (taxation of alcohol, for example), the proper extent of redistribution of income and wealth, and the relationship between public and private investment.

The committee dealt briefly with the total tax burden, stating that differences in revenue as a proportion of GNP were not large and that such differences were to a large extent balanced by differences in the level of services; differences in the distribution of the tax burden between different sectors and income groups might, however, have some effect on movements of capital and people. Similarly, it was the distribution of public expenditure rather than its total size that might have a distortive effect on competition. The committee went on to point out that disparities in tax structures also affect economic integration because of the effects on the relationship of costs, prices, and incomes.

The committee made a number of far-reaching recommendations, giving particular weight to tax transparency and rationalization of tax structures. In relation to direct taxation it proposed some harmonization of individual income tax: a single general (synthetic) tax with a common structure of scales (but not necessarily rates) and a uniform definition of taxable income. Frontier workers taxed in the country of employment should, it said, enjoy the personal allowances to which they would be entitled if they were domiciled there. Free movement of capital required harmonization of capital gains tax. There should be a separate and more closely harmonized tax on companies, integrated with the income tax system in relation to distributed profits. Interest payments and dividends should be subject to a common system of withholding tax, accompanied by a tax credit; distributions to another EC company should, however, be free of withholding tax. Double tax arrangements should be harmonized or replaced by a multilateral convention.

The abolition of tax frontiers required the introduction of an origin system of indirect taxation, said the committee, but that must be a long term aim in view of the differing degrees to which the public finances of the Member States relied on indirect taxation. Even if the destination system was retained, the existing systems of turnover tax should be replaced by a common system of VAT applied up to and including the wholesale stage at a more or less uniform rate, with a supplementary retail tax for those states which so desired for budgetary reasons. A move to an origin system would require alignment of excise duty structures and rates; under the destination system agreement on the scope and method of assessment of excise duties was necessary, with some harmonization of rates. Harmonization was necessary, however, in respect of goods used in production processes (such as sugar and alcohol). Road tax on commercial vehicles should be aligned, and the relationship between it and excise duty on motor fuels harmonized. There should also be broad harmonization of taxes on capital transactions and on transport. Finally, there should be some provision for financial transfers between Member States to offset, at least partly, the differences in their economic and financial strength.

The committee set out a three-stage timetable for the measures it recommended. In the first stage the most urgent matter was the harmonization of turnover tax. Withholding tax on dividends and interest, double tax arrangements and possibly excise duty structures should also be harmonized in this stage. The second stage would see harmonized company tax and income tax and the conclusion of a multilateral double tax convention. Unimportant excise duties would be abolished and the harmonization of excise duties studied. Finally, the third stage, in which all remaining proposals should be put into effect, would also bring the establishment of a common information system, a system of financial transfers, and a Community tax court. Measures concerning taxes on capital transactions, transport, and energy could be taken whenever appropriate in the integration process.

THE FIRST STEPS IN THE HARMONIZATION OF INDIRECT TAXATION

On the basis of the Neumark Report and the reports of the working parties, in November 1962 the Commission submitted to the Council a draft directive[5] on a common system of Value Added Tax to be applied as far as the wholesale stage, with the option for Member States of levying an additional retail tax. Tax was to be charged in the country of origin, which would make possible the elimination of tax frontiers. The proposal envisaged the introduction of the new system in stages: in a first stage of up to four years, cumulative taxes would be abolished; in a second stage a Community-wide system would be introduced; and in the third stage tax frontiers would be eliminated, which might require the approximation of rates and exemptions. In its opinion on the proposal the European Parliament proposed the elimination of the first stage, so that the new system would come into force at the end of 1967, and suggested common rules on exemptions. The Commission modified its proposal accordingly, and in April 1965 it also submitted a second draft directive on rules for the application of the common system.[6] Under the new proposals the common system was to be applicable to all stages of manufacturing, processing, and wholesale and retail trade; it would thus

[5] OJ 1964, 2512 (with the opinion of the Economic and Social Committee); version as amended by the European Parliament, OJ 1963, 2631.

[6] OJ 1966, 561 (with the opinion of the Economic and Social Committee); see also the Commission notice of 3 June 1964 indicating its intentions, OJ 1964, 1800.

establish competitive neutrality both within and between Member States. Exemptions and rates were to be left to the Member States until the elimination of tax frontiers required their harmonization.

The First and Second VAT Directives were adopted by the Council in April 1967. The Commission was requested to submit proposals before the end of 1968 for the harmonization necessary for the abolition of tax frontiers; the Council would decide on the proposals before 1 January 1970 if possible. The Commission was also to submit proposals on the application of VAT in agriculture; it did so in February 1968 (draft Third Directive, providing for flat-rate taxation of farmers who were not ready for the normal system and common reduced rates of tax on imports and exports of certain agricultural products and inputs). Further harmonization was made necessary by the Council Decision of 21 April 1970 on Community own resources; the attribution to the Community budget of a portion of VAT required a common basis of assessment for the tax, which would also prevent the Member States from applying the system in such a way as to favour particular goods or groups of persons.

The Commission accelerated its work on excise duties, particularly since it considered that the distortive effects of differences in excise duty structures would become more acute after the abolition of customs duties between Member States on 1 July 1968 and the harmonization of turnover tax. The needs of the common agricultural, transport, and energy policies also favoured harmonization. The Commission identified three categories: duties which should be harmonized (including alcohol, beer, sugar, tobacco, and petroleum products; further study was required for other drinks and sugar substitutes), those which need not (local taxes with no effect on trade between Member States), and those which should be abolished or could be integrated into the turnover tax system (salt, matches, etc.). Harmonization was to take place in two stages: first tax structures, then rates (on the abolition of tax frontiers); at the second stage it would also be necessary to consider the relationship between excise duties and VAT. The February 1967 tax harmonization programme thus called for harmonization of structures of duty on tobacco, spirits and wine, petroleum products, sugar and sweeteners, and beer. At the same time the Commission had some success in its efforts to persuade Member States to remove discriminatory aspects of their excise duty legislation (for example flat-rate taxation of imports without regard to the actual tax base, a practice held by the Court of Justice to be contrary to Article 95[7]). The Commission also studied the harmonization of road tax on passenger vehicles, partly in order to promote equal competitive conditions for manufacturers.

In 1969 the Council adopted the first of a series of directives harmonizing

[7] See Case 16/69, *Commission* v. *Italy* [1969] ECR 377.

tax and duty-free allowances for persons travelling from one state to another.[8] It was followed by directives on exemptions for small non-commercial consignments received from other countries.[9]

The Commission prepared draft legislation on indirect taxes on capital transactions. It studied three possibilities: abolition of capital duty (tax on contributions of capital to corporations) and stamp duty, abolition of stamp duty on bonds and foreign securities, and harmonization of capital duty, or harmonization of stamp duty and capital duty. For economic and technical reasons it chose the second, and submitted a draft directive in December 1964. In their opinions on the proposal the European Parliament and the Economic and Social Committee said that abolition of capital duty would have been preferable, but the proposal was ultimately adopted as Directive 69/335. The directive required the Commission to submit a proposal on common rates of duty. It did so in February 1971; the proposal was approved by the Council in December 1971 but not adopted until April 1973, in order to allow the new Member States to state their views. The Commission also examined the taxation of insurance contracts and considered the possibility of harmonizing taxes on stock exchange transactions. It prepared draft directives on both in 1970 but did not submit them; a proposal regarding tax on transactions in securities was submitted only in 1976.

EARLY MOVES TOWARDS HARMONIZATION OF DIRECT TAXATION

In 1962 the Commission began to study the harmonization of corporate taxation in so far as it affected the competitive position of businesses. Initially working parties were established to study bases of assessment and favourable tax treatment. The latter group was particularly concerned with tax avoidance through the use of tax havens. The Commission went on to study withholding tax, the taxation of distributed profits, and the elimination of double taxation. It became increasingly conscious of the obstacles created by differences in tax structures to the ability of business firms to operate throughout the Community and to the formation of larger industrial groups (cross-border mergers).

At the same time it was studying the question of capital movements, and its work in this field had important tax implications. Following the adoption in 1960 and 1962 of Council directives abolishing exchange restrictions on certain types of transactions,[10] it became apparent that the free movement of

[8] Directive 69/169, OJ 1969, L133/6 (English Spec. Ed. 1969 (I), 232); amended from time to time.

[9] Directive 74/651 (imports from Member States), OJ 1974, L354/57; and Directive 78/1035 (imports from non-member countries), OJ 1978, L366/34.

[10] First Council Directive for the implementation of Art. 67 of the Treaty, OJ 1960, 921 (English Spec. Ed. 1959–1962, 49); Second Council Directive 63/21 of 18 December 1962 adding to and amending the First Directive, OJ 1963, 62 (English Spec. Ed. 1963–64, 5).

capital raised serious issues. A group of experts under the chairmanship of Professor Claudio Segré was asked to study what needed to be done to establish a common European capital market and what its consequences would be for the Member States. The group devoted a chapter of its report[11] to tax obstacles to a single capital market. It identified three broad requirements of fiscal neutrality. First, the tax system should not influence the choice of place of investment. Secondly, it should not influence the choice whether to make a direct investment or invest through an intermediary such as an unit trust. Finally, in the long term the incentives for choosing different types of investment or methods of financing should be similar. There were also three broad categories of obstacles: double taxation (both internationally and in the case of investments made through intermediaries), tax preference for investment in the country of the taxpayer's residence, and differences from one country to another in the treatment of income accruing to non-residents. Accordingly, the group recommended that double taxation of investments by individuals should be eliminated by the adoption of multilateral arrangements or parallel national measures. The tax disadvantages of investing abroad through intermediaries should also be eliminated; fiscal transparency would probably require appropriate provisions in a multilateral double tax convention. Tax credits on dividend income should be extended to foreign dividend income or, better, a corresponding refund should be granted to non-resident shareholders (the group did not directly address the point that this apparent distortion arose from differences of approach to the taxation of company earnings in the hands of the company itself and of its shareholders). Disparities in the treatment of income accruing to non-residents were a particular problem for the bond market; it was necessary to abolish withholding tax or at least harmonize it at a low rate. Indirect taxes on the collection and transfer of capital constituted the most obvious direct impediment to a European capital market. The group noted that the Commission had already submitted a draft directive on capital duty, but thought that its abolition, along with stamp duty on the issue of securities, would be preferable.

In February 1967 the Commission submitted to the Council a tax harmonization programme containing measures relating mainly to direct taxation which were necessary for the establishment or functioning of the common market.[12] The most urgent measures were the elimination of obstacles to movements of capital (for example, double taxation of dividends and interest) and to the restructuring or concentration of companies within the Community (improved tax treatment of the parent/subsidiary relationship, cross-border mergers), and the achievement of equal competitive conditions in relation to investments (harmonized basis of assessment for company taxation). Further measures would include the harmonization of categories of taxable income,

[11] *The Development of a European Capital Market* (Brussels: EEC Commission, 1966).

[12] Bull. Supp. 8–67.

the approximation of rates, and co-ordination of tax collection. The Commission initially recommended standard rates of withholding tax (10 per cent for dividends and 25 per cent for interest) for both residents and non-residents, to be deductible against income tax in the country of residence; later it advocated the abolition of withholding tax on interest and measures to avoid double taxation of dividends. Since the main obstacle to cross-border mergers was the taxation of deemed capital gains, the Commission proposed a common system allowing Member States to safeguard revenue without impeding mergers. In January 1969 it submitted draft directives on cross-border mergers and on taxation of parent and subsidiary companies.

In 1970 a study of corporation tax and individual income tax in the Community was commissioned. In his report[13] Professor van den Tempel examined the manner in which profits were taxed in the hands of companies and their shareholders and the distortions to which disparities gave rise. He identified three systems applied in the Community: the classical system, under which profits are taxed independently in the hands of the company and of its shareholders (applied at the time in Luxembourg and the Netherlands, and in the United Kingdom), the dual-rate system, under which relief against economic double taxation is granted by applying a lower rate to distributed than to retained profits (West Germany), and the imputation or tax-credit system (France, Belgium), under which shareholders are granted relief on dividends by means of a tax credit representing at least part of the tax paid by the company. He also canvassed but rejected three other possible systems: the complete avoidance of economic double taxation of dividends (either by an extreme form of the dual-rate system in which no tax is charged on distributed profits or by an extreme form of the imputation system in which the tax paid by the company is fully credited against the shareholder's income tax), fiscal transparency (in which all company profits are treated as if they accrued to shareholders), and the deduction (in calculating the profit of the company) of a primary dividend corresponding to the return on debt financing. Each of the main systems had benefits at the national level. The dual-rate and tax-credit systems were roughly equivalent in effect, and were preferable in certain respects to the classical system, since they were more neutral in relation to the form of business organization and the choice of debt or equity financing, but they had the drawback of greater administrative complexity. However, only the classical system was suitable as a harmonized system in the Community, since only it offered the possibility of achieving capital export and import neutrality.

Tax provisions were also included in the 1970 proposal for a European

[13] A.J. van den Tempel, *Corporation Tax and Individual Income Tax in the European Communities* (Brussels: E.C. Commission (Studies, Competition—Approximation of Legislation Series no. 15), 1970.

company register: the European Company Statute.[14] It contained provisions on residence for tax purposes, transfer of residence without tax consequences and transfer of losses. Despite revision and resubmission in 1975 and 1989[15] the proposal has not been adopted.

THE PLAN FOR ECONOMIC AND MONETARY UNION

Additional impetus was given to the work on tax harmonization by the plan for economic and monetary union. In December 1969, at the end of the transitional period for the implementation of the EEC Treaty, a conference of Community heads of state or government adopted a resolution calling for further integration of the Community and its development into an economic and monetary union. A committee under the chairmanship of Pierre Werner, Prime Minister of Luxembourg, was asked to prepare a report on the achievement in stages of such a union.[16] In its report the committee referred, in relation to the abolition of tax frontiers, to the need for harmonization of VAT, certain excise duties, and taxes likely to influence movements of capital. It also called for the elimination of obstacles to a common capital market.[17]

In its contribution to the discussion[18] the Commission defined the objective as a frontier-free economic area with complete freedom of movement for goods, services, and factors of production. It suggested a three-stage process to be completed in 1978. With regard to taxation, the first stage (1970–1) included the introduction of VAT throughout the Community, the adoption of programmes for the approximation of excise duties and of VAT rates, and the adoption of measures to harmonize the taxation of dividends and interest and the structure of corporation tax. The second stage (1972–5) would see the harmonization of excise duties and VAT rates, of tax incentives for investment, and of the structure and basis of assessment of corporation tax. In the third stage (to begin in 1978 at the latest) tax frontiers would be eliminated and the free movement of capital established.

These discussions culminated in the adoption on 22 March 1971 of the Resolution of the Council and of the Representatives of the Governments of the Member States on the attainment by stages of economic and monetary union in the Community.[19] The union was to be established in stages over a

[14] OJ 1970, C124/1.

[15] COM(75)150; Proposal for a Regulation on the Statute for a European company, OJ 1989, C263/41.

[16] Council Decision 70/192 of 6 March 1970 on the procedure for economic and monetary co-operation, OJ 1970, L59/44 (English Spec. Ed., Second Series, X, 11).

[17] *Report to the Council and the Commission on the realization by stages of economic and monetary union in the Community*, Bull. Supp. 11–70.

[18] Commission memorandum to the Council on the preparation of a plan for the phased establishment of an economic and monetary union, Bull. Supp. 3–70.

[19] OJ 1971, C28/1 (English Spec. Ed., 2nd Ser., IX, 40).

period of ten years beginning on 1 January 1971; at the end of that period the Community was to constitute a single market (that is to say 'an area within which persons, goods, services, and capital move freely and with no distortion of competition'), form a single currency area, and possess the necessary legislative and administrative powers, subject to what is now called the principle of subsidiarity. In relation to tax, the resolution stated that the Council would adopt rules on the common basis of assessment for VAT; harmonize the scope, basis of assessment, and method of levying excise duties; harmonize taxes influencing capital movements (in particular taxes on interest and dividends); further harmonize company taxes; and consider the alignment of VAT and excise duty rates. A further resolution of 21 March 1972 stated that proposals submitted by the Commission relating in particular to fiscal harmonization would be given priority and that the Council would give a ruling on such proposals within six months of their being placed on its agenda.[20]

During the next few years the Commission's efforts were directed primarily towards the measures which the Council was to adopt by the end of 1973 for the establishment of Economic and Monetary Union (EMU): a draft directive on a standard basis of assessment for VAT and proposals for harmonization of excise duties, withholding tax on interest and dividends, and systems of company taxation. In 1972 it submitted a package of draft measures on excise duties.[21] Excise duties on tobacco, petroleum products, and alcoholic drinks were to be retained and harmonized; all others were to be abolished, except those which gave rise to no need for frontier tax adjustments. In 1973 it submitted the VAT proposal[22] and a draft directive on structures of excise duty on petroleum products.[23] With the exception of the first two stages of tobacco duty harmonization, which suffered delays and were significantly reduced in their scope, none of the excise duty proposals was adopted by the Council, and the Commission made increasing use of proceedings before the Court of Justice for infringement of Article 95 in order to eliminate discrimination in indirect taxation. In 1975 it also made a formal recommendation to the Member States not to raise levels of duty on wine.[24]

There was some delay in the submission of proposals on company tax, largely because of the complexity of the issues involved. A particular problem was the desire to find an appropriate way of avoiding economic double taxation of dividends. Although the main lines of the proposal on withholding tax and corporation tax structures were established by 1973, the proposal was not

[20] Resolution of the Council and of the Representatives of the Governments of the Member States of 21 March 1972 on the application of the Resolution of 22 March 1971, OJ 1972, C38/3 (English Spec. Ed., 2nd Ser., IX, 65).

[21] OJ 1972, C43; Bull. Supp. 3–72. [22] OJ 1973, C80/1. [23] OJ 1973, C92/36.

[24] Commission Recommendation 76/2 of 5 December 1975 to the Member States concerning the taxation of wine, OJ 1976, L2/13.

submitted until August 1975.[25] It provided for a common partial imputation system of company tax under which shareholders anywhere in the Community would receive a (reimbursable) tax credit; a narrow band of rates was set for both the tax and the credit. In the interest of combatting tax evasion a common rate of withholding tax was proposed.

The Commission was also coming to the view that harmonization of tax structures was not enough and that equal conditions of competition required some convergence of tax burdens on companies. A first step towards the latter would be a common basis for the calculation of taxable profits. However, the harmonization of taxes would be ineffective if there continued to be differences in the level of collection, and hence the effective tax burden; the Commission therefore studied the possibility of greater cross-border co-operation. Placing increased emphasis on tax evasion, which it said gave rise to abnormal capital movements and distorted competition, it advocated a strict regime for holding companies, particularly those established in tax havens outside the Community. This preoccupation with tax evasion, reflected in a Council Resolution of 10 February 1975,[26] resulted in a proposal for a mutual assistance directive which was adopted as Directive 77/799.[27]

STAGNATION IN THE 1970s

The dynamism shown by the Council at the time of the proposals on economic and monetary union was short-lived. A deteriorating economic climate and the accession of new Member States led to diminished enthusiasm for harmonization measures which promised increased growth tomorrow but the risk of lower revenues in some areas today. Very few of the measures proposed by the Commission in the early 1970s, in particular those relating to the abolition of tax frontiers, were adopted. The Commission made a number of efforts to break the deadlock. In June 1975 it submitted an Action Programme for Taxation, focussed primarily on matters of high priority but including longer-term measures which were regarded as necessary for greater integration. It urged the Council in particular to adopt the essential measures already submitted: a common basis of assessment for VAT, common systems of taxation for parent and subsidiary companies and for cross-border mergers,

[25] Proposal for a Council Directive concerning the harmonization of systems of company taxation and of withholding taxes on dividends, OJ 1975, C253/2.

[26] Council Resolution of 10 February 1975 on the measures to be taken by the Community in order to combat international tax evasion and avoidance, OJ 1975, C35/1.

[27] Council Directive 77/799 of 19 December 1977 concerning mutual assistance by the competent authorities of the Member States in the field of direct taxation, OJ 1977, L336/15. Extended to VAT by Council Directive 79/1070, OJ 1979, L331/8. Mutual assistance for the recovery of VAT claims was provided for by Council Directive 79/1071, OJ 1979, L331/10, amending Council Directive 76/308 on mutual assistance for the the recovery of EAGGF claims, agricultural levies and customs duties, OJ 1976, L73/18.

harmonized structures of company taxation, and harmonization of excise duties. In a communication submitted in August 1977 the Commission separately urged the Council to resume examination of the 1972 and 1973 excise duty proposals with a view to their immediate adoption, and in its November 1977 Communication on the Prospect of Economic and Monetary Union it emphasized the need for progress in relation in particular to indirect taxes, in order to make possible the elimination of tax frontiers.

In its 1980 report to the Council on the scope for convergence of tax systems in the Community[28] the Commission indicated the measures it considered urgent for the achievement of a true common market. Its two main objectives were the elimination of tax frontiers in indirect taxation, in order to create a real single market for goods, and the alignment of company tax burdens, in order to ensure fair conditions of competition for businesses and neutrality in relation to capital movements. Accordingly, in the field of VAT the harmonization of the basis of assessment should be completed, rates harmonized, and a financial compensation mechanism established to allocate revenue to the country of destination. The excise duty proposals should be adopted. In company tax, the 1975 proposal on harmonization of systems should be adopted, and rates and bases of assessment harmonized.

Mention should also be made of the Fredersdorf Report, prepared by the Economic and Social Committee following the publication of the Commission's 1975 Action Programme for Taxation.[29] This interesting report contained a broad survey of the existing tax situation and outlined the extensive harmonization which its authors considered necessary for the achievement of economic and monetary union; a single market for goods, services, capital, and labour; and, more generally, solidarity among Member States. It suggested that harmonization presented an opportunity to rationalize national tax systems, and that it would be necessary for the Member States to arrive at some political consensus on the desirable balance between direct and indirect taxation. The report recommended complete harmonization of excise duties and VAT (including uniform rates), transport taxes, and taxes on transactions; a high degree of harmonization of corporation tax and tax on dividends; and harmonization of payroll taxes. The origin principle should, it said, be applied in relation to indirect taxes, which would require some mechanism for financial adjustments between Member States in order to make up for the resulting shifts in revenue. Indirect taxes were to be harmonized by 1990, with the remaining tasks to be completed by 1995. The report emphasized the need for all the Community institutions to identify clearly the objectives which harmonization was to serve and the precise measures necessary in order to achieve them.

[28] Bull. Supp. 1–80.

[29] Information report of the section for economic and financial questions of the Economic and Social Committee on tax harmonization, Doc. CES 846/78, July 1978; published in [1978] *Intertax* 384 and 445.

Throughout this period work continued on VAT. After considerable discussion in the Council the 1973 proposal was adopted in May 1977 as the Sixth Directive, and the Commission went on to submit proposals on rules for second-hand goods (draft Seventh Directive)[30] and refunds for foreign taxable persons (draft Eighth Directive).[31] The latter was adopted in December 1979,[32] but the proposal on second-hand goods found no agreement in the Council and the proposal was ultimately withdrawn in November 1987. A number of other directives concerning the scope and application of the Sixth Directive were subsequently proposed and adopted: the Eleventh Directive excluding the French overseas departments from the territorial scope of the system[33] (proposed in December 1979 and adopted in March 1980); the Tenth Directive on the hiring out of movable tangible property[34] (proposed in April 1979 and adopted in July 1984); the Seventeenth Directive on the temporary importation of goods other than means of transport[35] (proposed in August 1984 and adopted in July 1985); the Twentieth Directive, allowing Germany to use the VAT system to compensate farmers for the dismantling of monetary compensatory amounts[36] (proposed in July 1984 and adopted in July 1985); the Thirteenth Directive on refunds for taxable persons outside the Community[37] (proposed in July 1982 and adopted in November 1986), and the Eighteenth Directive abolishing most of the existing derogations from the Sixth Directive (proposed in December 1984 and adopted in July 1989).[38] Further proposals by the Commission included draft directives on the deferred payment of VAT by taxable persons on imports from other Member States (draft Fourteenth Directive, July 1982),[39] expenditure in respect of which VAT is not recoverable (draft Twelfth Directive, July 1983),[40] the elimination of double taxation on imports by the final consumer (draft Sixteenth Directive, July 1984),[41] and special measures for small businesses (draft Twenty-second Directive, October 1986).[42] In May 1981 the Commission sent the Council a communication on a programme for the simplification of VAT procedures and formalities in intra-Community trade.[43]

Work also continued on company tax, though with no concrete results.

30 OJ 1978, C26/2.

31 OJ 1978, C26/5.

32 Directive 79/1072 on the harmonization of the laws of the Member States relating to turnover taxes—Arrangements for the refund of Value Added Tax to taxable persons not established in the territory of the country, OJ 1979, L331/11.

33 Directive 80/368—exclusion of the French overseas departments from the scope of Directive 77/388, OJ 1980, L90/41.

34 Directive 83/386, OJ 1984, L208/58.

35 Directive 85/362, OJ 1985, L192/20.

36 Directive 85/361, OJ 1985, L192/18.

37 Directive 86/560—Arrangements for the refund of Value Added Tax to taxable persons not established in Community territory, OJ 1986, L326/40.

38 Directive 89/465, OJ 1989, L226/21.

39 OJ 1982, C201/5 and C203/11 (identical).

40 OJ 1983, C37/8; amended OJ 1984, C56/7.

41 OJ 1984, C226/2; amended OJ 1986, C96/5.

42 OJ 1986, C272/12.

43 OJ 1981, C244/4.

Following the submission of the 1975 proposal on harmonization of systems of company tax, in November 1976 the Commission submitted a draft arbitration directive concerning taxation of transfers of profits between associated companies in different Member States.[44] In response to comments from the European Parliament on the 1975 proposal, the Commission submitted a further draft directive in July 1978 applying the same principles to collective investment organizations, in order to ensure equal treatment for direct investors and persons investing through such organizations. In 1980 it started preparatory work on the harmonization of rules on the calculation of taxable profits, and in September 1984 it submitted a draft directive on the carry-over of losses.[45]

It was during this period of stagnation in particular that the Court of Justice took a leading role in ensuring that the principles laid down in the Treaty in relation to taxation found full expression and in furthering the objective of economic integration. The unsuccessful proposals for the harmonization of indirect taxation were directed in large part at tax structures which were protectionist in their effect, and it was the Court of Justice that broke down many of those barriers through the application of Article 95. Much of the Court's fundamental case law on the meaning of tax discrimination and the scope of Article 95 was laid down in the late 1970s and early 1980s, and it dealt with issues on which the Council had been unable to reach agreement—for example, excise duties on alcoholic drinks (Case 168/78, *France*; Case 169/78, *Italy*; Case 170/78, *United Kingdom*; and Case 171/78, *Denmark*) and the treatment of imports of second-hand goods (Case 15/81, *Gaston Schul*).[46]

TOWARDS THE SINGLE MARKET

In the early 1980s, however, a new political consensus gradually developed; a desire to escape from the stagnation into which the Community had fallen. In June 1985 the Commission issued its White Paper on the completion of the internal market;[47] it outlined the existing physical, technical, and tax barriers to free movement of goods, people, and capital, and proposed measures for the elimination of those barriers, to be completed by the end of 1992—a date which took on almost talismanic significance. The Commission presented the White Paper to the meeting that month of the European Council in Milan, at which the Member States began the negotiations that led, by way of an intergovernmental conference, to the signature of the Single European Act; in its expansion of the possibility of majority voting in the Council the Single

[44] The proposal was ultimately agreed to in 1990 as a convention pursuant to Art. 220 of the Treaty; see Ch. 15.

[45] OJ 1984, C253/5; amendments to the proposal, OJ 1985, C170/3.

[46] See below, Ch. 3.

[47] COM(85)310.

European Act contributed to the achievement of the White Paper's objectives (although not in relation to tax, where the voting requirements remained unchanged). The White Paper called in particular for the elimination of tax frontiers; the measures it proposed included the alignment of rates of indirect tax. The Council's response was to instruct an *ad hoc* working party to determine what measures in relation to indirect taxes were necessary in order to establish the internal market by the end of 1992. The working party reported that if the removal of tax frontiers was considered necessary for the completion of the internal market there was no alternative to the Commission's proposals in the White Paper. That conclusion was accepted by the Council. Meanwhile the Commission submitted a draft standstill directive intended to ensure that national measures on VAT and excise duties did not diverge further before harmonization took place.[48]

The acceptance of the White Paper and the principles it contained gave new impetus to the harmonization process. New proposals were drawn up for VAT: the excise duty proposals were revamped and new proposals put forward. In August 1987 the Commission submitted a package of draft measures to the Council, accompanied by a general communication on the approximation of indirect tax rates and the harmonization of structures. The Commission proposed a two-rate system of VAT (in bands of 4–9 per cent for the reduced rate and 14–20 per cent for the standard rate) and common excise duty rates. Frontier tax adjustments were to be discontinued: VAT paid in other Member States would be deducted in the same way as internal VAT and financial adjustments between Member States would be made through a clearing house mechanism. There were also to be new rules on the place of supply of services. The proposals, which reflected the approach set out in the White Paper, were: a working paper on the establishment of a VAT clearing mechanism, a directive on the approximation of rates, amendments to the Sixth Directive to take into account the abolition of tax frontiers, a directive on the convergence of VAT and excise duty rates, and four directives on excise duty rates (tobacco, mineral oils, and alcohol).[49]

Reactions were varied. The Economic and Social Committee thought that the VAT proposals did not achieve sufficient harmonization soon enough, while the European Parliament advocated a maximum reduced rate of 9 per cent and minimum standard rate of 15 per cent. Most Member States found both the VAT and the excise duty proposals too inflexible, and in May 1989 the Commission submitted a further communication to the Council. It maintained its objective of approximation of rates in order to permit the abolition of tax frontiers, but took a more flexible approach. A transitional period of active convergence was to begin immediately and continue until the end of

[48] OJ 1985, C313/5.

[49] OJ 1987, C250/2 (VAT rates), 3 (convergence of VAT and excise duty rates), and 4 (alcohol), C251/3 and 4 (tobacco), C252/2 (frontiers), and C262/8 (mineral oils).

1992. The Commission proposed a minimum standard rate of VAT of 14 per cent, a reduced rate band (still 4–9 per cent), and the possibility of a zero rate for a restricted group of products; the clearing mechanism was replaced by payments to and from a central clearing account on the basis of intra-Community trade statistics. It stated that the excise duty proposals would be amended to take into account the wide divergence in rates and health, energy policy, and environmental concerns; in October 1989 it accordingly submitted proposals for minimum rates for all except certain petroleum products (in respect of which rate bands were considered necessary), with target rates for the longer term.[50] Target rates for petrol were proposed in February 1991.[51]

The VAT proposals continued to meet opposition in the Council, which took the view that the move to an origin system[52] presupposed conditions that could not be met before the end of 1992. It laid down guidelines for the simplification of formalities for businesses and the supervision of transactions. There were also particular difficulties regarding cars, mail order supplies, and supplies to exempt persons. In May 1990 the Commission accordingly amended its proposal on the abolition of tax frontiers to include provisions on transitional arrangements applicable until the end of 1996.[53] After discussion and further amendment the proposal was adopted as Directive 91/680.[54] These transitional arrangements were subsequently amended, clarified, and simplified by Directive 92/111.[55] In order to cut down on the risk of fraud under the transitional arrangements the Council also adopted Regulation 218/92 on administrative co-operation in the field of indirect taxation (VAT).[56] The regulation supplements the existing provisions of Directive 77/799, and provides for a common system of information exchange on intra-Community transactions.

A new proposal for a Seventh Directive on second-hand goods, antiques, and works of art, submitted in early 1989 after the original 1978 proposal had been withdrawn, was adopted by the Council in February 1994.[57] There was considerable agreement, meanwhile, on the gradual alignment of VAT rates. In December 1989 the Member States agreed not to depart from the 14–20 per cent band of standard rates, and in June 1991 they agreed to the essen-

[50] OJ 1990, C12/4 (cigarettes), 8 (other tobacco), and 12 (alcoholic beverages), and C16/10 (mineral oils).

[51] OJ 1991, C66/14.

[52] A common market system, according to Professor Biehl's classification.

[53] OJ 1990, C176/8.

[54] Council Directive 91/680 of 16 December 1991 supplementing the common system of VAT and amending Directive 77/388 with a view to the abolition of fiscal frontiers, OJ 1991, L376/1.

[55] Council Directive 92/111 of 14 December 1992 amending Directive 77/388 and introducing simplification measures with regard to VAT, OJ 1992, L384/47.

[56] OJ 1992, L24/1.

[57] Council Directive 94/5 of 14 February 1994 supplementing the common system of VAT and amending Directive 77/388—Special arrangements applicable to second-hand goods, works of art, collectors' items and antiques, OJ 1994, L60/16.

tials of what became Directive 92/77.[58] Under that directive, adopted in October 1992, from 1 January 1993 Member States must apply a standard rate no lower than 15 per cent and may apply up to two reduced rates, neither of which may be lower than 5 per cent, on specified categories of goods and services. Higher rates are abolished. Zero rates and special reduced rates may be retained during the transitional period.

Leaving aside the question whether the Community will in fact move to an origin system at the projected end of the transitional period, the VAT system is still not complete. Pending proposals include rules on passenger transport[59] and on gold held for investment purposes[60], amendments to the Eighteenth Directive on derogations from the common basis of assessment,[61] the draft Twelfth Directive on expenditure not giving rise to a right to deduction and the draft Twenty-second Directive on special arrangements for small businesses.

The new proposals on excise duty rates were followed in September 1990 by a set of proposals on structures (definitions of dutiable products, etc.) and on general arrangements for the holding and movement of goods subject to duty.[62] Under the latter, duty was to continue to be payable in the Member State where the goods were released for consumption; goods were to be moved between traders under suspension of duty in a system of tax warehouses. Even the minimum degree of harmonization necessary for the abolition of frontier checks was not easy to achieve, in view of the widely differing rates and indeed attitudes of the Member States—wine, cigarettes, and diesel were particularly controversial—but Directive 92/12 on general arrangements was adopted in February 1992[63] (further details were added in December 1992 by Directive 92/108[64]) and in October 1992 the Council adopted a package of directives on structures and rates of duty along with a decision authorizing the retention of certain existing derogations on mineral oils used for specific purposes.[65]

The White Paper did not represent a new departure in quite the same way for the harmonization of company tax, but the elimination of tax barriers to cross-border business activities was an important element of the completion of a single internal market. Further efforts were made to obtain the adoption of

[58] Council Directive 92/77 of 19 October 1992 supplementing the common system of VAT and amending Directive 77/388 (approximation of VAT rates), OJ 1992, L316/1.

[59] OJ 1992, C307/11. [60] OJ 1992, C302/9. [61] OJ 1992, C205/6.

[62] OJ 1990, C322/1 (general arrangements), 11 (alcoholic beverages), 16 (tobacco), and 18 (mineral oils).

[63] Council Directive 92/12 of 25 February 1992 on the general arrangements for products subject to excise duty and on the holding, movement, and monitoring of such products, OJ 1992, L76/1.

[64] Council Directive 92/108 of 14 December 1992 amending Directive 92/12 and Directive 92/81, OJ 1992, L390/124 .

[65] Council Directives 92/78 to 92/84 (structures and rates for tobacco, mineral oils, and alcoholic drinks) and Council Decision 92/510, OJ 1992, L316/5 *et seq.*; see Ch. 10.

the measures aimed at preventing double taxation—the merger, parent–subsidiary, and transfer pricing proposals. In April 1990 the Commission issued guidelines on company taxation[66] in which it stated that those measures, together with measures on transfers of losses and on payments of interest and royalties within groups of companies, were necessary for the completion of the internal market; it added that tax incentives should be made more transparent. It withdrew the 1975 proposal on the harmonization of company taxation and of withholding tax on dividends on the ground that it did not meet the needs of a more fully integrated market.

The merger and parent–subsidiary directives were adopted in July 1990; the transfer pricing proposal was adopted as a convention rather than as a directive.[67] In December 1990 the Commission submitted draft directives on interest and royalty payments between parent companies and subsidiaries and on arrangements for the taking into account of losses of subsidiaries and branches in other Member States.[68]

Following the adoption of legislation abolishing restrictions on capital movements,[69] in February 1989 the Commission put forward a proposal for a directive on a common system of withholding tax on interest income,[70] intended to prevent tax evasion and avoid the diversion of investment towards countries which did not charge withholding tax on interest paid to non-residents. Member States were to require the deduction of withholding tax at a minimum rate of 15 per cent from all payments of interest. They were free to apply a higher rate to residents than to non-residents; conversely, they were also free to refrain from levying withholding tax on payments to residents where the payment was automatically notified to the tax authorities and in other circumstances where the risk of tax evasion was remote. Recipients were to be entitled to a tax credit or, where appropriate, a refund in the State where they paid income or profits tax, and any necessary revenue adjustments were to be made between the States concerned. The proposal met strong resistance from certain Member States, and no agreement could be reached. Instead, attention was turned towards reinforcement of the existing measures for co-operation between tax authorities; meanwhile, Member States which applied withholding taxes found themselves under pressure to reduce or discontinue them in order to avoid capital flight.

66 SEC(90)601; published in [1990] *Intertax* 487 and in Bull. Supp. 4–91.

67 Council Directive 90/434 of 23 July 1990 on the common system of taxation applicable to mergers, divisions, and transfers of assets and exchanges of shares concerning companies of different Member States, OJ 1990, L225/1; Council Directive 90/435 of 23 July 1990 on the common system of taxation applicable in the case of parent companies and subsidiaries of different Member States, p. 6; Convention on the elimination of double taxation in connection with the adjustment of the profits of associated enterprises, p. 10.

68 OJ 1991, C53/26 and 30.

69 Council Directive 88/361 of 24 June 1988 for the implementation of Art. 67 of the Treaty, OJ 1988 L178/5.

70 OJ 1989, C141/5.

In late 1990 the Commission appointed a committee under the chairmanship of Mr Onno Ruding to study the impact of taxation on the location of investment and the allocation of profits between businesses in different countries.[71]

TAXATION OF INDIVIDUALS

As has been seen, the activities of the Community in the tax field have focussed mainly on the taxation of goods and on obstacles to the cross-frontier operations of companies. Taxation can also affect another of the 'four freedoms', freedom of movement for workers. There are bilateral agreements between Member States concerning the tax treatment of certain frontier workers but no rules of general application. In 1972 the Commission began to study the influence of taxation, in particular income tax, on the free movement of workers, but it was not until December 1979 that a draft directive was submitted to the Council, providing in particular that frontier workers should be taxed in their country of residence and that income from employment paid to other persons and pensions were to be taxed as if the recipient were resident in the State of his employment.[72] The proposal was subsequently withdrawn, since there was no agreement in the Council. It has therefore fallen once more to the Court of Justice to determine the consequences of the Treaty principles of free movement.[73]

In January 1989 the Commission proposed an amendment to Council Regulation 1612/68 on freedom of movement for workers within the Community.[74] In relation to taxation, it proposed an addition to Article 7 of the regulation to the effect that the criteria for granting tax advantages should not exclude facts or events occurring in another Member State. Although the amendment was intended to codify principles already laid down by the Court of Justice, it has not been adopted by the Council.

In December 1993 the Commission issued a recommendation concerning the tax treatment of individuals who are subject in one Member State to income tax on income from employment, pensions, or income from professional or business activities, but are resident in another Member State.[75] It

[71] The report of the committee is discussed in Ch. 14.

[72] Proposal for a Council Directive concerning the harmonization of income tax provisions with respect to freedom of movement for workers within the Community, OJ 1980, C21/6.

[73] See Ch. 16.

[74] Proposal for a Council Regulation amending Regulation 1612/68, OJ 1989, C100/6; Economic and Social Committee opinion, OJ 1989, C159/65; European Parliament opinion, OJ 1990, C68/88. Modifed proposal, OJ 1990, C119/10; the proposed addition to Art. 7 was not changed.

[75] Commission Recommendation 94/79 of 21 December 1993 on the taxation of certain items of income received by non-residents in a Member State other than that in which they are resident, OJ 1994, L39/22.

called on Member States to treat such individuals, where they receive the preponderant part of their income (defined as at least 75 per cent) in the state in question, no less favourably than their own residents with respect to income tax. Essentially that means granting them the various tax allowances to which they would be entitled if they were residents, except those concerning income which is not subject to tax in that state (such as interest income, normally taxed in the state of residence). Conversely, the Member State of residence may withhold from such persons the allowances to which they would normally be entitled, in order to ensure that they do not benefit from two sets of allowances and thus enjoy more favourable treatment than residents of either state. The recommendation, which has no binding effect, does not assist taxpayers who earn less than 75 per cent of their income in a state other than their state of residence. In an explanatory memorandum published with the recommendation, however, the Commission indicated its intention to pursue the issue before the Court of Justice.

Although some harmonization of income tax was recommended by the Neumark Committee, the Commission has frequently disavowed any intention to propose more general harmonization of personal income or wealth taxation, largely out of a concern for what is now referred to as subsidiarity.[76] If taxation is one of the most fundamental prerogatives of the State, then taxation of the income or wealth of individuals is its most sensitive aspect. However, in 1984 the Commission adopted a Memorandum on income taxation and equal treatment for men and women[77] in which it examined direct and indirect discrimination against women, particularly married women, in the tax systems of the Member States. Although both the Parliament and the Economic and Social Committee called for the submission of a draft directive on the matter, no such proposal has been put forward.

[76] See, e.g., the answers to Parliamentary Written Questions 309/70 of Mr Berkhouwer, OJ 1970, C150/9; 672/76 of Mr Cifarelli, OJ 1977, C27/31; 459/78 of Mr Howell, OJ 1978, C282/30; and 2756/87 of Mr Alvarez de Eulate Peñaranda, OJ 1988, C352/28.

[77] COM(84)695 final.

Indirect Taxation and VAT

3

The Tax Provisions of the Treaty: Articles 95 to 99

In Articles 95 to 98 the Treaty lays down a set of rules intended to prevent tax discrimination in relation to movements of goods between Member States, in particular in the application of frontier tax adjustments. The taxation of goods may not be used as a means of favouring domestic products, either by protecting them against imports or by providing disguised export subsidies. Articles 95 and 96 lay down the primary prohibitions of discrimination, and reflect the relevant provisions of the General Agreement on Tariffs and Trade (GATT).[1] In view of the complexity of the cumulative 'cascade' systems operated by most of the original Member States, and the consequent difficulty of ascertaining with any exactitude the amount of tax borne by goods to be exported and outright impossibility of determining the amount of tax borne by domestic goods corresponding to imports, Article 97 allowed Member States to establish average rates for products or groups of products. Finally, Article 98 prohibits Member States from making border tax adjustments in respect of direct taxation unless permitted to do so by the Council. Article 99 is broader in scope; it provides for the harmonization of indirect taxation to the extent necessary for the functioning of the single market.

ARTICLE 95

Article 95 of the EEC Treaty lays down a general prohibition on fiscal discrimination against products imported from other Member States. It is worded as follows:

> No Member State shall impose, directly or indirectly, on the products of other Member States any internal taxation of any kind in excess of that imposed directly or indirectly on similar domestic products.
>
> Furthermore, no Member State shall impose on the products of other Member States any internal taxation of such a nature as to afford indirect protection to other products.

[1] Under the second para. of Article III of GATT, 'The products of the territory of any contracting party imported into the territory of any other contracting party shall not be subject, directly or indirectly, to internal taxes or other internal charges of any kind in excess of those applied, directly or indirectly, to like domestic products. Moreover, no contracting party shall otherwise apply internal taxes or other internal charges to imported or domestic products in a manner contrary to the principles set forth in paragraph 1.' Para. 1 provides, *inter alia*, that internal taxation should not be applied in such a way as to protect domestic production.

[2] The second stage of integration under the Treaty began on 1 January 1962.

Member States shall, not later than at the beginning of the second stage,[2] repeal or amend any provisions existing when this Treaty enters into force which conflict with the preceding rules.

The function of Article 95 in the scheme of the Treaty is twofold: first of all, it complements the other provisions of the Treaty aimed at ensuring free movement of goods. Articles 9 to 17 of the Treaty, establishing the Customs Union, prohibit customs duties on imports and exports and all charges having equivalent effect in trade between Member States (including those of a fiscal nature). Articles 30 to 36 prohibit quantitative restrictions and all measures having equivalent effect in trade between Member States. These provisions do not by themselves suffice to preclude any possibility of protectionism, for it would be easy to replace a customs duty or quota with an internal tax equally restrictive in its effect. As a third line of defence, therefore, Article 95, based on the second paragraph of Article III of GATT, serves to eliminate that potential lacuna and preclude fiscal barriers to trade.[3]

Secondly, it has been observed[4] that Articles 95 to 99 are included in Part Three of the Treaty (Policy of the Community) and not in Part Two (Foundations of the Community) along with the other provisions on the free movement of goods. They are thus intended to contribute to the achievement of the wider aims of the Treaty set out in Articles 2 and 3. In accordance with those articles, Article 95 is aimed at the establishment of a single market for goods and seeks to ensure free competition by placing all products of Member States on an equal footing from the fiscal point of view.[5] Member States may not give domestic products an unfair competitive advantage by means of discriminatory taxation (although there is nothing to prevent reverse discrimination).[6] The objective is fiscal neutrality—Article 95 seeks to ensure complete neutrality of internal taxation as between imports and domestic products.[7] The purpose of the second paragraph of Article 95 in particular is to eliminate discrimination between products that are in 'legitimate confrontation'.[8]

Conversely, Article 95 allows Member States to ensure that foreign products bear as much tax as domestic products and thus do not derive unfair

[3] See Case 21/79, *Commission* v. *Italy* [1980] ECR 1; Joined Cases 142 and 143/80, *Amministrazione delle Finanze dello Stato* v. *Essevi and Salengo* [1981] ECR 1413.

[4] E.g. by A. J. Easson, in *Tax Law and Policy in the EEC* (London: Oceana, 1980), at para. 2.

[5] Case 15/81, *Gaston Schul* v. *Inspecteur der Invoerrechten en Accijnzen* [1982] ECR 1409, especially at para. 26.

[6] A Member State may thus discriminate against its own products. Presumably this was considered unlikely, and it may have been thought that where a Member State places its own products at a disadvantage that is a matter for it alone. That view may be considered unsound, however, on the ground that any diminution in economic efficiency within the Common Market affects all Member States.

[7] Case 168/78, *Commission* v. *France* [1980] ECR 347; Opinion of Advocate General Reischl in Case 26/80, *Schneider-Import* v. *Hauptzollamt Mainz* [1980] ECR 3469; Case 323/87, *Commission* v. *Italy* [1989] ECR 2275.

[8] Case 168/78, *Commission* v. *France*.

advantage from the fact that they have been exported free of tax from their country of origin. It assumes and permits the retention of a destination system of taxation (as, until now, has the rest of Community law on indirect taxes, in particular VAT). Member States are expected to allow exportation of products free of tax, so that it is for the Member State where they are imported to tax them at the level it considers appropriate for goods in its own economy.

The Article 95 prohibition raises delicate issues, since it impinges on the fiscal sovereignty of the Member States and has obvious revenue implications. Its formulation reflects an effort to balance Member States' freedom of action in establishing structures and rates of taxation and the interests of the Community in free trade. A good example of the difficult equilibrium to be maintained may be seen in the cases on differential taxation systems, discussed below. The attempt by a State to achieve a social or economic purpose by applying varying levels of tax may have an impact on flows of goods between Member States. This conflict between important interests—the free movement of goods and free competition on the one hand and legitimate choices of economic or social policy on the other—may be seen in an acute form in the cases on synthetic alcohol.[9] Particularly where both interests have a Community dimension the only real solution is ultimately harmonization.

Direct Effect

Article 95 was one of the first Articles of the Treaty to be held by the Court to have direct effect—that is to say, to be directly applicable in all Member States without any need for national implementing legislation.[10] Coupled with the principle that Community law takes precedence over inconsistent provisions of national law, that means that individuals and companies who are charged tax contrary to the prohibition on discrimination can challenge the tax in the national courts. The first and second paragraphs of Article 95 presented no problem in that respect, since they clearly create an unconditional obligation which is complete and legally perfect. The third paragraph was held to be a suspensory clause which merely allowed the Member States a period of grace; Article 95 has thus had direct effect since the beginning of the second stage of the transitional period, that is to say 1 January 1962.

Although it seems an obvious point, the Court has found it necessary to state that the application of Article 95 does not depend on prior harmonization pursuant to Article 99.[11] The two provisions have different objectives: Article 95 forbids discrimination, while Article 99 is available as a means of

[9] Case 140/79, *Chemial Farmaceutici* v. *DAF* and Case 46/80, *Vinal* v. *Orbat*, [1981] ECR 1 and 77 respectively.

[10] Case 57/65, *Lütticke* v. *Hauptzollamt Saarlouis* [1966] ECR 205.

[11] Case 171/78, *Commission* v. *Denmark* [1980] ECR 447; Case 55/79, *Commission* v. *Ireland* [1980] ECR 481.

reducing or eliminating barriers to trade caused by different schemes of taxation even in the absence of discrimination. Indeed, as a matter of principle the application of Article 95 is not in any way affected by harmonizing measures; it is a superior rule of Community law with which any secondary harmonizing legislation must comply. Consequently, national measures implementing the common VAT system—and the Community VAT directives themselves—remain subject to scrutiny under Article 95.[12] That does not, however, mean that the existence of harmonizing measures is entirely irrelevant from the point of view of Article 95; the existence of partial harmonization may provide an opening for the application of Article 95 in situations where it would otherwise have been inapplicable. In Case 15/81, *Gaston Schul*,[13] where the failure of the importing country to take into account VAT paid in the country of export was held to be contrary to Article 95, it was the fact that the tax was charged under the common system of VAT that enabled Article 95 to be applied. Had the tax been, for example, an excise duty levied under national legislation alone, there could have been no obligation for the authorities in the importing country to take tax already paid into account. The fact that double taxation in a (partly) harmonized context can constitute discrimination, while double taxation in other circumstances cannot, provides an illustration of the fact that there are many tax issues that can be dealt with only by harmonization. In Case 142/77, *Larsen*,[14] for example, the objection that the impact on exports of Danish legislation created a risk of double taxation was judged irrelevant, since the Treaty did not forbid double taxation as such.

The Relationship between Article 95 and other Articles of the Treaty

Article 95 does not operate in isolation. It interacts and overlaps with a number of other Treaty articles: the most significant are Articles 12 and 13, which prohibit customs duties and charges having equivalent effect in trade between Member States; Article 30, which prohibits quantitative restrictions on imports and measures having equivalent effect; Article 37, on state monopolies of a commercial character; and Articles 92 and 93, which regulate state aid. Because the effects of these various Articles and the criteria for their application are different it is necessary to distinguish their scope.

[12] Case 42/83, *Dansk Denkavit* v. *Ministeriet for Skatter og Afgifter* [1984] ECR 2649; Case 15/81, *Gaston Schul* v. *Inspecteur der Invoerrechten en Accijnzen* [1982] ECR 1409.
[13] Discussed in more detail below, p. 62.
[14] [1978] ECR 1543, see below.

Articles 12 and 13

One of the reasons originally adduced for the distinction between Articles 9 to 13 and Article 95 was that they have different timetables and different effects. Customs duties on exports and charges having equivalent effect were to be abolished by the end of the first stage, while customs duties on imports and charges having equivalent effect were to be phased out according to a complicated timetable during the transitional period (in the event their abolition was completed ahead of time, on 1 July 1968, a rare event in Community affairs). Discriminatory indirect taxation on products of other Member States, on the other hand, was to be eliminated by the beginning of the second stage. It would be illogical and impractical, it was said, to seek to apply to the same situation provisions which came into effect at different times. Moreover, it is often pointed out that customs duties and charges having equivalent effect are entirely unlawful, whereas discriminatory internal taxation is invalid only to the extent of the discriminatory effect.[15] Customs duties by their nature discriminate against imports, so there can be no question of them being unlawful only to a limited extent. Indeed, discrimination is not the issue in relation to customs duties and charges having equivalent effect; as the Court held in the *Diamantarbeiders* case, the justification for their prohibition is that 'any pecuniary charge—however small—imposed on goods by reason of the fact that they cross a frontier constitutes an obstacle to the movement of goods'.[16]

The distinction between internal taxation on the one hand and customs duties or charges with equivalent effect on the other is often a fine one, particularly where importation is a chargeable event in a system of internal taxation, and most of the early cases on Article 95 which came before the Court of Justice reflect the confusion experienced by national authorities in dealing with this matter. In the first case, the *Pain d'épices* case,[17] Article 95 was actually raised as a defence to an action brought by the Commission under Article 169 for breach of Article 12; it was argued that a tax on imports of a product similar to gingerbread was legitimate in order to offset an internal tax on rye, a raw material used in its production. The first clear statement of the distinction was given in Case 10/65, *Deutschmann* v. *Germany*,[18] where the Court held that Article 95 cannot apply to:

> a charge which is imposed either by reason of or at the time of importation and which, being imposed specifically on a product imported from a Member State to the

[15] See, e.g., Case 94/74, *IGAV* v. *Ente Nazionale per la Cellulosa e per la Carta* [1975] ECR 699, discussed below.

[16] Joined Cases 2 and 3/69, *Sociaal Fonds voor de Diamantarbeiders* v. *Brachfeld* [1969] ECR 211, at para. 14; see also Case 24/68, *Commission* v. *Italy* [1969] ECR 193, which makes the same remarks in relation to charges affecting exports.

[17] Joined Cases 2 and 3/62, *Commission* v. *Belgium and Luxembourg* [1962] ECR 425.

[18] [1965] ECR 469.

exclusion of a similar domestic product, has, by altering its price, the same effect upon the free movement of goods as a customs duty.

A charge imposed on the issue of import licences was thus a charge equivalent to a customs duty, contrary to Article 12, and not an internal tax subject to Article 95. Conversely, a system of general taxation applying without distinction to all categories of products, whether domestic or imported, is internal taxation subject to Article 95, even if it is charged at the time of importation.[19] A good example of this is VAT under the existing system of taxation in the country of destination. In Case 57/65, *Lütticke* v. *Hauptzollamt Saarlouis*,[20] therefore, the Court replied to a question on the combined effect of Articles 12 and 13 and Article 95 by pointing out that these Articles cannot be applied to the same case since they create different systems.

It remained for the Court to refine the *Deutschmann* definition and show in practical terms where the distinction was to be drawn. In Case 24/68, *Commission* v. *Italy*,[21] concerning a statistical levy charged on imports and exports, the Court laid down a more comprehensive definition of customs duties, charges having equivalent effect; and internal taxation, emphasizing that the abolition of customs duties between Member States is intended not simply to avoid protection but to ensure free movement of goods generally. The key passage is worth quoting in full (paragraphs 9 and 11):

> Any pecuniary charge, however small and whatever its designation and mode of application, which is imposed unilaterally on domestic or foreign goods by reason of the fact that they cross a frontier, and which is not a customs duty in the strict sense, constitutes a charge having equivalent effect . . . even if it is not imposed for the benefit of the State, is not discriminatory or protective in effect and if the product on which the charge is imposed is not in competition with any domestic product . . .
>
> It follows from Articles 95 *et seq.* that the concept of a charge having equivalent effect does not include taxation which is imposed in the same way within a State on similar or comparable domestic products, or at least falls, in the absence of such products, within the framework of general internal taxation, or which is intended to compensate for such internal taxation within the limits laid down by the Treaty.

The definition in Case 78/76, *Steinike and Weinlig* v. *Germany*[22] has a slightly different focus: the prohibition in Article 13(2) is, the Court held, aimed at tax demanded at the time of or by reason of importation which, being imposed specifically on imports to the exclusion of domestic products, has the same restrictive effect on the free movement of goods as a customs duty by increasing their price. Financial charges within a general system of internal taxation applying systematically to imports and domestic products according to the same criteria are not charges having equivalent effect. On the other hand, in Case C–163/90, *Legros* v. *Administration des Douanes*[23] the Court held that the

[19] Case 7/67, *Wöhrmann* v. *Hauptzollamt Bad Reichenhall* [1968] ECR 177.
[20] [1966] ECR 205. [21] [1969] ECR 193. [22] [1977] ECR 595.
[23] [1992] ECR I–4625.

octroi de mer charged on all goods entering the French overseas departments, whether from other countries or from metropolitan France, constituted a charge equivalent in effect to a customs duty because it constituted an obstacle to imports from other Member States.

A number of subsidiary questions nevertheless arose. The Court held at an early stage that an internal tax is not to be regarded as a charge equivalent in effect to a customs duty simply because there is no similar domestic product.[24] It must be considered to be internal taxation if it is applied on the basis of objective criteria to whole classes of imports and domestic goods irrespective of their origin.[25] Indeed, Article 95 itself does not prohibit internal taxation of imported goods which do not compete with domestic products (the early cases concern the importation into Germany of Mediterranean products such as citrus fruits). Internal taxation is by definition fiscal in purpose, and there is no reason to place certain imports in a privileged position simply because there are no domestic products to be protected. It has been argued, however, that an exorbitant tax which departed from the normal framework of internal taxation could be contrary to Article 12.[26]

Nor does the portion of internal taxation which exceeds the tax charged on the similar domestic product or is otherwise discriminatory become a charge equivalent in effect to a customs duty. This ought to be obvious, since otherwise Article 95 would be largely nugatory, but Advocate General Gand thought it necessary to point it out in Case 57/65, *Lütticke*. Indeed, the Commission itself raised this canard as late as 1980 in its submissions in Case 32/80, *Officier van Justitie* v. *Kortmann*.[27]

An apparent exception to the clear and rigid distinction between customs duties and internal taxation was established by the Court in Case 77/72, *Capolongo* v. *Maya*,[28] which concerned a parafiscal charge levied in a uniform manner on domestic and imported paper and cardboard, the proceeds being used to finance various activities in support of the domestic paper industry. Although there was no discrimination in the way in which the charge was levied, the Court went behind the appearance of equality and held that the destination of a charge must be taken into account. Where a charge is intended to support activities which specifically benefit taxed domestic products, the charge constitutes a net supplementary tax burden for the import but is offset by benefits received in respect of the domestic product. It may thus constitute a charge equivalent in effect to a customs duty, since in real

[24] Case 20/67, *Kunstmühle Tivoli* v. *Hauptzollamt Würzburg* [1968] ECR 199; Case 90/79, *France* [1981] ECR 283; Case 193/85, *Co-Frutta* v. *Amministrazione delle Finanze dello Stato* [1987] ECR 2085.

[25] See also Case 27/67, *Fink-Frucht* v. *Hauptzollamt München–Landesbergerstraße* [1968] ECR 223; Case 31/67, *Stier* v. *Hauptzollamt Hamburg-Ericus* [1968] ECR 235; Case 78/76, *Steinike and Weinlig*.

[26] Case 31/67, *Stier* v. *Hauptzollamt Hamburg-Ericus*, submissions of the Commission.

[27] [1981] ECR 251.

[28] [1973] ECR 611.

terms only the import is taxed. In Case 94/74, *IGAV*, and in Case 77/76, *Cucchi* v. *Avez*,[29] the Court refined and clarified the scope of the exception. There must be a clear connection between the duty charged on all products and the advantage provided to domestic products (thus a tax which was not earmarked for measures in support of the domestic product but was simply paid to the State revenue authorities would not be a charge having equivalent effect; the measures in support of the domestic product would then fall to be examined under the provisions of the Treaty on state aid). Most importantly, *Cucchi* makes it clear that the charges imposed on the domestic product must be made good in full for them to constitute a charge having equivalent effect; the *Capolongo* judgment did not address this point (indeed, the quotation in *Cucchi* of a rather generally worded passage from *Capolongo* gives rise to an apparent inconsistency in the later judgment), and in *IGAV* the Court simply said that the charges must be made good wholly or in part. It seems clear that the *Cucchi* refinement is necessary, since only if the charge on domestic products is fully compensated for by benefits which their producers receive can it be said that the tax is borne only by imports. Otherwise there is simply discriminatory taxation, as Advocate General Reischl pointed out in his Opinion in *Cucchi* and has now been established in a number of judgments[30]—the effect of the scheme is that the domestic product is taxed more lightly than the import. Depending on the facts of the case it may not always be clear whether and to what extent there is a benefit for domestic producers. For example, in Joined Cases C–78/90 to C–83/90, *Compagnie Commerciale de l'Ouest* v. *Receveur Principal des Douanes*[31] a tax on petrol was used to fund an energy conservation agency. The *Cucchi* rule was held applicable since it appeared that the agency paid subsidies for modifications to refineries, but there is some force in the French government's submission that measures intended to reduce demand for a product should not be regarded as a benefit to its producer.

The opposite phenomenon, that is to say discrimination against exports, may be seen in Case 51/74, *Hulst* v. *Produktschap voor Siergewassen*,[32] where the Court established a 'reverse-Capolongo' rule: a levy charged on both exports and domestic sales the proceeds of which are used to finance measures making domestic sales more attractive constitutes a charge equivalent in effect to a customs duty on exports. However, after defining a charge having equivalent effect to a customs duty in an orthodox manner (any charge levied at the

[29] [1977] ECR 987; see also its companion case, Case 105/76, *Interzuccheri* v. *Rezzano e Cavassa* [1977] ECR 1029.

[30] Beginning with Case 73/79, *Commission* v. *Italy* [1980] ECR 1533. See most recently Joined Cases C–149/91 and C–150/91, *Sanders Adour* [1992] ECR I–3899; Case, C–17/91 *Lornoy* v. *Belgium*; Case C–114/91, *Claeys* and Joined Cases C–144/91 and C–145/91, *Demoor Gilbert en Zonen* v. *Belgium* [1992] ECR I–6523, I–6559 and I–6613 respectively; Case C–266/91, *CELBI* [1993] ECR I–4337; and Case C–72/92, *Scharbatke* [1993] ECR I–5509.

[31] [1992] ECR I–1847.

[32] [1975] ECR 79.

time of or by reason of the export of goods which has the same restrictive effect as a customs duty on the free movement of goods), the Court stated rather baldly that an internal levy which falls more heavily on goods for export than on goods sold on the domestic market has an effect equivalent to a customs duty on exports. This is quite contradictory, since an internal levy clearly does not meet that definition. Moreover, the Court went on to state that Article 95 could apply to the same levy, 'if only by analogy' (there being no express provision on discrimination against exports). This is entirely inconsistent with the strict distinction drawn by the Court between the provisions on customs duties and those on indirect taxation. Are we to conclude that that distinction is only to be made in respect of imports? The answer is fairly clearly no. In a case decided shortly before *Hulst*, Case 27/74, *Demag* v. *Finanzamt Duisburg-Süd*,[33] the Court held that a special turnover tax charged at a low rate on exports during a period of balance of payments surplus (thus amounting to a partial withdrawal of the exemption of exports from internal taxation) constituted internal taxation within the meaning of Article 95 and could not therefore be a charge equivalent in effect to a customs duty.

Article 30

The distinction between the scope of Article 95 and that of Article 30 is clearer and easier to define: essentially, Article 95 is concerned with fiscal barriers to trade; Article 30 with non-fiscal barriers. In Case 74/76, *Iannelli & Volpi* v. *Meroni*[34] the Court stated that Article 30 does not extend to obstacles to trade covered by other Articles of the Treaty, so that it is necessary to have regard to the particular purpose of each provision and its distinct field of application. Article 30 might thus be regarded as a residual prohibition, and Article 95 as a *lex specialis* in relation to it.[35] It is important to bear in mind, however, that different aspects of the same scheme may fall under different provisions. For example, health inspections may be a barrier to trade outlawed by Article 30; where such inspections are permissible under Article 36, fees charged for them constitute internal taxation to which Article 95 applies.[36]

It follows from the clear distinction between Article 95 and Article 30 that the Article 36 derogation and the *Cassis de Dijon*[37] exception are not

[33] [1974] ECR 1037.

[34] [1977] ECR 557.

[35] See also Case 252/86, *Bergandi* v. *Directeur Général des Impôts* [1988] ECR 1343, at para. 33.

[36] Case 35/76, *Simmenthal* v. *Minister of Finance* [1976] ECR 1871; see also Case 50/85, *Schloh* v. *Auto Contrôle Technique* [1986] ECR 1855, concerning roadworthiness tests on imported cars. Similarly, a fee charged for an import licence or for health inspection of imports alone is a charge equivalent in effect to a customs duty, even where it is intended to offset charges for the inspection of (live) domestic animals—see Case 314/82, *Commission* v. *Belgium* [1984] ECR 1543.

[37] Case 120/78, *Rewe-Zentrale* v. *Bundesmonopolverwaltung für Branntwein* [1979] ECR 649.

available.[38] The absence of anything analogous to Article 36 in the provisions on taxation or any case law directly corresponding to *Cassis de Dijon* might be regarded as a lacuna. It is clear that there can be no such derogations with regard to customs duties and charges having equivalent effect, if only because they are not normally the least restrictive means of control, and in any event there must be few circumstances in which a duty imposed only on imports or exports, rather than an outright prohibition, could be justified on grounds of protecting some public interest.[39] However, states often use taxation as a means of influencing consumer behaviour which is less restrictive than an outright prohibition or quantitative restriction. Since the latter clearly could be covered by Article 36 or by the *Cassis de Dijon* exception, it seems perverse that there should be no similar dispensation in respect of taxation. On the other hand, it may be argued that the fact that the Member State in question simply applies higher taxation rather than a prohibition shows that there are no overriding considerations of public health, safety, or the like to be protected; moreover, the reasons of public policy advanced to justify higher taxation of imports often amount to simple protection of national industry.[40]

Close examination of the case law suggests that there may in fact be no such lacuna, at least in relation to the second paragraph of Article 95. That provision prohibits only taxation which results in unjustified discrimination; schemes of taxation which apply differential rates are considered legitimate so long as they are directed at objectives which are compatible with the Treaty, even if they may place some imported products at a disadvantage.[41] This is broader in its scope than the *Cassis de Dijon* exception since it does not presuppose the same overriding considerations of public policy.

As a final point on the distinction between Article 95 and Article 30 it should be added that a tax affecting imported products is not to be regarded as a measure equivalent in effect to a quantitative restriction solely because there is no similar domestic product.[42] In Case C–47/88, *Commission* v. *Denmark* the Court suggested that the imposition in those circumstances of such heavy taxation on the imported product (in that case cars, which are not manufactured in Denmark) that the free movement of goods was impeded could be contrary to Article 30.[43] However, in so far as that statement is based on the view that Article 30 is applicable whenever the flow of imports

[38] Case 32/80, *Kortmann*, cited above; Case 29/87, *Dansk Denkavit* [1988] ECR 2965.

[39] See, e.g., Case 7/68, *Commission* v. *Italy* [1968] ECR 423, in which an export duty on art treasures was held unlawful.

[40] See, e.g., Case C–105/91, *Commission* v. *Greece* [1992] ECR I–5871.

[41] See below for fuller discussion of this point.

[42] Case 27/67, *Fink-Frucht*, a case which resolved a number of fundamental issues.

[43] [1990] ECR I–4509, referring to Case 31/67, *Stier* v. *Hauptzollamt Hamburg-Ericus* [1968] ECR 235, in which the Court held that Member States could not levy such taxation but did not indicate on what basis they were prevented from doing so. In *Stier* the Commission had argued that tax which departed from the normal framework of internal taxation was a charge equivalent to a customs duty contrary to Art. 12.

into a Member State is hampered, irrespective of any discrimination in favour of domestic products, it may have been overtaken by the Court's reversal of its previous case law in Joined Cases C–267 and C–268/91, *Keck and Mithouard*.[44]

Article 37

There is some degree of overlap between Article 95 and Article 37, on state monopolies of a commercial character, which are frequently financed by charges levied on the products concerned. Article 37 falls at the end of the chapter of the Treaty which deals with the elimination of quantitative restrictions on the movement of goods between Member States. Its purpose is to prevent the operations of state (or delegated) monopolies which supervise or appreciably influence imports and exports from resulting in discrimination. As the Court held in Case 45/75, *Rewe* v. *Hauptzollamt Landau/Pfalz*,[45] that covers not only quantitative restrictions but all discrimination affecting the conditions under which goods are procured and marketed, including charges which result in discrimination against imports (an interpretation, said the Court, which corresponds to the second paragraph of Article 95). The *Rewe* case concerned the German monopoly for the marketing of spirits, under which spirits distilled in Germany were required to be sold to the monopoly at a price set by the authorities. Certain domestic spirits were exempt, but were subject to a tax composed of spirits duty applicable to all alcohol and an amount representing the administrative costs of the monopoly. Imports were also subject to a compensatory duty comprising the same elements. To levy a contribution to the running costs of the monopoly on imports alone would be contrary, the Court said, to Article 37 and Article 95, but to levy the same tax on both imports and domestic products, with part of the proceeds of the charge on domestic products going to the monopoly and the revenue from imports going to the state, was compatible with both those provisions. The conclusion would presumably be different if the proceeds from charges on all products went to the monopoly, since that would be a *Capolongo* or *Cucchi* situation, and the charge on imports would constitute a charge equivalent in effect to customs duty. Moreover, although the Court's discussion in *Rewe* of the relationship between Articles 37 and 95 remains valid, its conclusion that the portion of a charge which represents the running costs of the monopoly can be offset by a tax on imports is unsound, as it recognized in Case 4/81, *Hauptzollamt Flensburg* v. *Andresen*,[46] since a contribution to monopoly costs does not constitute internal taxation for the purposes of Article 95.

Is there any difference in effect between Articles 37 and 95 as regards taxation? In many cases the result would be the same whichever provision were

[44] [1993] ECR I–6097. [45] [1976] ECR 181. [46] [1981] ECR 2835.

applied. In cases where questions have been referred to the Court on both Articles 37 and 95 the Court has often preferred to look at the situation from the point of view of Article 95. While both provisions are aimed at eliminating discrimination, Article 95 is more general in its scope, since Article 37 is concerned only with matters 'intrinsically connected with the business of the monopoly'.[47] Indeed, it may be that this requirement of an 'intrinsic connection' in the later cases reflects a stricter view of the scope of Article 37 which would exclude its application to taxes on products not actually handled by the monopoly.[48] The fact that, unlike Article 95, Article 37 prohibits negative discrimination, that is to say discrimination against domestic products,[49] would thus not normally have tax implications.

Articles 92 and 93

There is also some overlap between Article 95 and the provisions of the Treaty on state aid, since both are at least in part directed towards the same objective, that is to say ensuring equal conditions of competition for domestic industry and that in other Member States. Where the same situation has elements of both state aid and discriminatory taxation, both sets of provisions must be complied with.[50] Thus where a tax charged on imports and domestic products alike is used to finance aid to domestic production it is no answer to say, as the Italian government argued in Case 73/79, *Commission* v. *Italy*,[51] that the financing of aid can be challenged only under Article 93. In that case the Court pointed out that Articles 92 and 93 and Article 95 pursue the same objective but are directed at different kinds of state measure. It had previously been held that aspects intrinsic to a scheme of aid should be examined under Articles 92 and 93, even if they might separately be contrary to other provisions of the Treaty, while those not necessary for attainment of the purpose of the aid or its proper functioning fell to be dealt with under those other provisions.[52] However, such a view might create a dangerous loophole if applied to Article 95, and it is clear that the Court's attitude is stricter: in Case 73/79 it held that a measure which may be regarded as aid is subject to Article 95 if it is carried out by means of discriminatory taxation.[53] Discriminatory taxation is not exempted from Article 95 simply because it forms part of an aid

[47] Case 148/77, *Hansen & Balle* v. *Hauptzollamt Flensburg* [1978] ECR 1787, again on the German monopoly equalization levy; Case 86/78, *Peureux* [1979] ECR 897; Case 17/81, *Pabst & Richarz* [1982] ECR 1331.

[48] Most recently, Joined Cases C–78/90 to C–83/90, *Compagnie Commerciale de l'Ouest* [1992] ECR I–1847.

[49] Case 86/78, *Peureux* v. *Directeur des Services Fiscaux de la Haute-Saône* [1979] ECR 897.

[50] E.g. Case C–266/91, *CELBI*, above, note 30.

[51] [1980] ECR 1533, concerning the sugar surcharge which had already been the subject-matter of Case 77/76, *Cucchi* and Case 105/76, *Interzuccheri*.

[52] Case 74/76, *Iannelli* v. *Meroni* [1977] ECR 557.

[53] *Contra* Advocate General Capotorti in Case 148/77, *Hansen*.

scheme and can therefore be challenged by other means. Furthermore, the discretion enjoyed by the Commission and the Council under Articles 92 and 93 cannot be exercised in a manner contrary to Article 95; thus the Commission cannot authorise discriminatory taxation as a form of aid.[54] Consequently, the fact that a Member State is authorized to grant aid does not mean that any manner of financing the aid whatsoever is compatible with Community law.[55]

Moreover, the manner in which an aid scheme is financed must be taken into account in determining whether it 'affects trade between Member States' for the purposes of Article 92. Aid financed by a charge which is contrary to Article 95 will be held to be incompatible with the common market for the purposes of Article 93(2).[56]

Scope of Article 95

Internal Taxation

In defining the scope of Article 95 it is as well to look first to its wording and consider the most significant concepts. The central point is that Article 95 is concerned with internal taxation on products. In distinguishing the respective scopes of Article 95 and the provisions on customs duties and charges having equivalent effect we have already seen what 'internal' means. It is therefore necessary to identify what is meant by taxation. In Case 10/65, *Deutschmann*, the German government argued that only taxes properly so called fell within the purview of Article 95, and not, for example, administrative charges. That is clearly much too restrictive a view; Advocate General Gand rejected it in that case on the ground that there was in any event too much variation in tax terminology in the Member States for national classifications to provide a helpful criterion. The Court has in fact taken a very broad view of the concept: taxation for the purposes of Article 95 includes not only taxes levied by central government but any fiscal or parafiscal levy imposed by or with the authority of any level of government, including levies charged by or for quasi-official bodies and allocated to a specific purpose.[57]

[54] Joined Cases 142 and 143/80, *Essevi and Salengo* [1981] ECR 1413. This is simply an illustration of the general principle that the Community institutions remain bound by primary Community law, that is to say, the Treaty.

[55] See Case 105/76, *Interzuccheri*.

[56] Case 47/69, *France* v. *Commission* [1970] ECR 487.

[57] See, e.g., Case 74/76, *Iannelli & Volpi* v. *Meroni*, a levy on paper products used by the Ente Nazionale per la Carta e la Cellulosa to finance support measures for domestic industry; Case 222/82, *Apple and Pear Development Council* v. *Lewis* [1983] ECR 4083, a levy on growers to finance the activities of the Council.

Taxes imposed directly or indirectly on Products

Article 95 is concerned with what is usually called indirect taxation, that is to say taxation of things rather than persons, and only with that which can be said to affect products in a fairly immediate manner. It does not permit the taxation of imported products in order to offset the burden of direct taxation on domestic manufacturers. The intent of the expression 'imposed . . . indirectly on . . . products' is to capture taxation of raw materials and intermediate products but not of factors of production (subject to the possible application of Article 98) or, for example, stamp duties levied generally on businesses as such.[58] The definition given by the Court in Case 28/67, *Mölkerei Zentrale Westfalen/Lippe* v. *Hauptzollamt Paderborn*[59] seems still to be valid:

> all taxation which is actually and specifically imposed on the domestic product at all earlier stages of its manufacture and marketing or which corresponds to the stage at which the product is imported from the other Member States, it being nevertheless understood that the effect of this taxation diminishes in proportion as the previous stages of manufacture and marketing become more remote and that this burden tends rapidly to become negligible.

This clearly includes excise duties, turnover taxes (including VAT), consumption taxes, sales taxes, and the like; it also includes fees for health inspections,[60] registration fees for pharmaceutical products,[61] and fees for roadworthiness tests on cars.[62] Article 95 also extends to taxes on the use of products rather than the products themselves. The Court was expressly asked to rule on this point in Case 252/86, *Bergandi* v. *Directeur Général des Impôts*,[63] concerning an annual tax on automatic game or amusement machines, and held that Article 95 must be interpreted widely so as to cover all taxation which directly or indirectly conflicts with the principle of equal treatment. It therefore prohibits any levy likely to discourage imports, including a levy on the use of products. The Court had already implicitly arrived at the same conclusion in the cases on the French annual car registration tax.[64] The broadest approach taken by the Court to the concept of a tax imposed indirectly on goods is that in Case 20/76, *Schöttle* v. *Finanzamt Freudenstadt*,[65] where it held that a tax on the carriage of goods by road fell within the scope of Article 95, as a tax which had an immediate effect on the cost of domestic and imported products; this is probably as far as the Court could decently go. In Case C–195/90, *Commission* v. *Germany*,[66] concerning a tax on foreign

[58] Cf Case 45/64, *Italy* (an Art. 96 case).
[59] [1968] ECR 143.
[60] Case 35/76, *Simmenthal.*
[61] Case 32/80, *Kortmann.*
[62] Case 50/85, *Schloh.*
[63] [1988] ECR 1343.
[64] Cf Case 112/84, *Humblot* v. *Directeur des Services Fiscaux* [1985] ECR 1367.
[65] [1977] ECR 247.
[66] [1992] ECR I–3141.

heavy goods vehicles, Advocate General Jacobs took the same approach on the basis that imports, even if they were sometimes carried by German lorries and sometimes by foreign lorries, were in any event hit more severely by the tax than domestic goods distributed in Germany, which would normally be carried only by German lorries. However, the Court did not find it necessary to rule on the Article 95 point.

In most cases there can be no serious question as to what are products and what are, for example, services. The Court has held, however, that savings deposits (and so, presumably, other financial 'products') fall under the provisions of the Treaty on freedom to provide services and the free movement of capital and are not products for the purposes of Article 95.[67]

The scope of Article 95 may also be defined negatively in terms of the internal charges or expenses which cannot be offset by taxation of imports. Often these are additional non-fiscal burdens which are borne by domestic products, and the Court has held more generally that there can be no compensation between a tax applied to imports and a charge of a different nature imposed, for example for economic purposes, on the domestic product.[68] There are various examples in the Court's case law. In the *Pain d'épices* case the tax held illegal was intended to compensate for the extra financial burden on domestic producers resulting from the high support price for rye in Belgium and Luxembourg. In Case 4/81, *Andresen*, a charge on domestic products to cover the administrative costs of the German spirits monopoly was held not to justify a corresponding tax on imports, although in Case 45/75, *Rewe*, Advocate General Reischl had been of the view that not to impose such a charge on imports would place them at an unacceptable competitive advantage. Monetary problems resulting from the rate of the green pound in Ireland could not be corrected by taxation of imports.[69] Fees for the inspection of (live) domestic poultry cannot be offset by a charge for inspection of imported poultry meat.[70] It might be thought an obvious point, but as recently as 1989 the Court was obliged to point out, in Case 323/87, *Commission* v. *Italy*,[71] that a tax could not be imposed on imports to offset a difference in production costs. Article 95 is not a justification for the imposition of countervailing duties.

Where a tax on imports is intended to offset a non-fiscal burden of that kind it will normally follow that the tax is a charge equivalent in effect to a customs duty, contrary to Article 12; but in some circumstances, where the tax is part of a scheme of taxation of a particular category of products, such as alcoholic beverages, it may simply be held to be discriminatory and thus contrary to Article 95.

[67] Case 267/86, *Van Eycke* v. *ASPA* [1988] ECR 4769.
[68] Case 45/75, *Rewe*, [1976] ECR 181.
[69] Case 55/79, *Commission* v. *Ireland* [1980] ECR 481.
[70] Case 314/82, *Belgium*. [71] [1989] ECR 2275.

Products of Other Member States

Article 95 is concerned with taxation of products of other Member States; reverse discrimination is thus unobjectionable, as the Court observed in Case 86/78, *Peureux*. Article 95 clearly applies to products imported from Community customs territory, that is to say the territory of the Member States as defined in Regulation 2913/92 of 12 October 1992 establishing the Community Customs Code.[72] France considers its overseas departments to be an integral part of its territory, but Article 227(2) provided for the gradual application of the Treaty to them. The provisions on, *inter alia*, the free movement of goods were applicable immediately, while the conditions for the application of the other provisions were to be determined by Council decision within two years of the entry into force of the Treaty. No general decision was made in that respect, but the Court held in Case 148/77, *Hansen & Balle* v. *Hauptzollamt Flensburg*,[73] (without deciding whether Article 95 was to be regarded for this purpose as one of the provisions relating to the free movement of goods, as the plaintiff had argued) that the remainder of the Treaty and secondary Community law were automatically applicable in the French overseas departments after the expiry of that two-year period.

Article 95 is nowhere expressly made applicable to the overseas countries and territories referred to in Part Four of the Treaty, but according to the Court's judgment in Case 91/78, *Hansen* v. *Hauptzollamt Flensburg*,[74] Article 5(1) of Council Decision 70/549 of 29 September 1970 on the association of the overseas countries and territories with the European Economic Community,[75] under which 'Member States shall refrain from any internal fiscal measure or practice that directly or indirectly leads to discrimination between their own products and like products originating in the countries and territories', may be 'juxtaposed' with Article 95, prohibiting discrimination in the application of internal taxation to domestic and imported products. In his Opinion in that case Advocate General Capotorti is rather more explicit, not to say comprehensible, stating that 'the principle embodied in Article 95 is extended in practice to products coming from such countries', thus derogating from the rule that the prohibition on tax discrimination does not apply to goods imported from non-member countries.

This liberal approach has not, however, been applied uniformly: the Court has held that provisions in association agreements with non-member countries which were similar to Article 95 (and often very similar to Article 5 of Decision 70/549) were not to be interpreted in the same way as Article 95. For example, in Case 104/81, *Hauptzollamt Mainz* v. *Kupferberg*,[76] the Court

[72] OJ 1992, L302/1. [73] [1978] ECR 1787. [74] [1979] ECR 935.

[75] OJ, English Spec. Ed., 2nd Ser. I (2), 164. Now, see Council Decision 86/283; OJ 1986, L175/1. The territories in question are dependencies of Member States.

[76] [1982] ECR 3641, following the line taken in relation to Art. 30 in Case 270/80, *Polydor* [1982] ECR 329. See most recently Case C–312/91, *Metalsa* [1993] ECR I–3751.

held that the existing case law on Article 95 was not applicable in relation to the prohibition of tax discrimination in Article 21 of the EEC–Portugal association agreement,[77] which provides that:

The Contracting Parties shall refrain from any measure or practice of an internal fiscal nature establishing, whether directly or indirectly, discrimination between the products of one Contracting Party and like products originating in the territory of the other Contracting Party.

Although Article 21 of the Agreement and Article 95 were directed at the same objective, the elimination of tax discrimination, they were worded differently and were to be interpreted in their own respective contexts. Since the Agreement on free trade and the EEC Treaty pursued different objectives—the Treaty sought to achieve a single market, with all the characteristics of a domestic market, uniting the national markets of the Member States, whereas the Agreement was intended merely to eliminate certain restrictions on trade—the Court's interpretation of Article 95 could not simply be applied by analogy to Article 21 of the Agreement, and the latter was therefore more restricted in its scope and effect. This has not been a consistent approach, however. In Case 17/81, *Pabst & Richarz* v. *Hauptzollamt Oldenburg*,[78] the Court treated Article 53(1) of the EEC–Greece Association Agreement as equivalent to Article 95, whose wording it closely resembled, on the basis that the intention of the Agreement was to prepare for the entry of Greece into the Community by a gradual adjustment to the requirements of Community law. The same conclusion must follow in relation to the EEA Agreement: Article 14 of the agreement is identical in its wording to the first and second paragraphs of Article 95, and the agreement itself is intended to create a broader single market (a 'homogenous European Economic Area' according to Article 1).

The Court has, on the other hand, gone well beyond the wording of Article 95 itself in an important respect—the treatment of goods originating in non-member countries but in free circulation in a Member State. The wording of Article 95 restricts its application to products *of* Member States, which would appear to exclude products imported into Member States from outside the Community. In this respect there is a curious difference between the scope of the provisions on customs duties and those on quantitative restrictions on the one hand and Article 95 on the other, since Article 9 makes it clear that the former provisions, which themselves simply prohibit customs duties and quantitative restrictions 'between Member States', are to apply to 'products originating in Member States and to products coming from

[77] Agreement of 22 July 1972 between the European Economic Community and the Portuguese Republic, annexed to Regulation 2844/72 of the Council of 19 December 1972 (OJ, English Spec. Ed. (31 December 1972), L301/166).

[78] [1982] ECR 1331.

third countries which are in free circulation in Member States'. This creates something of an anomaly, if we accept that at least one purpose of Article 95 is to serve as a back-up to the prohibitions in Articles 12, 13, and 30. The explanation may lie in Article 95's origin in Article III of GATT, an agreement intended to be of universal application, so that the question of goods from other countries would not arise, or in the fact that Article 95 is in the title of the Treaty on 'common rules', which is concerned above all with ensuring equal conditions of competition for industry in the Member States.

Whatever the origin of the anomaly, the Court resolved the problem by what may be regarded as a piece of judicial legislation in Case 193/85, *Co-Frutta* v. *Amministrazione delle Finanze dello Stato*.[79] It held that the aim of Article 95 is to ensure free movement of goods in normal conditions of competition by eliminating all forms of protection resulting from discriminatory internal taxation, and must therefore ensure complete neutrality between domestic products and products imported from other Member States. Its role is to preclude any circumvention of the prohibitions of customs duties and of quantitative restrictions by means of fiscal measures; not to apply Article 95 to products in free circulation would therefore be contrary to the spirit and system of the Treaty. In his Opinion in that case Advocate General Lenz had come to the contrary conclusion on the basis that Article 9 of the Treaty applied only certain provisions to goods in free circulation, not including Article 95, and that the purpose of Article 95 was to secure normal conditions of competition between Member States. He took a consciously narrow view on the ground that Article 95 restricted the fiscal sovereignty of Member States only to the limited extent necessary in order to promote intra-Community trade. Perhaps at least partly in reply to the latter point, the Court held that commercial policy in relation to non-member countries is a Community power (subject to any necessary measures under Article 115); Member States cannot discriminate against goods in free circulation.

Beneficiaries of Article 95

Since Article 95 prohibits fiscal discrimination against products imported from other Member States, importers of such products may naturally rely on it in order to challenge illegal taxation in the courts of the Member State of importation. In Case 68/79,[80] the Court was called upon to consider the situation, not uncommon in connection with the taxation of alcoholic drinks, where a country does have some small production of a drink which is predominantly imported—in the event, spirits other than aquavit in Denmark. Could domestic producers of these drinks who suffered the effects of discriminatory taxation directed against imports argue in the national courts that the

[79] [1987] ECR 2085.

[80] *Just* v. *Ministry for Fiscal Affairs* [1980] ECR 501.

tax was contrary to Article 95 and therefore could not be levied? The Court held that since Article 95 referred expressly to 'products of other Member States' it could not be relied upon by domestic producers. Domestic manufacturers of products which are caught by higher rates of tax aimed at imports cannot plead discrimination; Article 95, like most Articles of the Treaty, applies only where there is some transnational element in the case.

Applicability to Exports

The sections of the Treaty on customs duties and on quantitative restrictions include express prohibitions of restrictions on exports, as might be expected if the objective is to create a market with the characteristics of a domestic market. Article 95, however, simply prohibits higher taxation of imports than of domestic products; it is aimed solely at imports, and there is no corresponding provision prohibiting discrimination against exports, equivalent to Articles 16 and 34. For the literal-minded that might seem to be the end of the matter, but from a fairly early stage the Court has suggested that Article 95 could be applied by analogy to taxation of exports. Such a view may be inferred from rather cryptic remarks in Case 51/74, *Hulst* v. *Produktschap voor Siergewassen*,[81] where the Court referred to the principles underlying the prohibitions of discrimination in Article 95 and in Article 40(3) (common organizations of agricultural markets must exclude any discrimination between producers and consumers in the Community) and stated that a levy on flower bulbs could be contrary to those prohibitions 'if only by analogy' where exported goods were taxed more heavily than goods sold on the domestic market. In Case 46/76, *Bauhuis* v. *Netherlands*,[82] a case on fees for veterinary inspections of livestock intended for export which, it was argued, constituted measures equivalent in effect to customs duties on exports, the Court remarked in passing, without further discussion, that if the fees were also charged in respect of inspections of livestock intended to be sold on the domestic market they would form part of a general system of domestic charges and thus fall under the prohibition of discrimination in Article 95 rather than the prohibition of charges equivalent to customs duties on exports. Finally, in Case 222/82, *Apple and Pear Development Council* v. *Lewis*[83] a levy imposed by a fruit growers' association was held not to offend against either Articles 9 to 16 or Article 95 since it had no effect on imports and affected exported products in the same way as products sold on the domestic market; that does not necessarily imply, of course, that Article 95 is applicable to exports.

None of these judgments, however, states outright that Article 95 prohibits discrimination against exports. That proposition is established in Case 142/77, *Statens Kontrol med Ædle Metaller* v. *Larsen*,[84] concerning a Danish

[81] [1975] ECR 79. [82] [1977] ECR 5, at para. 25. [83] [1983] ECR 4083.
[84] [1978] ECR 1543.

charge on precious metals which was intended to cover the expenses of supervision and was levied on the quantities of metal consumed by each undertaking. Normally the charge was paid by the goldsmith who affixed his registered mark to the object in question, whether this was the goldsmith who actually worked the metal or one for whom the work was done on a contract basis, but in the case of objects exported without a Danish mark being affixed the charge was paid by the goldsmith who worked the metal. The charge was challenged, primarily on the basis that it was a charge equivalent in effect to a customs duty. Replying to a reference for a preliminary ruling, the Court pointed out that the charge covered all precious metal worked by Danish firms and therefore constituted internal taxation, not a charge equivalent in effect to a customs duty. However, although the wording of Article 95 is restricted to imports of products from other Member States, the Treaty seeks to ensure neutrality of internal taxation in relation to intra-Community trade generally. Article 95 must therefore be interpreted as prohibiting discrimination also where the export of a product is the chargeable event. 'It would . . . be incompatible with the system of the tax provisions laid down in the Treaty to hold that Member States, in the absence of an express provision . . . in the Treaty, are free to apply in a discriminatory manner a system of internal taxation to products intended for export to other Member States (paragraph 25)'. Citing *Hulst* as authority, the Court held that Article 95, taken together with the other tax provisions of the Treaty, prohibits tax discrimination against exports to other Member States. Under Article 95 a system of internal taxation must be applied without discrimination whatever the origin or destination of the products. However, there was no discrimination in this case, since the charge was applied to all transactions in precious metals.

For a lawyer from a common law background, at least, this judgment must be a surprising one, flouting as it does the plain words of the Treaty. The Court has often taken a dynamic approach to the interpretation of the Treaty, but only rarely has it taken creativity to the point of filling perceived lacunae. The judgment is all the more striking when it is considered that no argument on the application of Article 95 to exports was raised by the parties to the Danish proceedings or by the Danish government or the Commission in their written observations submitted to the Court (the question on Article 95 was actually referred to the Court on the basis that there was a possibility of discrimination against *imported* metal); the point appears to have been raised for the first time in the Opinion of Advocate General Capotorti, who referred to *Hulst* and *Bauhuis* as support for the proposition. Moreover, the ruling may, again from the point of view of an English lawyer, be considered to be vigorously *obiter*, since the Danish tax in question was held to entail no discrimination.

Nevertheless, the matter cannot be dismissed so easily, for the absence of any reference to exports in Article 95 is clearly a lacuna. As Advocate

General Capotorti pointed out, the possibility of fiscal discrimination against exports is a threat to the principle of free movement of goods. Such protection of the home market by customs duties or quantitative restrictions is prohibited by Articles 16 and 34 respectively; if Article 95 is at least in part a 'third line of defence' then surely it ought to forbid taxation having that effect. Why, then, does it not do so expressly? There are various possible explanations for the absence of any reference to exports in Article 95. It might be thought that discrimination against exports did not occur to the drafters of the Treaty as a possibility. It is clear, however, that, especially in times of shortage, a state may wish to retain goods for its domestic market, and in any event Articles 16 and 34 are directed at that possibility. Secondly, it might be thought to be a deliberate omission, on the basis that the Member States are at liberty to hamper their own industry if they wish. As has already been pointed out, this is unsound economics, and once again the same consideration would apply in respect of customs duties and quantitative restrictions. Thirdly, and more likely, it may be that the possibility of discrimination against exports was not contemplated in connection with provisions governing the retention of a destination system with border tax adjustments, where the main concern was to avoid distortion of competition arising from abuse of that system in relation to imports. In addition, the absence of any provision relating to exports in Article III of GATT, the model for Article 95, might mean that there was nothing to prompt the drafters of the Treaty to think of that possibility.

If we do not accept the extension of Article 95 to exports, how can fiscal discrimination against exports be avoided? The other provisions of the Treaty on internal taxation are of no assistance. Article 96, the only provision which is specifically concerned with exports, prohibits discrimination in favour of exports by means of excessive tax rebates. Nor do the provisions on customs duties or on quantitative restrictions offer a satisfactory solution. It has been suggested that Article 34 constitutes a general prohibition of measures restrictive of exports other than customs duties and equivalent charges. That is to say, whereas Article 30 cannot normally apply to fiscal measures since there is a specific provision governing them, there is no such specific provision in relation to exports, and so Article 34 may be applied as a general residual provision. That argument has the merit of simplicity, but it seems inconsistent with the structure of the Treaty, which envisages three discrete categories covering customs duties and equivalent charges, quantitative restrictions (i.e. quotas) and equivalent measures, and internal taxation. It is hard to conclude that internal taxation should constitute a separate category for some purposes but not for others. Nevertheless, the Court's apparent willingness in Case C–47/88, *Denmark*,[85] to contemplate the application of Article 30 to the taxa-

[85] [1990] ECR I–4509, above, note 43.

tion of goods which do not compete with domestic products and are thus not protected by Article 95 provides some support for this thesis. Advocate General Capotorti raised the possibility of applying Article 34 in his Opinion in *Larsen*, only to dismiss it, partly because of what he called this 'lack of harmony at the theoretical level' but also because of the difference in the consequences of the two sets of rules: measures equivalent to quantitative restrictions must be eliminated altogether, whereas internal taxation must merely be applied in such a manner as to avoid discrimination.[86]

A further possibility lies in the application of Articles 12 and 16, which prohibit customs duties on exports and charges having equivalent effect. The Court appeared to accept such a solution in Case 51/74, *Hulst*, stating that a levy which bears more heavily on export sales than on domestic sales has an effect equivalent to a customs duty. This is not altogether satisfactory, however, since it also stated that the same levy could be contrary to Article 95 'if only by analogy', and in any event such a solution would be inconsistent with the distinction between internal taxation and charges equivalent in effect to customs duties. The only exception would be the 'reverse-Capolongo' situation also referred to in *Hulst*, where the revenue from an internal levy is used to make sales on the domestic market more attractive.

There may be some considerations which would justify a different conclusion in respect of exports. It was observed above that one of the reasons put forward for the proposition that the same tax could not be subject to both the provisions on customs duties and those on internal taxation was that there were different timetables governing the application of the two sets of rules. That is not the case in respect of exports, for Article 16 requires the abolition of customs duties on exports and equivalent charges by the end of the first stage, while Article 95 requires inconsistent national provisions to be repealed by the beginning of the second stage; there is no effective difference in the two deadlines. But the objection that the provisions have different consequences stands, and the overriding consideration must surely be the structural incongruity.

It may be observed, finally, that this issue is of very little practical significance. A specific charge on exports will of course be a charge equivalent in effect to a customs duty; we are concerned here with internal tax charged at a higher rate on goods for export than on goods intended for the domestic market. However, in a destination system of taxation exports are generally altogether free of tax. Article 96, which assumes a destination system of taxation, allows Member States to exempt exports but does not require them to do so.[87] In most instances where the question of the applicability of Article 95 to

[86] It may be argued, however, that the amount of tax which does not exceed that on domestic goods and is thus non-discriminatory should not normally be regarded as a quantitative restriction, so that Advocate General Capotorti's objection is a largely formalistic one.

[87] And see Case 27/74, *Demag*, above, note 33. In relation to turnover tax, on the other hand,

exports has been adverted to even indirectly there was no actual discrimination, simply a failure to exempt exports fully from internal taxation (*Larsen* is an exception: there it was the identity of the person liable to pay the charge in certain cases that led to apparent discrimination). Where all goods are subject to tax at the same rates a failure to exempt exports cannot of itself amount to discrimination. The fact that the goods may then be subject to tax a second time in the state where they are imported does not mean that taxation by the first state is discriminatory.[88] It is only in relation to a harmonized scheme of taxation that Community law is concerned with this possibility of double taxation, and even then it is the country where the goods are imported that must take into account the tax already borne by the imported product.[89] At present, then, it would appear that the only hypothesis in which there could be tax discrimination against exports is that of a tax such as an excise duty charged on all goods of a certain type with no exemption for exports but instead a higher rate charged on goods intended for export.

Article 95—The Distinction between the First and Second Paragraphs

Article 95 contains two separate rules governing what are presented as two distinct situations. The first paragraph is concerned with the tax treatment of similar products and simply states that imports must not bear more tax than domestic products. The second paragraph prohibits taxation of imports in such a way as to protect 'other' products. The latter expression is usually taken to mean products which are not similar but nevertheless compete to some degree, so that the level of taxation on one may favour the other. This dichotomy represents a practical way of dealing with a situation which in reality is rather more complex: that is to say, there is a continuum of competitive relationships, from that between identical products at one extreme to that, at the other extreme, between products which cannot serve any of the same purposes and thus are not in competition at all. The importance of the distinction made in Article 95 lies in the fact that in both cases the ultimate question is whether the tax burden differs in such a way as to distort competition. Where two products are, if not identical, at least close substitutes for each other any difference in the burden of taxation will have a discriminatory or protective effect; the first paragraph of Article 95 thus prohibits any such difference. For products in a more remote competitive relationship the point

Art. 15 of the Sixth VAT Directive (see also Art. 10 of the Second Directive) requires exemption of exports, so that for a large segment of indirect taxation the question of excessive taxation of exports does not arise (the situation in that regard will change if and when the Community moves to an origin system).

[88] Or, for that matter, by the second: see Case C–72/92, *Scharbatke* [1993] ECR I–5509].

[89] See Case 15/81, *Gaston Schul*, below, note 114.

at which discrimination occurs is more difficult to ascertain, and so the second paragraph lays down a broad prohibition of indirect protection.

The Court has often been able to avoid having to decide whether products were similar or not, because in many of the cases before it the discrimination or protection was obvious. Nevertheless, Advocate General Reischl took a contrasting view in his Opinion in Case 168/78, *France*,[90] saying that the first and second paragraphs of Article 95 are independent provisions which apply in the alternative. He came to the rather curious conclusion, in a case involving taxation which was higher on typical foreign spirits than on typical French spirits, that the tax system was contrary to the first paragraph of Article 95 because all spirits were similar products, but that the second paragraph, had it applied, would not have been infringed since there was no evidence of protection. It was in that case and its sister cases on the taxation of various alcoholic beverages[91] that the Court first seriously addressed the distinction between the first and second paragraphs of Article 95. It stated that the first paragraph lays down the basic rule, prohibiting different taxation of similar products, while the second paragraph extends the same concept to indirect protection by fiscal means in relation to products which are not similar but still compete to some extent. The first paragraph entails a simple comparison of tax burdens, while the second paragraph is based on the more general criterion of the protective nature of the tax system. In the event the Court held that some of the products were similar but all were in competition with each other, so that Article 95 as whole was applicable. The Court could then examine whether the tax system was discriminatory or protective, that is to say whether there was a difference in the rules for levying tax and if so whether that difference might favour domestic products.

Article 95, First Paragraph

The first paragraph is concerned with similar products—not, it should be emphasized, identical products. The requisite degree of similarity must, like all fundamental concepts of Community law, be defined on a common basis and not, for example, on the basis of national tax classifications. In some early cases the Court had recourse to tax or Common Customs Tariff classifications. In Case 27/67, *Fink-Frucht*, for example, the Court stated that for the purposes of this provision similar products were normally those coming under the same fiscal, customs, or statistical classification.[92] While the appeal to a simple and easily verifiable criterion had some practical attraction the use of

[90] [1980] ECR 347.

[91] Case 169/78, *Italy* [1980] ECR 385, Case 170/78, *United Kingdom* (interlocutory judgment) [1980] ECR 417; and Case 171/78, *Denmark* [1980] ECR 447.

[92] See also Case 28/69, *Italy* [1970] ECR 187; as late as Case 45/75, *Rewe* Common Customs Tariff classification was still referred to as an 'important factor'.

classifications intended for other purposes was not satisfactory. That approach was expressly rejected in Case 168/78, *France*, and indeed by that time it had already given way to an approach focusing on the particular characteristics of the products and the needs or wishes of the consumer. As with many aspects of Article 95, the criterion of similarity has been explored most thoroughly in cases on the taxation of alcoholic drinks. Thus in Case 45/75, *Rewe*,[93] the Court held that the fact that two products contain the same raw material (alcohol) does not make them similar for the purposes of Article 95; similar products are those which at the same production or marketing stage have similar characteristics and meet the same consumer needs.

The 1978 alcohol cases[94] raised the issue of the similarity of various different kinds of spirits. France and Italy taxed grain spirits more heavily than those distilled from wine or fruit, and Italy, not having Caribbean colonies, also taxed rum more heavily. Denmark taxed aquavit and schnapps at a preferential rate. The three governments argued that the products were not similar because of the differences in the raw materials used, the manufacturing processes, the typical characteristics of the products (particularly their flavours), and consumer preferences. France emphasized the distinction between products drunk as aperitifs and those drunk as digestifs, while Denmark argued that aquavit was unique because it was drunk at meals with typical dishes. The Commission argued that all spirits were similar products, and Advocate General Reischl took the same view. While the Court's response represented a practical way of disposing of the issue, it was not an entirely happy one from the point of view of academic rigour. The Court observed that all the products in question had common features—they were products of distillation, alcoholic beverages for human consumption—but that some had distinct characteristics, stemming from the raw materials used, the manufacturing process, or added flavouring. The proposed distinctions between aperitifs and digestifs and on the basis of taste were not, it said, helpful. It concluded that some at least of the drinks were similar and the others were clearly in competition with each other so as to come within the second paragraph of Article 95, so that Article 95 should be applied as a whole. That, of course, made it necessary to enquire into the protective nature of the tax structures rather than simply determining whether more tax was payable on imports than on domestic products. The Court was able to hold, however, that in a tax system with differing levels of taxation the fact that products which were predominantly imported fell into the higher tax categories demonstrated the protective nature of the system.

The issue of similarity was raised again soon afterwards in Case 216/81,

[93] Above, note 45.

[94] Cases 168/78, *France*, 169/78 *Italy*, and 171/78, *Denmark* (although Case 170/78, *United Kingdom* is one of the same series of cases, it concerns solely the second para. of Art. 95).

Cogis v. *Amministrazione delle Finanze dello Stato*,[95] another case concerning discrimination between grape and grain in Italy, and this time the Court held that the first paragraph of Article 95 should be interpreted broadly. The expression 'similar products', it said, is a flexible one, covering products with similar characteristics which meet the same consumer needs—not identical products, but products which have a similar and comparable use, due regard being had to consumer habits in the Community as a whole.[96] In this case and in Case 106/84, *Commission* v. *Denmark*,[97] where it held that grape and fruit wine were similar products, the Court stated that in deciding whether products are similar it is necessary first to consider their objective characteristics such as their origin, the method of manufacture, and their organoleptic characteristics, especially taste and alcohol content, and then consider whether they can be used by consumers for the same purposes. A rough parallel may thus be drawn between this test and the test of demand substitutability used in defining the relevant product market for the purposes of the competition rules in Articles 85 and 86 of the Treaty.

While these criteria do seem to entail a broad definition of similarity, much can depend on the manner in which the question is addressed. The Court took a restrictive approach, for example, in Case 184/85, *Commission* v. *Italy*,[98] concerning an excise duty on bananas. It held that the organoleptic characteristics and water content of bananas and Italian fruit differed. For example, pears were thirst-quenching, while bananas were particularly good infant food; they were therefore not similar. There is some uncertainty, therefore, as to how broadly the first paragraph of Article 95 will be applied in any particular circumstances.

Equal Treatment

The basic principle in Article 95 is that there should be no tax preference for domestic products. In order to be consistent with the first paragraph of Article 95, therefore, the tax on imports need not necessarily be the same as that on domestic products, but the charge to tax may not be higher. Article 95 is infringed if the tax on imports and domestic products is calculated in a different manner or according to different criteria so that—even if only in some

[95] [1982] ECR 2701.

[96] Not, it should be repeated, consumer habits in the country in question, which cannot be used to justify discriminatory taxation—see Case 170/78, *United Kingdom* and Case 319/81, *Italy*.

[97] [1986] ECR 833. It may be noted that Common Customs Tariff classifications are described as irrelevant in this case.

[98] [1987] ECR 2013. Cf. Case 104/81, *Kupferberg*, in which port and German liqueur wine were held not to be 'like products' for the purposes of the EEC–Portugal agreement because they differed in their method of manufacture and characteristics (the German product was not fortified). For a comparable case on the definition of the relevant product market for the purposes of Art. 86 of the EEC Treaty see Case 27/76, *United Brands* v. *Commission* [1978] ECR 207.

cases—the domestic product bears less tax.[99] It is important to bear in mind in that respect that it is the tax that must be equal; the effect on the final price is irrelevant. It is no defence to say that the imported product is cheaper than the similar domestic product, so that a higher level of tax merely places them on the same footing, or conversely that in any event the imported product is more expensive, so that a higher level of tax does not alter the competitive relationship to an appreciable degree.

What is important is the actual effect of the tax system. The point of reference to which taxation of imports must be compared is the tax in fact charged on domestic products. While that is a fairly obvious remark, there have been cases in which difficulties of application arose. In one case[100] it was asserted that an apparently uniform scheme of taxation of wool resulted in discrimination because the degree of vertical integration in the Italian industry meant that a certain rate of tax was in practice applied only to imports. The case was dismissed on other grounds, but in his Opinion Advocate General Roemer stated (correctly, it is submitted) that where, owing to the legal structure of a business sector, a particular rate of tax is practically never applied, that charge is in fact non-existent for the domestic sector. In comparing tax burdens for the purposes of Article 95 it is the normal situation that must be taken into account. Recourse to the 'normal' situation may not always provide a simple answer, however; the treatment of imports in relation to graduated or differentiated systems of tax has given rise to an abundant case law.[101]

The most obvious instance of discrimination is a difference in the rates of tax applied, but the Court's inquiry does not stop there. Where the rate is uniform a difference in the basis of assessment may entail discrimination. In particular, it is important to ensure that goods are taxed at the same stage of processing. A tax which is charged at the same rate on raw materials or semi-finished products in the case of domestic goods but on finished products in the case of imports is contrary to Article 95.[102] Indeed, an apparently neutral basis of assessment may be discriminatory in its effect—one example is a Belgian flat-rate single-stage tax on transfers of standing, felled, or sawn timber, which was held to be discriminatory because imports were usually sawn timber and thus of higher value at the time of taxation.[103] A Member State cannot tax imports according to a flat-rate scale where the corresponding domestic products are taxed according to their actual value or, for example, alcohol content.[104]

[99] Case 45/75 *Rewe*, above, note 45.

[100] Case 7/69, *Commission* v. *Italy* [1970] ECR 111.

[101] See the discussion of differential tax schemes, below.

[102] Opinion of Advocate General Roemer in Case 7/69, *Italy*, above, note 100; Case 74/76, *Iannelli* v. *Meroni* [1977] ECR 557.

[103] Case 77/69, *Commission* v. *Belgium* [1970] ECR 237.

[104] Case 16/69, *Commission* v. *Italy* [1969] ECR 377, where imported potable spirits were taxed on the basis of a somewhat unlikely minimum alcohol content of 70%, whereas domestic spirits were taxed on their actual content, typically 40% to 45%.

More generally, equality is required in all aspects of the manner in which the tax is levied. The same exemptions and reductions must be available to imports as to domestic goods.[105] The tax must be calculated in the same manner.[106] For example, it is not legitimate to break down what would in a domestic context be a single transaction into two transactions in order to charge turnover tax twice.[107] The manner of payment can also be a source of discrimination. Where payment of tax may be deferred for a certain period in respect of domestic products but not of imports there is a difference in the actual effect of the tax, to the disadvantage of imports.[108] Some qualification of that rule is required, however, in relation to VAT. In Case 42/83, *Dansk Denkavit*,[109] a similar argument was put forward in order to challenge the fact that VAT on imports was payable within one month after the end of a one-month accounting period, whereas VAT on domestic transactions was payable within twenty days after a one-month accounting period following a three-month tax period. The Court held that Article 95 requires comparison of the tax burden at each production or marketing stage, taking into account the rate of tax, the basis of assessment, and the details of collection, including time limits for payment. Under the common VAT system, however, tax periods are not periods for collection but reference periods for calculating the net tax position of the taxable person. The tax position of imports is net from the time of importation, so no comparison can be made between tax periods in the internal VAT system and the taxation of imports.[110]

Even the penalties imposed for breaches must be uniform, or at least not out of proportion to each other. Case 299/86, *Drexl*,[111] concerned Italian legislation under which offences in relation to the payment of import VAT were subject to the penalties for smuggling rather than the much milder penalties for offences in relation to the payment of VAT on domestic transactions. The Italian government argued that the Member States had exclusive power to determine penalties for breaches of the law. The Court replied that although criminal law and the fixing of penalties for tax offences are in general a matter for the Member States, their power is limited by Community law where there is an impact on the neutrality of internal taxation; a system of penalties cannot be allowed to restrict fundamental Community freedoms. In this case it could legitimately be said that there was some difference in gravity between offences in relation to import VAT and those in relation to VAT on domestic

[105] Case 257/86, *Commission* v. *Italy* [1988] ECR 3249 (free samples of low value); Case 21/79, *Commission* v. *Italy* [1980] ECR 1 (regenerated waste oil).

[106] Case 45/75, *Rewe*, above, note 45.

[107] Case 54/72, *FOR* v. *VKS* [1973] ECR 193, where the German authorities sought to charge turnover tax on the full value of imported textile equipment on its installation, having already charged turnover equalization tax on importation.

[108] Case 55/79, *Commission* v. *Ireland* [1980] ECR 481.

[109] [1984] ECR 2649.

[110] See also Art. 10(3) of the Sixth VAT Directive.

[111] [1988] ECR 1213; see also Case C–276/91, *France* [1993] ECR I–4413.

transactions, but not so great a difference as to justify the disproportion in the severity of the penalties under the Italian legislation.

However, differences in the economic structures of firms subject to taxation are not in themselves a relevant factor in assessing equal treatment. For example, a flat-rate annual charge levied on all firms which place certain products on the market, such as a registration fee for pharmaceutical products, may constitute a greater burden in respect of imports than of domestic goods, particularly where there are several importers, since they pay the same fee on a smaller quantity. The Court has held[112] that that does not constitute discrimination against imports (arguably this situation does not fall under Article 95 at all, inasmuch as the tax is levied on firms as such, not on goods).

In Case 77/76, *Cucchi*, Advocate General Reischl stated that in assessing equal treatment it is necessary in every case to take into account not only the tax levied but also any benefits received in return. In that case the Court restricted itself to refining the *Capolongo* exception, but it took up the point in Case 73/79, *Italy*,[113] holding that where the proceeds of a tax levied on domestic and imported goods alike are used to finance activities to the benefit of the domestic product, the result may be that imports are indirectly subject to higher taxation. Italy argued that this approach could lead to formalism in the application of Article 95, since it could charge the same tax without earmarking the proceeds for the offending activities, then simply provide a corresponding sum from State funds as aid. The Court dismissed that argument briskly on the ground that it would be an entirely different situation. A more complete answer might have been to point out that that situation would fall to be examined under Articles 92 and 93, and in the event that the aid was considered compatible with the common market any resulting formalism would be nothing more than is inevitable in a complex society where taxes are rarely hypothecated.

The principle of equal treatment in taxation is taken to its logical conclusion in a (partly) harmonized system in Case 15/81, *Gaston Schul* v. *Inspecteur der Invoerrechten en Accijnzen*,[114] which concerned the importation into the Netherlands by a private individual of a boat bought by him from another private individual in France. Since the transaction was a private one there had been no refund of VAT on exportation; the Dutch authorities nevertheless charged import VAT, so that VAT was charged twice on the same goods. Had the same transaction taken place entirely in the Netherlands there would have been no charge to VAT there, since under the VAT system there is in principle no further taxation once goods have reached the retail stage.[115]

[112] Case 32/80, *Kortmann* [1981] ECR 251; Case 29/87, *Dansk Denkavit* v. *Minister for Agriculture* [1988] ECR 2965.

[113] [1980] ECR 1533.

[114] [1982] ECR 1409.

[115] Unless they come back into the commercial chain as used goods, in which case there are special problems—see below, Ch. 9.

Here, the Court addressed the question whether tax can be charged on importation where the same transaction (supply by a non-taxable person) within the country would not be taxable. It thus raised for the first time the question of double taxation in trans-frontier transactions. In reply to the objection that second-hand goods sold in the Netherlands bore residual VAT, so that the taxation of imports simply put them in the same position, the Court pointed out that the imported goods likewise bore residual VAT. Although the Member States are free to tax imports in the same way as domestic supplies, that is justified only in so far as the imported goods do not already bear VAT charged in the exporting country, since otherwise the tax on imported goods would be an additional charge not borne by domestic products. That, says the Court, follows both from the wording of Article 95, which prohibits not only the direct but also the *indirect* imposition of excessive tax on imports, and from Articles 2 and 3 of the Treaty, according to which the objective of the Treaty is a single market without frontier obstacles. The benefits of that single market must be available to private individuals as well as to businesses. Consequently, the VAT charged in the importing state must be reduced by the amount of residual VAT which was charged in the exporting country and not refunded on exportation. As a practical matter, it is for the importer to demonstrate the amount of tax borne by the goods. Although full neutrality is a matter for the legislature, Article 95 prevents the Member States from applying the VAT system to imports in a manner inconsistent with its principles.

This was an important step for the Court, since previously it had been concerned solely with the situation within the importing Member State. In other cases in which the possibility of double taxation had been raised it had held that the avoidance of double taxation was a matter for harmonization.[116] It must be emphasized, however, that the *Gaston Schul* solution is only possible in relation to a common system of tax, since otherwise the tax paid in the exporting Member State is no concern of the importing country.[117] The basic premise of a destination system of taxation is that goods are exported free of tax and the importing country may tax them as it will, subject of course to any prohibition of discrimination. The fact that the exporting state may, for example, have charged excise duty and not refunded it on exportation is quite immaterial. To oblige the importing country to make an allowance for excise duty paid in the exporting State would have the effect of shifting revenue to the latter, contrary to the logic of a destination system. Indeed, the same effect as regards revenue follows from the *Gaston Schul* judgment itself, since the VAT system does not allow for the refund of tax on exports by private individuals, and that gave rise to considerable debate.

Having laid down the basic principle that residual VAT paid in one

[116] See, e.g., Case 142/77, *Ædle Metaller.*

[117] See Case C–72/92, *Scharbatke* [1993] ECR I–5509.

Member State must be taken into account in the charge to tax on importation into another Member State, the Court then had to define the taxable amount and the residual amount of tax. In Case 47/84, *Staatssecretaris van Financiën* v. *Gaston Schul Douane-Expediteur* (*Schul II*),[118] it was argued that the VAT paid in the exporting State should be included in the taxable amount since it was part of the 'price paid . . . by the importer' (Sixth Directive, Article 11(B)(1)); the Commission, seeking a solution that would protect the revenue position of both States, also argued that the matter could be resolved only by harmonizing legislation. The Court did not agree, taking the view that Article 95 required it to set guidelines to avoid double taxation. The taxable amount is the import value of the goods *less* the residual amount of VAT. Where the import value is higher than the price paid in the exporting State, the residual amount is the amount of VAT actually paid; where the goods have declined in value, the residual amount of VAT must be reduced proportionately. The same principles apply where the transaction giving rise to the importation was not for consideration.[119] Moreover, the residual amount of VAT must also, it would appear, be taken into account in determining the fine payable in respect of an offence against the VAT rules on importation.[120]

In circumstances where this strict requirement of equal treatment cannot be applied, there is a more general requirement of proportionality. This may be seen, for example, in Case 32/80, *Kortmann*,[121] concerning a fee for registration of parallel imports of pharmaceutical products (under a simplified procedure, since the products were already registered by the main importer or manufacturer). The Court held that Article 95 required that there should be a reasonable proportion between the fee charged for the first registration and that charged for subsequent registrations (but not that there should be no fee at all).

Since Article 95 is directed at equal treatment for imports and domestic products it follows that it is only the discriminatory aspect or part of a tax that is unlawful. The contrary might be inferred from the Court's remarks in Case 28/67, *Mölkerei Zentrale*,[122] where it stated that it was for the national court to decide whether the illegality affected the whole tax or only the excess amount. That should, however, be interpreted as meaning that it is the national court that has the task of determining whether or not the tax is severable, not as allowing the national court to determine the effect of Article 95.

Finally, the reimbursement of an unlawful tax must not perpetuate the dis-

[118] [1985] ECR 1491.

[119] Case 39/85, *Bergeres-Becque* v. *Service Interrégionale des Douanes* [1986] ECR 259, which concerned the importation of a car received as a gift. Following the *Gaston Schul* cases the Commission issued a communication describing the approach it proposed to take in such matters; OJ 1986, C13/2.

[120] Case C-276/91, *France* [1993] ECR I-4413.

[121] Above, note 38.

[122] Above, note 59.

crimination. Case 17/81, *Pabst & Richarz* v. *Hauptzollamt Oldenburg*[123] concerned a compensatory tax on imports corresponding to a non-fiscal levy on domestic spirits. Following a finding by the Court of Justice that certain aspects of the German monopoly and tax system for spirits were unlawful[124] the German Government amended the system and refunded the amount of tax already paid on imports. However, it also paid a flat-rate refund on stocks of domestically produced spirits, and this was held to be wrong: if the same refund was paid on imports and domestic spirits the original discrimination in favour of domestic spirits subsisted.

Article 95, Second Paragraph

The second paragraph of Article 95 prohibits measures which discriminate against imports in favour of 'other' products, an expression which, as we have already seen, is taken to mean products which are in competition, partially, indirectly or potentially.[125] As the Commission put it in its application in Case 168/78, *France*, Article 95 as a whole seeks to eliminate all discrimination between products which are in any way in legitimate confrontation. Products compete if they are interchangeable or are capable of being substituted for each other. The products in question must simply have sufficient characteristics in common that they are an alternative choice for consumers in some circumstances.[126] In its interlocutory judgment in Case 170/78, *United Kingdom*, the Court referred to the underlying purpose of Article 95 and the other Articles of the Treaty which promote the free movement of goods. In defining the competitive relationship between products, it said, it is necessary to look not only at the present situation but also at the potential for further development in the substitution of products so as to develop the complementary features of the economies of Member States in accordance with Article 2 of the Treaty. The examination of possible substitution cannot therefore be restricted to existing consumer habits, and the tax system cannot be allowed to consolidate these habits, even in relation to what are perceived to be luxury items.[127] It is necessary to take into account the potential market in the absence of what is alleged to be protective taxation.

The interpretation of the expression 'other products' as meaning 'competing domestic products' may not necessarily be regarded as a compelling one; a more general interpretation could be a powerful instrument for ensuring free movement of goods. For example, let us suppose that a Member State

[123] [1982] ECR 1331.

[124] See, *inter alia*, Case 45/75, *Rewe*, above, note 45.

[125] Case 168/78, *France*; Case 184/85, *Italy*; Case 193/85, *Co-Frutta*; Case 27/67, *Fink-Frucht* speaks of an imported product which is in competition with domestic goods 'by reason of one or more economic uses to which it is put'.

[126] E.g., wine and beer—Case 170/78, *Commission* v. *United Kingdom* (interlocutory judgment) [1980] ECR 417.

[127] Final judgment in Case 170/78, *United Kingdom* [1983] ECR 2265; Case 319/81, *Italy*.

has a favourable tax scheme for certain goods imported from one other Member State or even from a non-member country; that could be challenged under Article 95 only if we interpret the second paragraph more broadly as prohibiting any tax discrimination against imports at all. More generally, we may raise the question of products which are not themselves in direct competition. Imports may be adversely affected by taxation of ancillary products. An obvious example is that of containers. A special tax on plastic bottles, perhaps for environmental reasons, may have an impact on the competitive position of imported drinks. What is the position of such a tax in relation to Article 95? The closest the Court has come to addressing that issue was in Case 27/67, *Fink-Frucht*, where it made the rather cryptic statement that protection may exist where the imported product bears a specific fiscal charge because of any 'economic circumstance in such a way as to protect economic activities distinct from those used in the manufacture of the imported product'.

Indirect Protection

Whereas the first paragraph of Article 95 prohibits higher taxation of imports than of similar domestic products, and thus entails a simple comparison of the levels of tax, the second paragraph takes a different approach: it prohibits taxation which results in indirect protection. The focus is thus squarely on the distortion of competition, the economic disadvantage caused by an additional tax burden. How, then, is it to be determined whether a tax is protective in effect? One way might be by providing direct statistical evidence of reduced demand for the imported product. In several cases the parties have adduced statistical evidence to show, for example, that the allegedly disadvantaged product had enjoyed an increase in demand, but the Court has generally held such evidence inconclusive on the ground that it cannot show what the position would have been in the absence of the alleged difference in treatment.[128] Nevertheless, such direct evidence of protection has had some appeal, and in at least one case the Court has referred to statistics to support its conclusion, on other grounds, that there was no protection.[129]

The more usual approach has been to say that it is unnecessary to demonstrate protection directly by means of statistics; it is sufficient that protection should be the likely effect of the difference in taxation. In its first case on this issue, Case 27/67, *Fink-Frucht*, the Court said that 'indirect protection contrary to the second paragraph would occur . . . if internal taxation imposed a heavier burden on the imported product'. In his Opinion Advocate General

[128] Case 216/81, *Cogis*, above, note 95. See also the Opinions of Advocate General Reischl in Cases 168/78, *France*, and 170/78 *United Kingdom* (interlocutory judgment); in Case 168/78 he suggested that the only way of showing the influence of the different taxation on consumers would be a public opinion poll.

[129] Case 356/85, *Commission* v. *Belgium* [1987] ECR 3299. See also Advocate General VerLoren van Themaat in Case 106/84, *Denmark*.

Gand said essentially the same thing in different words: the second paragraph is to be understood in a wide sense as covering any tax that increases the price of an import in relation to a competing domestic product. That implies that protection and discrimination are interchangeable concepts, which seems an entirely defensible proposition; any discrimination in taxation will by its nature have a protective effect. The Court has sometimes appeared, however, to regard them as distinct criteria which must both be met,[130] and that approach is also taken by some academic writers.[131] This difference in views may be merely terminological, and it is necessary to be clear what we mean by discrimination in this context. The treatment of similar products in a dissimilar manner constitutes discrimination, but so does the treatment of differing products in the same manner, or more generally any disproportion in the treatment of separate products having regard to the relationship between them.[132] Such a disproportion to the detriment of imports will, *ex hypothesi*, have a protective effect. For example, to apply the same tax by volume to beer and wine may amount to discrimination against beer and, where wine is a typically domestic product and beer normally imported, the result will be protection of the domestic market for wine.

In applying the second paragraph of Article 95 it is thus necessary, in order to identify discrimination, to determine the proper basis for comparison. That may not be an easy task, as many of the cases in which such an exercise has been attempted (explicitly or not) show. The most striking example of this is the Court's final judgment in Case 170/78, *United Kingdom*,[133] in which the parties had sought to identify the appropriate basis for comparing the taxation of wine and beer; the Court itself had asked for information on the manufacturing processes involved, but the parties did not think that helpful. The Commission said the proper basis was volume and alcoholic strength taken together, the United Kingdom said the average price of each drink was the correct criterion, while the Italian government argued that volume alone

[130] See, e.g., Case 200/85, *Commission* v. *Italy* [1986] ECR 3953, where the Court said that since a system of differential taxation applied in the same manner to domestic and imported products it was not discriminatory and, for essentially the same reasons, not protective in effect. In its interlocutory judgment in Case 170/78, *United Kingdom*, the Court found that the tax burden on wine seemed to be heavier than that on beer in relative terms but asked the parties to provide further evidence on the issue of protection; in its final judgment in that case, however, it clearly accepted that an additional tax burden on imports was protective in effect. In Case 171/78, *Commission* v. *Denmark*, where the Court applied Art. 95 without distinguishing between the two paras., it stated that it was sufficient 'to examine whether the application of a given national tax system is discriminatory or, as the case may be, protective, in other words whether there is a difference in the rate or the detailed rules for levying the tax and whether that difference is likely to favour a given domestic production'.

[131] E.g., D. Berlin, *Droit fiscal communautaire* (Paris: Presses Universitaires de France, 1988), at 163.

[132] See, e.g., the Opinion of Advocate General Lagrange in Case 13/63, *Italy* v. *Commission* [1963] ECR 165, at 190.

[133] [1983] ECR 2265.

should be taken into account, subject to a corrective factor of 1:1.5 to reflect the difference in the usual quantity consumed. The Court declined to express a preference for one criterion or another, since on any criterion wine was subject to an additional tax burden which afforded protection to domestic beer production. While that was sufficient to dispose of the case before the Court, it is open to the criticism that it did not provide a great deal of assistance to a Member State wishing to ensure that its tax system is fair to imports and consistent with Article 95.

The difficulty of ascertaining the appropriate basis of comparison in cases where the competitive relationship is more distant is perhaps one of the reasons the Court has had recourse to a variety of criteria in addressing the issue of protection. It may, for example, be shown that the tax mechanism is likely because of its inherent characteristics to bring about protection. In the 1980 alcohol cases,[134] where it applied both paragraphs of Article 95 without distinguishing between them, the Court simply held that the nature and structure of the tax systems were clearly protective, having regard to the relationship of competition and substitution between the products, inasmuch as domestic products generally fell within a favourable tax category while products which were mainly imported from other Member States were in an unfavourable category. Regard may be had to the total tax burden, as in the final judgment in Case 170/78, *United Kingdom*. However, in Case 356/85, *Commission* v. *Belgium*,[135] on the rates of VAT applicable to wine and beer, the Court stated that, whereas the first paragraph of Article 95 is based on a comparison of tax burdens, the second paragraph refers to the more general criterion of protection, so that it is necessary to examine the impact of taxation on competitive relationships and determine whether it has the effect of reducing demand for the imported product. Here the difference between the prices of wine and beer was held to be so great that the small difference in the tax rates had very little effect on the final price and so could have no influence on consumer behaviour. The Commission and the French government had argued that, once it was established that the products were in competition, any difference in tax rates on the same basis of assessment would be contrary to Article 95, and that approach certainly seems consistent with the bulk of the case law.[136] It seems more satisfactory, however, to say that this is an illustration of the difference between the first and second paragraphs of Article 95: the second paragraph requires the demonstration of at least a potential protective effect.

[134] Cases 168/78, *France*; 169/78, *Italy*; and 171/78 *Denmark*; Case 170/78, *United Kingdom* (interlocutory); see also the cases on taxation of motor vehicles, beginning with Case 112/84, *Humblot*.

[135] Above, note 129.

[136] See the cases cited above and Case 323/87, *Commission* v. *Italy* [1989] ECR 2275, in particular the Opinion of Advocate General Jacobs. In Case 277/83, *Commission* v. *Italy* the Court stated that even slight discrimination is sufficient to bring a tax under Art. 95.

Differentiated Systems of Taxation

Particular problems arise where a Member State has a graduated scheme of taxation for a particular product or for goods in general. National tax systems frequently include special low rates for favoured categories of goods or producers, or higher rates for luxury products. Until recently many Member States applied a higher rate of VAT to 'luxury' products,[137] and most apply a progressive scale of tax to, for example, motor cars or alcoholic drinks. Indeed, one of the main functions of modern excise duties is the manipulation of demand rather than simple revenue-gathering. Conversely, Member States may provide special tax advantages for categories of products, in order to encourage certain classes of producers or benefit consumers. It is of the essence of such schemes that similar or competing products be treated differently, for various social or economic reasons. How can this be reconciled with a rule which prohibits any measure that places imports at a disadvantage in relation to similar domestic products? In his Opinion in Case 45/75, *Rewe*,[138] Advocate General Reischl took the view that it was sufficient for imports to be taxed at the 'normal' rate, and Member States were entitled to give special tax incentives to, for example, domestic small firms. Yet the effect of that is that some domestic products will be taxed at a lower rate than all imports. It might be argued that if there is to be any difference in tax treatment Article 95 demands that imports should always benefit, that is to say that all imports should be taxed at the low rate in order to avoid any possibility of discrimination. In that case, however, imports will have an unfair advantage which is not justified by the considerations underlying the scheme. The Commission argued for such treatment of imports in Case 127/75, *Bobie*; the German Government replied that that would be tantamount to outlawing graduated systems of taxation, since no Member State could place its own industry at such a disadvantage. The middle way is to integrate imports into the scheme and apply to them the same criteria, so that in the aggregate they are treated in the same way as domestic products. That is essentially what the Court has done, but it is not a simple task. Since progressive tax scales and tariffs of luxury products are generally based on the domestic situation, imports may, intentionally or not, be ill served by the criteria used. The focus thus shifts to the criteria by which goods are treated more or less favourably; it is necessary to ensure, first, that those criteria can be applied to imports and, secondly, that they do not themselves place imports at a disadvantage. The scheme as a whole must be neutral as between imports and domestic products.

An instructive parallel may be drawn in this respect between the case law

[137] This would seem no longer to be possible following the entry into force of Directive 92/77/EEC—see Ch. 8.

[138] [1976] ECR 181.

on differential tax systems and the *Cassis de Dijon* case law[139] concerning Article 30 and the free movement of goods, sometimes referred to as the 'rule of reason'. The *Cassis de Dijon* exception concerns restrictive trading rules which, although apparently applicable without distinction to imports and domestic products alike, in fact affect imports more severely. Such rules, despite their apparent neutrality, fall within the Article 30 prohibition; the resulting obstacles to trade may, however, be excused if they are necessary in order to protect certain overriding public interests. Similarly, in relation to differential tax schemes the Court has held that the Member States may enact legislation which responds to their own social and economic priorities so long as the resulting tax burden is no heavier for imports than for domestic products, both viewed as a whole. The parallel is not an exact one, since Article 95 requires real neutrality of taxation, whereas the *Cassis de Dijon* exception allows foreign products to be placed at a disadvantage where the interest protected is sufficiently important. The important aspect, however, is the flexibility which the Court has been willing to display.

The Court first addressed these issues in Case 127/75, *Bobie Getränkevertrieb* v. *Hauptzollamt Aachen-Nord*,[140] which concerned a special low rate of tax on domestic beer produced by small breweries; imports were taxed at a rate just below the top rate for domestic beer and somewhat above the average. The Court's solution was a common-sense one: a Member State which chooses to grant special tax advantages for certain products must grant them without distinction to domestic products and imports alike. Member States are at liberty to give advantages to categories of products or classes of producers, but these must be available equally to products of other Member States, even where the advantages are granted for purely domestic social or economic reasons.[141] More generally, the Court has held in a series of cases that differentiated systems of taxation are permissible so long as they are based on objective criteria (for instance the raw material or the production method), they pursue legitimate social or economic objectives which are consistent with the Treaty, and there is no direct or indirect discrimination or protection in favour of domestic products.[142] Progressive taxation in particular is permissible.

The requirement of neutrality raises the question of the criteria for the scheme. In order for it realistically to be said that the tax advantages are equally available to imports the conditions of entitlement themselves must be such as can be met equally by imports; criteria which reflect specifically

[139] Case 120/78, *Rewe* v. *Bundesmonopolverwaltung für Branntwein* [1979] ECR 649.

[140] [1976] ECR 1079.

[141] See also Case 148/77, *Hansen & Balle* v. *Hauptzollamt Flensburg* [1978] ECR 1787; Case 26/80, *Schneider-Import* v. *Hauptzollamt Mainz* [1980] ECR 3469.

[142] Joined Cases 142 and 143/80, *Amministrazione delle Finanze dello Stato* v. *Essevi and Salengo* [1981] ECR 1413; Case 200/85, *Commission* v. *Italy* [1986] ECR 3953; Case 196/85, *Commission* v. *France (vins doux naturels)* [1987] ECR 1597; Case 252/86, *Bergandi* v. *Directeur Général des Impôts* [1988] ECR 1343.

national circumstances and thus favour national production are discriminatory in effect.[143] It may not always be easy to determine whether criteria are discriminatory in nature; in Case 196/85, *Commission* v. *France* (*vins doux naturels*) special tax advantages for producers of natural sweet wines had been extended, after pressure on the part of the Commission, to wine from other Member States whose production was traditional and customary. The Commission argued that that criterion discriminated against foreign wine because it was vague and left some discretion to the national authorities. The Court held that the criterion applied without distinction to French products and imports, and there was nothing to suggest that it was applied in such a way as to give preference to French products. Provisions applicable without distinction to imports and domestic products cannot be considered contrary to Community law simply because they *might* be used to discriminate. Where, on the other hand, the criteria and the operation of the scheme are obscure, so that the position of imports is unclear, it seems that there is an onus on the Member State concerned to demonstrate that the system is not protective in its effect.[144]

The use of discriminatory criteria, however, does not necessarily invalidate the scheme altogether. Where a scheme relies on some criteria which are truly general and others which imports cannot meet because of geographical considerations or the legislation applicable to their production in their country of origin, it appears that the latter may simply be ignored, so that imports which meet the general criteria are entitled to the tax advantage.[145]

Secondary criteria relating to supervision or verification can be a source of problems. The possible difficulty of ensuring that imports are in fact entitled to the benefit of the tax advantage cannot serve as a pretext for not applying it to them; it is for the Member State to choose criteria which can be met by imports and can be verified. The Member State may require proof that the conditions of entitlement have been fulfilled, but its evidentiary requirements may not be disproportionate or more strict for imports than for domestic products. A requirement of supervision in the Member State concerned is obviously unacceptable.[146] One option for a Member State which wishes to apply strict rules involving close supervision is to apply those rules only to domestic products and to apply a simpler criterion to imports. That has been held acceptable so long as the practical effect of the rules applied to imports is no less favourable than those applied to domestic products.[147] Evidence of compliance with conditions may be provided in the form of certificates issued

[143] See, e.g., Case 319/81, *Commission* v. *Italy* [1983] ECR 601.

[144] See Case C–152/89, *Commission* v. *Luxembourg* [1991] ECR I–3141 and Case C–153/89, *Commission* v. *Belgium* [1991] ECR I–3171.

[145] Case 153/80, *Rumhaus Hansen* v. *Hauptzollamt Flensburg* [1981] ECR 1165; Case 38/82, *Hauptzollamt Flensburg* v. *Hansen* [1983] ECR 1271.

[146] Joined Cases 142 and 143/80, *Essevi and Salengo*, above, note 142.

[147] Case 26/80, *Schneider-Import*, above, note 141.

by the authorities of the country of origin or another appropriate agency, and in that context a Member State may legitimately require that the imports be subject in the Member State of origin to controls equivalent to those applied in the importing State.[148]

Where the differential tax is aimed not at favouring particular producers or products but at introducing some degree of progressivity it may be difficult to find acceptably neutral criteria. Systems of registration tax or annual taxation for motor cars, for example, are typically based on engine size, but the criteria for higher or 'luxury' rates of excise duty or other taxes are usually more subjective. The Court has addressed this question chiefly in respect of alcoholic drinks, most notably in a series of cases against Italy. Case 319/81, *Commission* v. *Italy*, concerned the application by the latter of its highest rate of VAT to gin and spirits bearing a denomination of origin which was registered or otherwise protected in the country of origin; there was no such system of denominations in Italy. The Commission claimed that this was discriminatory, and one of Italy's defences was that it was at liberty to apply a higher rate to luxury goods because of the greater contributive capacity of their buyers. The Court agreed that a Member State may impose a higher rate on luxuries, but it must not discriminate in doing so. Although some denominations of origin may give products a reputation for quality, that does not necessarily make them luxury goods, especially where they do not have that character in the Member State of origin. Where habits of consumption in one Member State give certain foreign goods that character, taxation must not entrench those habits, for the purpose of the Treaty is to ensure that all consumers have as far as possible equal access to Community goods.[149] The issue was raised again in Case 278/83, *Commission* v. *Italy*: vat-fermented sparkling wine was taxed at the lower rate of VAT applicable to essential goods (10 per cent), bottle-fermented sparkling wine at the standard rate (18 per cent), and sparkling wines with a denomination of origin which were required by law to be fermented in the bottle were taxed at the higher rate (38 per cent). There were no Italian wines in the last category, and the Court simply held that the highest tax category was clearly so defined as to apply only to imports and protect domestic products. Advocate General Slynn, however, specifically addressed the question of the taxation of luxuries; he said that products made by broadly the same process, having the same characteristics, and put to the same use are normally in competition, and the fact that one of them has more prestige does not put it in a class apart. There must be a real difference between the product said to be a luxury and other products, particularly where there is no domestic manufacture of that product, and in that respect it is necessary to avoid entrenching habits of consumption.

[148] Case 196/85, *France* (*Vins doux naturels*), above, note 142.

[149] Case 319/81, *Commission* v. *Italy*, above, note 143. Cf Case 170/78, *Commission* v. *United Kingdom* [1983] ECR 2265 (final judgment).

That suggests that only products which would be regarded as luxury goods everywhere in the Community can be taxed more heavily. The Court has not given any indication of what criteria might be considered appropriate for identifying such goods.

In a progressive system, problems may arise where products at the higher end of the scale are not produced in the Member State concerned. While it is legitimate to continue to increase rates according to objective criteria,[150] the Court may hold that there is a protective effect where the choice of criteria or the rate of tax appear calculated to penalize imports. For example, in Case 112/84, *Humblot*,[151] a special annual road tax of a considerable amount was charged for cars with a power rating for tax purposes above that of the most powerful French cars; both that and the replacement scheme, under which such cars were subject to the normal system of road tax but that system included a sudden increase in the tax applicable in respect of cars with a rating above that of the most powerful French cars, were held contrary to Article 95.[152]

A system of differential taxation is clearly discriminatory where an advantage is granted to a single product which represents the bulk of domestic production[153] or where the scheme is structured in such a way as to give preference to domestic production[154] or exclude certain imports.[155] It may even offend against Article 95 where an advantage is given to one domestic product among many.[156] There is no discrimination, on the other hand, where a significant proportion of domestic production falls into each category,[157] and a system is not to be regarded as discriminatory solely because only imports fall into the most highly taxed category, although in the latter case the situation must be examined closely.[158] For example, in Case 200/85, *Italy*, on the taxation of diesel cars, the fact that the threshold for the application of a higher rate of tax was raised from an engine capacity of 2,000 cc to one of 2,500 cc at a time when an Italian manufacturer was about to market a diesel car with an engine capacity just under 2,500 cc was not sufficient to demonstrate discrimination where the increase also benefited

[150] Case 112/84, *Humblot*; Case C–132/88, *Commission* v. *Greece* [1990] ECR I–1567.

[151] [1985] ECR 1367.

[152] Case 433/85, *Feldain* v. *Directeur des Services Fiscaux* [1987] ECR 3521.

[153] Case 68/79, *Hans Just*, [1980] ECR 501; Case 106/84, *Commission* v. *Denmark*, above, note 97.

[154] Case 112/84, *Humblot*, and the other car cases; Case 252/86, *Bergandi*; Joined Cases 317/86, 48, 49, 285 and 363 to 367/87 and 65 and 78 to 80/88, *Lambert* v. *Directeur des Services Fiscaux* [1989] ECR 787.

[155] Cases 319/81 and 278/83, *Italy*, above.

[156] Case 277/83, *Commission* v. *Italy* [1985] ECR 2049 (it may be noted that the product concerned, marsala, accounted for 90% of Italian production of liqueur wine).

[157] Case 243/84, *John Walker* v. *Ministeriet for Skatter og Afgifter* [1986] ECR 875; Case 200/85, *Commission* v. *Italy* [1986] ECR 3953.

[158] Case 200/85, *Italy*; Case C–132/88, *Commission* v. *Greece*. Cf. Case 278/83, *Italy*.

many imported models and the higher rate of tax was applied to Italian-made petrol-engined cars. Case 243/84, *Walker*, is an interesting one in this respect, for it concerns a range of products competing more or less closely. In Denmark spirits such as whisky were taxed much more heavily than liqueur fruit wine, a Danish product. While the products were clearly not similar within the meaning of the first paragraph of Article 95, they did compete. Walker argued that whisky was for Scots or English people what liqueur fruit wine was for Danes; on any basis of comparison it was therefore overtaxed. The Court noted that the most lightly taxed product was Danish, but whisky was taxed not in a category by itself but with other spirits, many of them Danish. The system as a whole thus did not discriminate against imports, even if it could be said that whisky, viewed in isolation against Danish liqueur fruit wines, was taxed disproportionately heavily. The relevant comparison was between the treatment of domestic and imported alcoholic drinks as a whole.

The most extreme examples of the Court's attitude towards differentiated systems of taxation are Case 140/79, *Chemial Farmaceutici* v. *DAF*, and Case 46/80, *Vinal* v. *Orbat*.[159] They concerned an Italian special tax on denatured synthetic alcohol which was intended to ensure the continued existence of an outlet for agricultural alcohol. The result was to make the production of synthetic alcohol in Italy uneconomic, so that only imported alcohol was in fact caught by the tax. Importers and the Commission argued that synthetic alcohol and alcohol of agricultural origin were similar products and that the tax discriminated against imports. After repeating that Community law does not prohibit tax provisions which differentiate between products according to objective criteria in pursuit of a legitimate aim the Court held that the tax was not discriminatory, since although it hampered imports it also prevented profitable domestic production; provisions which impose a heavier burden on synthetic than on agricultural alcohol are not contrary to Article 95 if they apply without distinction to the two products, whether domestic or imported. Where the tax has had the result of eliminating domestic production it cannot be regarded as indirect protection of domestic agricultural alcohol simply because synthetic alcohol is exclusively an imported product. As Advocate General Reischl pointed out in Case 46/80, *Vinal*, this was not a case of protecting typical domestic products. Agricultural alcohol is produced in all Member States, and the existence of the tax appeared to be the sole reason for the lack of synthetic alcohol production in Italy. The decision to promote agricultural alcohol over synthetic was one within the Member States' independence in fiscal matters so long as there was no discrimination on the basis of the origin of either product. These cases bear perhaps the closest resemblance of any Article 95 cases to a *Cassis de Dijon* approach, since the result was effective exclusion of the foreign product.

[159] [1981] ECR 1 and 77 respectively.

These two cases may usefully be contrasted with Case 216/81, *Cogis*, in which the Italian government argued on the basis of *Chemial* and *Vinal* that it was entitled to tax grape spirits at a reduced rate in order to encourage the distillation of wine and thus ensure an outlet for grape products. Domestic and imported grain spirits were treated identically, but there was virtually no domestic production, at least partly, it said, because the tax made such production uneconomic. The Court rejected that argument, holding simply that grain and grape spirits were in competition and that taxation could not protect domestic products. One explanation for this apparent contradiction is that given by Advocate General Reischl both in this case and in *Vinal*: there is a distinction to be drawn between a choice of industrial policy and a difference of emphasis within agricultural policy. In other words, it is all right to protect farmers against scientists but not to protect Italian farmers against Scottish farmers.

Where the result of a differential tax system is discriminatory or protective it is no excuse that the intent is to favour agricultural production,[160] and discrimination cannot be justified by social considerations.[161] In his Opinion in Case 323/87, *Italy*, Advocate General Jacobs goes further; he suggests that the case law on differential tax systems is an anomaly which allows Member States to discriminate and should therefore be restricted in its application. The economic objectives appealed to by the Italian government in that case—to protect Italian wine growers—would best be met, he says, by Community measures. While it is true that these cases have frequently been relied on by Member States in support of discriminatory systems of taxation, it will be apparent from the above discussion that the Court has in general rejected such arguments where the system as a whole placed imports at a disadvantage and has in fact been restrictive in its approach. Differential tax systems should in no way be regarded as an exception to Article 95, for such schemes always remain subject to its requirements. For the Court to go further and outlaw differential systems of taxation altogether would, it may be suggested, impinge on the fiscal sovereignty of the Member States to an excessive extent and would not be justified by the objective of Article 95, that is to say the prohibition of discriminatory or protective taxation.

Where Advocate General Jacobs is surely right is in his suggestion that the objectives allegedly pursued by the Italian measures at issue in Case 323/87 would more appropriately be met by Community measures (indeed, in Case 216/81, *Cogis*, Advocate General Reischl pointed out that there already were measures at the Community level intended to assist both wine growers and cereals growers, and that national measures should not be allowed to detract from common policies). The suggestion may be taken further. One serious

[160] Case 16/69, *Commission* v. *Italy* [1969] ECR 377; Case 216/81, *Cogis*; Case 323/87, *Commission* v. *Italy*.

[161] Case 106/84, *Commission* v. *Denmark*, above, note 97.

criticism that may be made of this line of cases is that it entails some exportation of economic distortions. Where a Member State decides, for social or economic reasons which it considers important, to introduce a distortion of market conditions in favour of certain producers by granting tax advantages to their products, those tax advantages must be granted on the same terms to imports. However, economic conditions or priorities in the Member States where those imports are produced may be such as to make that distortion less desirable or even harmful there (the practical effect of the tax advantage in other Member States will of course depend on the importance of the market offered by the Member State granting the advantage and the importance of the production sector concerned in the other Member States). The application of Article 95 may thus have a perverse effect in some circumstances which can be cured only by Community harmonizing measures.

Recovery of Unlawfully Charged Tax

The procedural conditions for the recovery of unlawfully charged tax are governed by national rules, subject always to the prohibition of discrimination (both under Article 95 itself and more generally under Community law). Those rules must not be less favourable than the conditions applicable to similar domestic claims. In Case 240/87, *Deville* v. *Administration des Impôts*,[162] for example, the Court ruled incompatible with Community law French legislation which allowed recovery of the excess car tax which had been held unlawful in the *Humblot* line of cases[163] but restricted the time limit normally available for tax refund claims. The Court held that a Member State may not adopt procedural rules specifically aimed at making it more difficult to recover tax levied contrary to Community law. Indeed, the requirement is not merely one of equal treatment: it is well established in various areas of Community law that national rules aimed at preventing recovery of improper charges altogether or making it virtually impossible in practice are not permissible, even where the same rules are applied to purely domestic claims.[164]

A frequent problem is that of rules against unjust enrichment; many countries have rules denying recovery of excess tax where the result would be unjust enrichment of the taxpayer, usually because he has been able to pass the tax on to customers. This issue, it may be said in passing, is not as clear-cut as it may appear. Why should it be more objectionable for a business to enjoy a windfall than for the Treasury to enrich itself by means of an unlawful tax, which is the inevitable alternative? It may logically be argued that the

[162] [1988] ECR 3513.

[163] Case 112/84, *Humblot* v. *Directeur des Services Fiscaux* [1985] ECR 1367; Case 433/85, *Feldain* v. *Directeur des Services Fiscaux* [1987] ECR 3521; Joined Cases 76, 86 to 89 and 149/87, *Seguela and Others* v. *Administration des Impôts* [1988] ECR 2397.

[164] Cf. Case 199/82, *Amministrazione delle Finanze* v. *San Giorgio* [1983] ECR 3595.

reverse is the case, since in a normal competitive environment the business will be led to pass on its good fortune to its customers, if not necessarily to the same customers who ultimately bore the unlawful tax. This point is all the more compelling inasmuch as the business will also have suffered some loss by virtue of the reduced demand for its products caused by the higher taxation. Nevertheless, the Court has accepted that Community law does not require repayment where the result would be unjust enrichment and so does not prevent national courts from considering the possibility that charges may have been passed on to other persons.[165] However, once again the rules governing this may not make recovery of the improper charge unduly difficult. Thus in Case 104/86, *Commission* v. *Italy*, the Court held (referring to Case 199/82, *San Giorgio*) that rules placing the burden of proof on the taxpayer or special limitations on the form of evidence required (in the event, a rule requiring the taxpayer to provide documentary proof that the tax had not been passed on to other persons) were contrary to Community law.

The courts may take into account the harm that the taxpayer may have suffered as a result of the restriction of imports. They may not, on the other hand, take into account the extent of the possible liability on the part of the national Treasury.[166]

ARTICLE 96

Article 96 is the corollary to Article 95; it prohibits the concealed subsidisation of exports through the tax system. It is worded as follows:

> Where products are exported to the territory of any Member State, any repayment of internal taxation shall not exceed the internal taxation imposed on them whether directly or indirectly.

Like Article 95, therefore, it is premissed upon the retention of a destination system of taxation. Goods are normally to be taxed in the country where they are consumed, the importing country, and it follows that they may be exported free of tax. It is necessary, however, to ensure that exporters are not covertly aided by the 'repayment' of more tax than they have paid. Unlike Article 95, Article 96 has given rise to little litigation, perhaps at least partly because it is a much simpler provision—there is no comparison of different products, for example.

Many of the issues concerning the scope of Article 96 are identical to those already discussed in relation to Article 95—its place in the scheme of the Treaty, its purpose, and its relationship with other provisions of the Treaty—

[165] Case 68/79, *Hans Just* v. *Ministry for Fiscal Affairs* [1980] ECR 501; Case 104/86, *Commission* v. *Italy* [1988] ECR 1799.

[166] On both points, Case 68/79 *Hans Just*.

and need not be discussed again here. Article 96 certainly has direct effect, as it lays down a clear and unconditional obligation for Member States; the lack of any suspensory clause similar to that of the third paragraph of Article 95 means that it has had direct effect since the entry into force of the Treaty.

One important point, however, arises from the distinction between internal taxation and customs duties. While a tax imposed only on exported goods would constitute a charge equivalent in effect to a customs duty and thus offend against Article 12 of the Treaty, the mere fact that internal taxes and parafiscal charges are not refunded on export is not inconsistent with the system established by Articles 95 to 98. Article 96 merely permits Member States to refund tax; it does not compel them to do so, or to refund the full amount of tax paid.[167]

The main issue that has been addressed in the very few decided cases on Article 96 is the identification of the amount of tax paid and its character as tax imposed directly or indirectly on goods. Article 96 was first applied by the Court in Case 45/64, *Commission* v. *Italy*,[168] which concerned the refund, on exportation of certain manufactured products, of duties on iron and steel used in their manufacture and of a variety of duties and charges paid by manufacturers. The refund was paid at a flat rate according to the weight of the products. In a first judgment the Court held that tax imposed 'directly' on a product within the meaning of Article 96 was the tax imposed on the product itself; tax imposed 'indirectly' on the product was the tax imposed on raw materials or semi-finished products used in the manufacture of the final product. Most of the taxes which the Italian government purported to refund—registration, stamp and mortgage duties, licence and concession charges, taxes on vehicles and advertising—were taxes imposed on the manufacturer as such rather than on the products, and thus could not be refunded under Article 96. In so far as the system also concerned taxes on the products, it was necessary to ascertain whether or not the refund was always less than or equal to the amount of tax actually paid. Since the Italian government had introduced a flat rate scheme, it was incumbent upon it to demonstrate that the system always complied with Article 96; it was asked to provide the necessary information. In a second judgment four years later the Court found that the Italian system did not ensure that the amount refunded at the flat rate always remained within the limit laid down by Article 96. This approach was repeated by the Court in the Belgian and Luxembourg beer cases,[169] in which the amount of excise duty refunded on exports of beer took into account wastage at a flat rate.

[167] Case 27/74, *Demag* v. *Finanzamt Duisburg-Süd* [1974] ECR 1037; see also Case 2/73, *Geddo* v. *Ente Nazionale Risi* [1973] ECR 865 and Case 142/77, *Statens Kontrol med Ædle Metaller* v. *Larsen* [1978] ECR 1543, although neither of these refer expressly to Art. 96.

[168] [1965] ECR 857; second judgment [1969] ECR 433.

[169] Case C–152/89, *Commission* v. *Luxembourg* [1991] ECR I–3141 and Case C–153/89, *Commission* v. *Belgium* [1991] ECR I–3171.

ARTICLE 97

The principle lying behind Articles 95 and 96, that input tax should be repaid on exportation and that imports should be made subject to the same level of taxation as comparable domestic goods, assumes that it is possible to ascertain the amounts of tax in question. When the Treaty was concluded, however, most of the original Member States operated cumulative 'cascade' systems of turnover taxation under which it was very difficult to determine the amount of tax borne by particular goods at any stage of the production process (in order to refund that amount on exportation) and entirely impossible to state a uniform level of tax borne by comparable goods (in order to levy a compensatory tax on imports—since the amount of tax borne by any similar domestic product will vary according to the degree of vertical integration in the production process). In order to allow the system of border tax adjustments to function it was therefore considered necessary to allow the Member States to establish average rates of tax borne by products and grant refunds or charge compensatory tax at those rates. Article 97 accordingly provides that:

> Member States which levy a turnover tax calculated on a cumulative multi-stage tax system may, in the case of internal taxation imposed by them on imported products or of repayments allowed by them on exported products, establish average rates for products or groups of products, provided that there is no infringement of the principles laid down in Articles 95 and 96.
>
> Where the average rates established by a Member State do not conform to these principles, the Commission shall address appropriate directives or decisions to the State concerned.

The purpose of the provision was to make it possible to apply border tax adjustments while at the same time avoiding the risk of arbitrary levels of tax and refunds being used as a means of protection or as export subsidies. It was no doubt thought that the relative positions of domestic and foreign industries would be preserved by the application of an average rate; the lack of neutrality in relation to imports and exports would be no greater than the internal lack of neutrality. Nevertheless, in view of the system's lack of transparency it was effectively an invitation to discriminate: by setting a high 'average' rate or by taking a range of products subject to different levels of tax as a single group for the calculation of the average, a state could give disguised assistance to exports and place imports at a cost disadvantage. The proviso that the principles of Article 95 and 96 should continue to apply would, if taken literally, prevent the application of average rates altogether; otherwise, it could be of little effect. There was thus an internal contradiction from the beginning.

The interpretation of Article 97 was first brought before the Court for a decision in 1967. Its decision in Case 57/65, *Lütticke*, that Article 95 had direct effect had given rise to some confusion and a spate of litigation in the German courts, largely prompted by the supposition, notwithstanding the Court's statement to the contrary,[170] that Article 97 must also have direct effect since it was essentially an implementing provision governing the application of Article 95. In a number of cases referred by German courts, in particular Case 28/67, *Mölkerei Zentrale Westfalen/Lippe* v. *Hauptzollamt Paderborn*,[171] the Court held that Article 97 gave the Member States a discretion and therefore could not have direct effect. In the absence of Community rules, the fixing of average rates and the determination of groups of products were a matter for the Member States, subject to the Commission's supervision. Moreover, it was solely for the Commission, not for national courts, to examine whether the average rates set by Member States were consistent with Article 95. National courts could at most verify whether the conditions for the application of Article 97 were met, that is to say, that the state in question levied turnover tax under a cascade system and that it had exercised its discretion by establishing average rates. Even if those average rates could be shown not to correspond to the aggregate tax burden actually borne by domestic products, only the Commission could take action.[172]

The result was that companies and individuals had no recourse. They could not challenge tax assessments based on Article 97 in the national courts, and had no remedy against the Commission either, as one persistent German importer and litigant found out. In Case 4/69, *Lütticke* v. *Commission* the Court dismissed the applicant's claim for damages against the Commission for failure to ensure proper application of Article 97 in relation to turnover equalization tax paid by it in respect of imports of milk powder on the ground that the Commission had a discretion to assess the matters taken into account by the Member State in the calculation of average rates and the applicant had not shown that that discretion had been used incorrectly.[173] Lütticke had previously been unsuccessful in an action against the Commission for failure to take action against Germany under Article 169 of the Treaty for infringement of Article 95[174] but had succeeded at least in part in its challenge of tax assessments in the German courts under Article 95.[175]

The approach taken by the Court to Article 97 and its reluctance to intervene contrasts with its vigorous attitude to Articles 95 and 96. It is at least arguable that the proviso in Article 97 to the effect that the principles of Articles 95 and 96 should continue to apply placed a limit on the discretion of the Member States, and that national courts should therefore have been

170 [1966] ECR 205 at 211.

171 [1968] ECR 143. See also Case 25/67, *Milch-, Fett- und Eierkontor* v. *Hauptzollamt Saarbrücken* [1968] ECR 207.

172 Case 29/68, *Milch-, Fett- und Eierkontor* v. *Hauptzollamt Saarbrücken* [1969] ECR 165.

173 [1971] ECR 325.

174 Case 48/65, *Lütticke* v. *Commission* [1966] ECR 19.

175 In the proceedings which gave rise to Case 57/65, *Lütticke*.

able to apply Article 95 where rates which were claimed to be average rates authorized by Article 97 could be demonstrated not to reflect the real burden of tax on domestic products, quite independently of the express supervisory power given to the Commission.

The second paragraph of Article 97 empowers the Commission to take action where it finds that the average rates fixed by a Member State are contrary to the principles in Articles 95 and 96. The Commission adopted directives under that provision on a few occasions, in relation to combed wool in Germany,[176] agricultural products in Luxembourg,[177] and refined seed oil in Italy.[178] It also acted less formally, for example in relation to the German tax on milk powder, which was reduced following the Commission's intervention.[179]

It became apparent at an early stage that Article 97 was not being applied in a satisfactory manner. In June 1960 the representatives of the governments of the Member States meeting in the Council adopted a standstill agreement preventing further increases in border tax adjustments unless these were justified for technical reasons. Meanwhile, pending harmonization of turnover tax, the Commission began to study the standardized application of Article 97 by way of a common method of calculation. Since the introduction of a common calculation method went beyond its powers under the second paragraph of Article 97 the Commission did not itself issue a directive but proposed a Council Directive pursuant to Articles 99 and 100. Although a draft was prepared as early as 1961, the proposal was submitted only in 1967, and the Council adopted the directive establishing a common method of calculation[180] in April 1968, when VAT was already being introduced.

With the replacement of cascade turnover taxes by the common system of Value Added Tax Article 97 became a matter of purely historical interest. Only in the unlikely event of the accession of a new Member State which still practised a cascade system could Article 97 once again be applied during a transitional period.

ARTICLE 98

Articles 95 and 96 are concerned with taxation imposed on products, that is to say indirect taxation. However, direct taxes paid by producers have an obvious impact on their costs, and where the relative importance of indirect and direct taxation differs from one country to another producers may be

[176] Directive of 30 July 1962, OJ 1962, 2214.
[177] Directive 69/12/EEC, OJ 1969, L10/14.
[178] Directive 69/69/EEC, OJ 1969, L52/6.
[179] See the judgment in Case 4/69, para. 17, [1971] ECR at 338.
[180] Directive 68/221/EEC on a common method for calculating the average rates provided for in Article 97 of the Treaty, OJ 1968, L115/14 (English Spec. Ed. 1968(I), 114).

placed at a competitive disadvantage. Accordingly, although the general rule is that only taxes which are levied on domestic products may be imposed on the corresponding imports and refunded on exportation, Article 98 provides for a possible derogation:

> In the case of charges other than turnover taxes, excise duties and other forms of indirect taxation, remissions and repayments in respect of exports to other Member States may not be granted and countervailing charges in respect of imports from Member States may not be imposed unless the measures contemplated have been previously approved by the Council acting by a qualified majority on a proposal from the Commission.

Member States thus may not simply take such measures as they may consider necessary in order to ensure fair treatment for their industry, but must request the Commission to submit an appropriate proposal to the Council, which must then decide whether the proposed measure is justified. The exceptional nature of such a derogation is underlined by the fact that it may be granted only for a limited period. No proposal has ever been made pursuant to Article 98, and since the variations in the balance between direct and indirect taxation in the Member States have tended to narrow it seems unlikely that it will be used in the future.

ARTICLE 99

Articles 95 and 96 serve only to prohibit discrimination in taxation; they do not address the more complex obstacles to trade created by differences in the indirect tax legislation of the Member States. Article 99 therefore provides for the adoption of harmonizing measures. Originally that legislative power was expressed in vague terms, as follows:

> The Commission shall consider how the legislation of the various Member States concerning turnover taxes, excise duties and other forms of indirect taxation, including countervailing measures applicable to trade between Member States, can be harmonized in the interest of the common market.
>
> The Commission shall submit proposals to the Council, which shall act unanimously without prejudice to the provisions of Articles 100 and 101.

The meaning in particular of the reference to Articles 100 and 101 was the source of general puzzlement, without giving rise to practical difficulty. Following the amendment of Article 99 by the Single European Act, the Council may act where harmonization is necessary in order to ensure the establishment and functioning of the internal market—defined in Article 7a[181] of the Treaty, also inserted by the Single European Act, as an area without

[181] Art. 8a until the amendment of the Treaty by the Treaty on European Union.

internal frontiers in which the free movement of goods, persons, services, and capital is ensured in accordance with the provisions of the Treaty—before 31 December 1992. Article 99 now has the following wording:

> The Council shall, acting unanimously on a proposal from the Commission and after consulting the European Parliament and the Economic and Social Committee, adopt provisions for the harmonization of legislation concerning turnover taxes, excise duties and other forms of indirect taxation to the extent that such harmonization is necessary to ensure the establishment and the functioning of the internal market within the time-limit laid down in Article 7a.

The disappearance of the vague expression 'in the interest of the common market' in favour of a more precise form of words probably does not entail any real diminution in the powers of the Community institutions, since a measure which is in the interest of the common (or internal) market can be described as necessary for its functioning. It does, however, emphasize that harmonization for harmonization's sake is not a legitimate Community activity in this field.

A literal-minded reader might conclude that from 1 January 1993 Article 99 is spent and can no longer furnish the legal basis for legislation. On the analogy of the various provisions of the Treaty calling on the Council to take measures before the end of the transitional period it would appear, however, that the time limit imposes an obligation on the Community institutions to act within the prescribed period but does not deprive them of competence on its expiry. It follows that Article 99 can continue to be used as a legal basis where harmonization is perceived to be necessary for the functioning of the internal market after the end of 1992.

Unlike certain other Articles of the Treaty which give legislative power to the Council, such as Articles 100 and 101, Article 99 does not specify the type of measure that may be adopted. Accordingly, in its first proposal for a measure harmonizing excise duties the Commission put forward a draft regulation,[182] that is to say, a measure which took immediate effect as law in each Member State without the need for national implementing legislation (in contrast to the other main type of measure, a directive). The European Parliament criticized the choice of measure on the ground that national parliaments should be able to have a say in any matter affecting taxation. The objection seems misconceived, since the provisions of a directive are equally binding and the discretion of a national legislature is confined to determining the details of its implementation, but the Commission altered its proposal accordingly and its subsequent proposals for harmonizing measures under Article 99 have taken the form of directives. One regulation has been adopted

[182] Proposal for a Council Regulation on taxes other than turnover tax affecting the consumption of manufactured tobacco and for a Council Resolution on excise duties on manufactured tobacco, OJ 1967, 198/12.

in relation to procedural matters: Regulation 218/92 on administrative co-operation in the field of indirect taxation (VAT).[183]

By itself or in combination with Article 100, Article 99 is the legal basis for the legislation on indirect taxation discussed in subsequent chapters.

[183] OJ 1992, L24/1.

4

Basic Principles and Scope of the Common System of Value Added Tax

INTRODUCTION[1]

The First Directive of 11 April 1967,[2] in conjunction with the Second Directive[3] of the same date, required Member States to introduce, no later than 1 January 1970,[4] a common system of Value Added Tax to replace existing systems of turnover tax. Article 2 of the First Directive described the common system in the following terms:

> The principle of the common system of Value Added Tax involves the application to goods and services of a general tax on consumption exactly proportional to the price of the goods and services, whatever the number of transactions which take place in the production and distribution process before the stage at which tax is charged.
>
> On each transaction, Value Added Tax, calculated on the price of the goods or services at the rate applicable to such goods or services, shall be chargeable after deduction of the amount of Value Added Tax borne directly by the various cost components.
>
> The common system of Value Added Tax shall be applied up to and including the retail trade stage.

The above definition sets out the essential characteristics of a theoretical model to which the actual Community system aspires. According to that model, the tax applies at all commercial stages from production to retail and to all categories of goods and services. Although a tax on consumer expenditure, it is collected by traders, who add it to the selling price of their supplies. Multiple taxation is avoided by allowing traders, when calculating the tax due to the authorities, to deduct from the VAT which they collect from customers the VAT which they themselves have been charged by their suppliers. The effect of this mechanism is to ensure that, regardless of the number of com-

[1] For a fuller historical outline of the development of the Community's policy in the sphere of indirect taxation, see Ch. 2.

[2] 1st Council Directive on the harmonization of legislation of Member States concerning turnover taxes (67/227, OJ 1967, English Spec. Ed., 14).

[3] 2nd Council Directive on the harmonization of legislation of Member States concerning turnover taxes—Structure and procedures for application of the common system of Value Added Tax (67/228, OJ 1967, English Spec. Ed., 16).

[4] The implementation date was postponed until 1 January 1972 for Belgium and 1 January 1973 for Italy by the 3rd, 4th, and 5th Directives (69/463, 71/401, and 72/250 respectively).

mercial stages involved in the production and distribution process, the VAT burden on goods or services at any given moment is always equal to the VAT charged by the last supplier. Tax is definitively borne only by the final consumer who, not being a trader, has no right of deduction.

VAT was chosen by the Community legislature because, in contrast to the cumulative multi-stage taxes which preceded it, it was less likely to 'distort conditions of competition or hinder the free movement of goods and services within the common market'.[5] The tax was 'bound . . . to result in neutrality in competition, in that within each country similar goods bear the same tax burden, whatever the length of the production and distribution chain, and that in international trade the amount of the tax burden borne by goods is known so that an exact equalization of that amount may be ensured'.[6]

The system actually established by the First and Second Directives fell short of the model described in Article 2 in several respects:

(1) Member States could choose not to apply the tax at the retail stage.[7]
(2) Only the services listed in Annex B to the Second Directive were compulsorily taxable.[8]
(3) Subject to consultation, Member States were free to determine exemptions from tax.[9]
(4) Member States could, within limits, restrict or refuse deduction in respect of capital goods.[10]

Notwithstanding those deficiencies and the lack of harmonization of rates of tax, the common structures introduced by the First and Second Directives were sufficient to meet the immediate demands of the common market. In intra-Community trade the amount of tax to be remitted on exports under the destination system[11] could be readily identified, and importing Member States were able to impose a level of taxation on imports corresponding to that borne by equivalent domestic products at the same commercial stage. Neutrality of competition between similar goods and services sold within a Member State was also achieved to a significant extent. The main impetus for further harmonization, in the form of the Sixth Directive of 17 May 1977,[12] came from the Council's Decision of 21 April 1970[13] to finance the Community budget from the Communities' own resources from the beginning of 1975; Article 4 of that decision provided that the Community's own

[5] 2nd recital in the preamble to the 1st Directive.

[6] Ibid., 8th recital.

[7] Final para. of Art. 2 of the 1st Directive, prior to its deletion by the 6th Directive.

[8] Art. 6(2) of the 2nd Directive.

[9] Art. 10(3) of the 2nd Directive.

[10] Art. 17 of the 2nd Directive.

[11] Under the destination system the tax on goods and services is collected by, and accrues to, the Member State in which the goods or services are consumed.

[12] 6th Council Directive on the harmonization of the laws of the Member States relating to turnover taxes—Common system of Value Added Tax: uniform basis of assessment (77/388, OJ 1977 L145/1).

[13] Decision 70/243 on the replacement of financial contributions from Member States by the Communities' own resources (OJ 1970, English Spec. Ed. (I), 224).

resources should include VAT revenue calculated by applying a rate not exceeding 1 per cent to an assessment basis determined in a uniform manner according to Community rules. It was, however, also recognized that a greater degree of harmonization would serve to enhance the neutrality of the tax in both domestic and intra-Community trade.[14]

The Sixth Directive, which originally was to be implemented by 1 January 1978,[15] replaced the Second Directive, adopting many of the basic concepts with only minor amendments. It expanded the assessment basis by removing the Member States' option to exclude the retail stage from the scope of the tax[16] and by providing for compulsory taxation of services. It laid down a common list of exemptions from tax and established common rules in the important areas of immovable property and financial transactions. The Directive also laid down detailed rules determining the country in which services were to be deemed supplied and established special schemes for small undertakings, farmers, and travel agents.

The Sixth Directive, like the Second, was based on the destination system of taxation and retained the mechanism employed by the Second Directive for cross-frontier trade in goods, namely remission of tax on exports by the exporting Member State and taxation of imports by the importing state. Services, being intangible, do not lend themselves to taxation at frontiers, and so the Sixth Directive introduced rules locating services in the country of the supplier, customer, or place of performance depending on the category of service. Remission of tax on cross-frontier services was achieved by granting a trader in a Member State who supplied a service in another State a refund of the tax incurred on the cost components of the service.

In its White Paper of 29 June 1985 the Commission noted that fiscal frontiers within the Community were incompatible with the single Community market and in 1987 proposed[17] their abolition. The Commission proposed a switch to a system under which goods and services would be taxed in their country of origin but the tax would be redistributed between Member States in order to preserve the existing pattern of revenues under the destination system.[18] Following a lengthy legislative process, including a communication[19] from the Commission in 1989 and amended proposals in 1990[20] and 1991,[21]

[14] See in particular the 3rd and 4th recitals in the preamble.

[15] The 9th Directive (78/583) of 26 June 1978 extended the implementation period to 1 January 1979 for Denmark, Germany, France, Ireland, Italy, Luxembourg, and the Netherlands.

[16] The 4th para. of Art. 2 of the 1st Directive, deleted by Art. 36 of the 6th Directive.

[17] OJ 1987, C252/2. COM(87)322 final.

[18] Some commentators point out that the use of the term 'origin system' is a misnomer in relation to the proposed Community system under which tax is collected by, but does not accrue to, the State of origin.

[19] Communication to the Council and the European Parliament of 14 June 1989 on completion of the internal market and approximation of indirect taxes: COM(89) 260 final.

[20] OJ 1990, C176/8: COM(90)182 final.

[21] OJ 1991, C131/3: COM(91)157 final.

the Council decided, by Directives 91/680[22] and 92/111,[23] to retain the destination system in a modified form for a transitional period. Under the transitional arrangements goods sold by a trader in one Member State to a trader in another Member State continue to be relieved of tax in the state of the supplier, but are no longer subject to an import charge in the state of the customer. Instead the customer must account for tax on the acquisition on his internal VAT return. For retail sales to individuals the transitional arrangements introduce taxation in the country of origin: an individual from one Member State purchasing goods in another state pays tax in the State of purchase and may freely import the goods into his home State. The transitional rules take account of the concern that the differences in rates of tax applied by Member States may lead to 'cross-border shopping' by individuals and other persons with no right of deduction. Accordingly, special arrangements ensuring taxation in the country of consumption apply to several important categories of trade, in particular cross-border purchases by public authorities and other institutional purchasers, mail-order sales to individuals, new means of transport, and goods subject to excise duty. The rules for cross-frontier services, which were already dealt with under the Member States' internal systems, remain largely unchanged under the transitional arrangements.

The transitional arrangements are applicable until 31 December 1996. However, their period of application will be automatically extended pending the entry into force of definitive arrangements based on collection of tax in the country of origin. The Commission is to report to the Council on the operation of the transitional arrangements and submit proposals for a definitive system before 31 December 1994.

Numerous matters were left unresolved by the Sixth Directive and were the subject of further directives or proposals. Certain directives, in particular those concerning temporary importation within the Community, are no longer in force following the abolition of tax frontiers from 1 January 1993. The directives and proposals of continuing significance are referred to at the appropriate places in subsequent chapters; only the most important are mentioned here.

The Sixth Directive made no arrangements for the refund of tax to traders who incur VAT in a Member State in which they are not established and do not make supplies. For example, an exporter in one Member State may incur VAT in another Member State on trade fair expenses. The Eighth Directive of 6 December 1979[24] introduced arrangements for the refund of VAT in

[22] Council Directive 91/680 of 16 December 1991 supplementing the common system of VAT and amending Directive 77/388 with a view to the abolition of fiscal frontiers (OJ 1991, L376/1).

[23] Council Directive 92/111 of 14 December 1992 amending Directive 77/388 and introducing simplification measures with regard to VAT (OJ 1992, L384/47).

[24] 8th Council Directive on the harmonization of the laws of the Member State relating to turnover taxes—Arrangements for the refund of VAT to taxable persons not established in the territory of the country (Directive 79/1072, OJ 1979 L331/11).

such cases. Similar arrangements for non-Community traders were introduced by the Thirteenth Directive of 17 November 1986.[25]

Although the Sixth Directive laid down a common list of domestic exemptions, it allowed Member States to retain a series of transitional derogations, subject to the proviso that the Community's own resources were not to be reduced. The Eighteenth Directive of 18 July 1989[26] abolished many of those derogations, thus harmonizing further the assessment basis. In addition, the Sixth Directive provided for future clarification of the scope of several import exemptions. By Directive 83/181 of 28 March 1983[27] the Council defined the exemptions applicable on the final importation of goods.

A particularly thorny issue left unresolved by the Sixth Directive was approximation of rates of tax. The Commission saw approximation of rates as a precondition for the removal of fiscal frontiers. Some Governments, in particular the United Kingdom Government, preferred to retain the power to decide upon rates, arguing that market forces would lead to such alignment as was necessary. Some measure of agreement was finally reached by Directive 92/77,[28] which, *inter alia*, laid down a minimum rate to be applied until the provisional end of the transitional period on 31 December 1996.

A problem that has only recently been resolved is the treatment of second-hand goods, works of art, antiques, and collectors' items. Where such goods re-enter the commercial cycle after being sold to a final consumer and bearing tax definitively, they are liable to be subject to double taxation in the absence of special rules. In 1978[29] the Commission put forward a proposal for a Seventh Directive on the matter, which was subsequently withdrawn. A further Proposal, tabled in 1988[30] and in revised form in early 1989,[31] was finally adopted on 14 February 1994.[32] The Directive introduces special arrangements under which tax is charged on the dealer's margin rather than on the full sale price.

Interpretation of the VAT Legislation by the Court

In interpreting the Community VAT legislation the Court has relied heavily on the teleological method of interpretation. It has paid close attention to the

[25] 13th Council Directive on the harmonization of the laws of the Member States relating to turnover taxes—Arrangements for the refund of VAT to taxable persons not established in Community territory (Directive 86/560, OJ 1986 L326/40).

[26] 18th Council Directive on the harmonization of the laws of the Member States relating to turnover taxes—Abolition of certain derogations provided for in Art. 28(3) of the 6th Directive, 77/388 (89/465, OJ 1989, L226/21).

[27] Cited below at p. 163, footnote 79.

[28] OJ 1992, L316/1.

[29] Proposal of 11 January 1978, OJ 1978, C26, amended on 16 May 1979 (OJ 1979, C136).

[30] COM(88)846.

[31] 11 January 1989, OJ 1989, C76/10.

[32] Council Directive 94/5 supplementing the common system of VAT and amending Directive 77/388—special arrangements applicable to second-hand goods, works of art, collectors' items, and antiques, OJ 1994 L60/16.

description of the model system in Article 2 of the First Directive and to the considerations set out in the preamble to the directive, in particular the aim of achieving a tax which is neutral in domestic and intra-Community trade. It has been conscious that that neutrality depends first and foremost on its general application.[33] Thus, concepts forming the basis for the tax such as 'supply'[34] and 'taxable person'[35] have generally been construed broadly; conversely, exemptions limiting the scope of the tax have consistently been construed narrowly.[36] The neutrality of the tax also depends on its remaining constantly proportional to the price of goods and services regardless of the number of stages in the commercial chain. That principle explains the Court's insistence that no restrictions should be placed on traders' right of deduction other than those expressly provided for in the legislation.[37] It also informs the Court's interpretation of the concept of 'consideration' used as the basis for determining the taxable amount.[38]

The Court has employed the technique of giving independent Community-law meanings to basic terms, such as the 'supply of goods'[39] and 'consideration'.[40] This allows it to ensure a uniform interpretation of the legislation in keeping with its aims.

The Court has also laid great emphasis on the contextual or schematic method of interpretation. Individual provisions of the VAT legislation form part of a complex system of taxation, and their function is often best understood when they are read together with other provisions.[41]

THE TAXABLE EVENTS

Article 2 of the Sixth Directive provides that:

> The following shall be subject to Value Added Tax:
> 1. the supply of goods or services effected for consideration within the territory of the country by a taxable person acting as such;
> 2. the importation of goods.

The transitional provisions in Article 28a also subject to tax certain 'intra-Community acquisitions' of goods for consideration within the territory of the country.[42]

The common VAT system imposes a general tax on consumer expenditure

[33] 'A system of Value Added Tax achieves the highest degree of simplicity and of neutrality when the tax is levied in as general a manner as possible and when its scope covers all stages of production and distribution and the provision of services': fifth recital in the preamble to the 1st Directive.

[34] Below, p. 92 ff. [35] Below, p. 108 ff. [36] Below, Ch. 6. [37] Below, Ch. 7.

[38] Below, p. 119 ff. [39] See *Shipping and Forwarding Enterprise SAFE*, below, at p. 93.

[40] See *Coöperatieve Aardappelenbewaarplaats*, below, at p. 120.

[41] See, e.g., the judgment in *Balocchi*, below, at p. 209. [42] Below, p. 140 ff.

by taxing commercial supplies of all categories of goods and services. The taxation of imports from non-member countries and intra-Community acquisitions is secondary, being necessary to preserve the coherence of the Member States' internal systems under the destination system of taxation: foreign goods, which generally enter a Member State's territory free of VAT, must be subject to domestic taxation of a level corresponding to that borne by equivalent domestic goods. The taxation of goods coming from other Member States is merely a transitional measure necessary until the Community abandons the destination system for intra-Community trade in favour of arrangements based on collection of tax in the country of origin, as envisaged by Directive 91/680.

The common VAT system is based on the 'territoriality principle'. A Member State taxes supplies, intra-Community acquisitions of goods, and imports from non-member countries which are made *within its territory*. In order to understand the mechanism by which tax revenue is divided between Member States in accordance with the destination principle, the provisions of Articles 2 and 28a must be read in conjunction with the rules determining the place where supplies are deemed to be made and those governing exemptions for intra-Community supplies and exports to non-member countries. Those rules are considered in Chapter 5.

TERRITORIAL SCOPE OF THE COMMON VAT SYSTEM

Under Article 2 of the Sixth Directive VAT is chargeable on supplies of goods and services within 'the territory of the country'. Article 3(2)[43] defines that term by reference to the area of application of the EC Treaty as defined in respect of each Member State in Article 227. The reference to Article 227 is not particularly helpful at first sight since that Article defines the area of application of the Treaty differently for different purposes. It seems, however, that the relevant territories must be those to which the indirect tax provisions of the Treaty, in particular Article 99, apply.

Notwithstanding the fact that the tax provisions are not expressly mentioned in Article 227(2), concerning Algeria and the French overseas departments, the Court has interpreted the provision as meaning that the prohibition of fiscal discrimination in Article 95 applies to imports from the latter[44]; it should be noted, however, that for VAT purposes the overseas departments are expressly excluded from the territory of the country by Article 3(3) of the Sixth Directive.

The overseas countries and territories listed in Annex IV to the Treaty, to

[43] Art. 3, inserted by Art. 1(1) of Directive 91/680 and amended by Art. 1(1) of Directive 92/111.

[44] Judgment in Case 148/77, *Hansen* v. *Hauptzollamt Flensburg* [1978] ECR 1787.

which Article 227(3) refers, are concerned only by the association arrangements set out in Part Four of the Treaty. Moreover, by virtue of the second subparagraph of that provision, the Treaty does not apply at all to the overseas countries and territories having special relations with the United Kingdom but not included in Annex IV.

According to Article 227(4) the Treaty applies to the European territories for whose external relations a Member State is responsible. Although by virtue of this provision the Treaty applies to Gibraltar, the latter is excluded from the territorial scope of VAT by Article 28 of the United Kingdom Act of Accession. The fact that it is not listed in Article 3(3) of the Directive with the other excluded territories in the directive is anomalous but doubtless expedient.

Article 227(5) provides that the Treaty does not apply to the Faroe Islands[45] or the sovereign base areas of the United Kingdom in Cyprus and applies to the Channel Islands and the Isle of Man[46] only to the extent necessary to ensure the implementation of the arrangements for those islands set out in the Treaty of 22 January 1972 concerning the accession of new Member States to the EEC and to the Euratom.

Article 3(3) of the Sixth Directive excludes from the 'territory of the country', as defined by reference to Article 227 of the Treaty, certain territories of individual Member States which form part of the Community customs territory (second subparagraph)[47] and some which are outside that territory (first subparagraph).[48] The distinction between the two categories of excluded territories is important because special rules apply to imports of goods in free circulation from territories which are 'third countries' for VAT purposes only.[49]

By way of derogation from the general definition, under Article 3(4)[50] Monaco and the Isle of Man are not to be treated as third countries. Member States are to treat transactions originating in or intended for those territories as originating in or intended for France and the United Kingdom respectively.

THE SUPPLY OF GOODS AND SERVICES

Article 2 of the Directive subjects to VAT 'the supply of goods or services', terms defined in Articles 5 and 6 of the Directive respectively. Article 5(1)

[45] The declaration to the contrary contemplated by Art. 227(5)(a) was never made.

[46] However, see Art. 3(4) below.

[47] Spain: the Canary Islands; France: the overseas departments; Greece: Agio Opos. It should be noted that territories which form part of the customs territory but fall outside the territories of the Member States (e.g., Jungholz, Mittelberg, Monaco and San Marino) are excluded from the area of application of the tax by virtue of the reference to Art. 227 in Art. 3(2).

[48] Germany: the Island of Heligoland, the territory of Büsingen; Spain: Ceuta, Melilla; Italy: Livigno, Campione d'Italia, the Italian waters of Lake Lugano.

[49] Below, p. 161.

[50] Amended by Directive 92/111.

defines 'supply of goods' as 'the transfer of the right to dispose of tangible property as owner'. 'Supply of services' is residually defined in Article 6(1) as 'any transaction which does not constitute a supply of goods'.

The residual definition of services ensures the broad application of the tax to all forms of consumption. As both categories of supply are in principle taxable transactions, the distinction is of only limited importance in a domestic context. Its main relevance is in the sphere of international trade where there are significant differences in the rules determining the country in which transactions take place; moreover, only goods are subject to taxation on importation from non-member countries and to the intra-Community acquisition mechanism introduced by the transitional arrangements.[51]

Supplies of Goods

Transfer of the Right of Disposal

The two key elements in the definition of a 'supply of goods' are that the supply must be of 'tangible property' and that it must entail 'the transfer of the right to dispose of [the property] as owner'. The Court had occasion to consider the latter phrase in Case 320/88, *Staatssecretaris van Financiën* v. *Shipping and Forwarding Enterprise SAFE BV*.[52] In that case company A transferred to company B, under what was termed an 'economic conveyance', extensive rights of user and disposal over immovable property comprising land with an existing building. The legal title was retained by A and was to be conveyed later at B's request. After demolishing the building and preparing the site for development B transferred its rights in the property to C. At the same time A transferred the legal title direct to C. The issue in the case was whether A made the supply of the property when it executed the economic conveyance to B (in which case it made an exempt[53] supply of an old building with the land on which it stood) or when it subsequently transferred the legal title (in which case it made a taxable[54] supply of building land). The Dutch Government, although accepting that the transfer of economic ownership alone could qualify as a supply of goods, considered that, where the transfer of economic and legal ownership was agreed upon at the same time, the transfer of legal ownership prevailed and the earlier transfer of economic ownership was of no significance. The Court disagreed. It concluded that, in the light of the aim of securing the uniform application of the tax, the term 'transfer of the right to dispose of tangible property as owner' was not to be construed as referring to transfer of ownership in accordance with the procedures prescribed by national law but covered any transfer of tangible property by one party which empowered the other party actually to dispose of it as if

[51] See Ch. 5. [52] [1990] ECR I-285. [53] See below, p. 183.
[54] See below, p. 183.

he were the owner of the property. A supply of goods without transfer of the legal ownership was therefore possible. It was for the national court to determine whether on the facts the actual power of disposal had been transferred.

The phrase 'actual power' might lead one to conclude that the transfer of physical possession is sufficient to qualify as a supply of goods. However, the contrary is indicated by Article 5(4), which treats the transfer of possession as a supply of goods only in certain cases. The Court possibly meant that the transfer must comprise the legal power to dispose of the rights entailed by ownership but not necessarily the legal title itself. Reference to national law, presumably the proper law of the contract, is therefore necessary to determine whether the rights transferred under a particular contract satisfy that test.

Article 5(4) of the directive treats as a supply of goods:

(a) the transfer, by order made by or in the name of a public authority or in pursuance of the law, of the ownership of property against payment of compensation;
(b) the actual handing over of goods, pursuant to a contract for the hire of goods for a certain period or for the sale of goods on deferred terms, which provides that in the normal course of events ownership shall pass at the latest upon payment of the final instalment;
(c) the transfer of goods pursuant to a contract under which commission is payable on purchase or sale.

With respect to subparagraph (b), the Commission's Proposal[55] originally contained a further provision[56] including within the definition of a supply of goods certain leases of movable and immovable property which could not be terminated unilaterally by the user. In the case of movable property the lease, described as 'a contract for the use of the property', had to contain an option to purchase; in the case of immovable property the option to purchase was not mandatory, but the provision applied 'in particular' to leases containing such an option. Following criticism from the European Parliament and the Economic and Social Committee, the provision was dropped. In the Explanatory Memorandum to its 1974 amendments the Commission pointed to the practical problem that a failure to take up the option to purchase after the leasing had been treated as a supply would necessitate a tax adjustment; it concluded that it was more practical to treat leasing transactions as a supply of services. The wording of the final text of the directive provides no basis for treating as a supply of goods 'pure' leases which do not contemplate the ultimate transfer of ownership even if they transfer to the lessee the right to use goods for most of their expected useful life.[57] The scope of the phrase 'which

[55] The Proposal for the 6th Directive submitted on 29 June 1973, together with the Explanatory Memorandum, is published in Bull. Supp. 11–73. An amended proposal was submitted on 12 August 1974, OJ 1974, C121/34.

[56] Art. 5(2)(b) of the Proposal.

[57] It would seem preferable to regard Art. 5(3)(a) or (b) as the basis for the UK legislation which treats long leases of immovable property (of a term exceeding 21 years) as a supply of goods: see note 98 below.

provides that in the normal course of events ownership shall pass at the latest upon payment of the final instalment' in subparagraph (b) is unclear. The provision clearly encompasses credit sale agreements where the purchase price for the goods is payable by instalments and legal title to the goods passes upon payment of the final instalment. Credit sale agreements containing a clause reserving title under which the purchase price is payable in a single instalment must presumably also be covered. However, since the draft provisions concerning contracts for use incorporating an option to purchase were deleted, it might be wondered whether Article 5(4)(b) covers hire purchase contracts under which ownership of the goods only passes at the end of the hire contract if the hirer exercises the option to purchase. However, such contracts may be considered to contemplate that in the normal course of events ownership of the goods will pass at the end of the hire period, albeit by the device of the option. They are in substance merely a form of credit sale, the exercise of the option being almost automatic.[58]

By virtue of the transitional provision in Article 28(3)(e) Member States may continue to derogate from Article 5(4)(c).[59] This compromise seems to have been intended to allow certain Member States, in particular France, to continue to treat such transactions as supplies of services.[60]

Tangible Property

Article 5(2) provides that 'electric current, gas, heat, refrigeration, and the like' are to be considered tangible property.

Article 5(3) adds that Member States *may* treat as tangible property:

(a) certain interest[s] in immovable property;
(b) rights *in rem* giving the holder thereof a right of user over immovable property;
(c) shares or interests equivalent to shares giving the holder thereof *de jure* or *de facto* rights of ownership or possession over immovable property or part thereof.

The wording of Article 5(3) is somewhat peculiar. First, paragraph 3(a) appears to overlap with paragraph 3(b). Secondly, and more importantly, one might be led to infer from the generality of the term 'certain interests in immovable property' that it was left to the Member States to choose whether to treat the transfer of full title to land and buildings as a supply of goods or as a supply of services. However, it is difficult to see why such a transfer should be distinguished from the transfer of full title to other types of property. Moreover, the legislative history of Article 5 suggests that no such distinction was intended. In the Explanatory Memorandum to its Proposal for

[58] This view finds support in the UK law, which treats the transfer of possession under both conditional sale and hire-purchase agreements as a supply of goods.

[59] See also Art. 6(4), concerning the services of agents.

[60] See the Opinion of the Economic and Social Committee, OJ 1974, C139/15 at 17.

the Sixth Directive the Commission stated that, like the identical definition of the supply of goods in the Second Directive, the general definition in Article 5(1) of the Directive was intended to apply to both movable and immovable property. The Commission's Proposal made no mention of 'certain interests in immovable property', a phrase which seems to have been added during the Council deliberations. The Proposal provided, in a draft second subparagraph of Article 5(1), that the categories of interest referred to in paragraphs 3(b) and (c) of the final text were to be treated as the property to which they related. The Proposal therefore seems to have assumed that the transfer of full title to immovable property would constitute a supply of goods under the general definition and sought to extend that definition to certain lesser or more indirect interests which might otherwise have fallen outside the definition. Paragraph 3(a) may have been added to allow the Member States full discretion to include within the definition of the supply of goods other interests, not covered by the general definition or by subparagraphs (b) and (c).[61] That the word 'interests' is qualified by the adjective 'certain' makes clear that Member States may select such interests as they see fit for such treatment.

It appears from the Explanatory Memorandum to the Commission's Proposal that Article 5(3)(b) was prompted by the existence in the private law of Member States of rights *in rem* giving the owner the right of economic utilization (for example, 'usufruct', 'emphyteusis' and 'superficie'). The oral explanations given by the Commission recorded in the European Parliament's working documents[62] indicate that Article 5(3)(c) was intended to cover situations which arise especially in France and Italy involving immovable property societies (joint possession of flats in which the shareholders also live).

Other Clarifications or Extensions of the Definition

Article 5(5) allows Member States to treat as a supply of goods the supply by a contractor of movable property made or assembled from materials supplied wholly or partly by the customer himself (subparagraph (a)), and also the handing over of certain works of construction (subparagraph (b)). Both provisions are similar to provisions that were mandatory in the Second Directive[63] and in the Commission's Proposal for the Sixth Directive.[64]

With respect to contract work under Article 5(5)(a), the Court held, in Case 139/84, *Van Dijk's Boekhuis* v. *Staatssecretaris van Financiën*,[65] that the production of goods from customers' materials implied the production of a new article whose function was different from that of the materials provided. It followed that repairs, however radical, which simply restored an article to the function which it previously had did not amount to a supply of goods for the purposes

[61] See also note 57 above.
[62] PE 35.687/fin 52.
[63] See Art. 5(2)(d) and (e) of the 2nd Directive.
[64] Art. 5(2)(d) and (e) of the Proposal.
[65] [1985] ECR 1405.

of Article 5(5)(a). The different classification as goods or services possible under Article 5(5)(a) was liable to lead to double taxation or non-taxation in intra-Community trade under the transitional arrangements. Consequently, on certain conditions intra-Community supplies of this type are compulsorily treated as supplies of goods under Article 28a(5)(a) of the directive.[66]

With respect to Article 5(5)(b), it may be noted that Article 6 of the Proposal defined the term 'works of construction' broadly as including 'all works relating to buildings, bridges, roads, ports, and other structures fixed to the ground' and 'works on preparing and improving ground'. That definition was deleted from the final text. Moreover, the addition of the word 'certain' suggests that Member States are in principle free to choose which works of construction they wish to treat as goods.

Article 5(6) and (7) provides that a taxable person shall or may be deemed to make a supply of goods in certain cases; Article 5(8) allows Member States to disregard certain supplies of goods. These provisions are considered below together with similar provisions concerning services in Article 6.

Mixed or Composite Supplies

A common difficulty is to ascertain whether a mixed or composite supply of goods or, more often, goods and services is to be regarded as a single supply of either goods or services or several supplies which may carry different liabilities. For example, does a customer at a self-service launderette receive a single service, namely the use of the facilities for washing his clothes, or individual supplies of electricity, water, use of equipment, and so forth?[67] Does an airline passenger receive a composite supply of air transport or several supplies of transport, food, and drink?[68]

Little guidance is to be derived on this question from the case law. Reference is sometimes made in this connection[69] to Case 126/78, *Nederlandse Spoorwegen* v. *Staatssecretaris van Financiën*.[70] In that case the Court held that a cash-collection service undertaken by a transport company when delivering goods to consignees was a service ancillary to transport within the meaning of Annex B, item 5, of the Second Directive and hence, like the transport service, was compulsorily taxable under Article 6 of the Directive. However, as Advocate General Jacobs noted in Case C–281/91, *Muys*,[71] despite its apparent relevance the case did not concern the question whether the consideration

[66] See below, p. 145.

[67] See the English VAT Tribunal decision in *Mander Laundries Ltd* [1973] VATTR 136.

[68] See the English Court of Appeal decision in *British Airways plc* v. *Commissioners of Customs and Excise* [1990] STC 643.

[69] See, e.g., the Commission's observations in the Report for the Hearing in Case C–281/91, *Muys' en De Winter's Bouw-en Aannemingsbedrijf BV* v. *Staatssecretaris van Financiën* [1993] ECR I–5405.

[70] [1979] ECR 2041.

[71] Note 69 above.

for the two supplies constituted consideration for a single supply. The issue was whether the collection service, which was acknowledged to be a separate service, was so inextricably linked to the transport service that it was to be regarded as 'ancillary' to it for the purposes of the Second Directive, and hence as falling into the category of services which were compulsorily taxable.

What considerations might therefore be relevant? The most appropriate criterion, in the light of the character of the tax as a consumption tax and the aim of competitive neutrality, might be the perception of the customer. Does he think he is receiving a single supply or a collection of individual supplies? A customer (other, perhaps, than a scientist!) visiting a launderette perceives what he receives, not as a collection of individual services, but as the use of the washing facilities, primarily the washing machine. Similarly, the airline passenger is buying a flight for himself and, he hopes, his luggage to his chosen destination; anything else he receives is incidental, a mere component of the basic service provided. Some support for this approach may be derived from remarks made by Advocate General Jacobs in his Opinion in *Muys*, where he considered the consumer's viewpoint when concluding that the supply of credit by a supplier of goods or services constituted a separate supply from the main supply of goods or services.

The mere fact that certain supplies are grouped together or indicated separately in a contract or invoice surely cannot override the substantive position. A clear separation of an exempt supply may, however, be a condition for exemption. In *Muys* considerable emphasis was placed by the German and Dutch Governments in their observations, and by the Advocate General in his Opinion, on the requirement that the grant of credit by a supplier should be clearly dissociated from the main supply of goods or services in the contract of sale if it was to qualify for exemption as a separate supply under Article 13(B)(d)(1). The Advocate General also observed that under Article 13 Member States were permitted to lay down such further conditions as were necessary to prevent avoidance, evasion, or abuse; this might be particularly relevant to transactions between connected persons. Many supplies to final consumers, however, take place without any formal written contract. At most the detailed analysis of the supplies made, together with the terms and conditions, are set out on the invoice;[72] in the case of many retail transactions only a till receipt is issued. In *Muys* the concern of the Advocate General was to prevent the artificial conversion of part of the purchase price of goods or services into consideration for an exempt supply of credit. It does not seem unreasonable that he should have demanded some formal evidence of the separate credit transaction, since its existence is based purely on an economic analysis of the transaction. It is submitted that, in the case of other mixed transactions where there has been a verifiable supply of goods or services

[72] Under Art. 22(3)(b) an invoice to a taxable person must state clearly the relevant tax at each rate as well as any exemptions.

attracting exemption or lower rates of tax, a clear breakdown on the invoice or even on the till receipt should suffice, without prejudice to the right of Member States to adopt such measures to prevent avoidance or abuse as prove necessary.

Supplies of Services

Article 6(1) provides as follows:

> 'Supply of services' shall mean any transaction which does not constitute a supply of goods within the meaning of Article 5.
>
> Such transactions may include *inter alia*:
>
> —assignments of intangible property whether or not it is the subject of a document establishing title,
>
> —obligations to refrain from an act or to tolerate an act or situation,
>
> —the performance of services in pursuance of an order made by or in the name of a public authority or in pursuance of the law.

Terra and Kajus observe[73] that the use of the word 'may' in the second subparagraph was intended to indicate that the list is not exhaustive rather than to give Member States discretion whether to treat such transactions as services. Although this does not fully explain the need for the insertion of the word, which did not appear in the Proposal, one might have expected the use of a clearer formulation such as 'Member States may treat as'[74] if the intention had been to make the treatment optional.[75]

The broad definition of 'services' in Article 6(1) is consistent with the generality of the tax. The scope of the provision may not, however, be as limitless as its wording might suggest. In its written observations in *Polysar*[76] the French Government had regard in this connection to the primary aim of the common VAT system, namely to achieve competitive neutrality by eliminating factors likely to distort competition. It argued that, unlike debt interest or management fees, dividends were not reflected in the cost components of goods or services and did not constitute consideration for a provision of services since they amounted to a share of the profits. That analysis, although not entirely unassailable from an economic viewpoint, is noteworthy inasmuch as it reflects an attempt to look behind the formal requirements of the Directive and to examine the rationale for including a transaction within its scope. That approach is surely correct. Consider for example the case of a

[73] *A Guide to the Sixth VAT Directive* (Amsterdam: IBFD, 1991), Vol. A, 301.

[74] See Arts. 6(3) and 5(3), (5) and (7).

[75] It may be noted, moreover, that services of the first two types are dealt with expressly in Art. 9(2)(e) of the Directive, concerning the place of supply of services, without any suggestion that their treatment as services is optional. The third type of transaction corresponds to the equivalent transaction involving goods, which is the subject of a compulsory provision in Art. 5(4)(a).

[76] Below, p. 112. See the Report for the Hearing.

share or debenture issue. On a purely formal analysis the issue of the shares or debentures would qualify as a service by the company, namely the transfer of the shareholder's or lender's rights. However, the subscriber or lender is not in any sense purchasing a service from the company which would be a suitable subject for a tax on consumption. The economic benefit in fact flows the other way, and is paid for by dividends or interest payments. Moreover, VAT is a tax on turnover, and subscriptions for share issues and loans do not form part of an undertaking's turnover in any normal sense.[77]

A related issue is the extent to which reference should be made to national law for the purpose of defining services. As stated above, in the case of goods the Court's decision in *Shipping and Forwarding Enterprise SAFE*[78] indicates that reference to national law is necessary for the purpose of determining the nature of the rights transferred under a contract. The question whether the transfer of particular rights constitutes the transfer of the right of disposal as owner for the purposes of Article 5(1) is one of Community law. In the case of services, it is difficult to see why reference to national law should be necessary, since a service is not defined by reference to the transfer of particular rights defined by national law. It would surely be preferable to adopt an independent legal analysis of transactions which is consistent with the purpose and scheme of the Directive.

Private Use of Goods and Services

Article 6(2) of the Directive provides that:

> The following shall be treated as supplies of services for consideration:
>
> (a) the use of goods forming part of the assets of a business for the private use of the taxable person or of his staff or more generally for purposes other than those of his business where the Value Added Tax on such goods is wholly or partly deductible;
>
> (b) supplies of services carried out free of charge by the taxable person for his own private use or that of his staff or more generally for purposes other than those of his business.
>
> Member States may derogate from the provisions of this paragraph provided that such derogation does not lead to distortion of competition.

That provision should be read in conjunction with the parallel provision in Article 5(6), which reads as follows:

> The application by a taxable person of goods forming part of his business assets for his private use or that of his staff, or the disposal thereof free of charge or more generally their application for purposes other than those of his business, where the Value

[77] In this connection it may be noted that in his Opinion in *Sofitam*, below, p. 113, Advocate General Van Gerven took the view that the term 'turnover' in Art. 19(2) of the Directive was to be given its general economic meaning according to common usage.

[78] Above, note 52.

Added Tax on the goods in question or the component parts thereof was wholly or partly deductible, shall be treated as supplies made for consideration. However, applications for the giving of samples or the making of gifts of small value for the purpose of the taxable person's business shall not be so treated.

Articles 5(6) and 6(2)(a) are complementary. The former concerns the outright transfer of goods to non-business use, the goods ceasing to form part of the assets of the business, whereas the latter concerns the use for non-business purposes of goods which remain part of the assets of the business.[79] The provisions are intended to ensure that a taxable person who puts to private use business goods on which he has deducted VAT does not gain an unwarranted advantage by comparison with a final consumer.[80] The device employed is to invent a fiction whereby a taxable person who has deducted VAT on privately used business goods makes a taxable supply of goods (Article 5(6)) or services (Article 6(2)(a)), thus giving rise to an output-tax charge in respect of the private use.

Articles 5(6) and 6(2)(a) are expressly stated to operate only where the taxable person has deducted input tax on the goods wholly or in part. As the Court explained in Case 50/88, *Kühne* v. *Finanzamt München III*[81] in relation to Article 6(2)(a):

that provision is designed to prevent non-taxation of business goods used for private purposes and therefore requires the taxation of the private use of such goods only where the tax paid on their acquisition was deductible.[82]

In that case the Court held that no charge to tax arose under Article 6(2)(a) in respect of the private use by a taxable person of goods (a motor car) acquired second-hand without deduction of tax from a private individual, notwithstanding the fact that the taxable person had deducted tax on the costs incurred in connection with the maintenance and use of the goods. The tax rules applicable to the supply of business goods were to be distinguished from those concerning the taxable expenses incurred for their use and maintenance. The Court added that Article 6(2) had direct effect.

Private Use of Goods and Deduction of Input Tax

The drafting of Articles 5(6) and 6(2)(a) prompts a basic question. Under those provisions a taxable supply arises where VAT has been deducted wholly or partly on the goods. Does it follow that a taxable person is entitled to full input-tax deduction on the acquisition of goods intended for mixed use because the private use is treated as a taxable supply? That was the Court's

[79] See para. 5 of the Opinion of Advocate General Jacobs in Case C–20/91, *De Jong* v. *Staatssecretaris van Financiën* [1992] ECR I–2847.

[80] See, e.g., para. 15 of the judgment in *De Jong*.

[81] [1989] ECR 1925.

[82] Para. 8 of the judgment.

understanding of the mechanism in Case C–97/90, *Lennartz* v. *Finanzamt München III*.[83] In that case it was asked to consider, in relation to a motor car put to mixed use, whether the practice of the German tax authorities of disallowing any deduction of input tax where the business use of goods amounted to less than 10 per cent was compatible with the Directive. The Court held that in principle a taxable person who uses a motor car for both private and taxable business purposes is entitled to deduct input tax in full on the acquisition of the car however small the proportion of business use.[84] In so doing the Court opted for the Commission's and also the French and German Governments' understanding of the private-use mechanism. The German 10 per cent rule was in fact applied by the German tax authorities precisely because of the principle of full initial deduction, which they considered unjustified in cases of negligible business use. The French Government, which shortly beforehand had amended its legislation after the Conseil d'Etat had found it to be incompatible with the Directive,[85] had implemented the principle of full deduction coupled with subsequent periodic private-use charges but had obtained authorization under Article 27 of the Directive to apply, in derogation from the Directive, a 10 per cent rule similar to the German one. By implication the Court rejected the method then employed in the United Kingdom of a single input-tax apportionment on the acquisition of goods.

Private use of goods could equally have been accounted for by adjusting the initial deduction made by the taxable person. However, it seems that the device of a deemed supply was preferred, for reasons of 'impartiality and simplicity'.[86] It is true that the device of full deduction combined with an output-tax charge confers on the taxable person an unwarranted cash-flow advantage, inasmuch as he initially deducts VAT in full and is only later obliged to account for tax in respect of his private use. It might in fact have been appropriate for the Community legislator to incorporate in the Directive a minimum business use requirement such as the French and German.[87] However, apart from providing a relatively simple means of adjusting for changes in the proportions of business and private use, the output-tax mechanism has the advantage of allowing account to be taken of the full cost of the goods at the time when they are put to non-business use.[88]

In his recent Opinion in Case C–291/92, *Finanzamt Uelzen* v. *Armbrecht*[89] Advocate General Van Gerven none the less suggested that a taxable person who acquires an immovable property for mixed use may choose not to assign

[83] [1991] ECR I–3795.

[84] See para. 35 of the judgment.

[85] See *Compagnie Alitalia* [1990] 1–CMLR 248.

[86] See the Explanatory Memorandum accompanying the Proposal for a 6th Directive, above, 10.

[87] It should also be noted that Art. 17(6) of the 6th Directive allows Member States to disallow deduction of VAT on expenditure that does not strictly relate to the business: see below.

[88] See below, p. 105.

[89] Opinion of 15 September 1993, judgment not yet delivered.

the private part of the asset to his business. The issue in the case was whether a taxable person who supplied a guest house used partly for business and partly for private use could restrict the option for tax provided for by the German rules implementing Article 13C of the Directive[90] to the parts of the building used for business purposes or, in other words, whether the supply of the business parts constituted a separate item of supply for the purposes of Article 5(1). The Advocate General referred to the earlier case of *de Jong*,[91] in which the Court held that, where a builder acquired land in his private capacity and subsequently built a house on it for his private occupation, the charge for private use applied solely to the value of the building and not to the value of the land. The land never became part of the builder's business assets and hence could not be transferred to private use for the purposes of Article 5(6). The Advocate General concluded that, by analogy with that case, the private part of the guest house was to be treated separately for VAT purposes provided that the taxable person had evinced an intention to keep it outside the scope of VAT by refraining from deducting VAT on its acquisition and not charging VAT on its sale. He distinguished the *Lennartz* case on the basis that, unlike a motor car in respect of which it was not possible to determine precisely the parts put to business and private use, an immovable property could be precisely divided into a private part and a business part. The fact that the degree of business use might change after the sale was immaterial since it was the degree of business use by the vendor at the time of the supply by the vendor which was decisive.

Provided that the rules of the Directive are properly implemented, it is, however, unclear why a taxable person should make such a choice. The assignment of part of an immovable property irrevocably to private use offers the taxable person less flexibility than full immediate deduction of tax combined with periodic output-tax charges; moreover, the latter method is also reasonably straightforward to apply if the option to tax is implemented coherently.

Suppose, for example, that a taxable person acquires a guest house for £100,000 plus £10,000 VAT. The business and private proportions are respectively 90 per cent and 10 per cent in year one and 85 per cent and 15 per cent in year two. At the end of year one he builds an extension to the guest house costing £30,000 plus £3,000 VAT. At the end of year two he sells the guest house to another taxable person whose business and private use is respectively 95 per cent and 5 per cent in years three and four. The taxable person deducts in full the VAT of £10,000 at the beginning of year one and the £3,000 VAT at the end of that year but is then subject to an output-tax charge under Article 6(2)(a) in each of years one and two to take account of the varying degrees of private use of both the original building and the

[90] See below, at p. 183. [91] Above, note 79.

extension. The Member State should allow the taxable person to exercise the option to tax in respect of the property as a whole.[92] The vendor then exercises the option to tax, thus avoiding the clawback of tax which would arise under Article 20(2) of the Directive in the event of an exempt sale during the five- or ten-year adjustment period provided for by that provision. The purchaser is entitled to deduct the tax in full, but is subject to an output-tax charge in respect of his private use. Nevertheless, if the Advocate General Van Gerven's Opinion is followed by the Court, it may prove more advantageous for taxable persons to keep the privately occupied parts of an immovable property out of the business in view of the tendency of such property to appreciate.

Private Use of Services

In Case C–193/91, *Mohsche* v. *Finanzamt München III*[93] the Court was asked to consider a case concerning a situation which was the converse of that in *Kühne*. The issue was whether motor vehicle running costs on which no VAT was deducted (e.g., car insurance and tax) should be included in the charge for private use where VAT was deductible on the purchase of the motor vehicle. The Court held that the term 'use of goods' in Article 6(2)(a) did not include services ancillary to such use—the term covered only the use of the goods themselves. It offered little reasoning for its decision, merely observing that, unlike normal supplies which are taxable regardless of whether VAT was deductible on their cost components, private use was taxable only by way of exception. Further guidance may perhaps be derived from the Opinion of Advocate General Jacobs, whose conclusion was followed by the Court. The Advocate General considered that it followed from the principle laid down by the Court in *Kühne* that no charge for private use should be levied in respect of services or costs on which no tax was deducted. The Advocate General rejected the German Government's view that Mr Mohsche was to be equated with a person hiring a car from his business and, in the interests of neutrality, should suffer the same degree of double taxation. The purpose of Article 6(2)(a) was to place the taxable person in the position in which he would have been if he had acquired the goods as a private individual without any right of deduction. A private purchaser would not pay VAT on untaxed items and his tax burden on exempt items would be limited to the irrecoverable VAT incurred by the supplier. Since the operation of Article 6(2)(a) was dependent solely on tax having been deducted on the goods, the desired result could properly be achieved only by limiting the charge under that provision to the

[92] It appears that the German rules limit the option for tax to transactions 'carried out for another trader for the purposes of his business' (see point 2 of Advocate General Van Gerven's Opinion). It is unclear whether that expression covers transactions carried out for the purposes of taxable supplies deemed to arise under the German rules implementing Art. 6(2)(a) of the 6th Directive.

[93] Judgment of 25 May 1993, [1993] ECR I–2615.

use of the goods themselves. The private use of exempt or untaxed costs connected with such use would not therefore form the subject of the supply deemed to arise under the provision. The Advocate General added that this would not lead to tax avoidance by the taxable person in respect of *taxable* services connected with the use of goods (in respect of which VAT would normally be deductible), since his deduction entitlement in respect of such services would be restricted owing to the lack of taxable use.

The Advocate General's analysis has much to recommend it inasmuch as it leads to coherent treatment of costs ancillary to the use of goods. The treatment of such services does not depend—arbitrarily—on whether tax was deducted on the goods. The Advocate General suggested that the rationale for using the device of the deemed supply, namely allowing periodic adjustments in respect of private use, applied with less force to services which were generally consumed more quickly. He doubtless had in mind the vehicle running costs concerned in the case. It is submitted that a different analysis should apply to services involving additions or improvements to capital goods (e.g., construction services) which become incorporated in the value of goods. For the purpose of taxing the private use of goods the Directive expressly refers to their cost at the time of such use, thus taking into account the value of additions or improvements.[94] It seems therefore that, logically, VAT should in principle be deductible on such services. Let us suppose, for example, that a taxable person makes a taxable purchase of building land and deducts the VAT. He has a building erected on it by a third party mainly for the purpose of his taxable business activities, but also partly for non-business use. The non-business use of the building would then be taxable under Article 6(2)(a). The charge would, by virtue of Article 11(A)(1)(c), be based on the 'full cost' of providing the service, thus including the cost of the construction services. It is submitted that in such a case tax should remain fully deductible on the construction services since they would be referable in part to the taxable person's business supplies and in part to the deemed taxable supply under Article 6(2)(a).

On the Advocate General's analysis, there would, however, seem to be no provision in Article 6(2) for other services received from third parties, not incorporated in the value of goods, which are carried forward or capitalized as assets in company accounts. It is unclear whether Article 6(2) might be interpreted as extending to such services or whether private use thereof must be dealt with by a one-off restriction of the deduction entitlement. It may be noted that there is equally no provision for annual adjustment of deductions

[94] Art. 11(A)(1)(b) provides that the taxable amount in respect of supplies under Art. 5(6) is the purchase price of the goods or, in the absence of a purchase price, the cost price, *determined at the time of supply* (other language versions make it clear that both the purchase price and the cost price are to be determined at the time of the deemed supply). Similarly, Art. 11(A)(1)(c) provides that the taxable amount in respect of supplies under Art. 6(2) is the full cost of providing the service.

in respect of such services in Article 20(2) of the Directive, which applies only to capital goods.

In *Mohsche* Advocate General Jacobs also gave his views on the function of Article 6(2)(b). The latter did not apply to private use of services received from third parties but was intended to prevent a taxable person from benefiting from tax-free services provided by his own undertaking (i.e., to prevent 'value added' by the undertaking from escaping tax); this, in his view, was the explanation for the absence of any deductibility condition.

Self-supplies and Cessation of Trading

Article 5(7) provides that:

> Member States may treat as supplies made for consideration:
> (a) the application by a taxable person for the purposes of his business of goods produced, constructed, extracted, processed, purchased or imported in the course of such business, where the Value Added Tax on such goods, had they been acquired from another taxable person, would not be wholly deductible;
> (b) the application of goods by a taxable person for the purposes of a non-taxable transaction, where the Value Added Tax on such goods became wholly or partly deductible upon their acquisition or upon their application in accordance with subparagraph (a);
> (c) except in those cases mentioned in paragraph 8, the retention of goods by a taxable person or his successors when he ceases to carry out a taxable economic activity where the Value Added Tax on such goods became wholly or partly deductible upon their acquisition or upon their application in accordance with subparagraph (a).

Article 6(3) of the Directive provides:

> In order to prevent distortion of competition and subject to the consultations provided for in Article 29, Member States may treat as a supply of services for consideration the supply by a taxable person of a service for the purposes of his undertaking where the Value Added Tax on such a service, had it been supplied by another taxable person, would not be wholly deductible.

Under Article 11(A)(1)(b) the taxable amount in respect of supplies under Article 5(7) is the 'purchase price of the goods or of similar goods or, in the absence of a purchase price, the cost price, determined at the time of supply'. Article 11(A)(1)(d) taxes services covered by Article 6(3) on their open market value.

Article 5(7)(a) and Article 6(3) allow Member States to act to prevent the distortion of competition which might arise where a taxable person who would not be entitled to full deduction of VAT if he acquired goods or services from a third party (e.g., because the goods or services are used wholly or partly for exempt transactions) produces the goods or supplies the service within his own undertaking, thereby avoiding the cost of the non-deductible VAT. It is unclear why the words 'purchased' and 'imported', which did not appear in the proposal, were inserted after the various internal operations ('produced, constructed, extracted, processed') in the final text of Article 5(7)(a). A wholly or partly exempt taxable person who purchases or imports goods will normally pay VAT; if he does not, he will be in no better position than a taxable person who has the right to full deduction. Either way, there seems to be no need for anti-avoidance measures for purchased or imported goods.[95]

Article 5(7)(b) concerns the situation where goods are initially put wholly or partly to taxable use but are subsequently transferred to non-taxable use. It seems that in some cases the use of this provision is unnecessary since the distortion will be remedied by the adjustment of the initial deduction under the rules concerning capital goods in Article 20. However, the scope of those rules may be limited; moreover, by virtue of Article 11(A)(1)(b) the charge under Article 5(7)(b) takes account of the value of any work done or supplies received in connection with the goods up to the moment of the supply.

Article 5(7)(c) applies where a taxable person ceases trading. Terra and Kajus[96] suggest that this provision is redundant since the taxable person would be deemed to make a supply under Article 5(6). It is however perhaps not clear that cessation of trading necessarily means that business goods which the trader has been unable to dispose of are put to private or non-business use.

Article 5(8) provides that:

> In the event of a transfer, whether for consideration or not or as a contribution to a company, of a totality of assets or part thereof, Member States may consider that no supply of goods has taken place and in that event the recipient shall be treated as the successor to the transferor. Where appropriate, Member States may take the necessary measures to prevent distortion of competition in cases where the recipient is not wholly liable to tax.

Article 6(5) provides that:

> Article 5(8) shall apply in like manner to the supply of services.

It is apparent from the Explanatory Memorandum that the option in Article 5(8) was granted to Member States in the interests of simplicity and in order to avoid overburdening the resources of undertakings. The provision allows

[95] Although it seems that the UK relies on this provision to tax, by way of a self-supply charge, land exempted under the transitional provision in Annex F(16). This is presumably based on the notion that if the taxable person, rather than developing the land himself, acquired land with a new building already constructed on it, such an acquisition would not be covered by the transitional exemption, applicable solely to building land under the UK rules, and would therefore be liable to tax which would not be wholly deductible by the taxable person: see Ch. 6, note 43.

[96] *Guide*, 283.

Member States to dispense with a potentially large tax charge which would in any event generally be recoverable by the transferee. The extension of the provision to services by Article 6(5) allows the same treatment to be applied to, for example, transfers of intellectual property rights or agreements to refrain from certain activities.[97]

TAXABLE PERSONS

Article 2 of the Sixth Directive imposes VAT on supplies of goods or services made 'by a taxable person acting as such'. Article 4(1) of the Directive defines 'taxable person' broadly as:

> any person who independently carries out in any place any economic activity specified in paragraph 2, whatever the purpose or results of that activity.

Article 4(2) defines economic activity as comprising:

> all activities of producers, traders and persons supplying services, including mining and agricultural activities and activities of the professions. The exploitation of tangible or intangible property for the purpose of obtaining income therefrom on a continuing basis shall also be considered an economic activity.

Article 4(3) *permits* Member States to treat persons engaging in economic activities on an occasional basis as taxable persons and specifically mentions the supply of building land and new buildings.[98]

The broad definition of taxable person is in keeping with the character of VAT as a general tax on consumption. In short it is intended to cover *any* person carrying on *any* independent economic activity. The Court has given the term a correspondingly broad interpretation. For example, in Case 235/85, *Commission* v. *Netherlands*[99] the Dutch government argued that the official services performed by notaries and bailiffs in the Netherlands were not economic activities subject to VAT since they were not governed by normal economic laws but were performed in return for remuneration fixed by statute and involved services which individuals were required to use for reasons of public interest. The Court did not agree, holding that the notaries and bailiffs were taxable persons in so far as they provided services to private individuals in return for remuneration; the fact that their duties were conferred and regulated by law in the public interest was irrelevant. More recently, in Case C–186/89, *Van Tiem* v. *Staatssecretaris van Financiën*,[100] the Court emphasized that the exploitation of property in Article 4(2) referred to all operations,

[97] Also see Decision 93/204 (OJ 1993, L88) authorizing the UK to maintain until 31 December 1996 a measure derogating from Art. 5(8) and 21(1)(a) in relation to acquisitions by a company which is a member of a fiscal group for the purposes of Art. 4(4).

[98] For further discussion of the taxation of land and buildings, see below, p. 182 ff.

[99] [1987] ECR 1471. See also below, p. 114.

[100] [1990] ECR I–4363.

whatever their legal form, that were intended to obtain income on a continuing basis from the property. Thus the grant of building rights over immovable property for a specified period (eighteen years) in return for periodic remuneration qualified as an economic activity.

The words 'in any place' in Article 4(1) make it clear that it is immaterial where the activity is carried out. Thus, a person who carries on one of the activities listed in paragraph 2 is a taxable person even if he is established and carries on his activity in another Member State or outside the Community; numerous provisions of the Sixth Directive[101] and also the Eighth and Thirteenth Directives[102] are based on that premise.

Article 4(1) does not require the economic activity to be 'regularly' carried out. However, it seems reasonable to infer from Article 4(3), which gives Member States a discretion to tax occasional activities, that as a general rule a taxable person is one who carries on an economic activity on a regular basis. It may be noted that in the original proposal Article 4(1) was worded 'any person who independently and *regularly* carries out . . .'.[103] The distinction between regular and occasional activities was more important in the proposal since treatment as a taxable person was mandatory for specified types of occasional transaction.

The phrase 'whatever the purpose or results of that activity' indicates that it is immaterial whether the activity is carried on with a view to making a profit or actually makes a profit. The test is in principle an objective one based on the nature of the activity. An activity does not cease to be an economic activity merely because it is loss-making or carried on for charitable or philanthropic purposes. Thus, a private hospital is a taxable person even if it is run as a non-profit-making charity.[104]

The objective definition of economic activity must however be qualified in the light of two judgments of the Court. In Case 89/81, *Staatssecretaris van Financiën* v. *Hong Kong Trade Development Council*[105] the Court held that an activity consisting exclusively in providing services for no remuneration did not qualify as an economic activity. The issue in the case was whether the Amsterdam office of the Development Council, an organization founded with the object of promoting trade with Hong Kong, was a taxable person for the purposes of the Second Directive. The Council's activities in the Netherlands consisted in providing free of charge for traders information and advice about Hong Kong and also information concerning the European market for Hong Kong traders. The income of the Amsterdam office was provided in the form of a fixed annual grant from the Hong Kong government and a charge amounting to 0.5 per cent of the value of products imported to, and exported

[101] See, e.g., Arts. 9(2)(e) and 21(1). [102] Below, pp. 192–3. [103] Emphasis added.

[104] If that were not so, many of the provisions of Art. 13A of the Directive exempting activities carried out by private bodies in the public interest would be redundant.

[105] [1982] ECR 1277.

from, Hong Kong. The Court concluded that, where a person's activity consisted exclusively in providing services for no direct consideration, there was no basis of assessment and the activity was excluded from the scope of the tax; such a person was to be equated with a final consumer. The Court departed from the view taken by Advocate General VerLoren van Themaat, who considered the decisive factor to be the economic *nature* of the activities rather than the legal form or method of financing. In his view the test was whether the activities were of such a nature as might be engaged in by independent suppliers who operate for gain. He argued that in this case it was quite conceivable that a similar trade promotion service might be set up by Hong Kong trade and industry themselves or even by a resourceful undertaking; its remuneration might also be based on the volume of trade with Hong Kong and therefore be equivalent in economic terms to that provided by the 0.5 per cent charge.

The case is possibly unusual inasmuch as it arose because, contrary to the Community provisions, the Dutch legislation would have granted the Development Council the right of deduction if it had qualified as a taxable person notwithstanding the fact that it made no supplies for consideration. It would generally be of no interest for a person who does not make supplies for consideration to claim taxable status.[106] Possibly of more general importance are the Court's *dicta* in Case 50/87, *Commission* v. *France*,[107] a case concerning French legislation restricting the right to deduct input tax on immovable property let at low rentals. The legislation was designed primarily to prevent unjustified deduction of input tax in respect of non-commercial lettings between associated companies and by local authorities to associations with social objects or to firms setting up in their areas. The Court held that the French legislation was incompatible with the principle of full and immediate deduction of input tax under the Sixth Directive; however, it added, with respect to the problem of lettings at low rentals by local authorities, that there might be cases where, because of the amount of the rent, the leases must necessarily be regarded as 'involving a concession and as not constituting an economic activity'.

The Court's *dicta* suggest that an activity, such as the letting of immovable property, which by its nature would normally qualify as an economic activity may not do so in some cases because of the circumstances in which it is carried out. That approach must be correct. A balance must be sought between the need to prevent persons who are not genuinely trading from deducting tax on their purchases and the potential disruption of competitive neutrality resulting from non-taxation of genuine economic activity. The Directive reconciles those conflicting considerations in relation to many activities on the fringe of economic activity, such as hospital care, welfare, and education, by

[106] See also the Dutch case of *Polysar Investments Netherlands BV*, below, p. 112, which likewise arose because of the deficiencies in the Dutch legislation.

[107] [1988] ECR 4797.

exempting such activities when carried out by public-law bodies and allowing Member States to exempt them under certain conditions when they are carried out by private-law bodies.[108] It is none the less submitted that the tax authorities should be permitted, in relation to any activity, to examine whether the taxable person is genuinely trading, having regard to all aspects of the activity including not only its nature but also factors such as the level of consideration received or anticipated, its scale and degree of continuity, and whether it is carried on in a business-like manner or more by way of a hobby or recreation.[109]

Only supplies made by a taxable person 'acting as such' fall within the scope of the tax under Article 2. It is therefore necessary to distinguish between supplies which a taxable person makes in the course of his business and those made in connection with a non-business activity.[110] It is unclear whether individual transactions carried out in a plainly commercial context, but for an abnormally small consideration, may be singled out for exclusion from the scope of the tax on this basis. Would, for example, the letting of office premises at a peppercorn rent by a group property company to an exempt associated company fail to qualify as an economic activity? Or would the supply by a television retailer of a television to a member of staff for £1 be made as part of the retailer's economic activity? It would perhaps be preferable to remedy problems of abuse in a commercial context by specific anti-avoidance legislation enacted either at Community level or at national level under Article 27 of the Directive.[111] Arguably the concept of economic activity is too blunt an instrument to be used for this purpose.

[108] See Ch. 6.

[109] The question of what constitutes a business has given rise to considerable litigation in the UK courts. See, in particular, *Customs and Excise Commissioners* v. *Lord Fisher* [1981] STC 238, where Gibson J considered the following criteria relevant: whether the activity is a serious undertaking earnestly pursued; whether it is an occupation or function actively pursued with recognizable or reasonable continuity; whether it has a degree of substance; whether it is conducted in a regular manner and on sound and recognized business principles; and whether it is predominantly concerned with making taxable supplies for consideration of a kind commonly made by those who seek to profit by them. Many borderline cases have come before the UK VAT tribunals. See, e.g., *Michael Jackson Bloodstock Ltd* v. *Customs and Excise Commissioners* (LON 90/650 X (7863), where a company carrying on a bloodstock business was held not to be carrying on a business activity when it purchased horses purely for racing; *Haydon-Baillie* v. *Customs and Excise Commissioners* [1986] 2 CMLR 74, where it was held that the restoration of naval vessels for the purpose of exhibition and other exploitation was a business activity; *Atlas Marketing* v. *Customs and Excise Commissioners* [1986] 1 CMLR 71, where it was held that a would-be racing driver receiving sponsorship was engaged in a business activity.

[110] See, e.g., the English VAT Tribunal decision in *Stirling* v. *Customs and Excise Commissioners* [1985] VATTR 232, [1986] 2 CMLR 117, where the sale of a stamp collection and paintings effected in conjunction with a letting was held not to constitute a business activity. See also *Michael Jackson Bloodstock Ltd* v. *Customs and Excise Commissioners*, above, note 109.

[111] It may be noted that both the UK and Germany have specific legislation on transactions between connected parties authorized under Art. 27 of the Directive. The UK authorization was given by implied decision on 11 April 1987 and was extended to intra-Community acquisitions by Decision 92/546 (OJ 1992, L 351).

Acts Preparatory to Trading

In Case 268/83, *Rompelman* v. *Minister van Financiën*[112] the Court was asked to consider whether a person who acquired the future title to commercial premises under construction with the declared intention of letting the premises and making taxable supplies was, at that preparatory stage, acting as a taxable person. The Court held that the principle of neutrality demanded that preliminary investment expenditure incurred for the purposes of commencing a business must be regarded as an economic activity. If the activity did not commence until the property began to yield taxable income, this would create an arbitrary distinction between investment expenditure incurred before and during exploitation of the property. However, the tax authorities could require the declared intention to let the premises to be supported by objective evidence such as proof that the premises which it was proposed to construct were specifically suited to commercial exploitation. In *Lennartz* v. *Finanzamt München III*[113] the Court drew the general conclusion from the *Rompelman* decision that, where a person acquires goods for the purposes of an economic activity within the meaning of Article 4, he does so as a taxable person even if the goods are not used immediately for that economic activity.[114] It added that the question whether a person acquires goods as a taxable person depends on all the relevant circumstances, including the nature of the goods and the period between their acquisition and business use. Advocate General Jacobs, whose reasoning was followed closely by the Court, explained that where, as in *Rompelman*, the goods were 'specifically suited to commercial exploitation', little additional evidence was likely to be necessary; where, on the other hand, a person acquired goods which were equally suited to private use (such as a motor car), acquisition of the goods specifically for business purposes would be more difficult to substantiate if the goods were not so used immediately.

Holding Companies

In Case C–60/90, *Polysar Investments Netherlands BV* v. *Inspecteur der Invoerrechten en Accijnzen te Arnhem*[115] the question arose whether a purely passive parent company whose sole function was to hold shares in—and to act as a conduit for the distribution of profits from—foreign subsidiary companies forming part

[112] [1985] ECR 655. [113] Above, note 83.

[114] Para. 14 of the judgment. It is submitted that Advocate General Jacobs more correctly stated the principle in *Rompelman* when he concluded (at para. 33 of his Opinion in *Lennartz*) that 'a person acquiring goods for the purposes of an economic activity . . . does so in his capacity as a taxable person even if the goods are not immediately *used for generating supplies of goods or services*'. In *Rompelman* the Court stated that preparatory acts, such as the acquisition of assets, were to be treated as themselves constituting economic activity.

[115] [1991] ECR I–3111.

of the Polysar international group of companies constituted a taxable person. The Court considered that it did not, distinguishing the circumstances in *Van Tiem* on the ground that the mere acquisition and holding of shares did not constitute the exploitation of property for the purpose of obtaining income therefrom on a continuing basis, since any dividends received resulted from mere ownership of the property. It pointed out, however, that the position would be different where the shareholding was accompanied by direct or indirect involvement in the management of the companies. The fact that the company belonged to an international group of companies did not alter its non-taxable status since only persons established in the territory of the same Member State could be treated as a single taxable person for the purposes of Article 4(4).

In Case C–333/91, *SATAM SA* (now called *Sofitam*) v. *Ministre chargé du Budget*[116] the Court held that share dividends received by an active group holding company were to be excluded from the denominator of the fraction used to calculate the deductible proportion under Article 19(1) of the Directive.[117] The effect of the inclusion of the dividends would have been to reduce SATAM's deductible VAT. The basis for the judgment was that by virtue of the *Polysar* judgment dividends received from the holding of shares did not constitute the consideration for an economic activity and hence fell outside the scope of the tax and the deduction mechanism. The exclusion of dividends from the calculation of the deductible proportion was therefore necessary in order to preserve the neutrality sought by the deduction mechanism.

A first question arising from the *Polysar* judgment is whether a purely passive holding company making no supplies for consideration may be included in a fiscal group under Article 4(4) with associated taxable persons *established in the same Member State*. It may be noted that the Court considered that provision to be inapplicable because none of the holding company's subsidiaries was established in the same territory; it did not, however, suggest that the holding company's non-taxable status was itself an obstacle to grouping. Moreover, to allow a passive holding company to be included in a fiscal group with its subsidiaries would serve the interests of fiscal neutrality between economically comparable structures.

Secondly, although the *Polysar* and *SATAM* judgments are undoubtedly correct in their result, the Court's reasoning does not seem wholly satisfactory. It is submitted that the right of the two companies to deduct input tax should have been determined by the normal application of the deduction rules in Article 17 *et seq.* and not by artificially excluding their activities wholly or in part from the realm of economic activity. Notwithstanding Advocate General Van Gerven's remarks to the contrary in *Polysar*, a holding company of a commercial group is surely distinguishable from a private individual holding

[116] [1993] ECR I–3513. [117] Below, p. 194.

shares as an investment. It is the legal channel for the control and direction of the group, and its activity of acquiring, protecting, collecting profit distributions from, and disposing of investments in subsidiary and associated companies is carried on in a plainly commercial context.

That does not mean that a holding company should have an unrestricted right of deduction. The rules on deduction should apply in the normal way. In other words, the deductibility of input tax should depend on whether the inputs may be attributed to taxable outputs. In so far as the company makes no supplies for consideration, it should have no right of deduction under Article 17(2) unless it forms part of a fiscal group under Article 4(4). A particular question which arises here is the deductibility of input tax on legal and other fees incurred in connection with the acquisition, protection and sale of holdings. Whether a holding company or a fiscal group making taxable supplies may deduct such tax would depend, on this analysis, on whether the input tax is properly attributable to the company's or group's taxable supplies or to the ultimate exempt[118] disposal by the company or group of the holding. This question is likely to be considered by the Court in the pending Case C–4/94, *BLP*.[119]

Finally, it should be added that on this view the dividends received by SATAM were correctly excluded from the calculation of its input tax not, as the Court stated, because they did not constitute consideration for an economic activity but because they did not constitute consideration for a supply falling within the scope of the tax and because, in view of their high value in relation to the cost of collection, their inclusion would have distorted the input-tax calculation.

Independent Activity

The requirement of independence in Article 4(1) is further specified in Article 4(4), which excludes from the tax:

> employed and other persons . . . in so far as they are bound to an employer by a contract of employment or by any other legal ties creating the relationship of employer and employee as regards working conditions, remuneration and the employer's liability.

In Case 235/85, *Commission* v. *Netherlands*[120] the Dutch Government sought to argue that the activities of notaries and bailiffs were not independent because they were appointed by the Crown and were subject to disciplinary control by the public authorities; moreover, their conditions of work and remuneration were governed by statute. The Court was unimpressed. It held that notaries and bailiffs were not bound to the public authorities as employees

[118] See Art. 13(B)(d).
[119] *BLP Group Plc* v. *Commissioners of Customs and Excise.*
[120] [1987] ECR 1471.

since they were not integrated into the public administration. They carried out their activities on their own account and on their own responsibility; they were free, subject to the limitations imposed by statute, to arrange how they performed their work, and they themselves received the remuneration which made up their income. The existence of disciplinary control by the public authorities and the fact that their remuneration was determined by statute were not decisive. In Case C–202/90, *Ayuntamiento de Sevilla* v. *Recaudadores de las Zonas Primera y Segunda*[121] the Court was asked to consider the same question with respect to local tax collectors. The collectors were appointed by the municipality and were subject to its control. However, they maintained their own offices and were responsible for recruiting their own staff. Their remuneration was based on the tax collected. The Court observed first that the collectors did not receive a salary and were not linked to the municipality by a contract of employment. It then went on to consider whether the legal relationship with the municipality none the less created the relationship of employer and employee for the purposes of Article 4(4). As regards *working conditions*, there was no such relationship where the collectors independently organized the equipment and staff required to carry out their activities; the fact that the municipality could issue instructions to the collectors and exercise disciplinary control over them was not decisive. As regards *remuneration*, the collectors bore the economic risk of their activities in so far as their profit depended not only on the amount of tax recovered but also on the extent of their staff and other costs. Finally, as regards the *liability of the employer*, the fact that the municipality could be held liable for the actions of the collectors acting on its behalf was not sufficient. The decisive criterion was the liability arising from the contractual relations established by the collectors in the performance of their activity and their liability for damage caused to third parties when they were not acting as representatives of the public authority.

Public Authorities

Article 4(5) provides:

> States, regional and local government authorities and other bodies governed by public law shall not be considered taxable persons in respect of the activities or transactions in which they engage as public authorities, even where they collect dues, fees, contributions or payments in connection with these activities or transactions.
>
> However, when they engage in such activities or transactions, they shall be considered taxable persons in respect of these activities or transactions where treatment as non-taxable persons would lead to significant distortions of competition.
>
> In any case, these bodies shall be considered taxable persons in relation to the

[121] [1991] ECR I–4247.

activities listed in Annex D, provided they are not carried out on such a small scale as to be negligible.

Member States may consider activities of these bodies which are exempt under Article 13 or 28[122] as activities which they engage in as public authorities.

The idea underlying provisions is that public authorities are not to be treated as taxable persons when acting in performance of their basic public functions such as general administration, the administration of justice, national security, and defence. However, public authorities frequently engage in other activities, such as supplies of fuel and power, transport, education, telecommunications, broadcasting, etc., which fall within the realm of economic activity and might equally be performed by private traders. Given the wide variation between the Member States in the extent to which the public authorities are involved in such areas, the problem for the Community legislator was to find a workable criterion which would serve to define the limits of the tax and ensure its uniform application. The basic criterion in the first subparagraph of Article 4(5) focuses on the capacity in which the public authority acts. A public authority is a non-taxable person in respect of activities which it carries out *as a public authority*. The Commission's First Report states that the draftsmen of the Directive were unable to produce a Community definition of this criterion because of the widely differing scope of the public domain in the Member States.[123] This suggests that the Directive envisaged that the dividing line would be drawn by reference to national law. That point was confirmed by the Court in the Italian public authority cases,[124] where the Court held that a public authority acted in its public capacity for the purposes of Article 4(5) where it acted under the national public law regime rather than under the legal conditions applicable to private traders.[125] It was for the national court to apply that criterion, the fact that the legislature classified certain activities as 'administrative functions' merely constituting an indication that they might be subject to public law.

Taken alone the above criterion would have done little to ensure the uniform application of the tax. The second subparagraph of Article 4(5) therefore adds a second criterion, namely that public authorities must not be treated as non-taxable persons where this would lead to *significant distortions of competition.* That criterion is reinforced by the third subparagraph of Article 4(5), which

[122] See Ch. 6.

[123] *Commission's First Report to the Council on the application of the common system of Value Added Tax*, submitted on 14 September 1983 in accordance with Art. 34 of the 6th Directive: COM(83)426 final 30.

[124] Case 231/87, *Ufficio Distrettuale delle Imposte di Fiorenzuola d'Arda* v. *Comune di Carpaneto Piacentino* [1989] ECR 3233 and Case C-4/89, *Comune di Carpaneto Piacentino* v. *Ufficio Provinciale Imposta sul Valore Aggiunto di Piacenza* [1990] ECR I-1869.

[125] It should, incidentally, be noted that Art. 4(5) has been held to apply only to activities carried out directly by a public authority itself and not by private traders on its behalf: see *Commission* v. *Netherlands*, above, note 120, and *Ayuntamiento de Sevilla* v. *Recaudadores de las Zonas primera y segunda*, above, note 121; also *Commission* v. *Germany* [1985] ECR 2655.

adds that public bodies are in any case to be considered taxable persons in relation to a series of activities listed in Annex D[126] unless carried out on such a small scale as to be negligible. The Court has held that it is apparent from the structure of the provision that Member States are not *obliged* to exclude from taxation activities carried out on a negligible scale. The use of the words 'in any case' also indicates that Annex D is clarificatory and does not contain an exhaustive list of the activities in respect of which public authorities may be taxable.

In the Italian public authority cases the Court held that a public body was entitled to rely on Article 4(5) in order to resist taxation of activities not listed in Annex D in which it engaged as a public authority where non-taxation was not liable to give rise to significant distortions of competition. The significant distortion limitation placed on the rule was only conditional, and while it was true that its application involved an assessment of economic circumstances, that assessment was not exempt from judicial review. Conversely, it seems possible to conclude that, providing an appropriate remedy exists in national law, an aggrieved competitor of a public authority would be able to challenge the non-taxation of activities listed in Annex D or other activities whose non-taxation produces a significant distortion of competition.

Fiscal Groups

The second subparagraph of Article 4(4) provides that, subject to consultation of the VAT Committee:

> each Member State may treat as a single taxable person persons established in the territory of the country who, while legally independent, are closely bound to one another by financial, economic and organizational links.

It appears from the Explanatory Memorandum to the Commission's Proposal for the Sixth Directive that this provision was conceived as a means of simplifying administration for the tax authorities and combating abuse consisting in the splitting up of an undertaking into several taxable persons so that each may benefit from a special scheme. The United Kingdom used the provision to introduce legislation of the latter type in order to prevent traders from artificially subdividing businesses so as to avoid VAT registration under the special rules for small undertakings enacted by the United Kingdom under Article 24 of the Directive. A number of Member States, in particular Denmark, Germany, Ireland, the Netherlands, and the United Kingdom,

[126] The activities listed in Annex D are telecommunications; supply of water, gas, electricity, and steam; transport of goods; port and airport services; passenger transport; supply of new goods manufactured for sale; transactions of intervention agencies under common agricultural market organisations, trade fairs, and exhibitions; warehousing; activities of commercial publicity bodies; activities of travel agencies; staff shops, co-operatives, and industrial canteens; and commercial transactions of radio and television bodies.

have used Article 4(4) as the basis for legislation allowing or requiring associated companies to be grouped together as a single taxable person for VAT purposes.[127] Although the detailed arrangements vary, their basic effect is to create a single taxable person comprising all the legally distinct members of the group; thus, 'internal' supplies between members of the group are ignored, and the group accounts for VAT only on supplies made to third parties outside the group and deducts input tax only on supplies made to it by third-party suppliers. Such treatment may, as suggested in the Explanatory Memorandum, serve the interests of efficient tax administration. It may also produce tax savings for the traders concerned; in particular, the VAT cost arising from the non-deductibility of input tax on intra-group charges to wholly or partly exempt group members may be avoided.

Article 4(4) allows a Member State to extend such treatment solely to persons *established within its territory*. In its First Report the Commission expressed some concern regarding the 'international dimension' given to such groups under national legislation. According to the Commission, only the Dutch provisions expressly incorporated the territorial scope set out in the Directive. Since the German legislation specifically allowed undertakings established abroad to be included within a tax group, the Commission instituted infringement proceedings under Article 169 of the Treaty, which led to an amendment to the German legislation.[128] The Commission also indicated that it was considering whether the administrative provisions in Denmark, Ireland and the United Kingdom[129] permitted departures from the Directive.

In its Communication issued in May 1989[130] the Commission proposed the introduction of Community-wide fiscal units as part of its proposals for charging VAT in the country of the supplier and the establishment of a clearing mechanism for the redistribution of revenue. This would have made clearing unnecessary for a large number of transactions between associated companies. However, at its meetings in November and December 1989 the ECOFIN Council expressed reservations as to whether it would be possible to determine adequate legal criteria for eligibility for such treatment.

[127] The Commission's 1st Report (10–12) describes the arrangements introduced in those Member States. Some Member States (Germany and the Netherlands) make grouping automatic if the conditions of Art. 4(4) are fulfilled; others make it optional at the discretion of the taxpayer (Denmark and the UK) or at the discretion of the tax authorities (Ireland).

[128] See *Commission's Second Report to the Council on the Application of the Common System of Value Added Tax, COM (88) 799 Final, 6.*

[129] At the time the UK legislation required grouped companies to be 'resident' in the UK, a term not defined in the legislation. The relevant Customs and Excise leaflet stated that a company would be regarded as resident for this purpose if some part of its superior or directing authority was present in the UK; that condition was satisfied if one director with full voting rights was resident. The legislation has since been amended, although residence remains part of the test.

[130] COM(89)260.

CONSIDERATION AND THE TAXABLE AMOUNT

Supplies and Intra-Community Acquisitions

VAT, as a consumption tax, taxes expenditure on goods and services. Article 2 of the Sixth Directive reflects that characteristic by limiting the scope of VAT to supplies of goods or services 'effected for consideration'. Subject to a number of exceptions,[131] a supply made otherwise than for consideration falls outside the scope of the tax. Moreover, under the transitional arrangements for intra-Community trade, tax is normally chargeable on intra-Community acquisitions of goods only if they are made for consideration.[132]

In addition to its importance in defining the limits of the tax, the consideration received by the supplier also constitutes the normal basis for valuing supplies under Article 11(A)(1) of the Directive. Under that provision the taxable amount is 'everything which constitutes the consideration'.[133] Unlike the English text, other language versions of the Directive do not use the same term ('consideration') in both Articles. The French text, for example, uses the terms *à titre onéreux* in Article 2 and *contrepartie* in Article 11. However, the Court has closely linked the two concepts, in the sense that only something which is capable of valuation under Article 11 qualifies as consideration for the purposes of Article 2.

The Meaning of Consideration in Community VAT Law

The Sixth Directive does not define 'consideration', although Article 11 contains provisions applying the general definition of the taxable amount to specific items.[134] For the majority of commercial transactions, conducted in pursuance of an agreement stipulating a specific monetary price for the goods or services supplied, the rules of Article 11 are sufficient. None the less, in the absence of a definition of 'consideration', the Court has been obliged to define the limits of the term in several more unusual cases. A number of these have been referred to the Court by English courts, which have come to realize that consideration in Community VAT law differs in certain respects from the English common law concept.[135] In particular, since the latter does not incorporate any doctrine of adequacy, it is ill-equipped for use as a means of valuation.

It is, however, by no means only the English courts that have encountered difficulties. In fact the first—and still the leading—case on consideration was

[131] Above, at p. 100 ff.

[132] Art. 28a(1) of the 6th Directive, as amended by Directives 91/680 and 92/111.

[133] Below, p. 126.

[134] Below, p. 126 ff.

[135] See, e.g., Slade LJ in *Trafalgar Tours* v. *Customs and Excise Commissioners* [1990] STC 127, [1990] 3 CMLR 934.

referred to the Court by the Dutch Hoge Raad. In Case 154/80, *Staatssecretaris van Financiën* v. *Coöperatieve Aardappelenbewaarplaats*[136] the taxable person was an agricultural co-operative association operating a warehouse in which it stored potatoes for its members in return for an annual storage charge. The association refrained from making the storage charge to its members for two consecutive years. The Dutch tax authorities sought none the less to impose VAT in respect of the storage service provided by the association on the basis that the non-collection of the charge constituted consideration in the form of a reduction in the value of the members' shares in the association. The Court held that for the purposes of the Second Directive 'consideration' had an independent Community law meaning; its interpretation could not be left to the discretion of each Member State. While not actually defining the term, the Court laid down the following criteria:

(1) A direct link must exist between the service provided and the consideration received.
(2) The consideration must be capable of being expressed in money and constitute a 'subjective' value, inasmuch as the taxable amount is the consideration actually received and not a value assessed according to objective criteria.

Thus, an unascertained reduction in the value of the shares held by members of the co-operative did not qualify as consideration.

The criteria laid down by the Court were modelled closely on those proposed by the Commission in its written observations on the case. The Commission's view was prompted by the consideration that VAT should be charged only on the actual outlay of the consumer of the goods or services. That view is in keeping with the principle, laid down in Article 2 of the First Directive, that the tax should remain 'exactly proportional to the price of the goods or services', a fundamental characteristic of the VAT system serving to ensure its neutrality. It is clear that on the facts the test was not met since the association specifically chose not to make a charge for its services for the years in question, and a finding of consideration would have necessitated constructing notional consideration based on a 'normal' value for the service. The Commission pointed out that, in relation to domestic transactions, the use of a normal value for a transaction was reserved for measures designed to combat tax avoidance.[137]

The Court applied the test for consideration developed in *Aardappelenbewaarplaats* again in Case 324/82, *Commission* v. *Belgium*,[138] this time in the context of the Sixth Directive. There the Court held that Belgian legislation charging VAT on the basis of the list price of new cars irrespective of the price actually paid by the customer was contrary to Article 11 of the

[136] [1981] ECR 445. [137] See Art. 11(A)(1)(d). [138] [1984] ECR 1861.

Sixth Directive. The Court incidentally also concluded that the legislation went too far even to be authorized as an anti-avoidance measure under Article 27 of the Directive.[139]

Non-monetary Consideration

Payment for goods or services does not necessarily take the form of money[140] but may take another form such as a reciprocal supply of goods or performance of, or refraining to perform, some act. The competitive neutrality of the tax and uniformity of the tax base would be disrupted if such payments did not qualify as consideration. To satisfy the *Aardappelenbewaarplaats* criteria non-monetary consideration must, however, have a quantifiable monetary value for the supplier. In Case C–126/88, *Boots* v. *Commissioners of Customs and Excise*[141] the taxpayer, a retailer in the UK, operated a sales promotion scheme involving the use of money-off coupons. A customer making an initial purchase of goods ('the premium goods') received a coupon which could be used to obtain a price reduction equal to the face value of the coupon on a subsequent purchase of certain other goods ('the redemption goods'). In some cases Boots financed the promotion itself and in others it received reimbursement or, at least, a contribution from the manufacturer in exchange for the redeemed coupons. Customs and Excise decided that, regardless of who financed the promotion, the surrender of the coupon by the customer constituted non-monetary consideration for the supply of the redemption goods and, relying on section 10(3) of the VAT Act 1983,[142] assessed VAT on the open market value of the redemption goods (i.e., their normal retail selling price) even where Boots received no contribution from the manufacturer. The Court, which was asked to rule on the treatment at Boots' own promotions, took a different view. It held that the coupon was nothing more than a document incorporating the obligation assumed by Boots to grant a price reduction, that reduction constituting a 'discount' or 'rebate' expressly excluded from the taxable amount by Article 11(A)(3)(b) of the Sixth Directive.

That analysis was undoubtedly correct. By granting the discount Boots performed its side of the bargain entered into when the premium goods were sold, the coupon merely identifying the person to whom performance was due. Even if one were to accept the view—put forward by the United Kingdom—that the surrender of the voucher represented a benefit for Boots

[139] See Ch. 9, p. 223.

[140] The word 'consideration' in Art. 2 of the 6th Directive replaced the word 'payment' in Art. 2 of the 2nd Directive. It appears that the amendment, which was confined to the English text, involved no substantive change and was probably intended to make clear that non-monetary payments were included. See on this point Sir Gordon Slynn's Opinion in *Apple and Pear Development Council*, below, note 146.

[141] [1990] ECR I–1235.

[142] At the time s. 10(3) of the VAT Act 1983 read as follows: 'If the supply is not for a consideration or is for a consideration not consisting or not wholly consisting of money, the value of the supply shall be taken to be its open market value'. The provision has since been amended.

consisting in increased sales of the premium or redemption goods, that benefit still did not represent any additional value that was not already subject to tax. Taxing both the premium and the redemption goods on their full retail value would therefore have resulted in a tax charge that was disproportionate to the total price paid for the two sets of goods, contrary to Article 2 of the First Directive.

By way of contrast, non-monetary consideration was found by the Court to have passed in Case 230/87, *Naturally Yours Cosmetics Ltd* v *Commissioners of Customs and Excise.*[143] Here the taxable person was a company engaged in selling cosmetics to the public through independent sales agents. The company sold its products at wholesale prices to the agents, who sold the products at private parties which they encouraged their friends and acquaintances to organize. To induce the party hostesses to organize the parties, the agents gave them a pot of cream as a 'dating gift'. Where the agent used the cream as a dating gift she received it at a price considerably lower than the normal wholesale price (£1–50 rather than £10–14). Customs and Excise took the view that the company received additional, non-monetary consideration for the pots of cream supplied to its agents as dating gifts (namely the service of the agent in procuring the services of the party hostess), and accordingly assessed VAT on the open market value of the supplies pursuant to section 10(3) of the VAT Act 1983,[144] that is to say, on the normal wholesale price of £10–14.

The need to tax the wholesaler, Naturally Yours Cosmetics, on the full price of the dating gift, which necessitated constructing the provision of a service by the agent to the wholesaler, arose from the fact that the agents were not registered for VAT purposes or, in terms of the Sixth Directive, qualified for the United Kingdom exemption for small undertakings enacted under Article 24. The agent could not be taxed on the non-monetary consideration provided by the final consumer, the hostess, consisting in her services in organizing the party. Of more general importance is the judgment in Case C–33/93, *Empire Stores Ltd.* v. *Commissioners of Customs and Excise,*[145] in which the question arose whether a mail order firm's customers, private individuals, provided non-monetary consideration in the form of services to the firm. The case concerned two sales promotion schemes operated by the firm. Under the first scheme, referred to as the 'self-introduction scheme', Empire Stores allowed potential customers to choose from a list an article which was supplied without extra charge once they had filled in a form requesting personal details designed to establish their creditworthiness, had been approved by Empire Stores, and had placed an order for goods from its sales catalogue or made a first payment in respect of such an order. Under the second scheme, referred to as the 'introduce-a-friend scheme', Empire Stores offered an article

[143] [1988] ECR 6365. [144] Above, note 142.
[145] Judgment of 2 June 1994, not yet reported.

to existing customers who recommended one of their friends as a potential customer; it was supplied once the new customer had filled in the form, been approved by Empire Stores, and made a first payment relating to an order which she had placed. Under both schemes Empire Stores accounted for VAT in respect of the articles on the basis of their cost price. The Commissioners took the view that VAT ought to have been calculated on the basis of their tax-exclusive cost price plus 50 per cent, being the Commissioners' estimate of the prices which Empire Stores would have charged for the articles in question if they had been included in its sales catalogue, and raised assessments on that basis. The Manchester VAT Tribunal asked the Court, first, whether the supply of the article without extra charge ('the non-catalogue goods') was made for a consideration separate from the sum of money payable to the supplier for the catalogue goods ordered and, secondly, if so, how the taxable amount was to be determined. The Court, referring to its judgment in *Naturally Yours Cosmetics*, gave an affirmative reply to the first question and held that the taxable amount was the price paid by the supplier to acquire the non-catalogue goods. Its reply to the first question, in which it made no distinction between the two schemes, was based essentially on the VAT Tribunal's finding that the supply of the non-catalogue goods was made in consideration of the introduction of a potential customer and not in return for the purchase by that customer of catalogue goods. That finding, the Court said, was confirmed by the fact that the non-catalogue goods were not supplied each time an order was placed and that under the 'introduce-a-friend' scheme they were supplied not to the customer who had placed and paid for an order but to the person who introduced the customer to Empire Stores. The link was a direct one since if no service was provided by the potential or existing customer no goods were due from Empire Stores. As regards the second question, the subjective value of the customer's service could be identified and expressed in monetary terms. It was the value which Empire Stores, the recipient of the service, attributed to it which corresponded to the amount which it was prepared to pay for it, namely the price it had paid for the non-catalogue goods.

It is submitted that the replies to both questions are unsatisfactory. As regards the first question, the Court arguably should have distinguished between the two schemes. The 'introduce-a-friend' scheme unquestionably involved an exchange of supplies between the existing customer and the supplier. The former received the non-catalogue goods from the supplier in exchange for the service of introducing another person as a customer. The 'self-introduction' scheme, on the other hand, did not involve any act of agency on the part of the potential customer; the latter merely introduced herself as a customer. It must be clear that, in the absence of other factors, the mere fact of agreeing to be a customer cannot constitute additional consideration over and above the price paid for any supplies. What other factors then led the Court to conclude that the customer provided separate consideration in this case? The Court referred to the finding made by the national court that the supply of the non-catalogue goods was made in consideration of the introduction of a new customer and not in exchange for the purchase by the customer of catalogue goods. That finding, said the Court, was confirmed *inter alia* by the fact that the non-catalogue goods were not provided each time catalogue goods were ordered. However, there is a gap here in the chain of logic. The national Court's finding, based on the facts and on the English law of contract, does not of itself support the conclusion that, as a matter of Community VAT law, the non-catalogue goods were supplied in return for a service by the customer. It is submitted that, if the Court is to reply to specific questions by national courts based on particular transactions, it must conduct its own legal appraisal of the facts found by the national court in the light of the principles of the Community VAT legislation. There appeared in fact to be a material difference between the two schemes. Under the 'introduce-a-friend' scheme the conclusion that the supply of the non-catalogue goods constituted payment for the services of an agent is inescapable. Under the 'self-introduction' scheme, however, the gift was merely an introductory offer to a new customer. It is extremely common for a supplier to make a gift to a person when he first becomes a customer or periodically as a token of the customer's loyalty. Such gifts are undoubtedly linked to the fact of becoming or remaining a customer rather than to specific purchases, but as a general principle are not made in return for a service. It is true that in this case the customer had to complete a form providing personal details in order to receive the gift and become a credit customer. However, that requirement can more realistically be linked to the corresponding benefit received by the customer of being granted credit by the supplier. Indeed it is quite normal for suppliers to require potential credit customers to provide such details regardless of whether they receive a gift. Are we to conclude that the customer provides additional consideration in all such cases? It is submitted that the relevance of the national court's finding that the supply of the non-catalogue goods was linked to the introduction rather than to the first supply of catalogue goods was that the price paid for the first supply could not be regarded as consideration for both that supply and the supply of the non-catalogue goods. The supply of the non-catalogue goods was a gift, that is a supply for no consideration taxable on the basis of its cost pursuant to the combined provisions of Article 5(6) and Article 11.

As regards the second question, the Court examined the arrangement from the viewpoint of the recipient of the service. As already stated, however, the purpose of taking into account non-monetary consideration is to ensure uniformity of the tax base and to preserve competitive neutrality. If under the 'introduce-a-friend' scheme the value of the customer's service were not taxed, Empire Stores would have a competitive advantage over a supplier who paid agents a monetary commission for introducing new clients. It follows that the relevant value must be the price which Empire Stores would have had to pay for such a service, that is the price which the supplier of the service would charge for it. The value placed by the customer on her service is surely the price which she would have had to pay in order to purchase the non-catalogue goods, in other words their estimated retail value.

The judgment seems likely to create further uncertainty in the complex area of business promotion schemes, an area in which there has already been considerable litigation in the United Kingdom courts.

A Direct Link

The direct link requirement laid down in *Coöperatieve Aardappelenbewaarplaats* was considered further by the Court in Case 102/86, *Apple and Pear Development Council* v. *Commissioners of Customs and Excise*,[146] a case referred by the House of Lords. The taxpayer, a body established by statutory instrument to promote and improve the quality of apples and pears grown in England and Wales, was authorized to finance its activities by imposing a mandatory annual charge on growers at a rate fixed per hectare of planted land or according to the number of trees planted. The Court considered that the mandatory charge did not satisfy the direct link requirement. It considered three factors to be significant:[147]

(1) The benefit of the Development Council's activities accrued to the industry as a whole rather than to individual growers.
(2) No relationship existed between the level of benefits which individual growers obtained and the amount of the mandatory charge.
(3) The charge was imposed under statute rather than under contract and was recoverable whether or not any individual benefit was conferred.

Is any of those factors decisive individually? Does, first, the fact that a levy is imposed under statute of itself sever the requisite link with the supply? Such a view would be inconsistent with Article 4(5) of the Directive, which provides that public authorities are to be considered taxable persons in respect of the activities—of a predominantly commercial nature—listed in Annex D and more generally in respect of activities where treatment as a non-taxable person would lead to significant distortions of competition.[148] That provision would be frustrated if such supplies made by a public body were excluded from the scope of the tax wherever a Member State chose to introduce a statutory basis for the charges. Provided that a charge can be linked to specific supplies (e.g., power, telecommunications, transport), it surely constitutes consideration for VAT purposes even if it is made under statute or subordinate legislation. Does, secondly, a voluntary (contractual) payment which bears no direct relation to

[146] [1988] ECR 1443. [147] Paras. 14 and 15 of the judgment. [148] Above, p. 115 ff.

the level of benefits received by the individual concerned fail to satisfy the direct link requirement? The answer again must be that it does not. There seems to be no reason why supplies made for a flat-rate periodic charge should be treated differently for VAT purposes than supplies invoiced individually.[149] It may be concluded that it was the *combination* of the lack of individual benefit and the mandatory nature of the charge which was decisive.[150]

In Case C–16/93, *Tolsma* v. *Inspecteur der Omzetbelasting Leeuwarden*[151] the Court considered that the direct link test was not met where a barrel organ player received donations from passers-by whom he entertained. It held that services were supplied for consideration only 'if there is a legal relationship between the provider of the service and the recipient pursuant to which there is reciprocal performance, the remuneration received by the provider of the service constituting the value actually given in return for the service supplied to the recipient'.[152]

The Taxable Amount

Article 11(A)(1)(a) of the Sixth Directive defines the taxable amount broadly as:

> everything which constitutes the consideration which has been or is to be obtained from the purchaser, the customer or a third party for such supplies including subsidies directly linked to the price of such supplies.

Subsidies

Restricting consideration to subsidies which are 'directly linked to the price' of supplies conforms to the general notion of consideration already described. The effect is to exclude from the scope of the tax general subsidies granted without any specific reference to price, such as deficit or general operating subsidies. Whether the direct link criterion is appropriate from an economic viewpoint is questionable since the true consumption value of goods or services generally includes any subsidies received by the undertaking concerned. In its First Report[153] the Commission highlighted the fragility of the purely formal direct link test by pointing out that a Member State could easily alter the form in which a subsidy was granted, thereby removing it from the scope of the tax. The Commission's concern was that divergent treatment by Member States would interfere with the uniform collection of own resources. It suggested two

[149] In many cases it may in any event be preferable to regard the supply as that of the right to participate in the scheme or arrangement in question rather than as a supply of individual services. Thus, where a manufacturer enters into a warranty contract with his customers for a standard fee, even if he carries out no repairs for a particular customer, he has none the less made a taxable supply of the right to receive repair services.

[150] As Sir Gordon Slynn stated in his Opinion ([1988] ECR at 1461), the levy was more in the nature of an 'across-the-board tax than a true payment for services'.

[151] [1994] ECR I–743.

[152] Para. 14 of the judgment.

[153] At 37 to 39.

solutions: either a Community list of subsidies linked to price should be drawn up; or Article 11 should be amended so as to exclude from the taxable amount all types of subsidy other than those remunerating services supplied to final consumers. Having promised to review the matter, the Commission returned to it in its Second Report,[154] but without explanation appeared to abandon its earlier proposals and merely noted that the relevant words of Article 11 were to be given a strict and literal construction. Precisely what that means is unclear. Even within the limited logic of the provision, an excessively literal approach would make little sense. For example, a municipal subsidy to a local theatre based on the quantity of tickets sold seems as directly linked to price as a subsidy specifically expressed as a percentage of the ticket price. Both subsidies form part of the income for particular performances. Such subsidies may be contrasted with an annual grant which, although forming part of the general income of the theatre and possibly influencing the price of tickets, is too remote from particular supplies to form part of the consideration. The test is however likely to be difficult to apply in practice in many cases.

Credit Cards

Where a customer purchases goods or services by credit card, the supplier receives payment of the purchase price from the card issuer after deduction of the issuer's commission. In Case C–18/92, *Chaussures Bally* v. *Ministère des Finances*[155] the Court interpreted Article 11(A)(1)(a) to the effect that in the case of such sales the taxable amount was the full amount of the purchase price before deduction of the commission.[156]

Special Rules for the Valuation of Deemed Supplies

Article 11(A)(1)(b) to (d) lays down rules for the valuation of the supplies deemed to arise under the anti-avoidance provisions in Articles 5(6) and (7) and 6(2) and 6(3).[157]

Detailed Provisions on Particular Items

Article 11(A)(2) and (3) sets out a number of detailed provisions applying the general definition to specific items.

Article 11(A)(2) includes within the taxable amount any taxes, duties, levies, and charges, excluding the VAT itself. Incidental expenses such as commission, packing, transport, and insurance costs charged by the supplier are also included. In its First Report[158] the Commission noted that the practice of Member States differed on the question whether the finance element of hire-purchase payments constituted an incidental expense forming part of the taxable amount or a separate credit transaction qualifying for exemption under

[154] At 26 and 27.

[155] [1993] ECR I–2871.

[156] For the VAT treatment of the service supplied by the card issuer to the supplier of goods or services, see below, p. 187.

[157] Above, p. 100 ff.

[158] At 39.

Article 13(B)(d). In its Second Report the Commission stated that it had referred the question to the VAT Committee, which by a majority had concluded that, in the absence of any real loan agreement, the price supplement payable on a hire-purchase sale was to be included in the taxable amount for supplies of goods.[159] That analysis seems questionable on two counts. First, it is not clear that the term 'incidental expenses' covers the finance element of a hire-purchase contract. The Court has held that 'incidental expenses' do not include interest for late payment awarded by a court.[160] More significantly, in his Opinion in *Muys' en de Winter's Bouwgroep*[161] Advocate General Jacobs considered that the term likewise did not cover contractual interest in respect of the deferred payment of the purchase price under a contract of sale. That view seems correct. Interest on credit cannot be equated with commission, packing, transport, or insurance costs and, if not contractually distinct from the purchase price of goods or services, should be considered to fall directly under Article 11(A)(1)(a). It may be noted, secondly, that the correctness of the suggestion apparently made in the Commission's Second Report that there must be a separate loan agreement in a hire-purchase transaction, as distinct from contractually distinct finance clauses, also seems questionable in the light of the Advocate General's Opinion in *Muys*.[162]

Discounts and Reductions of the Taxable Amount

Article 11(A)(3) expressly excludes from the taxable amount discounts for early payment, and discounts and rebates allowed to the customer and *accounted for at the time of supply*. It also excludes reimbursement of expenses paid out on behalf of the customer.

Article 11(C)(1) provides, with respect to cancellation, refusal, or total or partial non-payment and price reductions granted *subsequent to the supply*, that 'the taxable amount shall be reduced accordingly under conditions which shall be determined by the Member States'. The wording of the provision suggests that the discretion allowed to the Member States is limited to defining the mechanism for making the requisite reduction to the taxable amount. It does not therefore seem to preclude the direct effect of the provision. In the particular case of total or partial non-payment, however, Article 11(C)(1) allows Member States to derogate from the above rule. The structure of the provision suggests that on this point the power to derogate extends to the principle of reduction itself.

Transitional Provisions

Under Article 28e[163] intra-Community acquisitions are to be valued on the same basis as supplies under Article 11(A). In particular the acquisitions for

[159] At 29.
[160] Case 222/81, *BAZ Bausystem* v. *Finanzamt München* [1982] ECR 2527.
[161] Above, p. 97.
[162] See point 11.
[163] Introduced by Directive 91/680 and amended by Art. 1(16) and (17) of Directive 92/111.

consideration deemed to arise under Article 28a(6) in respect of the use of goods dispatched from another Member State are to be valued in accordance with Article 11(A)(1)(b) and Article 11(A)(2) and (3). The same applies to the supplies deemed to arise in respect of transfers of goods to another Member State as referred to in Article 28c(A)(d). By virtue of the second subparagraph of Article 28e(1) excise duty is to be included in the taxable amount for acquisitions of dutiable goods in keeping with Article 11(A)(2)(a).

Imports

By virtue of Article 11(B)(1)[164] the taxable amount on importation is the customs value determined in accordance with the Community provisions in force. Under Articles 28 to 36 of Regulation 2913/92[165] establishing the Community Customs Code, the normal value for customs purposes is the transaction value, namely the price actually paid or payable for the goods when sold for export to the customs territory of the Community[166]; where the transaction value cannot be used, reference is to be made to one of the following values listed in order of preference: the transaction value of identical goods; the transaction value of similar goods; the value based on the unit price at which the imported goods are sold in the Community in the greatest aggregate quantity to persons unrelated to the seller; or a computed value.[167] By virtue of Article 11(B)(3)[168] the taxable amount is to include, in so far as not already included:

> taxes, duties, levies and other charges due outside the importing Member State and those due by reason of importation (excluding the VAT to be levied),

as well as incidental expenses, such as commission, packing, transport, and insurance costs incurred up to the first place of destination (as defined) within the territory of the importing Member State or such other place of destination within the importing state as is known when the chargeable event occurs.

Article 11(B)(5)[169] concerns the reimportation of goods that have undergone processing outside the Community.

Other Provisions

Article 11(C)(2)[170] concerns the valuation of transactions expressed in foreign currencies. Article 11(C)(3) sets out rules governing the treatment of returnable packaging costs.

Article 11(A)(4) and (B)(6)[171] lay down special rules for the taxation of

[164] As amended by Art. 1(5) of Directive 92/111.
[165] OJ 1992, L302.
[166] Ibid., Art. 29.
[167] Ibid., Art. 30.
[168] As amended by Directive 91/680.
[169] As amended by Directive 91/680.
[170] Amended by Directive 91/680.
[171] Added by Directive 94/5.

second-hand goods. These provisions are considered further in connection with the discussion of tax rates in Chapter 8.

MISCELLANEOUS MATTERS

Illegal Transactions

In Case 50/80, *Horvath* v. *Hauptzollamt Hamburg-Jonas*[172] the Court held that the introduction of the Common Customs Tariff no longer left Member States the power to apply customs duties to smuggled drugs which were destroyed immediately upon their discovery. There followed two cases, Case 221/81, *Wolf* v. *Hauptzollamt Düsseldorf*[173] and Case 240/81, *Einberger* v. *Hauptzollamt Freiburg* ('*Einberger I*'),[174] in which the illegal importation remained undetected until after the drugs had been disposed of. The Court held that the same principle none the less applied and that no customs debt arose upon the importation of drugs otherwise than through economic channels strictly controlled by the competent authorities for use for medical and scientific purposes. The Court reasoned that the importation and marketing of narcotic drugs otherwise than through strictly controlled channels were prohibited in all the Member States by virtue of international commitments.[175] A customs debt could not arise upon the importation of drugs which could not be marketed and integrated into the economy of the Community. It added that the introduction of the Common Customs Tariff, provided for in Article 3(b) of the Treaty, fell within the scope of the objectives assigned to the Community in Article 2 and the guidelines laid down in Article 29 for the operation of the customs union. Imports of illegal drugs fell wholly outside those objectives and guidelines.

In Case 294/82, *Einberger II*[176] the Court extended the principle established in those cases to VAT. Import VAT and customs duties displayed comparable essential features since they arose from the fact of importation of goods into the Community and their subsequent distribution through the economic channels of the Member States and since each constituted a component of the sale price calculated in a similar manner by successive traders. Their parallel nature was confirmed by the fact that Article 10(3) of the Sixth Directive authorized Member States to link the chargeable event and the date when the VAT on importation fell due with those laid down for customs duties. In Case C-343/89, *Witzemann* v. *Hauptzollamt München-Mitte*[177] the Court extended the case law on customs duties and VAT on drugs to imports of

[172] [1981] ECR 385. [173] [1982] ECR 3681. [174] [1982] ECR 3699.

[175] Single Convention on Narcotic Drugs 1961 (United Nations Treaty Series, 520 No. 7515), to which all the Member States are signatories.

[176] *Einberger* v. *Haupzollamt Freiburg* [1984] ECR 1177. [177] [1990] ECR I-4477.

counterfeit currency. The Court considered that its reasoning in the earlier cases applied with even greater force to counterfeit currency which, unlike narcotic drugs, were subject to a total prohibition on importation or marketing. In his Opinion in the case Advocate General Jacobs considered whether the rule against charging customs duties and VAT on drugs derived from the Treaty or from some general principle of law so that it could not be changed by the legislature. The question arose because, following the earlier cases, the Council had adopted Regulation 2144/87[178] which, with effect from 1 January 1989, provided that customs duty was payable on goods subject to measures of prohibition or restriction on importation, except for narcotic drugs not entering the economic channels strictly supervised by the competent authorities for use for medical and scientific purposes. Under the terms of the Regulation customs duty therefore became payable on imports of illegal goods other than drugs with effect from 1 January 1989. Although the facts of the case occurred prior to that date the Advocate General considered that it would serve the interests of legal certainty for the Court to indicate whether the legislature was empowered to change the position if it ruled against the imposition of customs duties on counterfeit currency. The Advocate General took the view that the Community legislature was free to intervene in the area and that by virtue of Regulation 2144/87 customs duty was payable on imports of counterfeit currency from 1 January 1989. Notwithstanding the Advocate General's remarks, the Court does not appear to have addressed the issue in its judgment.[179]

In Case 289/86, *Happy Family* v. *Inspecteur der Omzetbelasting*[180] and Case 269/86, *Mol* v. *Inspecteur der Invoerrechten en Accijnzen*[181] the Court, while observing that the principle of fiscal neutrality precluded a generalized differentiation between legal and illegal transactions, held that its reasoning in the *Einberger* cases applied to illegal transactions in narcotic drugs carried out within the territory of the country. That was so even in the case of soft, hemp-based drugs in respect of which the authorities applied a selective prosecution policy aimed primarily at large-scale dealers.

The Court considered a case falling the other side of the line in Case C–111/92, *Lange* v. *Finanzamt Fürstenfeldbruck*,[182] where it held to fall within the scope of the tax exports of goods to Eastern Europe made in contravention of an export ban decided within the framework of COCOM.[183] The Court held that, in contrast to previous cases, the goods were not such that all transactions were prohibited by reason of their nature or particular characteristics; all

[178] OJ 1987, L201/15. See Art. 2(2).

[179] The reference made by the Court in *Wolf* and *Einberger I* (and repeated in *Witzemann*) to Arts. 3(b) and 29 of the Treaty is not conclusive since, as Advocate General Jacobs pointed out (point 20 of the Opinion), the Court may have been seeking guidance from the Treaty for the purpose of interpreting the legislation rather than interpreting the Treaty itself.

[180] [1988] ECR 3655.

[181] [1988] ECR 3627.

[182] [1993] ECR I–4677.

[183] Co-ordinating Committee for Multilateral Export Controls.

that was prohibited was their export to certain destinations, owing to possible use for strategic purposes. Moreover, the exporting Member State could not withhold the export exemption provided for by Article 15.

The Compatibility of Other Taxes with VAT

Prior to its amendment by Directive 91/680, Article 33 of the Sixth Directive provided that:

> Without prejudice to other Community provisions, the provisions of this Directive shall not prevent a Member State from maintaining or introducing taxes on insurance contracts, taxes on betting and gambling, excise duties, stamp duties and, more generally, any taxes, duties or charge which cannot be characterised as turnover taxes.

No guidance is to be derived from the legislative history of this provision, which did not appear in the Commission's Proposal. It has however been the subject of numerous cases before the Court. In the first case, Case 295/84, *Wilmot*,[184] the Court was asked to consider the legality of a French solidarity levy and mutual assistance charge imposed upon the plaintiff company. The solidarity levy was introduced to finance certain social security benefits and was imposed on companies at a rate not exceeding 0.1 per cent of their turnover. The mutual assistance charge, which was levied for similar purposes, represented a specific proportion of the solidarity levy. The Court held the levy to be compatible with Article 33. The aim of that article, it stated, was to prevent the functioning of the common VAT system from being compromised by fiscal measures of a Member State levied on the movement of goods and services and charged on commercial transactions in a way comparable to VAT. It did not therefore prohibit a Member State from maintaining or introducing a non-fiscal charge introduced specifically to finance social funds and calculated on the basis of total annual turnover without directly affecting the price of goods or services.

The restricted view taken in *Wilmot* of what constitutes a prohibited turnover tax, namely whether the disputed tax has the effect of compromising the functioning of the common VAT system by imposing a charge on the movement of goods and services and on commercial transactions in a manner comparable to VAT, has been followed in later cases. In Case 252/86, *Bergandi*[185a] the Court held to be compatible with Article 33 a French tax on gaming machines levied at a flat annual rate per machine. The Court concluded that the characteristics of the French tax were not comparable to those of VAT as set out in Article 2 of the First Directive.[185b] In particular, the tax was not based on receipts but was charged solely by reason of the machine being placed at the disposal of the public, regardless of whether it was actu-

[184] *Rousseau Wilmot SA* v. *Organic* [1985] ECR 3759.

[185a] *Bergandi* v. *Directeur Général des Impôts* [1988] ECR 1343.

[185b] Above, p. 85.

ally used. A fixed-rate tax could only be regarded as a flat-rate tax on receipts if the rate was fixed on the basis of an objective estimate of the foreseeable receipts and if it was established that the tax could be passed on to the consumer in the price.[186] In *Wisselink*[187] the Court held that Article 33 did not preclude the Netherlands from introducing, at the time when it replaced its existing turnover tax system by VAT, a special consumption tax ('BVB') on the supply and importation of passenger cars. The Court observed first, in response to the taxpayer's argument that BVB was merely a disguised version of the old Dutch turnover tax, that the reasons for, and circumstances surrounding, the introduction of a tax were immaterial—what mattered were its objective characteristics. By introducing the BVB the Netherlands had not retained in part its old cumulative multi-stage turnover tax; the BVB was not at all comparable to that tax since it was levied at a single stage at the time of supply or importation. The Court went on to consider whether the BVB might none the less constitute a prohibited turnover tax under the *Wilmot* test. It noted that, although the BVB was a consumption tax whose basis of assessment was proportional to the price of passenger cars, it was not a general tax since it was charged only on two categories of specific products, namely passenger cars and motorcycles. Nor was it charged on the movement of goods and services or on commercial transactions in a manner comparable to VAT, since it was applied once only, upon its supply by the manufacturer or upon importation. The BVB paid was not deductible but formed an integral part of the cost price of the car; second-hand cars, other than those which were imported, were not subject to the BVB. Furthermore, the BVB did not jeopardize the functioning of the common VAT system since it was levied in addition to VAT and not in its place.

Other taxes held to be compatible with Article 33 are a German transfer tax on the purchase of land,[188] a French land registration duty,[189] a Belgian municipal tax on the receipts of dance halls and restaurants,[190] and an Italian levy on lawyers.[191] The sole case in which the Court has held a tax to be contrary to Article 33 is Case C–200/90, *Dansk Denkavit.*[192] By an Act of 18 December 1987 Denmark introduced a new tax known as the 'employment levy' with effect from 1 January 1988. The levy was intended to allow the state to finance certain social costs previously assumed by employers. The levy, which was replaced from 1 January 1992 by an increase in the rate of VAT, was charged at a rate of 2.5 per cent on the value of supplies of goods

[186] See also the similar ruling in Joined Cases 317/86, 48, 49, 285, 363 to 367/87, 65 and 78 to 80/88 *Lambert* v. *Directeur des Services Fiscaux de l'Orme* [1989] ECR 787.

[187] Joined Cases 93 and 94/88, *Wisselink* v. *Staatssecretaris van Financiën* [1989] ECR 2671.

[188] Case C–73/85, *Kerrutt* v. *Finanzamt Mönchengladbach-Mitte* [1986] ECR 2219.

[189] Case 208/91, *Beaulande* v. *Directeur des Services Fiscaux de Nantes* [1992] ECR I–6709.

[190] Case C–109/90, *Giant NV* v. *Gemeente Overijse* [1991] ECR I–1385.

[191] Case C–347/90, *Aldo Bozzi* v. *Cassa Nazionale di Previdenza ed Assistenza a favore degli avvocati e dei 'procuratori legali'* [1992] ECR I–2947.

[192] [1992] ECR I–2217.

and services made by undertakings qualifying as taxable persons for VAT purposes, as reduced by their purchases of goods and services. In the case of certain undertakings which were not taxable persons for VAT purposes, the levy was based on the total salaries paid, increased by 90 per cent. The levy was not charged on exports or imports; however, importers were not entitled to deduct the value of imports for the purposes of calculating the levy. The Court first of all confirmed the direct effect of Article 33. It then refined the *Wilmot* test by adding that those taxes, duties and charges which have the 'essential characteristics' of VAT must 'in any event' be regarded as being imposed on the movement of goods and services in a manner comparable to VAT.[193] A tax did not cease to be a turnover tax merely because it differed in certain respects from VAT. Notwithstanding the differences noted above the Danish tax remained essentially similar to VAT.

It is unclear whether the words 'in any event' disclose an intention to leave open the possibility that a tax which is not comparable to VAT may none the less be caught by Article 33. If so, this would constitute a welcome departure from the Court's reasoning in previous cases. It is submitted that it would have been open to the Court to take a broader view of the scope of Article 33, and in particular it is difficult to see why it has placed so much emphasis on the comparability of the various taxes under consideration with VAT. Article 33 does not prohibit value added taxes but turnover taxes. VAT was chosen as a replacement for the widely differing turnover taxes applied in the Member States because of its neutrality in domestic and intra-Community trade. That neutrality stems partly from the generality of the tax and partly from the fact that it always remains exactly proportional to the price of goods and services, so that at any commercial stage it is possible to identify precisely the turnover tax burden on goods and services. Somewhat ironically, it is taxes on goods or services which do not have all the characteristics of VAT that are more liable to frustrate that aim of fiscal neutrality. Particularly serious are general taxes, since they are liable to interfere with the fundamental aim of ensuring that the turnover tax burden on a Member State's goods and services is always an identifiable and identical proportion of their price. Owing to the specific nature of the taxes expressly permitted by Article 33 (taxes on insurance and gambling, stamp duties, and excise duties) the disruption which they cause to the VAT system is likely to be limited. The purpose of Article 33 was, it is submitted, to allow Member States to retain such specialized taxes while preventing them from introducing general turnover taxes of a type which VAT was intended to replace. The Court's decisions in this area may be justified on that ground.

Article 33 was amended by Directive 91/680 to take account of the removal of fiscal frontiers and the Community legislation on excise duties. The case law, however, seems unaffected by the changes.

[193] Para. 11.

5

Place of Supply and International Transactions

INTRA-COMMUNITY TRADE IN GOODS

The present rules for the taxation of trade in goods between Member States were introduced with effect from 1 January 1993[1] by Council Directives 91/680[2] and 92/111,[3] which substantially amended the rules applicable prior to that date.

Under the former rules goods exported from one Member State to another were generally relieved of VAT (by exemption together with a refund of input tax) in the exporting state and, like imports from non-member countries, taxed by the importing state upon importation into its territory. Traders were entitled to deduct VAT on imports on the same basis as VAT charged by their domestic suppliers.

The arrangements ensured that goods were taxed in the country of consumption while allowing the movement of goods across borders within the Community to be controlled by the national tax authorities. However, in its White Paper of 29 June 1985 the Commission noted that fiscal frontiers within the Community were incompatible with the single Community market and in 1987 put forward proposals[4] for their abolition. The Commission proposed to replace the existing arrangements by a system under which goods and services remained taxable in the country of origin. Tax would no longer be remitted on exports, and taxable persons would be entitled to deduct the foreign VAT charged by their suppliers on their internal VAT returns. Intra-Community transactions would in effect be treated like transactions within a single state. Since, however, tax would continue to accrue to the country of consumption as under the destination system, a clearing house mechanism for redistribution of revenue between Member States was proposed. Following a lengthy legislative process, including a communication[5] from the Commission in 1989 and amended proposals in 1990[6] and 1991,[7] the Council adopted Directives 91/680 and 92/111, amending the Sixth Directive.

The amended Sixth Directive embodies a compromise between the

[1] By virtue of Art. 4 of Directive 92/111 Member States were authorized to delay implementation of certain provisions of that Directive until 1 January 1994.

[2] OJ 1991, L376/1.

[3] OJ 1992, L384/47.

[4] OJ 1987, C252/2: COM(87)322 final.

[5] Communication to the Council and the European Parliament of 14 June 1989 on completion of the internal market and approximation of indirect taxes, COM(89)260 final.

[6] OJ 1990, C176/8: COM(90)182 final.

[7] OJ 1991, C131/3: COM(91)157 final.

Commission's original 1987 proposal and the Council's insistence that fiscal frontiers be removed without, for the time being, abandoning the destination principle. In the earlier part of its preamble Directive 91/680, like the 1987 Proposal, envisages the introduction of an origin-based system of collection preserving the existing patterns of revenue under the destination system.[8] However, the Directive contains no actual provisions to that effect. It limits itself to establishing transitional arrangements based mainly on the destination principle, leaving the introduction of definitive, origin-based arrangements for a future directive. The intention to change the arrangements again in due course none the less influences the structure of the amended Sixth Directive. The transitional provisions are partitioned off in a new Article 28 (a to n of the Directive), even those which amend (transitionally) the general provisions of the Directive.[9] Directive 91/680 also makes a number of definitive amendments to the general provisions of the Directive; however, these are confined to amendments likely to remain in place under the definitive system. The somewhat bizarre result is that the general provisions of the Sixth Directive, as they now stand, no longer of themselves embody a coherent scheme of taxation—they do so only when read in conjunction with the very long and detailed transitional provisions in Article 28a to n.

Under Article 28l of the Sixth Directive, as amended, the transitional arrangements are applicable for a period of four years until 31 December 1996. However, the period of application of the arrangements is automatically extended until the entry into force of the definitive system. The Commission is to report to the Council on the operation of the transitional arrangements and submit proposals for a definitive system before 31 December 1994.

Summary of the Transitional Arrangements

In view of the considerable complexity of the transitional provisions, it may be helpful to summarize the main arrangements before considering the provisions in more detail. The more detailed discussion is followed by several examples illustrating the main rules.

The purpose of the transitional arrangements is to remove tax frontiers within the Community while continuing to ensure that the majority of trade in goods is taxed in the country of consumption. The arrangements are basically as follows:

> Since 1 January 1993 VAT has ceased to be charged on imports of goods from other Member States and has been imposed under Member States' internal systems. The arrangements embody two basic principles:

[8] 7th recital.

[9] E.g., Arts. 28g and 28h replace Arts. 21 and 22 respectively by new, temporary Arts.

(a) Trade between taxable persons continues to be taxed in the country of consumption. Goods purchased by taxable persons from suppliers in other Member States continue to be relieved of tax (by exemption together with a refund of input tax) in the State of the supplier but are now taxed as an 'intra-Community acquisition' in the state of the customer, who enters the acquisition on his internal VAT return. He is entitled to deduct VAT on his acquisitions on the same basis as VAT charged by his domestic suppliers.

(b) Tax frontiers for private individuals and non-taxable legal persons have, in principle, been superseded by taxation in the country of origin. However, that principle must be read subject to a series of special arrangements designed to prevent 'cross-border shopping'; in the case of purchases by non-taxable legal persons, the scope of those arrangements is such that they in fact largely supplant the rule.

Special Arrangements to Prevent Division of Trade

A major concern during the legislative process was that, in the absence of harmonized rates of tax, private individuals and non-taxable legal persons such as government departments and local authorities, all of whom must bear tax definitively on their purchases, might be induced to purchase goods from other Member States applying lower rates of tax. Mail-order companies selling goods to private individuals might be induced to relocate to lower-tax Member States. Special arrangements were therefore made to ensure that the following important categories of sales to non-taxable persons remained taxable in the country of consumption:

(i) Distance sales to individuals: where a supplier arranges for his goods to be transported to another Member State to a customer who is a private individual, he is deemed to make a taxable supply in the state of the customer unless his total annual sales to individuals in that state fall below a certain threshold. Thus, for example, a mail-order firm with significant sales to other Member States must account for tax to the authorities in those states.

(ii) Non-taxable legal persons: where non-commercial bodies such as government departments and local authorities make purchases of goods exceeding a certain threshold from suppliers in other Member States, they are obliged to account for tax on such intra-Community acquisitions in the same way as taxable persons.

(iii) New means of transport (certain boats, aircraft, and land vehicles): irrespective of who the customer is, the sale of such goods is exempt with refund of tax in the country of the supplier and is taxable as an intra-Community acquisition in the state of arrival. Member States are obliged to lay down the detailed arrangements for collection of tax required by the extension of the acquisition mechanism to private individuals.

(iv) Goods subject to excise duty (mineral oils, alcohol and alcoholic beverages, and manufactured tobacco): the VAT arrangements mirror those for excise duty in Council Directive 92/12, which establishes the principle that excise duty is payable in the country of consumption unless the goods are acquired by private individuals for their own use and transported by them. Such goods therefore fall to be taxed in the country of consumption under the exemption/acquisition or distance sales mechanism, without the benefit of the *de minimis* provisions which restrict the application of those mechanisms in the case of normal goods.

Assembled and Installed Goods

Under the former rules special provision was made for goods assembled or installed by the supplier at the customer's premises to take account of the fact that the total value of such a transaction comprises not only the value of the parts supplied and imported into the state of assembly or installation but also the assembly work performed at the customer's premises. Those special rules have been retained under the transitional arrangements. Thus, such supplies are excluded from the exemption/acquisition mechanism, and instead the supplier is deemed to make a taxable supply in the state in which the goods are assembled. If they so wish, however, Member States may transfer responsibility for payment of the tax to the customer.

Fiscal Control

The rules concerning the place of supply and the exemption/acquisition mechanism for intra-Community trade are closely linked to the reporting requirements imposed on taxable persons by the amended Article 22 of the Directive. In the absence of controls at borders, fiscal control by the national authorities over the movement of tax-free goods must be exercised through returns made by taxable persons. In particular, proper control of the exemption/acquisition mechanism depends on the national authorities being able to carry out sample checks matching exempt supplies in one Member State with taxable acquisitions in another by reference to the VAT identification numbers of the supplier and purchaser. The detailed reporting requirements laid down by Article 22 are summarized in Chapter 8.

The Transitional Arrangements in More Detail

The Regime for Private Individuals and Assimilated Persons

The central feature of the new rules is the abolition of the taxable event of importation in intra-Community trade in goods. Article 2 of the Directive, unamended by Directive 91/680, continues to impose VAT on 'the importation of goods'. However, Article 7, as amended,[10] restricts the concept of importation to entry of goods into the Community. Private individuals are in principle free to purchase goods in another Member State and to take them back to their home state without further payment of VAT. However, they are obliged to pay tax on the goods in the Member State of purchase, since the supply of the goods no longer qualifies for exemption in that state.[11]

The regime for private individuals extends to certain taxable persons and non-taxable legal persons whose purchases fall below a certain threshold, namely farmers covered by the flat-rate scheme,[12] persons whose supplies do not give rise to deduction (such as insurance companies with no non-EC customers, hospitals, and other wholly exempt bodies), and non-taxable legal persons, in so far as their intra-Community acquisitions do not (and did not in the preceding calendar year) exceed a threshold of (at least) ECU 10,000. Unless such persons specifically opt for the general scheme they are spared the VAT-accounting obligations entailed by the intra-Community acquisition mechanism and are assimilated to private individuals.[13] They therefore pay tax in the country of origin unless the distance sales mechanism applies.

The mechanism applies where a supplier arranges transport of the goods to a private individual or assimilated person. Article 28b(B)(1) provides:

> By way of derogation from Article 8(1)(a) and (2), the place of supply of goods dispatched or transported by or on behalf of the supplier from a Member State other than that of arrival of the dispatch or transport shall be deemed to be the place where the goods are when dispatch or transport to the purchaser ends, where the following conditions are fulfilled:
>
> —the supply of goods is effected for a taxable person eligible for the derogation provided for in the second subparagraph of Article 28a(1)(a), for a non-taxable legal person who is eligible for the same derogation or for any other non-taxable person,

[10] Art. 1(2) of Directives 91/680 and 92/111.

[11] The export exemptions in Art. 15(1) and (2) of the amended Directive are restricted to supplies of goods transported outside the Community, and there is no applicable transitional exemption in Art. 28.

[12] Such persons do not have the right of deduction but flat-rate compensation for the tax incurred on their purchases of goods and services is received either by the farmer or his purchaser: see Ch. 9.

[13] Although Art. 28a(1)(a) of the Directive refers to intra-Community acquisitions by such persons below the threshold, the acquisitions are not subject to VAT (p. 142 ff., below) and the supply to them is not exempt.

—the supply is of goods other than new means of transport and other than goods supplied after assembly or installation, with or without a trial run, by or on behalf of the supplier.

The reference to taxable or non-taxable legal persons eligible for the derogation provided for by the second subparagraph of Article 28a(1)(a) extends the distance sales mechanism to the persons assimilated to private individuals.[14] The provision thus preserves the principle of taxation in the country of consumption for distance sales of significant value to private individuals and assimilated persons, and prevents possible distortions resulting from differences in VAT rates. Article 28b(B)(2) lays down a threshold for the application of the distance sales mechanism, thus allowing suppliers to make occasional cross-border sales without needing to account for VAT in other Member States. The mechanism does not apply to distance sales where the total VAT-exclusive value of a supplier's distance sales to a particular Member State does not (and did not in the preceding calendar year) exceed ECU 100,000. This proviso does not apply to goods subject to excise duty, which are covered by the distance sales mechanism regardless of the level of a supplier's sales. Member States may reduce the ECU 100,000 threshold to ECU 35,000 'where the Member State fears' that the higher threshold would lead to serious distortions of the conditions of competition. Member States exercising this option are required to inform the authorities of the Member State of dispatch or transport, its effect being to remove the relevant supplies from the latter Member State's tax jurisdiction. By virtue of Article 28b(B)(3) taxable persons may opt to waive the *de minimis* provision, subject to detailed rules laid down by the Member State concerned.[15] The option is in any case to apply for two calendar years.

Intra-Community Acquisitions

Unlike private individuals taxable persons regularly submit tax returns to the authorities. By taxing the act of acquiring goods from other Member States it was possible to arrange for taxable persons to record and account for tax on their internal returns. This mechanism was extended to acquisitions by non-taxable legal persons, thus bringing within its scope the very significant expen-

[14] The wording of Art. 28b(B)(1) is curious, since on a literal reading the generality of the phrase 'any other non-taxable person' makes the specific reference to 'non-taxable legal person who is eligible for the same derogation' unnecessary. It seems, however, that the former phrase is not as broad as it might appear and does not cover other non-taxable *legal* persons. The only non-taxable *legal* persons covered by the distance sales mechanism are therefore those falling under the derogation in the second subpara. of Art. 28a(1)(a); other non-taxable legal persons must pay tax under the intra-Community acquisition mechanism.

[15] Presumably such rules should be limited to what is necessary to ensure the proper exercise of the option. It seems that in practice Member States allow taxable persons to opt on a country-by-country basis.

diture of government departments and public authorities. It was evidently considered that, unlike private individuals, non-taxable legal persons could reasonably be required to submit declarations when they purchased goods from other Member States. Thus, Article 28a(1)(a) provides that tax is chargeable on:

intra-Community acquisitions of goods for consideration within the territory of the country by a taxable person acting as such or by a non-taxable legal person where the vendor is a taxable person acting as such . . .

The term 'intra-Community acquisition of goods' is defined in Article 28a(3) as:

acquisition of the right to dispose as owner of movable tangible property dispatched or transported to the person acquiring the goods by or on behalf of the vendor or the person acquiring the goods to a Member State other than that from which the goods are dispatched or transported.

The taxable event of an acquisition is thus the counterpart, in the country of the acquirer or arrival, of the exempt supply in the country of dispatch.[16] It is defined in terms which correspond to the definition of a 'supply of goods' in Article 5(1) ('the transfer of the right to dispose of tangible property as owner'), except that an intra-Community acquisition is limited to movable property presumably because immovable property cannot be transported from one Member State to another. Like a 'supply of goods', an 'intra-Community acquisition' must be regarded as having an independent Community law meaning, and it seems that the provisions of Article 5 and case law concerning the supply of goods must be relevant.[17] Reference to national law remains necessary in so far as it determines what rights have been acquired. It is submitted that for this purpose reference should be made to the proper law of the contract or transaction.[18]

Non-taxation of Acquisitions from Certain Suppliers

Under the first subparagraph of Article 28a(1)(a), there is a chargeable intra-Community acquisition of goods only:

[16] By virtue of the first sentence of Art. 8(1)(a), unamended by Directive 91/680, goods transported to the customer are deemed to be supplied in the country in which they are situated when transport begins.

[17] See Ch. 4.

[18] Reference to national law is also necessary in cases where Community law allows Member States to choose whether to classify a transaction as a supply of goods or services. The applicable tax law is that of the Member State of acquisition. Art. 28a(7) provides that 'Member States shall take measures to ensure that transactions which would have been classed as "supplies of goods". . . if they had been carried out within the territory of the country by a taxable person acting as such are classed as 'intra-Community acquisitions of goods.' The provision also counters the risk of non-taxation arising from divergent interpretations of the provisions defining goods and services.

where the vendor is a taxable person acting as such who is not eligible for the tax exemption provided for in Article 24 and who is not covered by the arrangements laid down in the second sentence of Article 8(1)(a) or in Article 28b(B)(1).

Those conditions call for some brief explanation:

The vendor must be a taxable person acting as such. As in a purely domestic situation there is no further tax charge on the cross-frontier sale or resale of goods by a private individual.[19]

The tax exemption in Article 24 allows Member States to exempt the turnover of small undertakings.[20] Undertakings covered by the exemption may be equated with private individuals in that they neither charge VAT on their supplies nor deduct VAT on their purchases. Their customers therefore bear the hidden VAT of the country of origin contained in the price of their goods.

The second sentence of Article 8(1)(a) deems goods which are installed or assembled by the supplier to be supplied in the country in which the installation or assembly is carried out. Since the supplier makes a taxable supply in the country of arrival, it is unnecessary to tax the acquisition of the goods by the customer.

As already mentioned, Article 28b(B)(1) establishes the distance sales mechanism, which applies, *inter alia*, to supplies to certain taxable persons and non-taxable legal persons making limited cross-frontier purchases. Under the distance sales mechanism the supplier makes a taxable supply in the country of arrival, thus making a chargeable intra-Community acquisition unnecessary.

Non-taxable Intra-Community Acquisitions

By way of derogation from the first subparagraph, the second subparagraph of Article 28a(1)(a)[21] provides that tax is not chargeable on intra-Community acquisitions made by taxable persons or non-taxable legal persons under the conditions set out in paragraph 1a of Article 28a. Paragraph 1a[22] refers to:

intra-Community acquisitions of goods whose supply within the territory of the country would be exempt under Article 15(4) to (10)[23] (subparagraph (a)); and

intra-Community acquisitions by a taxable person for the purposes of his agricultural, forestry, or fisheries undertaking subject to the flat-rate scheme in Article 25, by a taxable person who carries out only supplies of goods or services in respect of which VAT is not deductible, or by a non-taxable legal person, where the total value of the acquisitions (excluding VAT and exclud-

[19] See however the special arrangements for occasional sales of means of transport, below, p. 145.

[20] See Ch. 9.

[21] As amended by Art. 1(10) of Directive 92/111.

[22] Inserted by Art. 1(10) of Directive 92/111.

[23] Below, p. 168.

ing acquisitions of new means of transport and goods subject to excise duty) does not exceed, during the current calendar year, a threshold which may not be less than the equivalent of ECU 10,000 and did not exceed that threshold in the previous calendar year (subparagraph b).

As already mentioned, in so far as their acquisitions remain below the specified threshold, the persons referred to in subparagraph (b) are excluded from the tax charge under the acquisition mechanism and are assimilated to private individuals. They pay tax in the country of origin unless the supply is caught by the distance sales mechanism, which is specifically extended to such persons.[24] However, Member States are obliged to allow such persons the right to opt for taxation under the general scheme, i.e., taxation of the goods as an acquisition, and are to lay down detailed rules for the exercise of that option.

Although this derogation applies equally to goods subject to excise duty and new means of transport, the acquisition of such goods by the taxable and non-taxable legal persons qualifying for the derogation falls to be taxed under separate provisions.

Goods Subject to Excise Duty

The VAT arrangements for goods subject to excise duty follow the principles underlying the excise duty arrangements in Council Directive 92/12[25] and are designed to take advantage of the procedures which that Directive establishes for controlling the movement of goods under duty-suspension arrangements.[26] The definition in Article 33(2)[27] of the Sixth Directive is the same as in the Excise Duty Directive, namely mineral oils, alcohol and alcoholic beverages, and manufactured tobacco. The VAT arrangements are as follows:

> Where dutiable goods are supplied by a taxable person to another taxable person or a non-taxable legal person, they fall within the general exemption/acquisition mechanism provided for by Article 28a(1)(a), in conjunction with Article 28c(A)(a).

Where an acquisition by a taxable or non-taxable legal person escapes taxation under the general exemption/acquisition mechanism, it falls to be taxed under the specific provision for dutiable goods in Article 28a(1)(c).[28]

[24] Above, p. 139. By virtue of Art. 28c(A)(a), second subpara., supplies to persons qualifying for the derogation in the second subpara. of Art. 28a(1)(a) are excluded from exemption in the Member State of departure. Thus, tax remains payable in that State, unless the distance sales rules require the supplier to account for tax in the Member State of arrival of the goods.

[25] Directive of 25 February 1992 on the general arrangements for products subject to excise duty and on the holding, movement, and monitoring of such products (OJ 1992, L76/10), amended by Directive 92/108, OJ 1992, L390/124.

[26] See Ch. 10.

[27] As amended by Art. 1(23) of Directive 91/680.

[28] Inserted by Art. 1(10) of Directive 92/111. A corresponding exemption of the supply in the country of departure is to be found in Art. 28c(A)(c), inserted by Art. 1(12) of Directive 92/111.

The distance sales mechanism remains applicable to dutiable goods transported by the seller to private individuals. It should be noted that the derogation for supplies below a certain threshold in Article 28b(B)(2) does not apply to such goods.

The combined effect of those provisions is to ensure that, in keeping with the arrangements for excise duty, all intra-Community trade in dutiable goods, except goods purchased for private use transported by private individuals themselves, is taxed in the country of consumption.

The separate acquisition mechanism in Article 28a(1)(c) for supplies to taxable and non-taxable legal persons assimilated to private individuals should be read in conjunction with Article 22(11),[29] which requires Member States to adopt arrangements for declaration and payment of tax in the case of such acquisitions. The intention is that Member States should make use for this purpose of the obligations laid down with regard to excise duties.[30] The acquisition of dutiable goods by taxable and non-taxable legal persons who would otherwise not need to be identified for VAT purposes (because their intra-Community acquisitions did not exceed the threshold in the second subparagraph of Article 28a(1)(a)) may thus be avoided.

New Means of Transport

In the case of new means of transport the taxable event of acquisition is extended, by virtue of subparagraph (b) of Article 28a(1), to acquisitions not only by taxable and non-taxable legal persons assimilated to private individuals but also by private individuals themselves. The extension of the acquisition mechanism is prompted by the possibility of introducing special procedures for collecting the tax[31] without requiring such persons to be identified for VAT purposes. Thus, Article 22(11)[32] requires the Member States to adopt arrangements for declaration and subsequent payment.

The term 'new means of transport' is defined in Article 28a(2) and covers all but very small motorized land vehicles, vessels, and aircraft, other than the vessels and aircraft listed in Article 15(5) and (6).[33] Means of transport are not considered 'new' if they were supplied more than three months (or six months in the case of motorized land vehicles) after the date of first entry into service *and* they have travelled more than 6,000 kilometres in the case of land vehi-

29 As inserted by Art. 28h of Directive 91/680 and subsequently amended by Art. 1(20) of Directive 92/111.

30 See the Explanatory Memorandum to the Commission's Proposal for Directive 92/111 (note relating to point 13), COM(92)448 final. The exemption/acquisition provisions for dutiable goods refer expressly to compliance with the formalities in Directive 92/12.

31 E.g., declaration and payment at the time of registration.

32 Contained in the transitional provision in Art. 28h.

33 Broadly, commercial vessels used on the high seas, vessels used for sea rescue or inshore fishing and warships; aircraft used chiefly by airlines on commercial routes.

cles, sailed for more than 100 hours in the case of vessels, or flown for more than forty hours in the case of aircraft.[34]

By virtue of Article 28a(4) any person who from time to time makes an intra-Community supply of a new means of transport is to be regarded as a taxable person. Such a person therefore makes an exempt supply with entitlement to a refund of input tax. Limits are, however, placed on the right of deduction to prevent avoidance of tax: the right of deduction does not arise until the supply is actually made and the deductible tax is limited to the amount of tax for which he would be liable on the supply if it were not exempt. But for such rules, tax could be avoided by cross-border exchanges for minimal consideration.

Deliveries of Contract Work

The delivery of 'contract work' is defined in Article 5(5)(a) as:

> supplies under a contract to make up work from customer's [sic] materials, that is to say delivery by a contractor to his customer of movable property made or assembled by the contractor from materials or objects entrusted to him by the customer for this purpose, whether or not the contractor has provided any part of the materials used.

By virtue of Article 5(5)(a), unamended by Directive 91/680, Member States may choose whether to treat such deliveries as a supply of goods or a supply of services.

Under the transitional arrangements it was necessary to ensure that, where contract work was carried out for a customer in another Member State, the option given to Member States by Article 5(5)(a) did not result in non-taxation or double taxation of the work and that, in accordance with the destination principle, the value of the contractor's work was taxed in the Member State to which the goods were returned.

Article 28a(5)(a) treats as a supply of goods effected for consideration:

> the delivery to another taxable person of contract work, as defined in Article 5(5)(a), physically carried out within a Member State other than that within the territory of which the customer is identified for purposes of Value Added Tax.

The provision operates only where the materials used were sent by the customer from the Member State in which he is identified for VAT purposes and the work is returned to the customer in that Member State.[35]

The scheme is as follows: when the customer sends the raw materials to the contractor, there is neither a supply nor an acquisition since there is no transfer or acquisition of the right to dispose of the goods as owner.[36] When the

[34] Art. 28a(2)(b), as amended by Directive 94/5: below, p. 220.

[35] First and second indents of Art. 28a(5)(a).

[36] Moreover, by virtue of the fourth indent of Art. 28a(5)(b) the transfer of goods to another Member State for the purposes of contract work carried out in the state of arrival is excluded.

contractor returns the finished goods to the customer, the contractor makes a supply under Article 28a(5)(a), exempted under Article 28c(A)(a), and the customer makes a taxable acquisition.[37] By virtue of Article 28e(1), in conjunction with Article 11(A)(1)(a), the taxable amount is the amount invoiced by the contractor for the contract work.

Where the conditions mentioned in Article 28a(5)(a) are not met (for example, where the customer is not a taxable person or where the goods are not returned to the customer's Member State but are sold elsewhere by the customer), the transaction falls to be taxed under the general rules of the transitional arrangements.

In order to permit administrative control Article 22(2)(b), inserted by Article 28h, requires the contractor and the customer to keep a register of goods covered by these special provisions.[38]

Transfers of Goods to Other Member States

Article 28a(5)(b) treats as a supply of goods effected for consideration the 'transfer by a taxable person of goods from his undertaking to another Member State'. Such a transfer covers the dispatch or transporting, by or on behalf of the taxable person, of any tangible property to another Member State for the purposes of his undertaking.

By virtue of Article 28c(A)(d), in conjunction with the amended Article 17(3)(b), the deemed supply is exempt[39] in so far as it would be exempt if carried out for another taxable person. Accordingly, Article 28a(6) provides that an intra-Community acquisition for consideration includes:

> the use by a taxable person for the purposes of his undertaking of goods dispatched or transported by or on behalf of that taxable person from another Member State within the territory of which the goods were produced, extracted, processed, purchased, acquired . . . or imported by the taxable person within the framework of his undertaking into that other Member State.

Prior to 1 January 1993 goods transferred from one Member State to another were subject to import VAT even where the transfer was between two establishments of the same taxable person. The transitional arrangements use the acquisition mechanism to retain taxation of such goods in the state to which they are transferred. The concept of a transfer is broadly defined, so that any movement of business goods by a taxable person to another Member

from the scope of the deemed supply under Art. 28a(5)(b) (transfer by a taxable person of goods from his undertaking to another Member State).

[37] Art. 28a(7) requires Member States to treat as acquisitions transactions which would qualify as supplies of goods if they had been carried out within its territory.

[38] Below, p. 208. Owing to difficulties in the application of the rules on contract work the Commission and the Member States agreed upon simplified arrangements: see *International VAT Monitor*, Dec. 1993, 19.

[39] But gives rise to the right of deduction.

State is caught unless specifically excluded. However, the arrangements are aimed primarily at two categories of transfer:

The transfer of goods to another Member State to be held as stocks there: The inclusion of such transfers within the acquisition mechanism ensures that they fall under the system of administrative control in the same way as sales direct to customers.

The transfer of capital goods to another Member State for use in the taxable person's business: In the absence of special provisions, a taxable person would be able to purchase assets for an establishment with a limited deduction entitlement in one Member State through an establishment with a greater deduction entitlement in another Member State. For example, a bank whose activities in Germany were mainly taxable (owing to the exercise of the option to tax financial transactions granted to taxable persons by the German legislation under Article 13C) would be able to purchase a computer, deduct the VAT on it, and transfer it to its UK establishment whose activities were mainly exempt (no option to tax being available under the UK legislation).

Article 28a(5)(b) excludes from the scope of the deemed supply transfers to other Member States made in connection with the following transactions:

the supply of assembled goods and goods covered by the distance sales mechanism;
the supply of goods on board ships, aircraft, or trains;
supplies exempted under Article 15 or 28c(A);
the supply to the taxable person of contract work carried out in the other Member State;
the supply of a service to the taxable person involving work carried out in the other Member State;
temporary use of the goods in the other Member State by the taxable person for the purpose of supplying services;
temporary use of the goods, for a period of up to twenty-four months, in another Member State in which the import of the same goods from a third country would qualify under the arrangements for temporary importation for full exemption from import duties.[40]

If a transfer ceases to qualify under one of the above exceptions, it is deemed to be carried out at the moment when the conditions are no longer met.[41]

Exempt Supplies

Article 28c(A)(a) exempts:

supplies of goods, as defined in Articles 5 and 28a(5)(a), dispatched or transported by

[40] Indents 1 to 7 of Art. 28a(5)(b).
[41] Final subpara. of Art. 28a(5)(b), inserted by Art. 1(10) of Directive 92/111.

or on behalf of the vendor or the person acquiring the goods out of the territory referred to in Article 3 but within the Community, effected for another taxable person or a non-taxable legal person acting as such in a Member State other than that of the departure of the dispatch or transport of the goods.

The exemption is thus the counterpart to the taxable acquisition provided for by Article 28a(1)(a). In order for a supply to qualify for exemption both the destination of the goods and the customer must be in another, although not necessarily the same, Member State. Although by virtue of Article 28b(A)(1) a customer is deemed to acquire goods in the Member State to which they are sent, Article 28b(A)(2) deems the place of acquisition to be within the territory of the Member State which issued the customer's VAT identification number unless the customer can show that he has been subject to tax in the Member State to which the goods are sent. Thus, even where a supplier can show that goods are transported to another Member State, the supply qualifies for exemption only if the customer acquires the goods under the VAT identification number of another Member State, unless the customer can show that he has been subject to tax in respect of a taxable acquisition in the state of arrival.

It is apparent from the terms of the exemption that it does not apply to supplies effected for private individuals. Under the scheme of the transitional arrangements private individuals pay tax in the country of the supplier, unless the supply is caught by the distance sales mechanism. The second subparagraph of Article 28c(A)(a) also excludes from the exemption supplies of goods by taxable persons exempt from tax under Article 24 (small undertakings) and supplies effected for the persons assimilated to private individuals, namely taxable persons or non-taxable legal persons qualifying for the derogation under the second subparagraph of Article 28a(1)(a).[42]

Article 28c(A)(b) exempts:

supplies of new means of transport, dispatched or transported to the purchaser by or on behalf of the vendor or the purchaser out of the territory referred to in Article 3 but within the Community, effected for taxable persons or non-taxable legal persons who qualify for the derogation provided for in the second subparagraph of Article 28a(1)(a) or for any other non-taxable person.

Intra-Community supplies of new means of transport to taxable persons and non-taxable legal persons are exempt by virtue of the general exemption in subparagraph a of Article 28c(A). Subparagraph (b) is thus intended to extend that exemption to supplies to private individuals and to the taxable and non-taxable legal persons assimilated to private individuals. The counterpart to this exemption is to be found in Article 28a(1)(b), which extends the taxable event of acquisition for new means of transport to acquisitions by private individuals and assimilated persons. Means of transport therefore fall under the exemption/acquisition mechanism whoever the purchaser is.

[42] Above, p. 139.

Article 28c(A)(c)[43] exempts intra-Community supplies of dutiable goods effected, under the conditions laid down in Directive 92/12, for the taxable persons or non-taxable legal persons assimilated to private individuals. This provision is the corollary of Article 28a(1)(c), which subjects to tax the intra-Community acquisition of dutiable goods by such persons.

Article 28c(A)(d)[44] exempts supplies of goods as defined in Article 28a(5)(b) which would qualify for exemption if they were carried out for another taxable person. This exemption concerns supplies deemed to arise when a taxable person transfers goods from his undertaking to another Member State. The exemption is the counterpart to Article 28a(6), which provides that an intra-Community acquisition of goods for consideration is to include the use by a taxable person for the purposes of his undertaking of goods transported by him from another Member State.

Article 28k[45] provides for the retention, until 30 June 1999, of tax-free shops for travellers on intra-Community flights or sea crossings.

Exempt intra-Community Acquisitions of Goods

Article 28c(B)(a) exempts:

> the intra-Community acquisition of goods the supply of which by taxable persons would in all circumstances be exempt within the territory of the country.

This provision, which is modelled on the import exemption in Article 14(1)(a), is designed to ensure equal treatment of domestic and intra-Community transactions. Read literally the phrase 'in all circumstances' suggests that there must be a general exemption for the relevant supply: the exemption may not be limited to certain suppliers or customers or be subject to an option to tax. However, interpreted in that way, the provision would be liable to infringe Article 95 of the Treaty by discriminating against products of other Member States. Moreover, the other language versions of the provision support a different interpretation. The French term '*en tout état de cause*' and the German term '*auf jeden Fall*', for example, would be more accurately rendered as 'in any event' or 'in any case'. It seems, therefore, that the intention of the provision is to exempt intra-Community acquisitions in so far as the equivalent domestic transaction would be exempt.

Subparagraph (b) exempts acquisitions of goods the importation of which would in all circumstances be exempt under Article 14(1).[46]

Subparagraph (c) exempts acquisitions where under Article 17(3) and (4) the person acquiring the goods would in all circumstances be entitled to full

[43] Inserted by Art. 1(12) of Directive 92/111.
[44] Inserted by Art. 1(12) of Directive 92/111.
[45] Amended by Directive 94/4, OJ 1994, L60/14.
[46] Below, p. 163.

reimbursement of the VAT due in respect of the acquisition under Article 28a(1). The purpose of this provision is to exempt acquisitions of goods which are subsequently used for making exempt supplies to other Member States or non-member countries or supplies outside the territory of the Member State of intermediate acquisition. By virtue of Article 17(3) and (4), as amended by Article 28f, a taxable person established in another Member State or outside the Community would be entitled to a refund under the Eighth or Thirteenth Directive[47] of tax incurred on goods used for the purpose of such transactions. The exemption of intermediate acquisitions removes the need for such persons to claim a refund of tax, while allowing the movement of goods to be monitored.

Place of Supply and Acquisition of Goods

The various rules regarding the country in which transactions are deemed to take place have been largely dealt with in considering the various mechanisms provided for by the transitional arrangements. However, it may be useful to summarize them here:

Goods dispatched or transported to the customer: the place where transport begins (Article 8(1)(a), first sentence);

Goods transported from a non-member country supplied by the importer or subsequent suppliers: the Member State of import (Article 8(2), as amended by Article 1(5) of Directive 91/680);

Goods not dispatched or transported: the place where the goods are when the supply takes place (Article 8(1)(b));

Goods assembled or installed for the customer by the supplier: the place of assembly or installation (Article 8(1)(a), second and third sentences, as amended by Article 1(3) of Directive 91/680);

Goods covered by the intra-Community distance sales mechanism: the place of arrival (Article 28b(B));

Goods supplied on board ships, aircraft or trains during the part of a transport of passengers effected in the Community: the point of departure of the transport of the passengers.[48]

For intra-Community acquisitions of goods there are two rules. The acquisition is deemed to take place:

(1) at the place of arrival (Article 28b(A)(1)),

[47] Below, p. 192.

[48] Art. 8(1)(c), replaced by Art. 1(4) of Directive 92/111. The Commission is entrusted with submitting a report or proposals on the place of taxation of goods supplied for consumption and services provided for passengers on board.

(2) without prejudice to rule 1, in the Member State which issued the VAT identification number under which the acquisition was made, *unless* the acquirer establishes that the acquisition has been subject to tax in accordance with rule 1 (first subparagraph of Article 28b(A)(2)).

If the acquisition is taxed under rule 1 after being taxed under rule 2, the Member State which issued the VAT identification number must reduce the taxable amount accordingly (second subparagraph of Article 28b(A)(2)).

Examples of the Appliction of the Rules

Acquisitions made in the Member State of arrival in connection with triangular transactions covered by Article 28c(E)(3)[49] are normally deemed to take place in the state of arrival (third subparagraph of Article 28b(A)(2)[50]).

The application of the main rules and mechanisms may be illustrated by several simple examples:

(1) A French company sells a commercial property in France to a person residing in Germany. The goods consist of immovable property and hence fall outside the intra-Community acquisition mechanism. By virtue of Article 8(1)(b) the property is deemed to be supplied in France.

(2) A German company exports goods (which require no installation or assembly at the customer's premises) to a number of other Member States. It adopts the following export arrangements:

   (a) It exports goods to the United Kingdom through an independent importer established in the UK who buys the company's goods under its UK VAT identification number, transports them to its warehouse in the UK, and then sells them on the UK market. Here there are two separate supplies: A first supply by the exporter to the importer and a second supply by the importer to the ultimate customer. The first supply is deemed to be made in Germany under the first sentence of Article 8(1)(a). It is exempt but gives rise to the right of deduction by virtue of Article 28c(A)(a) and Article 17(3)(b), as amended by Article 28f. The United Kingdom importer makes a taxable intra-Community acquisition of the goods under Article 28a(1)(a). The acquisition is deemed to occur in the United Kingdom because the goods are situated there when transport to the acquirer ends for the purposes of Article 28b(A)(1); moreover, the importer acquires the goods under its United Kingdom VAT identification number in accordance with Article 28b(A)(2). The importer may deduct the VAT payable in respect of the acquisition under Article 17(2)(d), as amended by Article 28f, since it makes a taxable supply of the goods to the customer.

[49] Below, p. 152.

[50] Inserted by Art. 1(11) of Directive 92/111.

(b) The company sells and transports its goods to customers in France direct, the customers purchasing the goods under their French VAT identification numbers: The position of the German exporter is the same as in the preceding example. The French customer makes a taxable acquisition in France under Article 28a(1)(a) and may deduct the VAT in respect thereof if he puts the goods to taxable use.

(c) In Italy the company maintains stocks of goods at a warehouse which it uses to satisfy customer demands as they arise: The transfer of the goods from Germany to Italy is deemed to constitute a supply under Article 28a(5)(b). The deemed supply qualifies for exemption in Germany under Article 28c(A)(d). The company makes a taxable acquisition in Italy under Article 28a(6). It may deduct the VAT paid on the acquisition if the goods are used for making taxable sales.

(3) (a) An individual residing in France buys a computer in Luxembourg and returns with it to France: The supply to the individual is made in Luxembourg under Article 8(1)(a) and does not qualify for exemption. He is free to import the computer into France without payment of VAT.

(b) A mail order company established in Luxembourg makes distance sales of small computers to individuals in other Member States. It annual sales to France amount to the equivalent of ECU 200,000 and its sales to each of several other Member States to the equivalent of ECU 5,000: By virtue of Article 28b(B)(1) the company's sales to France are deemed to be made in France and the company must appoint a tax representative to account for the tax. Since the other sales fall below the minimum threshold laid down by Article 28b(B)(2), the company may choose, under Article 28b(B)(3), whether it wishes to pay tax in Luxembourg or the Member State of the customer.

(c) A (non-taxable) public authority in France buys from a Luxembourg firm a large computer (without installation) costing the equivalent of ECU 500,000: By virtue of Article 28a(1)(a) the authority makes a taxable acquisition of the computer in France (since the purchase is too costly to qualify under the derogation in the second subparagraph of Article 28a(1)(a)). The supply of the computer by the Luxembourg firm is exempt under Article 28c(A) and qualifies for refund of input tax under Article 17(3).

Triangular Transactions

During the year following the adoption of Directive 91/680 it was realized that the application of the transitional arrangements would give rise to particular problems with respect to so-called 'triangular transactions'. This is the term used to denote the situation where goods are purchased from a trader in Member

State A by a trader identified for VAT purposes in Member State B, but are transported direct to the latter's customer in Member State C. In the absence of simplifying provisions the intermediate trader in state B would either have to allow the seller in state A to invoice the ultimate customer in state C direct (which would involve the disclosure to the seller of confidential information concerning the final customer and price) or have to acquire the goods in state A or C and make an onward sale to the customer (which would involve being identified for tax purposes or appointing a fiscal representative in those states).

Directive 92/111 introduced provisions to simplify the VAT treatment of such transactions with effect from 1 January 1994.[51] Article 28c(E)(3), as amended by that Directive, provides that, where a taxable person identified in another Member State and not established within the territory of the country makes an intra-Community acquisition of goods within the territory of the country for the purpose of making a supply within that territory to a customer who is a taxable or non-taxable legal person identified there for VAT purposes, and the goods have been transported direct from a Member State other than the one in which the taxable person making the acquisition is identified for VAT purposes, no VAT is chargeable on the acquisition, provided that liability for payment of the tax on the supply has been transferred to the customer under the third subparagraph of Article 21(1)(a).[52]

Thus, in the above example the intermediate trader in Member State B would make a non-taxable acquisition in Member State C, followed by a supply in that state in respect of which the customer would account for tax.[53]

By virtue of the third subparagraph of Article 28b(A)(2)[54] the intra-Community acquisition is deemed to have been subject to tax in the Member State of arrival in accordance with paragraph (1) of that provision where Article 28c(E)(3) applies and the acquirer has complied with the declaration obligations in the last subparagraph of Article 22(6)(b). The effect of this is that the goods are not deemed to be acquired in the Member State which issued the identification number under the first subparagraph of Article 28b(A)(2). In the above example, therefore, the intermediate trader would make no acquisition in Member State B in which he is identified for VAT purposes. His only acquisition would be the non-taxable acquisition in Member State C.

The last subparagraph of Article 22(6)(b)[55] requires that in such cases the taxable person making the acquisition should mention on his recapitulative statement[56] the VAT identification number under which he made the acquisition and the subsequent supply in the state of arrival, the VAT identification number of the consignee to whom the subsequent supply was made and for each consignee the total value of supplies made in the state of arrival.

[51] Art. 4(2) of Directive 92/111. [52] As replaced by Art. 1(19) of Directive 92/111.

[53] It appears that the acquisition would be exempted by Art. 28c(B)(c).

[54] Inserted by Art. 1(11) of Directive 92/111.

[55] Subpara. added by Art. 1(20) of Directive 92/111. [56] Below, p. 209.

PLACE OF SUPPLY OF SERVICES

Services, being intangible, do not lend themselves to control or taxation at borders. Consequently, even prior to 1 January 1993 cross-frontier services were taxed under the Member States' internal systems. Little change was therefore necessary under the transitional arrangements. The Sixth Directive creates a series of fictions locating supplies in particular countries according to the type of service or the location and status of the customer. A taxable person established in one Member State providing services in another Member State has the right of deduction in his state of establishment, thus ensuring full remission of VAT in that State.[57]

The relevant provisions are set out in Article 9. The basic rule, contained in Article 9(1), is that a service is supplied where:

> the supplier has established his business or has a fixed establishment from which the service is supplied or, in the absence [thereof], the place where he has his permanent address or usually resides.

Article 9(1) serves as a residual category encompassing any services not covered by any of the special rules dealt with below. Many of the most common international services are singled out for special treatment under those rules, so that Article 9(1) services are in practice mainly domestic. However, as a matter of law it is immaterial where they are actually supplied or consumed or where the customer is established or resides—they are always taxed in the country of the supplier.

Article 9(2) lays down a series of special rules which may be summarized as follows:

(1) Services connected with immovable property are supplied where the property is situated (Article 9(2)(a));
(2) Transport services are supplied where the transport takes place having regard to the distance covered (Article 9(2)(b))[58];
(3) Services connected with cultural, artistic, sporting, scientific, educational, entertainment, or similar activities, ancillary transport activities such as loading, unloading, or handling,[59] and also valuations of, or work on, movable tangible property are supplied where the services are physically carried out (Article 9(2)(c));
(4) The following services are supplied where the customer is established if the customer is established outside the Community or the customer is a taxable person established in another Member State:

[57] See below, p. 191.

[58] This rule has been amended by the transitional arrangements: see below, p. 156.

[59] The rules on ancillary transport activities have also been amended by the transitional arrangements: see below, p. 156.

transfers and assignments of intellectual and commercial property rights;
advertising;
professional and consultancy services, data processing, and the supply of information;
banking, financial, and insurance transactions (excluding hire of safes);
supply of staff;
the hiring out of movable tangible property except for all forms of transport;
refraining from activities or waiver of rights referred to above;
agency in respect of the above activities (Article 9(2)(e)).

From the preamble and the rather muddled legislative history[60] of Article 9 it may be inferred that the legislative aims were essentially simplicity and avoidance of competitive distortions with respect to the most important categories of cross-frontier services. The preamble to the Sixth Directive states that:

although the place where a supply of services is effected should in principle be defined as the place where the person supplying the services has his principal place of business, that place should be defined as being in the country of the person to whom the services are supplied, in particular in the case of certain services supplied between taxable persons where the cost of the services is included in the price of the goods.

In the 'advertising cases'[61] the Court, referring to the preamble, observed in relation to Article 9(2)(e):

the Community legislature considered that, in so far as the customer habitually sells goods or provides services advertised in the State where he is established, and charges the relevant VAT to the final consumer, the VAT charged on the advertising service should itself be paid by the customer to that State. That explanation constitutes one of the factors which must be taken into account in interpreting the term 'advertising services' in Article 9(2)(e).[62]

[60] The rules on the place of supply of services underwent considerable change during the legislative process. In the Proposal all services except those relating to immovable property and transport services were deemed supplied at the place where the supplier was established (Art. 10). The Explanatory Memorandum stated that this choice was made for reasons of simplicity and to avoid difficulties of interpretation which might arise from the use of concepts such as the place of utilization or exploitation. However, Art. 16(10) of the Proposal granted exemption with refund of tax in respect of a series of services not dissimilar to the list in Art. 9(2)(e) of the Directive. Like the rule in Art. 9(2)(e), the exemption in Art. 16(10) depended, in the case of intra-Community services, on the customer being a taxable person who would account for tax on the services. The Explanatory Memorandum stated, with respect to the proposed Art. 16(10), that the application of the general rule of taxation in the country of the supplier would make Community supplies of such services subject to distortions of competition *vis-à-vis* those in non-member countries and would lead to distortion of competition within the Community because differences in rates of tax would mean that the competitive position of suppliers would vary according to the state in which they were established. The final text of the Directive included a further series of services, namely those in Art. 9(2)(c), whose place of supply depends on their place of performance. Article 9(2) was subsequently amended by the 10th Directive (84/386, OJ 1984, L208/58).

[61] Judgments in Case 68/92, *Commission* v. *France* [1993] ECR I–5881, Case 69/92, *Commission* v. *Luxembourg* [1993] ECR I–5907 and Case 73/92, *Commission* v. *Spain* [1993] ECR I–5997.

[62] See, e.g., para. 15 of the case against France, authors' own translation.

Those considerations prompted the Court to interpret the term 'advertising services' broadly.

The rationale for Article 9(2)(e), as expressed in the preamble and by the Court, seems valid only in so far as services are provided to exempt or partly exempt customers. Where the customer is fully taxable the place of taxation does not alter the allocation of revenue between Member States, nor would it be advantageous for such a customer to 'shop' for lower VAT rates. None the less the provision is a sensible one since, if such services were taxable in the country of the supplier, the customer would be unable to deduct the VAT on his internal return and would be forced to rely on the (much slower) refund procedure under the Eighth Directive.

Since divergent interpretation of Article 9 by the Member States is liable to lead to double taxation or non-taxation, the need for legal certainty seems paramount. It is therefore particularly regrettable that the Sixth Directive did not define the services in question more closely. The deficiencies of the Directive are highlighted by the numerous problems of interpretation that have arisen.[63] Unfortunately there seems little prospect of further clarificatory work for the moment since the Commission is presumably more concerned with adapting Article 9 to an origin-based system.

The Transitional Arrangements

Directive 91/680 introduced transitional rules for intra-Community transport of goods, services ancillary thereto, and certain services of intermediaries. As stated above, according to the general rule in Article 9(2)(b) transport services are supplied where the transport takes place, having regard to the distances covered. By way of derogation from that rule, Article 28b(C)(2) provides that the place of supply of services in the intra-Community transport of goods shall be the place of departure; however, under Article 28b(C)(3) where such services are rendered to customers identified for VAT purposes in a Member State other than that of departure, they are deemed to be supplied in the Member State which issued the customer with the VAT identification number under which the service was rendered to him. 'Intra-Community transport of goods' means 'transport where the place of departure and the place of arrival are situated within the territories of two different Member States'. Such transport may therefore pass through or over non-Community territory. Under Article 28b(C)(4) Member States need not apply the tax to that part of the

[63] See the discussion in the 1st Report (at 32–5) concerning the hiring of movable property, forms of transport, advertising services, services of consultants and experts, and data processing. As regards forms of transport see also the 2nd Report (at 21) and Case 51/88, *Hamann* v. *Finanzamt Hamburg-Eimsbüttel* [1989] ECR 767, where the term was held to include a pleasure boat; see also the Proposal for a 19th Directive, which seeks to introduce a provision into Art. 9 under which forms of transport would include 'pallets and containers, and equipment and apparatus capable of being drawn or pushed in order to perform a contract for transport or towing'.

transport corresponding to journeys over waters not forming part of the territory of the Community.

Article 9(2)(c) continues in principle to govern ancillary transport services such as loading, handling, and similar activities, deeming them to be supplied where the services are physically carried out. However, Article 28b(D) provides that services ancillary to the intra-Community transport of goods, rendered to customers identified for VAT purposes in a Member State other than the one in which the services are physically performed, are deemed to be supplied in the Member State which issued the customer with the VAT identification number under which the service was rendered to him.

Services of intermediaries acting in the name and for the account of other persons, rendered in connection with the transport of goods, would normally fall to be taxed in the country of the supplier under Article 9(1) of the Directive. However, under Article 28b(E)(1) and (2) such services are taxed according to rules which correspond to the rules governing services in intra-Community transport and ancillary services. Article 28b(E)(3) concerns services of intermediaries forming part of transactions other than the transport services referred to in Article 28b(E)(1) and (2) and Article 9(2)(e) services. By way of derogation from Article 9(1), such services are supplied in the country where they are carried out; however, if the customer is identified for VAT purposes in another Member State, the services are supplied in the State which issued the VAT identification number under which the customer received the service.

Article 9(3) allows Member States to depart from the normal rules in certain circumstances in order to avoid double taxation, non-taxation, or the distortion of competition.

Examples of the Application of the Rules

The application of the rules concerning the place of supply of services may be illustrated by several examples:

(1) A Paris estate agent sells a property in France for an American customer based in New York. The service concerns immovable property situated in France and is therefore supplied in France under Article 9(2)(a).

(2) A London-based road haulage company transports goods from London to Munich via Belgium and Luxembourg for a customer identified for VAT purposes in Spain. The service is deemed to be supplied in Spain under the transitional rule in Article 28b(C)(3).

(3) A Madrid-based conference organizer holds a one-day conference on EC VAT law at a large Hamburg hotel. Such services are covered by Article 9(2)(c) and are therefore supplied in Germany where they are physically carried out.

(4) A London-based art expert travels to Germany to value a newly discovered Rembrandt painting for a German taxable person. His service,

consisting in the valuation of movable tangible property for the purposes of Article 9(2)(c), is supplied in Germany where it is physically carried out.

(5) A United Kingdom accountancy firm provides advice on United Kingdom tax law to its associated firm in France. The service is covered by Article 9(2)(e) and is therefore deemed to be supplied in France where the customer is established.

The Concept of a Fixed Establishment

Both Article 9(1) and Article 9(2)(e) employ the concept of 'fixed establishment' for the purpose of linking supplies to a particular country. Services covered by Article 9(1) are supplied where the supplier 'has established his business or has a fixed establishment from which the service is provided'. Services covered by Article 9(2)(e) are supplied where 'the customer has established his business or has a fixed establishment to which the service is supplied' where the customer is established outside the Community or is a taxable person established in another Member State.

The concept of establishment is also relevant for other purposes. Article 21[64] of the Directive, concerning the persons liable for payment of the tax, distinguishes between taxable persons according to whether they are established within national territory or abroad. Moreover, the Eighth and Thirteenth Directives permit taxable persons to claim a refund of tax from the authorities of a Member State only if they are not established within its territory.[65]

In its Second Report[66] the Commission stated that the VAT Committee was asked to consider two possible interpretations of the concept of establishment: a fixed installation from which transactions could be carried out; or premises not having the capacity to carry out transactions, such as an information or administrative office. A large majority of the committee considered that a fixed establishment was to be defined without reference to the capacity to effect taxable transactions. Accordingly, in its Proposal for a Nineteenth Directive[67] the Commission sought to insert a new paragraph 4(a) in Article 9(2) in the following terms: 'the expression 'fixed establishment' in this Article means any fixed installation of a taxable person, even if no taxable transaction can be carried out there'.

The Court has taken a different view of the concept of establishment in Article 9(1). In Case 168/84, *Berkholz* v. *Finanzamt Hamburg*,[68] the plaintiff was an advertising agency which also installed and operated gaming machines, juke-boxes, and the like. It operated most of its machines in public houses in Schleswig-Holstein and Hamburg (Germany), but also had some gaming

[64] As amended by Directives 91/680 and 92/111.

[65] See below, p. 192.

[66] At 22.

[67] OJ 1984, C347/5. Amendments to the Directive were proposed in COM(87)315 final.

[68] [1985] ECR 2251.

machines on board two ferry boats owned by the Federal German Railways which plied between Germany and Denmark. The machines were maintained, repaired, and replaced at regular intervals by Berkholz's employees, who also emptied the machines in conjunction with staff of the German Railways and counted the takings. It was estimated that approximately 10 per cent of the turnover generated by the gaming machines arose when the vessels were in the German port, 25 per cent during passage through German territorial waters, and the remainder on the high seas, in Danish territorial waters or in the Danish port. However, the German tax authorities sought to charge German VAT on the entire turnover generated on the two ferries, deeming it to have arisen at Berkholz's place of business in Hamburg in accordance with Article 9(1) of the Sixth Directive. Berkholz took the view that its services were provided from a fixed establishment located on board the ferries. It therefore regarded only 10 per cent, or at most a further 25 per cent, as being subject to German VAT. The Court held, first, that the Sixth Directive did not restrict the Member States' freedom to tax services provided outside their territorial jurisdiction on board seagoing ships over which they have jurisdiction. Secondly, it was for the tax authorities in each Member State to determine from the range of options set forth in the Directive which point of reference was most appropriate to determine tax jurisdiction over a given service. The place where 'the supplier has established his business' was 'a primary point of reference inasmuch as regard is to be had to another establishment from which the services are supplied only if the reference to the place where the supplier has established his business does not lead to a rational result for tax purposes or creates a conflict with another Member State'. Services could not be deemed to be supplied at another establishment unless it was 'of a certain minimum size and both the human and technical resources necessary for the provision of the services are permanently present'. The installation on board a seagoing ship of gaming machines which were maintained intermittently did not qualify as such.

The VAT Committee's view and the definition of fixed establishment in the Proposal for a Nineteenth Directive make little sense in the context of Articles 9(1) and 9(2)(e). Even if a taxable person having its seat in one Member State were regarded as having a fixed establishment in another Member State simply by virtue of having a representative office there, the establishment could not in any event be 'one from which the service is supplied' for the purposes of Article 9(1) or one 'to which the service is supplied' for the purposes of Article 9(2)(e). Different views are possible, however, with respect to Article 21 and the Eighth and Thirteenth Directives. The view might be taken that any fixed installation, even one without the capacity to make supplies, constitutes a sufficient presence to bring a foreign taxable person within the scope of the VAT-accounting requirements for residents. The contrary view might be that a foreign taxable person should not be required to account for tax as a resident of a Member State when his fixed establishment there does not have the capacity to make taxable supplies and that a uniform interpretation of the establishment concepts in Article 9, 21, and the Eighth and Thirteenth Directives is preferable.

The *Berkholz* judgment might be understood as expressing a reluctance on the part of the Court to refer to secondary establishments. The Court's words must, however, be read in the light of the circumstances of the case, in which a taxable person sought to escape the Community's tax jurisdiction by creating national establishments outside Community territory. It is submitted that, in a genuine case in which a supplier or customer has several business establishments all capable of performing services, the most appropriate method of determining the place of supply for the purposes of Article 9(1) or 9(2)(e) would be to identify the establishment of the supplier whose resources were primarily used for supplying the service or the establishment of the customer which made primary use of the service. Consider the following case:

> A London solicitor provides legal advice concerning United Kingdom industrial law to the management of the Manchester factory of a French manufacturer whose head office is in Paris. Whether the solicitor's service falls to be taxed in the United Kingdom under Article 9(1) or in France under Article 9(2)(e) depends on whether the service is deemed to be supplied to the secondary establishment in Manchester or the Paris head office. In such a case it would clearly be more appropriate to link the supply to the French company's secondary establishment in the United Kingdom—the only connection with France is the residence of the company, and the advice is provided to the management of the manufacturer's United Kingdom establishment for the purposes of its United Kingdom business. Article 9(1) therefore applies rather than Article 9(2)(e).

The position would be the same even if the solicitor were asked to send his invoice to the French head office. If formal invoicing and payment arrangements could alter the substantive position, taxable persons would be practically free to choose the jurisdiction in which they wished supplies to be taxed, or even to escape tax altogether by rendering invoices to establishments outside the Community.

However, the position may not always be so clear. What if the solicitor provided the same advice to the company's central legal department in Paris? Although the advice would undoubtedly be related in part to the United Kingdom business, its immediate use might be by staff in Paris to prepare reports on the United Kingdom business or even reports of a more general nature concerning the company's operations. In such circumstances the French authorities might reasonably take the view that this went beyond a purely formal invoicing arrangement and that there were no grounds for departing from the primary point of reference, namely the principal establishment in France.

TRADE IN GOODS WITH NON-MEMBER COUNTRIES

Imports

By virtue of Article 2 of the Sixth Directive tax is chargeable on 'the importation of goods'. Article 7(1)[69] of the Directive defines 'importation' as:

(a) the entry into the Community of goods which do not fulfil the conditions laid down in Articles 9 and 10 of the [EC Treaty] or, where the goods are covered by the [ECSC Treaty], are not in free circulation;
(b) the entry into the Community of goods from a third country, other than the goods covered by (a).

Subparagraph (a) covers the importation of goods which are not in free circulation in the customs territory of the Community. Subparagraph (b) must be read in connection with Article 3 of the Directive, which gives 'third country' a special meaning for the purposes of the Sixth Directive. 'Importation' thus includes the entry of goods which are in free circulation for customs purposes but come from territories which are outside the territorial scope of the common VAT system.

The place of import is normally the Member State within whose territory the goods are when they enter the Community.[70] However, where goods covered by Article 7(1)(a) are, on entry into the Community, placed under one of the customs arrangements referred to in Article 16(1)(B)(a),(b),(c), or (d), under temporary import arrangements with total exemption from import duties[71] or under external transit arrangements,[72] the place of import is the Member State in which they cease to be covered by the arrangements.[73]

Similarly, where goods covered by subparagraph (b) are placed under one of the procedures in Article 33a(1)(b) or (c)[74] the place of import is in the Member State where the procedure ceases to apply.[75] By virtue of Article 33a(1)(b), goods from third territories forming part of the Community customs territory which enter the Community in a Member State other than the place of arrival are to circulate under the internal Community transit procedure.[76]

[69] As replaced by Art. 1(2) of Directive 91/680 and amended by Art. 1(2) of Directive 92/111.
[70] Art. 7(2), as amended.
[71] See Art. 137 ff. of Council Regulation 2913/92 (OJ 1992, L302/1).
[72] See Art. 91 ff. of Council Regulation 2913/92. The procedure allows the movement from one point to another within the customs territory of the Community of (a) non-Community goods, without such goods being subject to import duties and other charges or to commercial policy measures, and (b) Community goods which are subject to a Community measure involving their export to a third country and in respect of which the corresponding customs formalities for export have been carried out.
[73] Art. 7(3), first subpara., as amended by Art. 1(3) of Directive 92/111.
[74] Now contained in Art. 1(23) of Directive 92/111.
[75] Second subpara. of Art. 7(3), amended by Art. 1(3) of Directive 92/111.
[76] See Art. 163 ff. of Regulation 2913/92. The procedure allows the movement of goods from one point to another in the customs territory of the Community passing through the territory of a third country without any change in their customs status.

Article 33a(1)(c) requires Member States to ensure that such goods are placed, where appropriate, under arrangements equivalent to the customs arrangements in Article 16(1)(B)(a), (b), (c), and (d) or temporary import arrangements with full exemption from import duties.

In addition, Article 33a(2) equates goods exported to third countries for VAT purposes with goods exported out of the customs territory for the purposes of export formalities and provisions regarding reimportation of goods temporarily exported.

Import Exemptions

General

Prior to its amendment by Directives 91/680 and 92/111, Article 14(1)(a) to (j) of the Sixth Directive laid down a series of exemptions applicable to imports of goods from other Member States and from non-member countries. The explanatory memorandum accompanying the Proposal for a Sixth Directive explained that the exemptions mainly concerned goods exempted under the domestic scheme, although account was also taken of the general principles of the customs legislation with a view to co-ordinating VAT and customs arrangements and thus simplifying the administration. Although the considerations underlying customs exemptions were not necessarily the same as those governing VAT exemptions, in many cases (such as imports under diplomatic arrangements, temporary imports, transit and warehousing, traveller's allowances, small consignments, etc.) the aim pursued and economic justification were identical.

Article 14(2) required the Commission to submit to the Council proposals for rules clarifying the scope of the exemptions in Article 14(1) and detailed rules for their implementation. Pending the entry into force of such rules Member States were authorized to maintain their national provisions in force on matters related to the exemptions, adapt their national provisions to minimize distortions of competition, in particular non-taxation or double taxation, and use whatever administrative proposals they considered most appropriate to achieve exemption.[77] A number of directives defining import exemptions were adopted, only some of which were stated to be clarificatory measures based on Article 14(2).

Directives 91/680 and 92/111 on the transitional arrangements deleted entirely the exemptions in subparagraphs (b), (c), and (f) of Article 14(1) and restricted the remaining exemptions to imports from non-member countries. The Directives also repealed in their entirety the provisions, or at least the VAT provisions, of a number of the directives that had been adopted in this

[77] National measures adopted for this purpose were to be notified to the Commission, which was to inform the other Member States.

area[78] and repealed others as far as relations between Member States are concerned.[79]

Individual Exemptions

Imports of Goods Qualifying for Domestic Exemption

Article 14(1)(a) exempts the:

> final importation of goods of which the supply by a taxable person would in all circumstances be exempted within the country.

It seems, in the light of the other language versions, that the phrase 'in all circumstances' would, as in the case of the equivalent intra-Community exemption in Article 28c(B)(a),[80] be better understood as 'in any event' or 'in any case'. On that view imports from non-member counties are exempt in so far as the equivalent domestic transaction would be exempt, in particular under Article 13 of the Directive.

Goods in Transit

Article 14(1)(b), concerning the importation of goods under a declaration for transit arrangements, was repealed by Article 1(11) of Directive 91/680. The exemption was replaced by a transitional exemption in Article 28c(D), which provides as follows:

> Where goods dispatched or transported from a third territory are imported into a Member State other than that of arrival of the dispatch or transport, Member States shall exempt such imports where the supply of such goods by the importer as defined in Article 21(2) is exempt in accordance with paragraph A.
>
> Member States shall lay down the conditions governing this exemption with a view to ensuring its correct and straightforward application and preventing any evasion, avoidance or abuse.

[78] Art. 2 of Directive 91/680 repealed the VAT provisions of the following directives: 74/651 on the tax reliefs to be allowed on the importation of goods in small consignments of a non-commercial character within the Community (OJ 1974, L354/57), as last amended by 88/663 (OJ 1988, L382/40); 83/182 on tax exemptions within the Community for certain means of transport temporarily imported into one Member State from another (OJ 1983, L105/59); 83/183 on tax exemptions applicable to permanent imports from a Member State of the personal property of individuals (OJ 1983, L105/64), as amended by 89/604 (OJ 1989, L348/28). Art. 1(24) repealed in its entirety the 17th Council Directive (85/362) of 16 July 1985 on the harmonization of the laws of the Member States relating to turnover taxes—exemption from VAT on the temporary importation of goods other than means of transport (OJ 1985, L192/20).

[79] Council Directive 83/181 of 28 March 1983 determining the scope of Art. 14(1)(d) of Directive 77/388 as regards exemption from VAT on the final importation of certain goods (OJ 1983, L105/38), as last amended by Directive 89/219 (OJ 1989, L92/13). As regards its provisions on VAT, also Council Directive 69/169 of 28 May 1969 on the harmonization of provisions laid down by law, regulation, or administrative action relating to exemption from turnover tax and excise duty on imports in international travel (OJ 1969, English Spec. Ed., (I), 232), as last amended by Directive 91/191 (OJ 1991, L94/24). Directive 92/111 also repealed Art. 6 of the Directive.

[80] See above at p. 149.

The application of the exemption may be illustrated by the following examples:

> An importer established in Germany imports goods from a non-member country through a United Kingdom port for sale in Germany: By virtue of Article 28a(5)(b) he is deemed to make a supply when he transfers the goods from the United Kingdom to Germany. The supply is exempt under Article 28c(A), with the consequence that the importation of the goods into the United Kingdom is exempt under Article 28c(D). He makes a taxable acquisition of the goods in Germany under Article 28a(6).
>
> Where the German importer sells the goods to a customer in France and transports them directly from the United Kingdom, the supply to the customer is deemed to take place in the United Kingdom under Article 8(2)[81] and is exempt under Article 28c(A). The importation of the goods into the United Kingdom therefore qualifies for exemption under Article 28c(D). The customer makes a taxable acquisition in France.

In both cases the importer will have a VAT identification number in the United Kingdom and must comply with the declaration obligations in respect of the supply to the other Member State.

Temporary Imports

Until 1 January 1993, when it was amended by Directive 91/680, Article 14(1)(c) exempted

> importation of goods declared to be under temporary importation arrangements, which thereby qualify for exemption from customs duties, or which would so qualify if they were imported from a third country.

The Seventeenth Council Directive[82] was adopted to define the scope of the temporary importation exemption in Article 14(1)(c) and the common arrangements referred to in Article 16(3) for relieving from VAT supplies of goods subject to temporary importation arrangements.

Article 14(1)(c) and the Seventeenth Directive were repealed by Directive 92/111. As explained above, Article 7(3) of the Sixth Directive, as amended,[83] provides that, where goods are placed under arrangements for temporary importation with total exemption from import duty, the place of import is the Member State within whose territory the goods cease to be covered by the arrangements. By virtue of Article 10(3) the chargeable event is in principle postponed until that moment.

Exemption on Final Importation

Article 14(1)(d), as amended, exempts:

[81] As amended by Art. 1(5) of Directive 91/680.

[82] Above, note 78.

[83] Art. 1(2) of Directive 91/680 and Art. 1(3) of Directive 92/111.

final importation of goods qualifying for exemption from customs duties other than as provided for in the Common Customs Tariff. However, Member States shall have the option of not granting exemption where this would be liable to have a serious effect on conditions of competition.

According to the Explanatory Memorandum accompanying the Proposal for a Sixth Directive, the exemption was intended to apply to goods qualifying for non-tariff exemption from customs duties, i.e., under one of the exemptions provided for by Member States, subject to their own conditions, in the introductory notes to their national customs tariffs. A Community system of reliefs from customs duties was subsequently established by Council Regulation 918/83,[84] although Member States were authorized to retain certain reliefs applied by virtue of conventions to which they were signatories. Directive 83/181 of the same date, determining the scope of the VAT exemptions applicable under Article 14(1) to the final importation of certain goods, is closely linked, but not identical, to the customs regulation.[85] It likewise allowed Member States to retain certain reliefs which concerned only the signatory Member States. The directive provides for common exemptions in the following areas:

importation of personal property belonging to individuals coming from non-member countries;
school outfits, scholastic materials, and other scholastic household effects;
imports of negligible value;
capital goods and other equipment imported on the transfer of activities;
importation of certain agricultural products and products intended for agricultural use;
importation of therapeutic substances, medicines, laboratory animals and biological or chemical substances;
goods imported for charitable or philanthropic organizations;
importation in the context of certain aspects of international relations;
importation of goods for the promotion of trade;
goods imported for examination, analysis or test purposes;
other miscellaneous matters including certain documents and publications, materials for the stowage and protection of goods during transport, litter, fodder, and feedingstuffs for animals during transport, fuel and lubricants present in motor vehicles and special containers, goods intended for memorials to war victims and funerary articles.

[84] OJ 1983, L105/1.

[85] Note 79, above. The preamble to the Directive indicated that, while it was desirable to achieve the greatest possible degree of uniformity between the systems for customs duties and VAT, account had to be taken of the different objectives and structure of customs duties and VAT. The Commission's First Report explained, in relation to the then proposed instruments, that certain reliefs could not be transposed automatically to the VAT system for fear of distorting conditions of competition. This applied particularly to the customs exemptions for goods of an educational, scientific and cultural nature.

By virtue of Article 2(1) of Directive 91/680, the Directive ceased to have effect as regards relations between Member States on 31 December 1992.

By virtue of Article 1(8) of Directive 92/111 the exemption in Article 14(d) was extended to imports under Article 7(1)(b) which would have qualified for exemption if imported under Article 7(1)(a).[86]

Re-importation of Goods

Article 14(1)(e), as amended by Directive 91/680, exempts:

> reimportation by the person who exported them of goods in the state in which they were exported, where they qualify for exemption from customs duties.

The relevant customs provisions are now contained in Articles 185 to 187 ('returned goods') of Regulation 2913/92 establishing the Community customs code.[87]

Re-importation of Goods after Work

Article 14(1)(f), concerning re-importation of goods after the performance of work on them in another Member State, became obsolete from 1 January 1993 and was deleted by Article 1(11) of Directive 91/680. In this connection it should be noted that under the fifth indent of Article 28a(5)(b) of the amended Sixth Directive the transfer of goods to another Member State for the purpose of the performance of work on them in that state is specifically excluded from the scope of the supply which is deemed to arise on the transfer of business goods to another Member State. The work is taxable as a service in the state where it is performed under Article 9(2)(c).

Other Import Exemptions

Article 14(1)(g)[88] contains an exemption for imports under diplomatic and consular arrangements of goods qualifying for exemption from customs duties, imports by international organizations recognized as such by the host country on the terms laid down by the relevant convention or agreement and by armed forces into Member States which are parties to NATO.

Article 14(1)(h) exempts on certain conditions the import into ports of catches by sea fishing undertakings.

Article 14(1)(i) is a technical provision exempting the supply of services, in connection with the importation of goods where the value of such services is included in the taxable amount in accordance with Article 11(B)(3)(b). The exempt supply also gives rise to a refund of input tax under Article 17(3)(b).[89] Article 11(B)(3)(b)[90] includes within the taxable amount incidental expenses such as commission, packing, transport, and insurance costs incurred up to the first place of destination in the importing Member State. The exemption

86 See above, p. 161.

87 OJ 1992, L302.

88 Amended by Art. 1(11) of Directive 91/680.

89 Now contained in Art. 28f, inserted by Directive 91/680.

90 As amended by Art. 1(8) of Directive 91/680.

thus prevents the double taxation which would otherwise arise from that provision.

Article 14(1)(j) exempts the importation of gold by central banks.

Exports and Transactions linked to International Goods Traffic

Article 15 of the Sixth Directive[91] lays down a series of exemptions for exports from the Community and related transactions. Supplies qualifying for exemption under this Article give rise to the right of deduction under Article 17(3)(b).[92] Such exemptions therefore entail total remission of VAT .

The Sixth Directive does not lay down provisions concerning the evidence of export to be presented by the taxable person. However, like Articles 13 and 14, Article 15 states that the exemptions are to be granted under conditions which the Member States shall lay down for the purpose of ensuring the correct and straightforward application of such exemptions and of preventing any evasion, avoidance or abuse. It seems therefore that Member States are entitled to demand evidence of exportation, such as an air waybill, shipped bill of lading, certificate from the transporter, or evidence of postage.

The main export exemptions are those in Article 15(1) and (2). Article 15(1)[93] exempts:

> the supply of goods dispatched or transported to a destination outside the Community by or on behalf of the vendor.

Article 15(2)[94] exempts:

> the supply of goods dispatched or transported to a destination outside the Community by or on behalf of a purchaser not established within the territory of the country, with the exception of goods transported by the purchaser himself for the equipping, fuelling and provisioning of pleasure boats and private aircraft or any other means of transport for private use.

For these purposes 'the Community' means the territory of the Member States as defined for VAT purposes in Article 3(2) and (3). Exports to third countries situated outside the Community VAT territory but within the customs territory therefore qualify for exemption.

The reference to the purchaser being established outside the 'territory of the country' in paragraph 2 is puzzling. It might have been thought that the logic of the transitional arrangements would demand the replacement of that phrase by 'outside the Community'. The Commission's proposal to that effect in the Proposal for Directive 92/111[95] appears, however, to have been

[91] As amended by Art. 1(12) to (19) of Directive 91/680 and Art. 1(9) of Directive 92/111.

[92] As embodied in Art. 28f of the Directive, as amended by Directive 91/680.

[93] As amended by Directive 91/680.

[94] As amended by Directive 91/680.

[95] Point 8 of COM(92)448 final.

rejected by the Council.[96] The wording of the exemption suggests that the requirement is merely that the purchaser should not be established in the same Member State as the supplier claiming exemption.

The second and third subparagraphs of Article 15(3)[97] envisage a Commission proposal on rules specifying the scope and practical arrangements for implementing the exemption in relation to supplies made at the retail stage of goods to be carried in the personal luggage of travellers and lays down provisions to be applied pending the introduction of such rules.

The remaining exemptions in Article 15, which were subject to various amendments by Directives 91/680 and 92/111, concern:

work on movable property acquired or imported for the purpose of undergoing such work and exported from the Community (paragraph 3[98]);
the supply, modification, repair, maintenance, chartering, and hiring of certain sea-going vessels and of aircraft used by airlines on international routes, and certain supplies of goods and services connected therewith (paragraphs 4 to 9[99]);
supplies of goods and services under diplomatic and consular arrangements, to international organizations and their members and for forces and civilian staff of NATO countries (paragraph 10[100]);
supplies of gold to central banks (paragraph 11);
goods for export as part of humanitarian, charitable, or teaching activities (paragraph 12[101]);
supply of services, including transport and ancillary operations, except services exempted under Article 13, directly connected with export of goods or imports covered by Article 7(3) or Article 16(1), Title A (paragraph 13[102]);
services supplied by brokers and intermediaries forming part of transactions covered by Article 15 or of transactions carried out outside the Community (paragraph 14[103]).

Article 16(1) of the Directive permits Member States, subject to consultation of the VAT Committee, to lay down a series of exemptions linked to

[96] Moreover, the reference to third country in Art. 15(3), as amended by Directive 91/680, was similarly replaced by 'territory of the country' in Directive 92/111.

[97] Inserted by Art. 1(9) of Directive 92/111.

[98] Replaced by Art. 1(14) of Directive 91/680 and further amended by Art. 1(9) of Directive 92/111.

[99] Amended in part by Art. 1(9) of Directive 92/111. Pending the adoption of common rules specifying the scope and practical arrangements for these exemptions Member States may limit their extent.

[100] Amended by Art. 1(15) and (16) of Directive 91/680 and Art. 1(9) of Directive 92/111. Member States may limit this exemption.

[101] Amended by Art. 1(17) of Directive 91/680.

[102] Replaced by Art. 1(9) of Directive 92/111.

[103] Amended by Art. 1(19) of Directive 91/680.

international goods traffic provided that the transactions are not aimed at final use and/or consumption and that the VAT charged on entry for home use corresponds to that which should have been charged if they had been taxed on import or within the territory of the country. The exemptions concern[104] imports of goods intended to be placed under warehousing arrangements other than customs (Article 16(1)A)[105]; supplies of goods intended to be:

(a) produced to customs and, where applicable, placed in temporary storage;
(b) placed in a free zone or in a free warehouse;
(c) placed under customs warehousing arrangements or inward processing arrangements;
(d) admitted to territorial waters in connection with the operation of drilling or production platforms;
(e) placed under warehousing arrangements other than customs (Article 16(1)B)[106];

supplies of services relating to the supplies of goods referred to in B (subparagraph 16(1)C); supplies of goods and services carried out in one of the places listed in B (subparagraph 16(1)D); supplies of goods referred to in Article 7(1)(a) (i.e., not in free circulation) still subject to arrangements for temporary importation with total exemption from import duty or to external transit arrangements, supplies of goods referred to in Article 7(1)(b) (i.e., goods in free circulation but from outside the VAT territory) still subject to the internal Community transit procedure under Article 33a, and related supplies of services (Article 16(1)E).

Article 16(2)[107] allows Member States, subject to consultation of the VAT Committee, to opt to exempt intra-Community acquisitions of goods and imports for, and supplies of goods to, a taxable person intending to export them outside the Community as they are or after processing, together with supplies linked with his export business, up to a maximum equal to the value of his exports during the preceding twelve months. Member States exercising the option must apply similar treatment to exempt intra-Community supplies. The view expressed by Terra and Kajus[108] that this is essentially a simplification provision designed to avoid the need for VAT refunds to exporters seems convincing.

[104] The exemptions were substantially amended by Art. 1(20) of Directive 91/680.

[105] Exemption of imports of goods placed under customs arrangements is no longer necessary following Directive 91/680 since Art. 7(3), in conjunction with Art. 10(3), postpones importation and the charging of tax until such goods cease to be covered by the arrangements: above, p. 161.

[106] By virtue of Art. 16(1a), inserted by Art. 28c(E) as replaced by Directive 92/111, Member States exercising the option under Art. 16(1)B must extend it to intra-Community acquisitions of goods.

[107] As amended by Art. 28c(E), itself replaced by Directive 92/111.

[108] *A Guide to the Sixth VAT Directive* (Amsterdam: IBFD, 1991), 787.

6

Domestic Exemptions

GENERAL

Article 10(3) of the Second Directive left Member States free, subject to the consultations provided for in Article 16, to lay down whatever domestic exemptions they thought fit. The primary aim of the Sixth Directive, however, was to establish a uniform basis for collection of the Community's own resources. This implied uniform rules on exemptions.[1] The list which the Commission drew up in its Proposal for the Sixth Directive was based on:

(1) the exemptions already existing in the Member States; and
(2) the concern to keep the number of exemptions as small as possible.[2]

The latter concern reflects the fact that exemptions in domestic trade are liable to undermine the neutrality of VAT by limiting its scope and interfering with the deduction mechanism. Where he makes an exempt supply, a taxable person is placed in the position of a final consumer: he neither charges VAT on the supply, nor is he entitled to deduct the VAT incurred on the goods and services used for making it. The consequent disruption of the deduction mechanism and double taxation may be illustrated by the following examples concerning a lessor of commercial premises and his business tenant. In the first example the lessor makes a taxable letting,[3] and in the second an exempt letting. The basic figures are the same for ease of comparison.

(1) Taxable letting of commercial premises
Lessor's position

Purchase price of premises		200,000
VAT @ 10%	20,000	
Deductible VAT	(20,000)	
Net VAT cost		—
Total cost to lessor		200,000

[1] See Explanatory Memorandum to the Proposal for the 6th Directive. By virtue of Art. 2(1) of Regulation 1553/89 (OJ 1989 L155/9), transactions exempted under Art. 13 to 16 of the 6th Directive are excluded from the VAT resources base.

[2] See Explanatory Memorandum.

[3] Art. 13(C)(a) allows Member States to grant taxable persons the right to opt for taxation of otherwise exempt lettings.

Annual rental (assuming a 5% return)	10,000
VAT @ 10%	1,000
	11,000

Position of fully taxable tenant

Gross annual cost to tenant	11,000
Deductible VAT	(1,000)
Net annual cost to tenant	10,000

(2) Exempt letting of commercial premises

Lessor's position

Purchase price of premises	200,000
Irrecoverable VAT @ 10%	20,000
Total cost to landlord	220,000
Annual rental (assuming a 5% return) (Exempt from VAT)	11,000

Tenant's position

Annual cost to tenant (No VAT recoverable)	11,000

In the first example the tax operates in the normal way. Provided that he uses the premises for the purpose of making taxable supplies, the tenant may deduct the VAT charged by the lessor. In the second example the tenant cannot deduct the VAT which the lessor was unable to recover and therefore passed on in the rent. When the tenant subsequently charges VAT on supplies to his customers, the rental component of the price of his supplies will be taxed for a second time without any allowance for the VAT definitively borne on the rental payments. There is in addition likely to be an element of tax on tax because, if the tenant wishes to make the same profit in both examples, the £1,000 irrecoverable VAT will itself form part of the taxable price of the tenant's goods or services. The tax burden on the tenant's goods or services thus ceases to be proportionate to the price paid.

Exemptions relating to domestic transactions are dealt with in Article 13 of the Sixth Directive. Article 13(A) lays down a series of exemptions in areas such as the postal services, public broadcasting, health, education, social welfare, and religious, cultural, and political affairs. The Explanatory Memorandum to the Commission's proposal merely states that the Part A exemptions were based broadly on those already existing in the majority of Member States. The nature of the exempt supplies indicates that they are ones which are considered to merit exemption for social and political reasons. Article 13(B) lays down exemptions concerning, *inter alia*, insurance, transactions in land and buildings, banking and financial transactions, postage and fiscal stamps, and gambling. The Explanatory Memorandum states, somewhat unhelpfully, that the Part B exemptions concern specific fields where exemption is 'justified for reasons of general policy common to all the Member States'. Little precise explanation is available for many of them. It seems, however, that, in addition to economic and other policy considerations, the practical and administrative complexity of taxing the transactions concerned may have been a major influence. Both the Part A and the Part B exemptions are mandatory, although Member States are permitted to grant taxable persons the right to opt for taxation of certain supplies covered by Part B.

Evasion, Avoidance, and Abuse

In the case of both Part A and Part B exemptions Member States must lay down conditions 'for the purpose of ensuring the correct and straightforward application of such exemptions and of preventing any possible evasion, avoidance, or abuse'. This provision was evidently prompted by the particular risk of abuse associated with exemptions. For example, in Case C–281/91 *Muys*[4] Advocate General Jacobs pointed out that it would be possible for a supplier and his customer who were connected persons to abuse the exemption relating to the grant of credit in Article 13(B)(d)(1) by artificially converting the consideration for a taxable supply of goods into consideration for an exempt grant of credit by inflating the interest rate. Problems may arise in assessing whether measures adopted for this purpose comply with the principle of proportionality. It is, for instance, unclear whether in the example given by the Advocate General a Member State would be entitled to disregard the credit transaction on the ground of its artificiality or could be thought to remedy the abuse satisfactorily by imposing a market rate of interest.

Narrow Construction

As exceptions to the general scheme of the Directive, the exemptions in Article 13 have consistently been construed narrowly by the Court.[5] A narrow construction is justified since it serves to limit the disruption to the VAT system. The rule of strict construction means that the precise wording of particu-

[4] *Muys' en De Winter's Bouw- en Aannemingsbedrijf BV* v. *Staatssecretaris van Financiën* [1993] ECR I–5405: see point 12 of the Opinion.

[5] See, e.g., the judgment in *SUFA*, below, where the Court stated that 'the terms used to specify the exemptions envisaged by Art. 13 of the Sixth Directive are to be interpreted strictly since they constitute exceptions to the general principle that turnover tax is levied on all services supplied for consideration by a taxable person'.

lar exemptions is given more weight than is customary in the interpretation of Community legislation.

The exemptions in Article 13, and in particular those in Article 13(A), are closely defined in terms of the nature of the supplies, the identity of the supplier, and sometimes the recipient of the supply. The Court has paid particular attention to this feature of the drafting of the exemptions. Thus, in Case 348/87, *SUFA*[6] it held that an exemption[7] applicable only to independent groups of persons supplying services to their members did not extend to the supply of services by one foundation to another. In Case 353/85, *Commission* v. *United Kingdom*[8] the Court, noting that Article 13 expressly listed the cases in which the supply of *goods* was exempt, held that the exemption for 'the provision of medical care' in Article 13(A)(1)(c) covered only supplies of services and did not extend to goods other than minor supplies indissociable from the medical care.

The emphasis placed on the precise wording of particular exemptions also makes comparison of the different language versions important. Thus, for example, in Case 107/84, *Commission* v. *Germany*[9] the Court reviewed the different language versions of Article 13(A)(1)(a) before concluding that the term 'public postal services' referred to the postal authority itself rather than to postal activities.

Direct Effect of the Exemptions

The question whether and to what extent the various exemptions in Article 13 may be relied on by individuals before national courts in the absence of proper implementation in national law is complicated partly by the varying degrees of precision in their wording and partly by the uncertainty of the law on the doctrine of direct effect. We confine ourselves here to a number of general comments. There are certainly numerous individual exemptions which unquestionably meet the criteria of being unconditional and precise. Moreover, there are no general conditions attaching to the Article as a whole capable of barring the direct effect of its provisions. In Case 8/81, *Becker*,[10] the Court held Article 13(B)(d)(1) to have direct effect notwithstanding the introductory rider in Article 13(B) requiring Member States to lay down conditions for the purpose of ensuring the correct and straightforward application of the exemptions and of preventing evasion, avoidance, or abuse. That provision, said the Court, did not deprive the exemption of direct effect since it did not affect the definition of its subject-matter.

However, some exemptions (Article 13(A)(1)(b), (c), (g), (h), (i), (n)) leave Member States a degree of discretion in defining some or all of the bodies

6 *Stichting Uitvoering Financiële Acties* v. *Staatssecretaris van Financiën* [1989] ECR 1737.

7 Art. 13(A)(1)(f).

8 [1988] ECR 817.

9 [1985] ECR 2655.

10 *Becker* v. *Finanzamt Münster-Innenstadt* [1982] ECR 53.

qualifying for exemption. This may not be fatal if the taxable person seeking to rely on the exemption falls within a category which automatically qualifies under the terms of the exemption or, arguably, a category which has been designated as qualifying by the Member State concerned. For example, there seems no reason why an old people's home which is recognized as having charitable status should not be able to rely on the exemption in Article 13(B)(1)(g) for public bodies and 'other organizations recognized as charitable by the Member States concerned'.

In a number of the provisions the scope of the exempt services or goods is unclear. Where the lack of clarity may be resolved by judicial interpretation this should not of course deprive them of direct effect. However, the use of imprecise phrases such as 'certain cultural services',[11] 'certain services closely linked to sport',[12] or 'subject to conditions and limitations laid down by each Member State'[13] in some provisions would seem to be beyond judicial repair.

Transitional Exemptions

Complete agreement on a common list of exemptions could not be reached at the time when the Sixth Directive was adopted. Consequently, Article 28(3) allows Member States to continue, for a transitional period,[14] to tax transactions exempt under Article 13 or 15 set out in Annex E to the Directive (subparagraph (a)), to continue to exempt the activities set out in Annex F under conditions existing in the Member State concerned (subparagraph (b)), and to grant taxable persons the option to tax exempt transactions under the conditions set out in Annex G. The power given to Member States under subparagraphs (a) and (b) is limited to retaining measures already in force. By virtue of Article 2(2) of Regulation 1553/89,[15] transactions in respect of which the above options are exercised are taken into account for the purposes of the VAT resources base; the transitional exemptions under subparagraph (b) do not therefore reduce the Community's own resources. A number of the transitional derogations were abolished by the Eighteenth Directive of 18 July 1989.[16] This Chapter mentions only those derogations which remain following that Directive. In July 1992 the Commission tabled a proposal for the abolition of many of the remaining derogations permitted under the Sixth and Eighteenth Directives.[17] The proposal has yet to be adopted by the Council.

[11] Art. 13(A)(1)(n). [12] Art. 13(A)(1)(m). [13] Art. 13(B)(f).

[14] An initial period of five years, apparently subject to automatic extension (Art. 28(4)).

[15] See note 1 above. [16] Directive 89/465 (OJ 1989, L226/21).

[17] Proposal for a Council Directive on the harmonization of the laws of the Member States relating to turnover taxes: abolition of certain derogations provided for in Art. 28(3) of Directive 77/388 and in the second subpara. of Art. 1(1) of Directive 89/465, COM(92)215 final of 2 July 1992. For a detailed analysis of the Proposal, see Van Thiel, *International VAT Monitor*, April 1993, 2.

COMMENTS ON PARTICULAR EXEMPTIONS

In the remainder of this chapter we comment on individual exemptions. Our intention is to provide useful background rather than an exhaustive analysis of every exemption.

1—Article 13 (A)

Public Postal Services

Article 13(A)(1)(a) exempts:

the supply by the public postal services of services other than passenger transport and telecommunications services, and the supply of goods incidental thereto.

The transitional provision in Article 28(3)(b), in conjunction with Annex F, Point 5, permits Member States to continue to exempt telecommunications services supplied by the public postal services, and supplies of goods incidental thereto. By virtue of Annex G(1)(b) Member States maintaining this exemption may allow the taxable person the right to opt for taxation of such services. Article 28(3)(b), in conjunction with Annex F, Point 17, allows Member States to retain a general exemption for passenger transport.[18]

In *Commission* v. *Germany*[19] the Court held that the exemption applied only to services provided directly by the public postal authority and did not extend to 'indirect postal activities' performed under statute by transport undertakings on behalf of that authority. However, the Court added that:

the directive has specifically avoided influencing the manner in which the Member States organise their postal systems. Postal activities are still exempted even if they are carried out by a licensed undertaking. The provision restricts the exemption solely to the supply of services by the postal authority, whether it is a body governed by public law or a licensed undertaking.[20]

The scope of that dictum is not entirely clear. While there seems little doubt that an undertaking licensed to carry out all the functions traditionally carried out by the public-law postal authority would continue to qualify for exemption, the position is less clear if only certain activities of the postal authority are privatized (e.g., bulk mail or parcel post) or if a number of undertakings are licensed to compete in certain areas of the postal market.

[18] Special arrangements for passenger transport have been proposed by the Commission: Proposal for a Council Directive amending Directive 77/388 as regards the arrangements applicable to passenger transport, COM(92)416 final of 30 September 1992.

[19] [1985] ECR 2655.

[20] Para. 16 of the judgment. See also the Opinion of Advocate General Darmon at 2661.

Medical Exemptions

Article 13(A)(1)(b) to (e) exempt the following:

(b) hospital and medical care and closely related activities undertaken by bodies governed by public law or, under social conditions comparable to those applicable to bodies governed by public law, by hospitals, centres for medical treatment or diagnosis and other duly recognised establishments of a similar nature;
(c) the provision of medical care in the exercise of the medical and paramedical professions as defined by the Member State concerned;.
(d) supplies of human organs, blood and milk;
(e) services supplied by dental technicians in their professional capacity and dental prostheses supplied by dentists and dental technicians.

Under Article 28(3)(b), in conjunction with Annex F, Point 10, Member States may continue to exempt transactions of hospitals not covered by Article 13(A)(1)(b); by virtue of Article 28(3)(c), in conjunction with Annex G, they may also grant hospitals the option to tax such transactions. Article 28(3)(a), in conjunction with Annex E(2), allows Member States to continue to tax the transactions in Article 13(A)(1)(e); those which allow an option to tax may maintain that option.

The Commission's First Report[21] states that the scope of the expression 'or under social conditions comparable to those applicable to bodies governed by public law' in subparagraph (b) was the subject of inconclusive discussions in the VAT committee. In its Proposal for a Nineteenth Directive the Commission suggested amending the provision so as to extend exemption to all hospital care.[22]

With respect to subparagraph (c), the Court held in Case 353/85, *Commission* v. *United Kingdom*[23] that this exemption covered services provided outside hospitals or similar establishments within the framework of a confidential relationship between the patient and the person providing the care, a relationship which was normally established in the consulting room of that person. The exemption applied only to supplies of services and does not extend to goods (e.g., corrective spectacles supplied by opticians) other than minor supplies indissociable from the medical care. Subparagraph (c) was to be distinguished in this respect from the exemptions in subparagraphs (d) and (e), which expressly concerned or extended to supplies of certain goods.

It seems that the services of dentists, as distinct from those of dental technicians, fall to be exempted under subparagraph (c) rather than (e). This point may be significant inasmuch as there is no transitional provision applicable to subparagraph (c).

[21] At pp. 44–5. [22] Art. 1(3): COM(84)648 final and COM(87)315 final.
[23] [1988] ECR 817.

Independent Groups of Persons

Article 13(A)(1)(f) exempts:

services supplied by independent groups of persons whose activities are exempt from or are not subject to Value Added Tax, for the purpose of rendering their members the services directly necessary for the exercise of their activity, where these groups merely claim from their members exact reimbursement of their share of the joint expenses, provided that such exemption is not likely to produce distortion of competition.

This rather obscure exemption started life in the Commission's Proposal as a further medical exemption, concerning 'services supplied by independent professional groups of a medical or like nature to their members for the purposes of their exempted activities',[24] but was broadened without explanation during the legislative process to cover cost-sharing arrangements by other persons carrying on exempt or non-taxable activities. The Court had occasion to consider the exemption in *SUFA*.[25] SUFA was entrusted with making the practical arrangements for the lotteries organized by another foundation ('ALN') on behalf of the social and cultural institutions affiliated to it. All expenses incurred by SUFA were reimbursed by ALN whose only activity was to distribute the proceeds of the lotteries between the affiliated institutions. The tax authorities accepted that ALN was covered by the exemption but considered that SUFA was not. The Court, upholding the tax authorities' view, held that the exemption did not cover the case where one foundation supplied services exclusively to another foundation, neither of the foundations being a member of the other.

Welfare and education

Article 13(A)(1)(g) to (j) exempt the following:

(g) the supply of services and of goods closely linked to welfare and social security work, including those supplied by old people's homes, by bodies governed by public law or by other organisations recognised as charitable by the Member State concerned;
(h) the supply of services and goods closely linked to the protection of children and young persons by bodies governed by public law or by other organisations recognised as charitable by the Member State concerned;
(i) children's or young people's education, school or university education, vocational training or retraining, including the supply of services and of goods closely related thereto, provided by bodies governed by public law having such as their aim or by other organisations defined by the Member State concerned as having similar objects;
(j) tuition given privately by teachers and covering school or university education.

[24] Art. 14(A)(1)(f) of the Proposal. [25] See note 6, above.

The exemption in subparagraph (j), unlike those in subparagraphs (g), (h), and (i), is not subject to the restrictions provided for in Article 13(A)(2) in relation to private-law bodies.[26] The question has been raised[27] whether subparagraph (j) might cover groups of private teachers acting as a single entity for VAT purposes; if so, their activities would be exempt even if carried out on a fully commercial basis. No help is to be gleaned from the *travaux préparatoires*—no individual exemption for private tuition was proposed. However, although the English, French, and German texts have slightly different connotations[28] they arguably all seem to be referring to tuition given by individual private teachers either as part of or in connection with school or university education. A contrary view would, moreover, seem to deprive of all meaning the words 'other organizations defined by the Member States concerned as having similar objects' in subparagraph (i), since a private school could claim exemption under subparagraph (j).

Article 13(A)(1)(k) exempts:

> certain supplies of staff by religious or philosophical institutions for the purpose of subparagraphs (b), (g), (h) and (i) of this Article and with a view to spiritual welfare.

Other language versions[29] make it clear that the exemption applies where staff is supplied for the purpose of the *activities mentioned* in the subparagraphs concerned. Moreover, the word 'certain' appears to be a gratuitous addition in the English text. It appears that the phrase 'and with a view to spiritual welfare' is intended to qualify the preceding words; this reading is supported in particular by the French text.[30]

Non-profit-making Organizations

Article 13(A)(1)(l) exempts:

> supply of services and goods closely linked thereto for the benefit of their members in return for a subscription fixed in accordance with their rules by non-profit-making organisations with aims of a political, trade-union, religious, patriotic, philosophical, philanthropic or civic nature, provided that this exemption is not likely to cause distortion of competition.

This exemption, which did not appear in the original Proposal for the Sixth Directive, seems to have been inserted at the suggestion of the Economic and Social Committee, which thought it appropriate to make provision for exemp-

[26] Below, p. 181.

[27] See Terra and Kajus, *A Guide to the Sixth VAT Directive* (Amsterdam: IBFD, 1991), 604.

[28] *les leçons données, à titre personnel, par des enseignants et portant sur l'enseignement scolaire ou universitaire*; *den von Privatlehrern erteilten Schul- und Hochschulunterricht.*

[29] See, e.g., the French and German texts.

[30] *pour les activités visées sous . . . et dans un but d'assistance spirituelle.*

tion of trade unions and professional organizations in so far as they did not engage in competitive operations, such as commercial transactions or the giving of advice involving payments separate from the general contribution and varying according to the extent of the services rendered. It also considered that exemption should be extended to churches and equivalent institutions in so far as their activities were not already governed by public law.

In its First Report[31] the Commission noted that differences of interpretation had arisen with respect to the term 'trade-union', which was said to be more specific than the equivalent French term 'syndicale'.[32] The issue seemed mainly to be whether subscriptions paid by trade or professional associations and employers' organisations were covered by the exemption. The Commission thought the problem of limited significance because, in the light of the Court's judgments in *Aardappelenbewaarplaats*[33] and *Hong Kong Development Council*,[34] the subscriptions of organizations which merely acted as the collective voice of their members did not constitute consideration for services rendered. Only where the subscriptions were consideration for individually identifiable services rendered to members did they fall within the scope of the tax. It is unclear whether that analysis is correct, and in any event few organizations of this kind limit themselves to being the voice of their members; most provide general information and advice to their members through technical releases and other means and offer a range of other membership benefits. Notwithstanding the Commission's remarks the precise scope of the exemption may therefore be a matter of some significance. In proposing the exemption the Economic and Social Committee clearly envisaged that it would extend to professional organizations. Moreover, the extension of the exemption to such bodies and to trade and employers' organizations would not be inconsistent with the nature of the other organizations listed. For the moment, however, the position remains unclear.

Sport

Article 13(A)(1)(m) exempts:

> certain services closely linked to sport or physical education supplied by non-profit-making organisations to persons taking part in sport or physical education.

In its Proposal for a Nineteenth Directive[35] the Commission suggested deleting the word 'certain' in order to make the exemption more precise.[36] By

[31] At 45.

[32] Or equivalent term used in other language versions (e.g., *syndicale* (Dutch), *sindacale* (Italian)). The German text, which uses the term *gewerkschaftliche*, appears to be closer to the English.

[33] Case 154/80, *Staatssecretaris van Financiën* v. *Coöperatieve Aardappelenbewaarplaats* [1981] ECR 445.

[34] Case 89/81, *Staatssecretaris van Financiën* v. *Hong Kong Trade Development Council* [1982] ECR 1277.

[35] Above, note 22.

[36] Art. 1(3)(b) of the Proposal.

virtue of Article 28(3)(b), in conjunction with Annex F, Point 1, Member States may also continue to exempt admission to sporting events.

Cultural Services

Article 13(A)(1)(n) exempts:

> certain cultural services and goods closely linked thereto supplied by bodies governed by public law or by other cultural bodies recognised by the Member State concerned.

The Commission's original proposal was much more precise than the final exemption inasmuch as it listed the cultural bodies qualifying for exemption. The Commission sought again in its Proposal for a Nineteenth Directive to persuade the Council to replace subparagraph (b) by a more detailed provision.[37] It should be noted that Member States may continue to exempt services supplied by authors, artists, and performers under the transitional provision in Article 28(3)(b), in conjunction with Annex F, point 2. An option to tax may be offered under Annex G(1)(b).

Fund-raising

Article 13(A)(1)(o) exempts:

> the supply of services and goods by organisations whose activities are exempt under the provisions of subparagraphs (b), (g), (h), (i), (l), (m) and (n) above in connection with fund-raising events organised exclusively for their own benefit provided that exemption is not likely to cause distortion of competition. Member States may introduce any necessary restrictions in particular as regards the number of events or the amount of receipts which gave entitlement to exemption.

Ambulance Services

Article 13(A)(1)(p) exempts:

> the supply of transport services for sick or injured persons in vehicles specially designed for the purpose by duly authorised bodies.

Radio and Television

Article 13(A)(1)(q) exempts:

> activities of public radio and television bodies other than those of a commercial nature.

By virtue of Article 4(5) a public radio or television station is not to be considered a taxable person in respect of activities in which it engages as a public

[37] See Art. 1(3)(c) of the Proposal.

authority. Member States may treat as such activities those which are exempt under subparagraph (q). However, such a body must be treated as a taxable person in respect of activities mentioned in Annex D, namely transactions other than those specified in Article 13(A)(1)(q), i.e., commercial broadcasting and other activities. Thus, the non-commercial activities of a public radio or television body are either non-taxable or exempt[38] and its commercial activities are taxable. The non-commercial activities are presumably limited to its public broadcasting function. Taxable commercial activities may include advertising, video and book sales, sales of programme rights, etc. By virtue of the transitional provision in Article 28(3)(a), in conjunction with Annex E, Point 7, Member States may continue to tax the transactions otherwise exempted under this subparagraph.

Other Provisions

Under Article 13(A)(2)(a) Member States may choose to make the granting of the exemptions in subparagraphs (b), (g), (h), (i), (l), (m), and (n) to bodies not governed by public law[39] subject to one or more of the following conditions: that they are not profit-making; that they are run essentially on a voluntary basis; that they charge approved or comparatively low prices; and that the exemption is not likely to distort competition to the disadvantage of commercial enterprises. Article 13(A)(2)(b) provides that no exemption is to be granted (to any person) under those subparagraphs in respect of supplies of goods and services which are not essential to the transactions exempted and whose basic purpose is to obtain additional income by carrying out transactions which are in direct competition which those of commercial enterprises.

2—Article 13 (B) and (C)

Insurance

Article 13(B)(a) exempts:

insurance and reinsurance transactions, including related services performed by insurance brokers and insurance agents.

There is nothing in the *travaux préparatoires* to explain why it was chosen to exempt all insurance transactions. It is clear, however, that taxation of the

[38] It may be noted that this potential difference in treatment can lead to divergent application in the Member States of the rules on the place of supply of services in Art. 9 and hence double or non-taxation. In intra-Community transactions the rule in Art. 9(2)(e) (taxation where the customer is established) applies only where the customer is a taxable person. The VAT Committee reached a compromise solution whereby Art. 9(2)(e) would apply to services supplied to such public broadcasting organizations even where they are classified as non-taxable rather than exempt: see the Commission's Second Report, 23.

[39] See also the second para. of Art. 1 of the 18th Directive, which extends this provision to services covered by Art. 13(A)(1)(m) and (n) carried out by public bodies.

insurance sector would have been particularly complex. While it would be legitimate to tax the pure insurance element of insurance premiums, taxation of the savings or investment element involved in many policies would not be justified. Moreover, it would be inappropriate to treat gross insurance premiums as normal taxable turnover since the insurer's net receipt is the premium less the actuarial cost of providing the insurance cover to the insured person. Although such difficulties are not insurmountable, outright exemption of insurance certainly represents a simpler solution. Like betting and gaming,[40] insurance lends itself more to special taxes, and it is expressly provided in Article 33 that the Directive is without prejudice to the maintenance or introduction of taxes on insurance contracts.

The meaning of the terms 'related services', 'insurance brokers', and 'insurance agents' is not wholly clear. Presumably professionals such as accountants, solicitors, and estate agents who not only advise on insurance matters but also arrange insurance with insurers would qualify as brokers. It is possible that the term 'related services' must be narrowly construed as covering only those services which are *directly* related to the insurance, in particular the arranging of it.

Land Transactions

Article 13(B)(b), (g), and (h) exempts:

(b) the leasing or letting of immovable property excluding:
  1. the provision of accommodation, as defined in the laws of the Member States, in the hotel sector or in sectors with a similar function, including the provision of accommodation in holiday camps or on sites developed for use as camping sites;
  2. the letting of premises and sites for parking vehicles;
  3. lettings of permanently installed equipment and machinery;
  4. hire of safes.

  Member States may apply further exclusions to the scope of this exemption.

(g) the supply of buildings or parts thereof, and of the land on which they stand, other than as described in Article 4(3)(a).

(h) the supply of land which has not been built on other than building land as described in Article 4(3)(b).

Article 13(C), entitled 'Options', provides:

Member States may allow taxpayers a right of option for taxation in cases of:

(a) letting and leasing of immovable property;

(b) the transactions covered in B . . . (g) and (h) above.

Member States may restrict the scope of this right of option and shall fix the details of its use.

[40] Below, p. 188.

Unless VAT is seen as a tax on consumer expenditure rather than a tax on consumption of goods and services, it is not obvious that it should be imposed on land, which is neither produced nor consumed. None the less land may be the subject of economic activity which enhances its value; in particular, it may be cleared and prepared for development through the laying of foundation roads, levelling, installation of drainage and utilities. Plots of building land may be used to satisfy the needs of individuals (residential premises), in which case they are in the nature of consumer goods, or the needs of business, in which case they are a means of production whose cost is reflected in the price of goods and services.[41] The solution adopted in Article 13(B)(h) of the Sixth Directive is to tax supplies of building land while exempting supplies of other categories of land.[42] Once building land has a building constructed on it, it becomes attached to the building for VAT purposes until the building is demolished, when it is reconverted into building land.

Buildings also pose special problems. New buildings must be taxed since they are the product of economic activity and, like building land, are in the nature of consumer goods or means of production. Once they are completed and occupied, the production process ends and they are in effect 'consumed'; they may however change hands many times during their life and be used for private or business use. The scheme of the Sixth Directive is to tax new buildings and the land on which they stand,[43] but to exempt subsequent supplies during the remainder of their lifetime. The criterion chosen for determining whether a building is new is normally that of first occupation. Thus, by virtue of the reference in Article 13(B)(g) to Article 4(3)(a), the 'supply before first occupation of buildings or parts of buildings and the land on which they stand' is excluded from exemption. Article 4(3)(a) however permits Member States to apply other criteria within certain limits.

The exemption in subparagraph (g) applies to residential and commercial property alike, although supplies of old residential property generally fall outside the scope of the tax because they are made by private individuals. Under Article 13(C)(b) Member States may allow taxable persons an option to tax otherwise exempt supplies of land or land and buildings. That option is of

[41] See Explanatory Memorandum to the Proposal for the 6th Directive, 9–10.

[42] However, see note 43 below.

[43] Although the transitional provision in Annex F(16) permits Member States to continue to exempt supplies of buildings and land described in Art. 4(3), it seems that the UK has relied on this provision to continue to exempt building land even though, following the Court's judgment in the 'zero-rating' case (below, p. 204), it now taxes new commercial buildings together with the land on which they stand. It may be noted however that the UK, apparently on the basis of Art. 5(7)(a) (see Ch. 4, note 45), imposes a self-supply charge on a developer in respect of both land and buildings where he subsequently puts them to non-taxable use, thus effectively taxing the building land at a later stage where VAT would not be wholly deductible: see the preamble to Council Decision 89/466. It should also be noted that Annex E(11) permits the continued taxation of supplies covered by Art. 13(B)(g) in so far as they are made by taxable persons who were entitled to deduction of input tax on the building concerned.

particular importance in the commercial property sector. In some circumstances it may work to the advantage of a taxable person to opt to tax a supply in order to be able to reclaim the input tax incurred on the acquisition of a building or in respect of work performed on it. For example, let us suppose that a taxable person buys an office building from a developer for the purposes of his business, paying VAT on the acquisition. Provided that his business consists in making taxable supplies, he is entitled to deduct in full the VAT incurred on the building. However, if two years later he decides to sell the building, he will normally make an exempt supply under Article 13(B)(g). The consequence of this is that his initial deduction will be adjusted under Article 20 of the Directive, and he will suffer a clawback of a large proportion of the VAT deducted.[44] If, on the other hand, he opts to tax the supply, there will be no adjustment of his initial deduction. The exercise of the option to tax will have no adverse consequences for the customer if he is a taxable person entitled to deduct the VAT charged. The purpose of the option to tax is thus to allow the deduction mechanism to operate normally in the case of immovable property transactions between taxable persons.

As is to be expected, Article 13(B)(b), concerning the letting of immovable property, follows a similar pattern to subparagraphs (g) and (h). Subject to the specified exceptions or such others as may be laid down, lettings of immovable property are exempt but an option to tax may be granted to taxable persons under Article 13(C)(a). Thus, a new building which, instead of being sold, is the subject of an exempt letting is definitively taxed at the moment of the letting, since the lessor has no right of deduction.[45] The tenant thus bears tax indirectly through the lease payments just as he would do directly if he purchased the new building. If the tenant is a taxable person with the right of deduction, it may be preferable for the lessor to opt to tax the letting, so that he can recover the input tax incurred on the construction costs and pass it on to the tenant in a recoverable form.

In Case C–63/92, *Lubbock Fine* v. *Commissioners of Customs & Excise*[46] the Court held that the exemption for the letting of immovable property in Article 13(B)(b) extended to the surrender of a lease by a tenant to his immediate landlord for a consideration. The United Kingdom could not rely on the final sentence of Article 13(B)(b) ('Member States may apply further exclusions to the scope of this exemption') to exclude surrenders from the scope of the exemption since the relations created by a lease could not be broken up in that manner.

[44] See below, p. 196.

[45] See in this connection Art. 5(7)(a), which allows a Member State to require a developer who puts a building to wholly exempt use (e.g., an exempt letting) to make a self-supply of the building, thus ensuring that the non-deductible input tax relates to the full value of the building (and not just the VAT on materials and services).

[46] Judgment of 15 December 1993, [1993] ECR I–6665.

In Case 173/88, *Skatteministeriet* v. *Henriksen*[47] the Court held that the phrase 'letting of premises and sites for parking vehicles' in Article 13(B)(b)(2) covered the letting of all places designed to be used for parking vehicles, including closed garages. As an exception to the exemption in Article 13(B)(b) the provision placed such lettings under the general rules of the Directive and was not therefore to be construed narrowly. However, such lettings were not to be excluded from exemption if they were closely linked to exempt lettings of immovable property.

Technical Exemption

Article 13(B)(c) exempts:

> supplies of goods used wholly for an activity exempted under this Article or under Article 28(3)(b) when these goods have not given rise to the right to deduction, or of goods on the acquisition or production of which, by virtue of Article 17(6), Value Added Tax did not become deductible.

This provision is intended to prevent the double taxation which would otherwise occur where a taxable person disposes of goods on which he did not deduct tax either because they were used wholly for exempt transactions or because they fell into a category of expenditure (for example, luxury, amusement, or entertainment expenditure) in respect of which deduction is disallowed by the Member State concerned under Article 17(6).[48] The provision appears to operate only where no tax at all was deducted. It is not clear how the exemption fits in with the rules concerning the adjustment of deductions in respect of capital goods in Article 20. By virtue of those provisions, if a taxable person makes a taxable disposal of goods within the adjustment period following a period of exempt use, his initial zero deduction entitlement is increased to take account of the taxable disposal. However, the view might be taken that the disposal is exempt under Article 13(B)(c) because the goods were used wholly for an exempt activity and there was no initial deduction. It seems preferable to regard the capital goods provisions as taking precedence over the exemption in Article 13(B)(c) and to allow the deduction mechanism to operate normally. The exemption is still meaningful in view of the limited scope of the adjustment mechanism in Article 20.

Curiously the exemption applies only to the supply of goods. It is unclear why it does not extend to the use of goods.

[47] [1989] ECR 2763. [48] See below, p. 194.

Banking and Finance

Article 13(B)(d) exempts:

1. the granting and the negotiation of credit and the management of credit by the person granting it;
2. the negotiation of or any dealings in credit guarantees or any other security for money and the management of credit guarantees by the person who is granting the credit;
3. transactions, including negotiation, concerning deposit and current accounts, payments, transfers, debts, cheques and other negotiable instruments, but excluding debt collection and factoring;
4. transactions, including negotiation, concerning currency, bank notes and coins used as legal tender, with the exception of collectors' items; 'collectors' items' shall be taken to mean gold, silver or other metal coins or bank notes which are not normally used as legal tender or coins of numismatic interest;
5. transactions, including negotiation, excluding management and safekeeping, in shares, interests in companies or associations, debentures and other securities, excluding:
   —documents establishing title to goods,
   —the rights or securities referred to in Article 5(3);
6. management of special investment funds as defined by Member States.

General

The combined effect of those provisions is to exempt most mainstream banking and financial services, including lending and credit transactions, operation of bank accounts, dealings in money, securities for money or orders for payment, currency transactions, dealings in securities such as shares, stocks, bonds, government bills, etc., as well as investment fund management. The exemptions do not, on the other hand, extend to certain ancillary activities of banks and other financial institutions such as debt collection, credit control, and accounting services; equipment leasing; executor and trustee services; investment, financial, and taxation advice; nominee services; company administration services; and safe custody services. The precise reasons for the exemptions are unclear. Various explanations are possible, including economic and policy considerations, the practical and administrative complexity of taxing financial services (many of which are financed out of differences between lending and borrowing rates[49]), or even reservations as to whether credit and investment transactions may properly be subject to a tax on consumption. Whatever the reasons, the report of the Economic and Social Committee reveals that there was disagreement over the matter within the Committee, some members considering that all banking transactions, including the making of advances and the granting of credit, should be taxed,

[49] See IFS Commentary 32, *Tax Reform for the Fourth Term* (London).

others taking the view that such transactions should be exempt. The Directive embodies a compromise, inasmuch as Article 13(C)(b) allows Member States to grant taxable persons the option of taxing transactions exempted under (B)(d).[50]

Banking and financial services are deemed, by virtue of Article 9(2)(e),[51] to be supplied in the country where the customer is established if the latter is a taxable person established in another Member State or a person (whether taxable or not) established outside the Community. By virtue of the rules in Article 17(3) such services, except for fund management services exempt under subparagraph (a)(6), give rise to deduction of input tax if they are supplied to customers outside the Community. For reasons not explained in the *travaux préparatoires* fund management services never give rise to deduction of input tax.[52]

Subparagraph (d)(1)

In *Muys*[53] the Court accepted that the exemption in subparagraph (d)(1) applied to credit granted not only by banks and similar institutions but also by a trader to his customer.[54] However, where a taxable person purported to grant credit in respect of a payment on account due under the contract before the date of the main supply, this did not constitute a separate credit transaction for the purposes of subparagraph (d)(1). The supposed interest constituted part of the consideration for the main supply.

Subparagraphs (d)(2) and (3)

Payment cards involve two distinct relationships, one between the issuer of the card and its holder, and the other between the issuer and the supplier of the goods and services. In its First[55] and Second[56] Reports the Commission stated that the VAT Committee unanimously considered that the service provided by the issuer to the holder constituted a payment facility exempted under Article 13(B)(d). With respect to the service provided by the issuer to the supplier, while initially some members were inclined to see it as a form of (taxable) advertising, ultimately it was concluded almost unanimously that it

[50] Table 3 in Annex II to the Commission's First Report indicated that the option was available in Germany, Belgium, and France, subject to varying conditions set out in the table.

[51] See above, p. 154 ff.

[52] Terra and Kajus, '*Guide*', suggest that this was an oversight since subpara. (d)(6) was added at the final stages of the legislative process. However, that view is difficult to reconcile with the Council's failure to correct the omission when it replaced Art. 17(3) by a transitional provision in Directive 91/680. See also Ch. 7, note 8.

[53] See note 4 above.

[54] On the question whether a separate loan agreement is necessary for a transaction to qualify for exemption, see above, pp. 127–8.

[55] At 49 and 50.

[56] At 35.

should be seen as exempt under Article 13(B)(d)(2) and (3).[57] In its Proposal for a Nineteenth Directive the Commission seeks the abolition of the option to tax in respect of 'services rendered by financial institutions in issuing or managing payment cards or other similar documents'. The purpose of the proposal is to avoid divergent treatment, particularly with respect to the service provided by the issuer to the supplier.[58]

Subparagraph (d)(4)

Collectors' items are specifically excluded from exemption. However, by virtue of the transitional provision in Annex F(26) Member States may continue to exempt transactions concerning gold other than gold for industrial use.[59] The Commission's First Report[60] states that the VAT Committee concluded that the transitional exemption covered gold coins but was unable to agree on criteria for the application of the exemption to such coins.[61]

Postage Stamps

Article 13(B)(e) exempts:

> the supply at face value of postage stamps valid for use for postal services within the territory of the country, fiscal stamps and other similar stamps.

Betting and Gambling

Article 13(B)(f) exempts:

> betting, lotteries, and other forms of gambling, subject to conditions and limitations laid down by each Member State.

The Explanatory Memorandum to the Proposal for the Sixth Directive[62] states that this exemption is based purely on practical considerations, gaming and lotteries being better suited to specific taxes rather than a tax on added value. Accordingly Article 33 of the Directive expressly authorizes the maintenance or introduction of taxes on betting and gambling. The Proposal[63] provided for unqualified exemption of 'gaming and lotteries'. However, the final text of the exemption, which is qualified by the words 'subject to conditions

[57] See also the judgment in *Chaussures Bally*, above at p. 127, in which the Court seems to have assumed that the issuer's service was exempt. The point was however not directly in issue in the case, which was concerned with the taxable amount for the main supply of goods.

[58] 2nd Report, 35.

[59] On 27 October 1992 the Commission proposed the introduction of a special scheme of taxation: Proposal for a Council Directive supplementing the common system of VAT and amending Directive 77/388: special scheme for gold, COM(92)441 final.

[60] At 48 and 49.

[61] See also the remarks concerning platinum nobles in the 2nd Report, 35 and 36.

[62] At 16.

[63] Art. 14B(k).

and limitations laid down by each Member State', allows Member States to select the transactions which they wish to exempt. In his Opinion in Case C–38/93, *Glawe* v. *Finanzamt Hamburg-Barmbek-Uhlenhorst*,[64] Advocate General Jacobs noted however that Member States choosing to tax gambling transactions were obliged to comply with the general provisions of the Directive, including the rules on the taxable amount. The Court, following the Advocate General, held that the taxable amount in the case of slot machines consisted in the net takings emptied from the machine after payment of winnings rather than the total stakes inserted.[65]

Other Transitional Exemptions

In addition to those mentioned above the following transitional exemptions remain after the Eighteenth Directive:

services supplied by authors, artists, performers, lawyers, and other members of the liberal professions, other than the medical and paramedical professions, in so far as these are not services specified in Annex B to the Second Council Directive (Annex F(2));

services supplied by undertakers and cremation services, together with goods related thereto (F(6));

transactions carried out by blind persons or workshops for the blind provided that these exemptions do not give rise to significant distortion of competition (F(7));

the supply of goods and services to official bodies responsible for the construction, setting out, and maintenance of cemeteries, graves, and monuments commemorating war dead (F(8));

the supply of water by public authorities (F(12));

the supply, modification, repair, maintenance, chartering, and hiring of aircraft, including equipment incorporated or used therein, used by State institutions (F(23));

the supply, modification, repair, maintenance, chartering, and hiring of warships (F(25));

the services of travel agents referred to in Article 26, and those of travel agents acting in the name and on the account of the traveller, for journeys within the Community (F(27)).[66]

64 [1994] ECR 1.

65 The Advocate General's Opinion contains an interesting analysis of the application of VAT to gambling transactions: see in particular para. 14 ff. of the Opinion.

66 The Portuguese Republic is permitted by Art. 2 of the 18th Directive to defer abolition of certain exemptions until 1 January 1994.

7

The Right of Deduction

The right of a taxable person to deduct from the output VAT payable on his supplies the input VAT incurred on the goods and services used for making those supplies is the corollary of the principle that VAT is chargeable at every stage of production and marketing. It plays an essential part in ensuring, in accordance with Article 2 of the First Directive, that the tax remains 'exactly proportional to the price of the goods and services, whatever the number of transactions which take place in the production and marketing process before the stage at which tax is charged'.

Under the Community VAT system the right of deduction arises immediately and in full regardless of whether the expenditure is of a revenue or a capital nature[1] and regardless of the level of consideration received for the supplies for which the goods or services are used. The latter point was established by the Court in Case 50/87, *Commission* v. *France*,[2] where it held to be incompatible with the Sixth Directive French legislation which precluded total and immediate deduction of input tax on let immovable property where the rental income was less than one fifteenth of the property's value.

The detailed rules concerning the right of deduction are contained in Articles 17 to 20 of the Sixth Directive. Those articles have been replaced in part by transitional provisions contained in Article 28f.[3]

Under Article 17(1) the right to deduct arises at the time when the deductible tax becomes chargeable; VAT incurred on most supplies of goods and services thus becomes deductible at the moment when the goods or services are supplied. Under Article 17(2) a taxable person's right of deduction extends to VAT incurred on the following transactions:

VAT due or paid on goods or services supplied to him by another taxable person liable for tax within the territory of the country (subparagraph (a)),

VAT due or paid on imported goods within the territory of the country (subparagraph (b)),

VAT due on the fictitious supplies deemed to arise under Articles 5(7)(a) and 6(3) and the fictitious intra-Community acquisitions arising under Article 28a(6) (subparagraph (c)),

[1] See, however, Article 17(7) of the 6th Directive which allows Member States, after consulting the VAT Committee, to refuse or limit deduction of VAT on all or some capital goods or other goods for cyclical economic reasons. This rather vague provision has yet to be interpreted by the Court. For further discussion, see Terra and Kajus, *Guide*, p. 132.

[2] [1988] ECR 4797.

[3] Introduced by Directive 91/680 and amended by Art. 1(18) of Directive 92/111.

VAT due on general intra-Community acquisitions under Article 28a(1)(a) (subparagraph (d)).

Under subparagraph (a) a taxable person is entitled to deduct VAT only on supplies *made to him*. Thus a third party (that is to say a person other than the recipient of the supply) furnishing consideration for a supply under Article 11(A)(1) is not entitled to deduct the VAT charged. However, in Case 165/86, *Intiem*,[4] the Court held that, where a taxable person purchased goods for the purposes of his economic activity, he was entitled to deduct the VAT on those goods even though they were physically delivered to the taxable person's employees. The goods or services must be supplied by another taxable person acting in that capacity. A taxable person acquiring goods from a private individual is not entitled to deduct the residual VAT which may be contained in the value of the goods.[5]

Under Article 17(2) a taxable person has the right to deduct VAT on goods and services only 'in so far as [they] are used for the purposes of his taxable transactions'. In principle therefore he is not entitled to deduct VAT on goods and services used for transactions that are exempt or are outside the scope of the tax of a Member State. None the less he may, by virtue of Article 17(3), deduct or receive a refund of VAT incurred on the transactions mentioned in paragraph 2 in so far as the goods and services are used for the following export or intra-Community transactions:

Transactions relating to economic activities carried out in another country in respect of which VAT would have been deductible if they had been carried out in the territory of the country (17(3)(a)): For example, a taxable person established in a Member State may deduct the VAT incurred on goods and services used for performing a service which he is deemed, under Article 9 of the Directive, to perform in another Member State or outside the Community. The foreign transaction might equally be a supply of goods assembled on site at the customer's premises or one covered by the distance sales mechanism.

Transactions which are exempt under Article 14(1)(i), 15, 16(1)(B), (C), (D), or (E) or 16(2), or 28c(A) and (C)[6] (17(3)(b)): With the exception of Article 14(1)(i), which is a technical exemption concerning imports,[7] these provisions all relate to the exemption of exports of goods, international transport, or operations associated with international goods traffic or intra-Community supplies;

[4] *Leesportefeuille 'Intiem' CV* v. *Staatssecretaris van Financiën* [1988] ECR 1471.

[5] Case C-165/88, *ORO Amsterdam Beheer BV and Concerto BV* v. *Inspecteur der Omzetbelasting, Amsterdam* [1989] ECR 4081.

[6] The reference to Art. 28c(C) was added by Art. 1(18) of Directive 92/111.

[7] See above, p. 166.

Banking, insurance and financial transactions exempt under Article 13(B) (a) and (d) (1) to (5)[8] where the customer is established outside the Community or where the transactions are directly linked with goods to be exported to a country outside the Community (17(3)(c)): this again is effectively an 'export' exemption since, where banking, financial, and insurance transactions are carried out for a customer established outside the Community, they are deemed, under Article 9(2)(e), to be supplied where the customer is established. Such services, however, remain exempt without any refund of input tax where they are supplied to a taxable person established in another Member State and hence are deemed, under Article 9(2)(e), to be supplied in that State.[9]

In some cases a taxable person who incurs VAT under the conditions mentioned in Article 17(3) may be established in another Member State or outside the Community, and may not submit regular returns to the authorities in the state where he incurred the VAT. For example, an export trader in one Member State might incur VAT on travel and other expenses while attending a trade fair in another Member State or visiting a customer there. Article 17(4) provides that taxable persons established in another Member State may claim a direct refund of tax under the arrangements laid down in the Eighth Directive;[10] taxable persons established outside the Community may avail themselves of similar arrangements made by the Thirteenth Directive.[11]

Article 2 of the Eighth Directive requires Member States to refund to any taxable person who is not established in the territory of the country but who is established in another Member State any VAT charged to him in respect of services or movable property supplied to him by other taxable persons in the territory of the country, or charged in respect of the importation of goods into the country, in so far as such goods and services are used for the purposes of the transactions referred to in Article 17(3)(a) and (b) of the Sixth

[8] It should be noted that there is no right of deduction in respect of Art. 13(B)(d)(6) services ('management of special investment funds') performed for non-Community customers. There seems to be no explanation for this in the *travaux préparatoires*. It is not clear whether the exclusion of such services indicates an intention that they should also be excluded from the scope of Art. 9(2)(e) of the Directive and covered by Article 9(1).

[9] What is not clear is whether a right of deduction would arise in respect of such services under Art. 17(3)(a) where the taxable person has exercised an option to tax his services under Art. 13(C)(b). This would be anomalous since it may give the taxable person an unfair advantage over competitors with no right to opt in the Member State in which the supply is deemed to be made. The answer is probably that a Member State cannot grant an option in respect of services supplied in another Member State since it has no jurisdiction over such services.

[10] 8th Council Directive (79/1072) of 6 December 1979 on the harmonization of the laws of the Member States relating to turnover taxes—arrangements for the refund of VAT to taxable persons not established in the territory of the country (OJ 1979, L331/11).

[11] 13th Council Directive (86/560) of 17 November 1986 on the harmonization of the laws of the Member States relating to turnover taxes—arrangements for the refund of VAT to taxable persons not established in Community territory (OJ 1986, L326/40).

Directive or of services where the customer is solely responsible for payment of tax pursuant to Article 21(1)(b) of that Directive. Article 1 of the Eighth Directive defines 'a taxable person not established in the territory of the country' as a taxable person who, during the relevant period,[12] had in that country neither the seat of his economic activity nor a fixed establishment from which business transactions are effected nor, failing which, his domicile or normal place of residence *and* who during the same period made no supplies of goods or services deemed to have been supplied in that country, with the exception of (a) transport services and services ancillary thereto exempted under Article 14(1)(i), 15, or 16(1)(B),(C), and (D) of the Sixth Directive, and (b) services in respect of which tax is payable solely by the customer under Article 21(1)(b)[13] of that Directive; by virtue of the last subparagraph of Article 17(4) of the Sixth Directive,[14] that exception is extended to supplies of goods and services to persons designated to pay the tax in accordance with Article 21(1)(a).[15] Since a foreign taxable person would not otherwise have to register as a taxable person in a Member State in respect of such supplies (because they are exempt or responsibility for payment has been shifted to another person), it is logical to ignore them for the purposes of the Eighth Directive and allow him to claim a direct refund of tax incurred in that Member State. If he is established in the State or makes other categories of supplies there, he must reclaim any tax incurred by registering as a taxable person there, or appointing a tax representative.[16] Indent (c) of the last subparagraph of Article 17(4) provides that the Eighth and Thirteenth Directives do not apply to supplies of goods which are, or may be, exempted under Article 28c(A) when the goods are dispatched or transported by the acquirer or for his account. The Explanatory Memorandum[17] to the Commission's Proposal for Directive 92/111 states without further explanation that this is an anti-avoidance provision.

The Thirteenth Directive, although laying down basic conditions similar to those in the Eighth Directive, leaves the Member States greater discretion with respect to the detailed arrangements. Moreover, it allows Member States to make the refunds conditional upon the granting by non-member states of comparable advantages regarding turnover taxes.[18]

Article 17(2) confers the right of deduction solely on taxable persons acting in that capacity. A taxable person has no right of deduction in respect of

[12] As defined in the first and second sentences of the first subpara. of Art. 7(1) of the Directive.

[13] See below, p. 206.

[14] Inserted by Art. 1(18) of Directive 92/111.

[15] See below, p. 206.

[16] Reference is made to Arts. 3 to 9 of the 8th Directive, as amended by the 13th Directive, for the detailed rules governing the refunds. Also see the Commission's Report of 31 October 1985 (COM(85)586 final), submitted pursuant to Art. 12 of the Directive, on the operation of the schemes introduced in Member States and proposals for improving the Directive.

[17] Point 20 of COM(92)448 final.

[18] Art. 2(2).

goods which he acquires wholly for purposes other than those of his business even if subsequently he puts those goods to business use.[19] However, a person who acquires goods with the intention of using them for the purposes of his business does so in his capacity as a taxable person even where the goods are not used immediately for the purpose of making business supplies.[20] Where, in addition, he is able to demonstrate that he intends to use the goods for the purposes of transactions giving rise to the right of deduction, he has the right to immediate deduction of the input tax incurred on those goods in accordance with Article 17(1).[21] The extent of the evidence required to prove the intention to use goods for the purposes of a taxable economic activity depends on the particular circumstances, including the nature of the goods and the period between acquisition and use.[22] It is submitted that the same principles must apply *mutatis mutandis* to services which are purchased with a view to making subsequent business supplies.

Article 17(6) envisages a decision by the Council on expenditure not qualifying for deduction. It adds that VAT shall in no circumstances be deductible on expenditure that is not strictly business expenditure, such as that on luxuries, amusements, or entertainment. Pending the entry into force of common rules Member States are permitted to retain all the exclusions from deduction provided for in national law on the entry into force of the Sixth Directive. A proposal for a Twelfth Directive on expenditure not eligible for deduction was submitted to the Council on 25 January 1983,[23] but has yet to be adopted. In his Opinion in *Lennartz*[24] Advocate General Jacobs suggested that Article 17(6) could not be relied on to justify the retention of a general rule disallowing deduction of tax where business use amounted to less than 10 per cent. In his view the discretion retained by the Member States related specifically to the matters on which agreement could not be reached, namely the categories of expenditure on which VAT should not be deductible.

Article 17(5) contains provisions for the apportionment of input tax incurred on goods and services used partly for transactions in respect of which VAT is deductible and partly for transactions in respect of which it is not. The normal method of apportionment under the Directive is that contained in Article 19(1), namely an apportionment based on the ratio between turnover giving rise to the right of deduction (numerator) and total turnover (denominator). Subsidies of a type other than those included in turnover under Article 11(A)(1)(a) may, at the discretion of Member States, be included in the denominator as turnover not giving rise to deduction, thus reducing the

[19] Case C–97/90, *Lennartz* v. *Finanzamt München III* [1991] ECR I–3795, para. 8 ff.
[20] Ibid., para. 13 ff. See also the Opinion of Advocate General Jacobs at point 33.
[21] Ibid., judgment and Opinion.
[22] Para. 19 ff. of the judgment. See also the Opinion at point 41 ff.
[23] OJ 1983, C37/8. Amended on 20 February 1984, OJ 1984, C56/7.
[24] Above, noter 19, points 78–9.

deductible proportion of the input VAT. Conversely, the Court has held that share dividends received by a holding company are to be excluded from the denominator of the fraction.[25] Under Article 19(2) turnover from the sale of capital goods used in the business and incidental real estate and financial transactions are excluded from the calculation of the deductible proportion. Such transactions do not form part of the taxable person's regular business activity, and their inclusion would therefore distort the turnover ratio used for calculating the deductible proportion.[26] The proportion is fixed on an annual basis.[27] Generally a provisional proportion is fixed on the basis of the previous year's figure, and the deduction made on that basis is adjusted when the definitive proportion is fixed.[28] Since apportionment on the basis of total turnover can frequently produce a distorted result, Article 17(5) allows Member States considerable discretion to authorize or compel taxable persons to use certain other methods, in particular sectorial accounting or apportionment on the basis of the use of the goods or services.

The effect of the above rules may be illustrated by a simple example: A bank purchases a building for £2 million plus £200,000 VAT.[29] 40 per cent of the building is used to house a department responsible for its taxable equipment-leasing business; the remainder of the building is used by staff involved in lending and other exempt transactions. The bank has £300 million exempt turnover and £100 million taxable turnover. Under the normal method laid down by Article 19 the bank would be entitled to deduct one quarter (£100 million/£100 million + £300 million) of the input tax on the building (£50,000). A Member State would be entitled (but not obliged) to allow the bank to base its apportionment on the use of the building. The bank would then be entitled to deduct 40 per cent of its input tax (£80,000).

The Commission's First Report[30] recorded that certain Member States had adopted administrative practices deviating from Article 19 whereby the gross margin was substituted for turnover in the denominator of the fraction in respect of certain financial transactions exempted by Article 13(B)(d). The VAT Committee almost unanimously rejected the use of the gross margin with respect to interest on credit; however, considerable support was found

[25] Case C-333/91, *SATAM SA* (now called *Sofitam*) v. *Ministre chargé du Budget* [1993] ECR I-3513.

[26] See the Explanatory Memorandum accompanying the Proposal for the 6th Directive. The wording of Art. 19(2) is peculiar since it separately excludes 'capital goods used by the taxable person for the purposes of his business', 'transactions specified in Art. 13(B)(d), in so far as these are incidental transactions' and 'incidental real estate and financial transactions'. On the face of it there is some overlap between those categories. As Terra and Kajus (*A Guide to the Sixth VAT Directive* (Amsterdam: IBDF, 1991), 938) suggest, it seems that the latter category of 'incidental real estate and financial transactions' must refer to real estate transactions, other than disposals of capital goods used in the business, and financial transactions other than those in Art. 13(B)(d) (in particular the various taxable financial transactions).

[27] Second subpara. of Art. 19(1).

[28] Art. 19(3).

[29] A 10% VAT rate is assumed for ease of calculation.

[30] At 56.

for its use with respect to dealings in securities and exchange transactions. In the draft Nineteenth Directive the Commission proposed that the amount included in the denominator should be reduced by the purchase price of transfers of currency and securities exempted under Article 13(B)(d)(4) and (5).[31]

In the case of capital goods it was thought necessary to make provision in the Sixth Directive for subsequent adjustment of the initial deduction made upon the acquisition of such goods in order to take account of changes of use in subsequent years. Article 20(2) provides for an adjustment period of five years, which may be extended to ten years for immovable property. During the five-year period, which commences with that in which the goods are acquired or manufactured, adjustments are made in respect of one-fifth of the input tax on the goods to reflect variations in the deduction entitlement. For example, let us suppose that in the above illustration the taxable use of the building (and the bank's deduction entitlement) increased from 40 per cent to 60 per cent in year two but then reduced to 30 per cent in year three. In the event of the goods being covered by rules enacted under Article 20(2) the bank, having deducted £80,000 in year one, will be entitled in year two to deduct a further £8,000, that is to say 20 per cent (i.e. 60 per cent − 40 per cent) × ⅕ × £200,000, but will suffer a clawback of £4,000 in year three, that is to say 10 per cent (i.e., 40 per cent − 30 per cent) × ⅕ × £200,000. The same process continues each year until the end of the adjustment period or for as long as the goods are retained. Under Article 20(3), if the taxable person makes a supply of the goods during the adjustment period, they are deemed to be used wholly for taxable or exempt business use (depending on whether the supply is taxable or exempt) for the remainder of the adjustment period. Thus, if in year four the bank, exercising an option to tax allowed by the Member State concerned under Article 13(C)(b),[32] disposes of the building by way of a taxable supply, it will be entitled to a further single deduction in respect of years four and five of £48,000, that is to say 60 per cent (i.e., 100 per cent − 40 per cent) × ⅕ × £200,000 × 2. Conversely, an exempt disposal of the building would trigger a clawback of £32,000, that is to say 40 per cent (i.e., 40 per cent − 0 per cent) × ⅕ × £200,000 × 2.

Article 20(4) leaves it to the Member States to define capital goods[33] and determine the amount of tax to be taken into account for this purpose. They are also free, on the one hand, to adopt measures designed to prevent unjustified advantages and, on the other, to permit administrative simplifications. Article 20(5) provides that if the practical effect of not applying the adjustment rules in a Member State would be 'insignificant', that Member State may, subject to consultation of the VAT Committee under Article 29, refrain

[31] See Art. 1(8) of the Proposal.

[32] See above, p. 182 ff.

[33] As regards the definition of capital goods for the purposes of the 2nd Directive, see Case 51/76, *Nederlandse Ondernemingen* v. *Inspecteur der Invoerrechten en Accijnzen* [1977] ECR 113.

from applying them having regard to the need to avoid distortion of competition, the overall tax effect in the Member State concerned and the need for due economy of administration. It seems clear that Article 20(5) does not deprive Articles 20(2) and (3) of direct effect, since the economic assessment required in order to determine the significance of not applying the rules is not immune from judicial review.[34] Article 20(4), on the other hand, appears to leave Member States considerable discretion with respect to the definition of the concept of capital goods and the amount of tax to be taken into consideration for adjustment. The extent of that discretion is unclear, however, since an excessively broad construction of Article 20(4) would render Article 20(5) meaningless.

Article 20(2) merely adjusts the amount of the initial deduction made under Article 17 and cannot create an entitlement where none arose originally. Thus it does not operate where a taxable person acquires goods wholly for non-business purposes (and hence not as a taxable person for the purposes of Article 17(2)) and subsequently transfers them to business use.[35] However, according to Advocate General Jacobs,[36] the fact that initially no VAT is deductible on goods acquired by a taxable person for wholly exempt business use does not preclude adjustment under Article 20(2) if the goods are subsequently put to taxable use; what is involved is merely adjustment of the amount of the initial entitlement.

The rules governing the exercise of the right of deduction are set out in Article 18 of the Directive.[37] Article 18(1) lays down the formalities which must be complied with by a taxable person in order to make the various categories of deduction under Article 17(2). Article 18(2) provides that a taxable person is to effect deduction of tax by subtracting from the total amount of VAT due for a given period the total amount of tax in respect of which the right of deduction has arisen during the same period. It thus embodies the principle of immediate deduction. The transitional provision in Article 28(3)(d) permitted Member States to continue applying provisions derogating from that principle. The only Member State to make use of this provision was France, which delayed deduction by one month. In addition, Article 2 of Directive 92/111 permits the Kingdom of Spain and the Italian Republic to derogate from the principle within certain limits for a non-extendable period of two years from 1 January 1993.

Member States are to determine the conditions and procedures whereby a taxable person may be authorized to make a deduction which he has not

[34] See with respect to a similar condition in Art. 4(5) the judgments in Case 231/87, *Ufficio Distrettuale delle Imposte di Fiorenzuola d'Arda* v. *Comune di Carpaneto Piacentino* [1989] ECR 3233 and Case C–4/89, *Comune di Carpaneto Piacentino* v. *Ufficio Provinciale Imposta sul Valore Aggiunto di Piacenza* [1990] ECR I–1869.

[35] See para.12 of the judgment in *Lennartz*, note 19, above.

[36] Point 35 of the *Lennartz* Opinion.

[37] Amended by Art. 28f, inserted by Directive 91/680.

made in accordance with Article 18(1) and (2).[38] Where for a given period the input tax deductible exceeds the output tax due, Member States may make a refund or carry the excess forward to the following period. A refund or carry-forward may however be refused if the amount of the excess is insignificant.[39]

[38] Art. 18(3).

[39] Art. 18(4).

8

Payment of Tax, Rates, and Administration

CHARGEABLE EVENT AND CHARGEABILITY OF TAX

The provisions concerning the chargeable event and the moment when the tax becomes chargeable are set out in Article 10 of the Sixth Directive, as amended by Article 1(6) of Directive 91/680, and in Article 28d of the Sixth Directive, inserted by Directive 91/680 and amended by Article 1(14) of Directive 92/111.

The 'chargeable event' is defined as the occurrence by virtue of which the legal conditions necessary for tax to become chargeable are fulfilled.[1] The tax becomes 'chargeable' when the tax authority becomes entitled under the law at a given moment to claim the tax from the person liable to pay, notwithstanding that the time of payment may be deferred.[2]

The two concepts are important for several purposes. In principle the chargeable event determines the rate of tax applicable to a transaction, although in some cases the moment when the tax becomes chargeable is also relevant.[3] The right to deduct tax charged on a transaction arises at the time when the deductible tax becomes chargeable.[4] That moment also determines the return on which a transaction, whether taxable or exempt, is recorded[5] and hence indirectly the date on which the tax due on taxable transactions is payable to the tax authorities.[6]

In principle the chargeable event occurs and the tax becomes chargeable at the same time, namely when the goods are delivered or the services are performed; supplies of goods, other than hire purchase and credit sales covered by Article 5(4)(b), and supplies of services which give rise to successive statements of account or payments are deemed to be completed at the time when the periods to which such statements or payments pertain expire.[7] However, where a payment on account is made before the goods or the services are performed, the tax becomes chargeable on the amount received at an earlier moment than the chargeable event, namely upon receipt of payment.[8] In addition Member States have the option of providing that the tax shall

[1] Art. 10(1)(a). [2] Art. 10(1)(b). [3] Below, p. 205. [4] Art. 17(1).

[5] Art. 22(4)(a), contained in Art. 28h of the Directive inserted by Directive 91/680.

[6] It should be noted that the tax due on taxable transactions is not handed over at the moment when the tax becomes chargeable but at the end of, or after, the return period together with the tax due on other transactions in the period and after deduction of allowable input tax which became chargeable in the period.

[7] Art. 10(2), first subpara. [8] Second subpara. of Art. 10(2).

become chargeable, for certain transactions or for certain categories of taxable person, no later than the invoice date, the date on which the price is received, or within a specified period from the date of the chargeable event where an invoice is not issued or is issued late.

By way of derogation from the above rules tax becomes chargeable for intra-Community supplies of goods exempted under Article 28c(A) on the fifteenth day of the month following that during which the chargeable event occurs.[9] However, where the invoice is issued before that date tax becomes chargeable on the invoice date.[10] Corresponding rules apply to intra-Community acquisitions, for which the chargeable event occurs when the acquisition is effected. An acquisition is effected when the supply of similar goods is effected within the territory of the country.[11] The tax becomes chargeable on the fifteenth day of the month following that during which the chargeable event occurs,[12] unless an invoice is issued before that date.[13] The coincidence of the exempt supply and the intra-Community acquisition facilitates the matching of the two transactions for fiscal control purposes.

In the case of imports the chargeable event occurs and the tax becomes chargeable when the goods are imported. Where on entry into the Community the goods are placed under one of the arrangements referred to in Article 7(3),[14] the chargeable event occurs and the tax becomes chargeable only when the goods cease to be covered by those arrangements. However, where imported products are subject to customs duties, to agricultural levies, or charges having equivalent effect established under a common policy, the chargeable event occurs and the tax becomes chargeable when the chargeable event for the Community duties occurs and the duties become chargeable. Where imported goods are not subject to any of the aforesaid duties Member States are to apply the provisions in force governing customs duties for the purpose of determining the chargeable event and the moment when the tax becomes chargeable.[15]

RATES

The Sixth Directive originally contained few provisions on rates of tax, limiting itself mainly to harmonization of the basis of assessment. In particular no standard rate of tax was fixed, nor was there any limit on the number of higher or lower rates. The only requirements were that the rate applicable to imports should be the same as the domestic rate and that any lower rate

[9] Art. 28d(4).
[10] Art. 28d(4), second subpara., replaced by Art. 1(15) of Directive 92/111.
[11] Art. 28d(1). [12] Art. 28d(2).
[13] Art. 28d(3), replaced by Art. 1(14) of Directive 92/111.
[14] See above, p. 161. [15] Art. 10(3), as amended by Art. 1(6) of Directive 91/680.

should be fixed at a level which would normally be sufficient to permit deduction from the output VAT charged of all the input VAT deductible under Article 17.[16] The latter requirement had to be read subject to the transitional provision in Article 28(2), which permitted Member States to retain reduced rates and zero rates[17] applicable at 31 December 1975 on certain conditions. Closer alignment of rates was, however, seen by the Commission as a prerequisite for the removal of fiscal frontiers within the Community. The Commission, aware of the budgetary consequences of complete harmonization for some Member States,[18] initially proposed[19] a standard-rate band of between 14 and 20 per cent and a reduced-rate band of between 4 and 9 per cent, no provision being made for zero rates of tax.[20] Those proposals proved controversial, disagreement focusing mainly on the width of the bands, the products to be covered by the reduced rates and the question of zero rates.[21] At the same time the Commission's original 1987 proposals for the abolition of fiscal frontiers through the introduction of a system of taxing goods and services in their country of origin were also meeting resistance. In its Communication of 14 June 1989,[22] in which it sought to break the deadlock by proposing transitional arrangements based on the destination principle, the Commission also modified its original proposals on rates by suggesting a minimum standard rate rather than a standard-rate band and by relaxing somewhat its position on zero rates. The debate continued, some Member States (notably the United Kingdom) taking the view that no legislative measures to align rates were necessary since market forces would exert the necessary pressure for alignment.[23] None the less, in June 1991 the Council was able to reach a measure of agreement on many aspects of the rate structure, issuing a statement including a declaration by Member States that, as from January 1993, they would apply a standard rate of VAT not lower than 15 per cent.[24] The compromise finally reached in Directive 92/77,[25] amending the Sixth Directive with effect from 1 January 1993, was to lay down a minimum standard rate for a period of four years, coinciding with the initial period of

[16] Art. 12(4), second sentence. The requisite rate, sometimes referred to as 'the sponge rate', was thought to be around 5%.

[17] More correctly, exemptions with refund of the tax paid at the preceding stage.

[18] In 1987 the standard rates applied in the Member States varied from 12% (Spain and Luxembourg) to 25% (Ireland).

[19] See COM(87)320 *Final: Completion of the internal market: approximation of indirect tax rates and harmonization of indirect structure. Global communication from the Commission.* Also COM(87)321 *Final: Proposal for a Directive completing the common system of Value Added Tax and amending Directive 77/388/EEC—Approximation of rates.*

[20] As applied particularly in the UK and Ireland.

[21] See COM (89)260 final, 4.

[22] COM(89)260 final: *Communication from the Commission to the Council and to the Parliament—Completion of the internal market and approximation of indirect taxes.*

[23] For a wide-ranging discussion of the arguments see the draft Report of 21 February 1991 of the European Parliament's Committee on Economic and Monetary Affairs and Industrial Policy.

[24] ECOFIN, 24 June 1991.

[25] OJ 1992, L316/1.

validity of the transitional arrangements. The text of the relevant provisions was further amended by Article 1(7) of Directive 92/111.

The amended Sixth Directive thus lays down a minimum standard rate of 15 per cent applicable until 31 December 1996. The Council is to decide unanimously before 31 December 1995 on the minimum rate to be applied after that date on the basis of the report to be prepared by the Commission on the operation of the transitional arrangements and proposals on the definitive system.[26] Member States may also apply up to two reduced rates of at least 5 per cent to the supplies listed in Annex H.[27] The requirement, existing under the original rules, that the tax resulting from application of the reduced rates should normally permit deduction of all input tax deductible is retained.[28] The provision for higher rates under the original rules was deleted.[29] The Council is to review the scope of the reduced rates every two years from 1994 on the basis of a report from the Commission and, acting unanimously on a proposal from the Commission, may decide to alter the list in Annex H.[30]

Member States may apply a reduced rate to supplies of natural gas and electricity provided that no risk of distortion of competition exists. A Member State must give prior notice to the Commission, which is to give a decision on the existence of such a risk. No distortion is deemed to exist if the Commission fails to adopt a decision within three months of the notification.[31] It is unclear what legal significance attaches to such a decision or what action a Member State should take if it disagrees with it.

The Directive contemplates the future adoption of special rules for the following items:

> second-hand goods, works of art, antiques, and collectors' items (before 31 December 1992);

[26] Art. 12(3)(a), first and second subparas., as replaced by Directive 92/111. It is unclear whether, in the absence of such a decision, any legal obligation regarding a minimum rate would continue to exist after 31 December 1996. It is possible that the provision might be construed to the effect that an extension of the transitional period without any further decision on rates would also entail continuance of the legal obligation concerning the minimum rate.

[27] Last subpara. of Art. 12(3)(a), as replaced by Directive 92/111. Annex H defines in detail the supplies eligible for reduced rates. Broadly the various categories are: (1) foodstuffs; (2) water; (3) pharmaceutical products; (4) medical equipment, aids for the disabled, and children's car seats; (5) transport of passengers; (6) books, newspapers, and periodicals; (7) admission to places of culture and entertainment; (8) writers, composers, and performing artists; (9) housing as part of a social policy; (10) non-capital goods and services used in agriculture; (11) hotels and camping sites; (12) admission to sporting events; (13) use of sporting facilities; (14) charities; (15) undertakers and cremation; (16) medical and dental care; (17) street cleaning, and refuse collection and waste treatment.

[28] First sentence (previously second sentence) of Art. 12(4).

[29] Art. 1(2) of Directive 92/77, deleting the first sentence of Art. 12(4).

[30] Last subpara. of Art. 12(4), inserted by Art. 1(3) of Directive 92/77.

[31] Art. 12(3)(b).

agricultural outputs other than those falling within Category 1 of Annex H (before 31 December 1994);
gold (before 31 December 1992).[32]

Member States applying reduced rates in respect of the abovementioned agricultural outputs may continue to do so until 31 December 1994.[33]

The envisaged arrangements for second-hand goods, etc., were adopted by Directive 94/5,[34] which introduced a new Article 12(3)(c). Under the first subparagraph of that provision Member States may also apply a reduced rate to imports of works of art, collectors' items, and antiques as defined in the Article 26a(A), introduced by the Directive. Where they avail themselves of this option they may, under the second subparagraph, also apply the reduced rate to supplies of works of art effected by their creator or his successors in title or on an occasional basis by a taxable person other than a taxable dealer where the works have been imported by the taxable person himself, or where they have been supplied to him by their creator or his successors in title, or where they have entitled him to full deduction of VAT.

Where a Member State did not, on 1 January 1993, avail itself of the option to apply reduced rates of tax, it may reduce the taxable amount for imports of works of art, collectors' items, and antiques provided that the VAT due on the reduced amount is at least 5 per cent of the normal taxable amount.[35] Member States may extend that option to the supplies referred to in the second subparagraph of Article 12(3)(c).[36]

Directive 92/77 also replaced the transitional provision in Article 28(2) with an entirely new provision. The transitional arrangements, laid down in subparagraphs (a) to (f), are essentially as follows:

(a) Zero rates and reduced rates lower than 5 per cent which were legally in force on 1 January 1991 and satisfy the conditions laid down in the last indent of Article 17 of the Second Directive (i.e., were granted for clearly defined social reasons and for the benefit of the final consumer) may be retained.[37]

(b) Reduced rates not lower than 5 per cent may be applied to goods and services other than those listed in Annex H in respect of which zero rates

32 Articles 12(3)(c) to (e).

33 Art. 12(3)(d), second subpara. The wording of the provision suggests that, in the absence of agreement, a standard rate must be applied from 31 December 1994, although the position is far from clear. See the comments of Terra, *International VAT Monitor*, January 1993, 2 and 3, where reference is made to differing interpretations by the German and French delegations.

34 For a summary of the provisions of the Directive, see below, p. 219 ff.

35 Art. 11(B)(6), inserted by Directive 94/5. See also Art. 28(1a), inserted by Directive 94/5, which allows the UK to apply a 2.5% effective minimum rate until 30 June 1999.

36 Art. 11(A)(4), inserted by Directive 94/5.

37 Special provision is made for Ireland in respect of the supply of energy products for heating and lighting. Although not expressly stated, subparagraph (a) presumably applies only to supplies covered by Annex H.

or reduced rates lower than 5 per cent were legally applied at 1 January 1991.

(c) Member States required by the Directive to increase their standard rate, as applied at 1 January 1991, by more than 2 per cent may apply a reduced rate below 5 per cent (but not a zero rate) in respect of the goods and services listed in Annex H and also restaurant services, children's clothing, children's footwear, and housing.
(d) Reduced rates applied at 1 January 1991 to restaurant services, children's clothing, children's footwear, and housing may be retained.
(e) Member States which at 1 January 1991 applied a reduced rate to supplies of goods and services other than those in Annex H may apply a reduced rate not lower than 12 per cent to such supplies.
(f) Special provision is made for certain regions of Greece.

On the basis of a report from the Commission the Council is to review the above transitional provisions before 31 December 1994 and, on the basis of a Commission proposal, adopt measures to remedy significant distortions of competition.[38]

With respect to Article 28(2)(a), above, the requirements laid down by the last indent of Article 17 of the Second Directive were considered by the Court in Cases 415 and 416/85, *Commission* v. *Ireland and United Kingdom*.[39] The Commission challenged certain zero rates of tax applied by the United Kingdom and, to a more limited extent, Ireland in areas such as agriculture, construction, fuel and power, and sewerage and water on the ground that they went beyond what was permitted by the transitional provision in the former Article 28(2), which likewise referred to the conditions in Article 17. With respect to the term 'clearly defined social reasons' the Court held that the identification of social reasons was in principle a matter of political choice for the Member States and could be the subject-matter of supervision at the Community level only in so far as, by distorting that concept, it led to measures which because of their effects and their true objectives lay outside its scope. The Court did not hold any of the zero rates to be illegal on the basis of that condition. It held in particular that the zero-rating of private housing in pursuance of the United Kingdom's social policy in housing matters, namely facilitating home ownership for the whole population, was legitimate. As regards the term 'for the benefit of the final consumer' the Court held that the final consumer was the person who acquired goods or services for personal use rather than an economic activity and hence bore the tax. However, in addition to supplies made to the final consumer, supplies made at a stage higher in the production or distribution chain which was sufficiently close to the final consumer to be of advantage to him were also to be considered to be for his benefit. Accordingly the Court held to be unlawful a number of zero rates applied

[38] Art. 28(2)(g). [39] [1988] ECR 3097 and 3127.

by the two Member States in respect of supplies to persons other than final consumers, in particular in the areas of construction and utilities. Only in respect of agricultural produce did it accept that zero-rating higher in the commercial chain had the requisite degree of proximity to benefit the final consumer.

Both subparagraphs (a) and (b) of Article 28(2) require that the reduced rates or zero rates should be 'in accordance with Community law'. That phrase would appear to make the separate reference to the conditions of Article 17 of the Second Directive in subparagraph (a) redundant, since a measure not conforming to those conditions would not be in accordance with Community law. Equally, the absence of such a reference in subparagraph (b) does not remove the need to comply with those conditions; moreover, a measure conforming to the conditions in Article 17 is presumably not 'in accordance with Community law' if it was not already in force at 31 December 1975.[40]

The rate of tax applicable to taxable transactions is normally that in force at the time of the chargeable event.[41] However, the rate applicable to supplies of goods or services is that in force at the moment when the tax becomes chargeable where there is a payment on account[42] or the Member State exercises the option[43] to make the tax chargeable at a date other than that of the chargeable event.[44] In the case of imports covered by the second and third subparagraphs of Article 10(3) the rate applicable is that in force at the time when the tax becomes chargeable.[45] Special arrangements are provided where there is a change in rates.[46]

The rate of tax applicable to the intra-Community acquisition of goods is that in force when the tax becomes chargeable.[47] The tax rate applicable is that applied to the supply of like goods within the territory of the country.[48] Subject to the above-mentioned options concerning works of art, collectors' items, and antiques, the rate applicable to imports of goods is that applicable to the supply of like goods within the territory of the country.[49]

PERSONS RESPONSIBLE FOR PAYMENT OF THE TAX

Article 21(1)[50] of the Sixth Directive specifies the persons who are responsible for paying tax under the internal system (i.e., on supplies and intra-Community acquisitions within the Community). The rules are as follows.

[40] It will be noted that in subpara. (b) the phrase 'in accordance with Community law' qualifies 'at 1 January 1991 . . . applied'. The condition therefore seems to be that the measures should have been lawfully applied at that date under the existing rules.

[41] Art. 12(1).

[42] Second subpara. of Art. 10(2).

[43] Third subpara. of Art. 10(2).

[44] Art. 12(1)(a).

[45] Art. 12(1)(b), replaced by Art. 1(6) of Directive 92/111.

[46] Art. 10(2).

[47] Art. 28e(3), as renumbered by Art. 1(17) of Directive 92/111.

[48] Ibid.

[49] Art. 12(5), replaced by Directive 94/5.

[50] As contained in the transitional provision in Art. 28g, as amended by Art. 1(19) of Directive 92/111.

Supplies of Goods and Services

The general rule is that the taxable person making the supply must pay the tax on it.[51]

Where the taxable supply of goods or services is made by a taxable person established abroad, Member States may make someone else liable for payment, for example a tax representative or the customer.[52] This rule applies, for example, where a taxable person established abroad is deemed, by virtue of Article 9(2)(a) or (c), to provide services within the territory of a Member State or is deemed to make supplies of goods there under the distance sales mechanism or the rules for assembled goods.

In the case of triangular transactions covered by Article 28c(E)(3),[53] responsibility for paying the tax is in principle shifted to the taxable person or non-taxable legal person to whom the supply of goods is made, provided that certain conditions are fulfilled.[54] However, Member States may derogate from that rule where the taxable person has appointed a tax representative within their territory.

Member States have a general option of making someone other than the supplier jointly and severally liable for the tax.[55]

Where a taxable person established abroad provides, within the territory of a Member State, services covered by Article 28b(C),(D), and (E) (i.e., services connected with intra-Community transport of goods and services of intermediaries) to persons identified for VAT purposes within that territory or services covered by Article 9(2)(e) (i.e., services taxed where the customer is established), responsibility for paying the tax is shifted to the customer by virtue of Article 21(1)(b). However, Member States retain the option of making the supplier jointly and severally liable.

Article 21(1)(c) contains a catch-all provision whereby any person who mentions VAT on an invoice or other document serving as an invoice is liable for payment.

Imports and Intra-Community Acquisitions

On importation, the person liable is the person designated or accepted as such by the importing state. For acquisitions, the normal rule is that the person effecting the acquisition is liable for payment. Where an acquisition is made by a person established abroad, Member States have a discretion to make someone else responsible for payment of tax, for example a tax representative. They may also provide that someone other than the person effecting the acquisition is jointly and severally liable for payment of the tax.[56]

[51] Art. 21(1)(a), first subpara.

[52] Art. 21(1)(a), second subpara.

[53] See above, p. 152 ff.

[54] Third subpara. of Art. 21(1)(a).

[55] Final subpara. of Art. 21(1)(a).

[56] Arts. 21(2) and 21(1)(d).

OBLIGATIONS OF THE PERSON LIABLE FOR PAYMENT

Prior to its amendment by Directives 91/680 and 92/111, Article 22 of the Sixth Directive laid down only basic requirements concerning invoicing, reporting, and payment obligations; the detailed rules were left largely to the Member States. The scope for fraud under the transitional arrangements, which abolished tax frontiers but retained intra-Community sales exemptions, necessitated the introduction at Community level of detailed accounting and reporting requirements to allow the national tax authorities to exercise administrative control on the basis of the internal VAT-reporting system. Under this heading we summarize the main requirements laid down by Article 22[57] and the principal features of the system of co-operation established between the tax authorities.

VAT Identification Numbers

Subject to certain exceptions, Member States are now required to issue VAT identification numbers to all taxable persons who within their territory make supplies of goods or services giving them the right of deduction.[58] They must also issue identification numbers to taxable persons who qualify for the flat-rate scheme for farmers, taxable persons with no right of deduction, and non-taxable legal persons, in so far as such persons do not qualify for the derogation from the acquisition mechanism laid down by the second subparagraph of Article 28a(1)(a) or do qualify but have opted for that mechanism.[59] Member States must also issue an identification number to any taxable person who, within their territory, effects intra-Community acquisitions for the purposes of economic activities carried out abroad.[60]

The identification numbers are to have a prefix in accordance with ISO International Standard 3166—alpha 2—by which the Member State of issue may be identified.[61]

Invoicing and Accounting Requirements

Taxable persons are required to issue an invoice or document serving as an invoice in respect of:

[57] Contained in the transitional provision in Art. 28h of the Directive, as inserted by Directive 91/680 and amended by Directive 92/111.

[58] Art. 22(1)(c), as amended by Art. 1(20) of Directive 92/111.

[59] Second indent of Art. 22(1)(c).

[60] Third indent of Art. 22(1)(c), inserted by Art. 1(20) of Directive 92/111. This amendment is explained in the Proposal for the latter Directive—COM(92)448 final (point 21).

[61] Art. 22(1)(d).

supplies of goods or services to another taxable person or a non-taxable legal person;
supplies of goods under the distance sales mechanism and exempt intra-Community supplies;
payments on account received before the supply is made.[62]

Certain requirements are laid down with regard to the content of invoices. Invoices must state clearly the price exclusive of tax and the relevant tax at each rate as well as any exemptions. In addition invoices relating to specified intra-Community transactions must indicate both the supplier's and the customer's VAT identification number.[63]

Member States are to lay down the criteria that determine whether a document may be considered an invoice.

In Joined Cases 123 and 334/87, *Jeunehomme and Others* v. *Belgian State*[64] the Court held that Article 22, as it stood prior to Directive 91/680, merely laid down minimum requirements and that Member States were entitled to require additional information to ensure the correct levying of the tax and permit supervision by the tax authorities, provided that such information was limited to what was necessary for that purpose. The particulars required should not, by reason of their number or technical nature, render the exercise of the right to deduction practically impossible or excessively difficult. That ruling, although given on the basis of the original text of Article 22, would seem to be unaffected by Directives 91/680 and 92/111.

Taxable persons are required to keep detailed accounts for inspection by the authorities, and must in particular keep registers of goods sent to another Member State for the purposes of contract work, the performance of work on the goods, or temporary use. They must also keep a register of all materials despatched to them from another Member State for the purpose of contract work.[65]

Reporting and Payment Requirements

Taxable persons are required to submit periodical VAT returns providing all the information needed to calculate the tax that has become chargeable and the deductions to be made. The return must also indicate for the period in question the total value of:

their exempted intra-Community supplies of goods;
their supplies of assembled goods and distance sales deemed to be made in other Member States;

[62] Art. 22(3)(a).

[63] Art. 22(3), as amended by Art. 1(20) of Directive 92/111. Specific requirements are laid down with respect to new means of transport and triangular transactions.

[64] [1988] ECR 4517.

[65] Art. 22(2).

their intra-Community acquisitions;
their supplies of assembled goods and distance sales where the goods have come from other Member States;
supplies in respect of which liability for payment of tax is shifted to them under the arrangements for triangular transactions.[66]

When submitting their returns taxable persons must normally pay the net amount of VAT due. Member States may, however, set a different date for payment or demand an interim payment. In Case C–10/92, *Balocchi*,[67] the Court held, in relation to the former Articles 10 and 22(4) and (5), that it was lawful for Member States to base interim payments on the previous year's turnover even though the latter might exceed the figure for the period covered by the interim payment, provided that the taxable person could substitute an estimate of the actual figure and was not penalized for underestimates made in good faith. However, the Court held to be unlawful legislation which required taxable persons making monthly payments to make by 20 December of each year an interim payment of 65 per cent of the amount due for December in the previous year or of the estimated amount due for that month in the current year. The Court reasoned that the slightest variation in turnover or error of estimation would lead to the payment of an amount in excess of the amount due at 20 December, which was contrary to the principle that tax should be demanded only in respect of transactions already carried out.

In addition to the periodical return, Member States may require taxable persons to submit a yearly statement, including in particular all the details given on the periodical returns.[68] The statement is to provide all the information necessary for any adjustments that need to be made. Although not specified, such adjustments might, for example, include adjustments to the taxable person's deduction entitlement under Article 20 or in respect of the private use of goods under Article 6(2)(a).

In relation to intra-Community transactions, each taxable person identified for VAT purposes must, in addition, submit a quarterly recapitulative statement of the acquirers identified for VAT purposes to whom he has made supplies of goods exempted under Article 28c(A)(a) (the general intra-Community supply exemption) and (d) (the exemption for deemed supplies comprising transfers of business goods) and of consignees identified for VAT purposes in contract work or triangular transactions.[69] The statement must indicate:

[66] Art. 22(4), as amended by Art. 1(20) of Directive 92/111.

[67] Judgment of 20 October 1993, *Balocchi* v. *Ministero delle Finanze dello Stato*, [1993] ECR I–5105.

[68] Art. 22(6)(a).

[69] First subpara. of Art. 22(6)(b), inserted by Art. 1(20) of Directive 92/111.

the VAT identification number under which he made supplies exempted under Article 28c(A)(a);
the customer's VAT identification number, indicating where appropriate that the supplies consisted in the delivery of contract work;
the total value of supplies for each customer;
for deemed supplies consisting in the transfer of business goods to another Member State exempted under Article 28c(A)(d), the taxable person's VAT identification numbers in the States of departure and arrival and the value of the goods transferred;
the amounts of any price adjustments under Article 11(C)(1);
in the case of goods sent by a taxable person to another Member State with a view to the supply to him in that state of contact work, a statement to that effect together with the VAT identification numbers of the taxable person and the supplier of the contract work;
in the case of triangular transactions, the VAT identification number under which the taxable person made the acquisition and the subsequent supply in the state of arrival, the VAT identification number of the consignee to whom the subsequent supply was made and for each consignee the total value of supplies made in the state of arrival.[70]

Member States may require the statements to be filed on a monthly basis or require that they give additional particulars.[71] The Council, acting on a proposal from the Commission, may authorise Member States to simplify the obligations concerning recapitulative statements in certain cases.[72]

In the case of exempted supplies of new means of transport made to purchasers not identified for VAT purposes or by persons treated as taxable persons by virtue of making occasional supplies of such goods, Member States must require the vendor to communicate all the information necessary for control purposes.[73]

Member States may require taxable persons effecting intra-Community acquisitions under Article 28a(1)(a) and (6) to submit monthly or less frequent statements giving details of such acquisitions.[74]

Other Provisions

Member States must take measures to ensure that non-taxable legal persons who are liable for tax in respect of intra-Community acquisitions under Article 28a(1)(a) comply with the above obligations relating to declaration and payment.[75] The same applies to persons who, by virtue of Article 21(1)(a) and

[70] Third to sixth subparas. of Art. 22(6)(b), as amended or inserted by Art. 1(20) of Directive 92/111.
[71] Art. 22(6)(c).
[72] Art. 22(12). See, as regards the UK, Decisions 92/621 (OJ 1992, L408) and 93/609 (OJ 1993, L292).
[73] Art. 22(6)(d).
[74] Art. 22(6)(e).
[75] Art. 22(10).

(b), are liable to pay the tax instead of a taxable person established abroad or are jointly and severally liable for the tax.[76]

Member States are to adopt the arrangements for declaration and subsequent payment in the case of intra-Community acquisitions of goods subject to excise duty and of new means of transport in so far as the acquisitions are covered by the specific acquisition provisions applicable to those goods.[77] They may in addition impose other obligations which they deem necessary for collection of the tax and prevention of evasion, subject to the requirement of equal treatment for domestic and intra-Community transactions and provided that they do not involve any formalities connected with the crossing of frontiers.[78] They may, on the other hand, release certain taxable persons from some or all obligations.[79]

Fiscal Control and Co-operation between Tax Authorities

The accounting and reporting obligations summarized above are an essential element in the system of fiscal control established by Regulation 218/92.[80] That Regulation, which supplements the provisions on mutual assistance in Directive 77/799,[81] provides for a common system for the exchange of information on intra-Community transactions. The Regulation requires Member States to maintain an electronic database for the purpose of storing the information collected from the recapitulative statements submitted by taxable persons within its territory. A Member State is therefore able to obtain quickly the value of the intra-Community supplies received by customers identified for VAT purposes within its territory and verify that the customer has declared the supplies as taxable acquisitions. A Member State may also request details of individual transactions, including invoice numbers, dates, and values. The above requirements concerning invoices and returns ensure the availability of such information.

Those requirements, which serve the purposes of fiscal control, were supplemented by extensive statistical requirements introduced by Council Regulation 3330/91.[82] The abolition of fiscal frontiers meant that intra-

[76] Art. 22(7).

[77] Art. 22(11), as amended by Directive 92/111. See further above at p. 144 (new means of transport) and p. 143 (goods subject to excise duty).

[78] Art. 22(8).

[79] Art. 22(9).

[80] Regulation 218/92 on administrative co-operation in the field of indirect taxation, OJ 1992, L24/1. For a detailed analysis of this regulation, see Terra, 'Removal of fiscal frontiers—Administrative cooperation in the field of indirect taxation (VAT)', *International VAT Monitor*, June 1992.

[81] OJ 1977, L336, 15, amended by Directive 79/1070, OJ 1979, L331/11, and Directive 92/12, OJ 1992, L76/1.

[82] Council Regulation 3330/91 of 7 November 1991 on the statistics relating to the trading of goods between Member States, OJ 1991, L316/1.

Community trade statistics could no longer be compiled on the basis of import documentation. The Regulation establishes a new system of collection known as 'intrastat' providing for the submission of detailed returns by consignors and consignees.[83]

THE VAT COMMITTEE

Article 29 of the Sixth Directive sets up an Advisory Committee on VAT consisting of representatives of the Member States and the Commission.[84] The Commission provides the chairman of the committee and the necessary secretarial support.[85] The functions of the Committee are to consider points subject to the consultation procedure laid down by certain provisions of the Directive as well as questions raised by members concerning the application of the VAT legislation.

The Sixth Directive requires Member States formally to consult the VAT Committee where they wish to exercise the options provided for by the following provisions:

Article 4(4) concerning single taxable persons;
Article 6(3) concerning self-supply of services;
Article 16(1) and (2) on exemptions linked to international traffic in goods;
Article 17(7) permitting the exclusion of all or some goods from the system of deductions;
Article 20(5) permitting non-application of the adjustment rules applicable to capital goods;
Article 24(1) concerning special schemes for small undertakings.

The agenda and minutes of the VAT Committee are considered confidential. The Commission is however permitted to outline the results of the Committee's work without stating the position of individual delegations.[86] The Commission's First and Second Reports contain many references to the opinions of the Committee, or a majority of the Committee, on particular points of interpretation. While the Committee is undoubtedly a useful forum for the exchange of views by national authorities on problems of practical implementation, its opinions do not have any legal status. Even their persuasive value in proceedings before the Court is undermined by the vague descriptions given of them and the absence of reasoning capable of judicial consideration.

[83] For a analysis of the intrastat requirements, see Terra, *International VAT Monitor*, April and June 1992 and February 1993.

[84] Art. 29(1).

[85] Art. 29(2).

[86] See Jim Somers, 'The EC VAT Committee', *International VAT Monitor*, March 1993, where the author discusses the workings of the Committee in detail and criticizes its reluctance to disclose its workings.

It has been argued, however, where the Sixth Directive requires a Member State formally to consult the VAT Committee, prior consultation is a condition of the legality of the national measures adopted.[87]

[87] See Terra and Kajus, *Guide*, 1202.

9

Special Schemes and Derogating Measures

SMALL UNDERTAKINGS

Article 24(1) of the Sixth Directive allows Member States, subject to consultation of the VAT Committee, to introduce simplified procedures for small undertakings such as flat-rate schemes for charging and collecting the tax, provided that they do not lead to a reduction thereof. Article 24(2) allows Member States temporarily to retain exemptions or graduated tax relief introduced under Article 14 of the Second Directive. Annual turnover limits for exemptions may be increased up to ECU 5,000, whereas the ceiling for graduated relief may not be increased, nor may the conditions for its grant be made more favourable. Member States not previously granting exemptions or graduated relief may grant exemption subject to a maximum turnover limit of ECU 5,000 and grant graduated relief to taxable persons whose annual turnover exceeds the ceiling fixed for exemption. Member States applying an exemption to taxable persons whose turnover is equal to or higher than ECU 5,000 are permitted to increase it in order to maintain its value in real terms. Taxable persons exempt from tax under Article 24(2) are entitled neither to deduct nor to charge tax.[1] Article 24(3)[2] and (4) lay down more detailed provisions with respect to the reliefs in Article 24(2). Taxable persons eligible for exemption from tax may opt either for the normal VAT scheme or for the simplified procedures under Article 24(1), in which case they are entitled to any graduated relief provided for under national legislation.[3]

As the Commission observed in its First Report, the foregoing rules produce rather curious anomalies. Member States which upon entry into force of the Sixth Directive applied an exemption ceiling of less than ECU 5,000 or which introduced an exemption were allowed to increase the ceiling up to that figure but were not authorized to exceed it, even to take account of inflation.[4] Member States which, like the United Kingdom and Ireland, already applied an exemption of more than ECU 5,000 upon entry into force of the

[1] Art. 24(5).

[2] Amended, with respect to supplies of new means of transport and supplies by foreign persons, by Art. 28i, now contained in Art. 1(21) of Directive 92/111.

[3] Art. 24(6).

[4] None the less the Commission noted that Germany, which applied an exemption of less than ECU 5,000 prior to entry into force of the 6th Directive, raised it to ECU 7,900 on 1 January 1980.

Directive were authorized to maintain its value in real terms.[5] The Commission noted similar anomalies with respect to graduated relief.

Article 24(8) instructed the Commission to report to the Council on the application of Article 24 at four-yearly intervals from 1 January 1982, if necessary making proposals for amendments. The Commission issued a report on 15 December 1983 summarizing the various exemptions, reliefs, and flat-rate schemes applied by the Member States.[6] Further to that report it submitted to the Council a Proposal for a Directive amending Article 24.[7] The Proposal required Member States to grant exemption to taxable persons with an annual turnover of less than ECU 10,000 and gave them the option of extending the turnover limit to ECU 35,000.[8] It also required Member States to introduce a common simplified scheme for businesses with a turnover of less than ECU 200,000.[9] Taxable persons eligible for exemption could opt for the normal or simplified scheme[10] and those eligible for the simplified scheme could opt for the normal scheme.[11] Member States were entitled to retain their existing exemption or simplified schemes provided that they were no less favourable to small and medium-sized businesses.

FLAT-RATE SCHEME FOR FARMERS

Article 25 of the Sixth Directive empowers Member States to lay down special rules for agricultural, forestry, and fisheries undertakings[12] (hereinafter 'flat-rate farmers'), intended to relieve them of the accounting, invoicing, declaration, and payment obligations incumbent on other taxable persons.[13] Originally devised solely for small farmers for whom the normal scheme of the Directive or the simplified procedures provided for in Article 24(1) would give rise to difficulties, the flat-rate scheme has been liberally applied by the Member States.[14] Article 25 replaces the normal deduction mechanism by flat-rate compensation for input VAT granted in proportion to the farmer's

[5] Both the UK and Ireland made full use of that power.

[6] COM(83)748 final.

[7] Proposal submitted on 9 October 1986, OJ 1986, C272/12, amended by a further proposal submitted on 4 November 1987, OJ 1987, C310/3.

[8] Proposed Art. 24(1).

[9] Proposed Art. 24(6), as amended by the Proposal of 24 November 1987.

[10] Proposed Art. 24(5).

[11] Proposed Art. 24(6a), inserted by the Proposal of 4 November 1987.

[12] As defined by the Member State concerned within the framework of the production activities listed in Annex A to the Directive: Art. 25(2).

[13] See Explanatory Memorandum accompanying Proposal for the 6th Directive.

[14] Commission's 1st Report, 19–20. The Commission considered that an output or turnover ceiling should be introduced.

outputs. The flat-rate percentages, which are fixed by the Member States,[15] are applied by virtue of Article 25(5)[16] to the VAT-exclusive price of:

supplies of agricultural products[17] and services[18] by the flat-rate farmer to taxable persons (wherever established) other than those eligible within the territory of the country for the flat-rate scheme;
exempt intra-Community supplies of agricultural products to non-taxable legal persons not excluded from the intra-Community acquisition mechanism under the second subparagraph of Article 28a(1)(a).[19]

In the case of supplies covered by Article 25(5), the flat-rate compensation, which excludes all other forms of deduction, is paid either by the customer or by the public authorities, at the discretion of the Member State concerned. Where the Member State opts for payment by the customer, taxable customers may deduct the flat-rate compensation as input tax. In the case of taxable persons or non-taxable legal persons[20] who make intra-Community acquisitions of products from flat-rate farmers, Member States are to refund the flat-rate compensation to the foreign customer according to a method of their choice, and in particular may apply Article 17(4) of the Directive, concerning refunds of tax to taxable persons not established in the territory of the country.[21] Subject to certain conditions Member States are also to provide for refunds in respect of exempt supplies of agricultural products to taxable purchasers established outside the Community and supplies of agricultural services to taxable customers established in other Member States or outside the Community.[22]

In the case of supplies other than those covered by Article 25(5), in particular supplies to individuals, the flat-rate compensation is deemed to be paid by the purchaser or customer[23]; whether in such cases the farmer can actually raise his prices to cover the flat-rate percentage depends of course on market conditions.

[15] Art. 25(3). The percentages are to be based on macro-economic statistics for flat-rate farmers in the preceding three years and are not to be used to obtain for flat-rate farmers refunds greater than the VAT charged on inputs. Member States may fix varying compensation percentages for forestry, for the different sub-divisions of agriculture and for fisheries. See also the judgment in Case 3/86, *Commission* v. *Italy* [1988] ECR 3369.

[16] Now contained in the transitional provision in Art. 28j(2) of the 6th Directive, inserted by Directive 91/680.

[17] Defined as goods produced by an agricultural, forestry, or fisheries undertaking as a result of the activities listed in Annex A to the Directive: Art. 25(2).

[18] Defined as services as set out in Annex B supplied by the flat-rate farmer using his work force and/or the equipment normally available in his undertaking: Art. 25(2).

[19] Above, p. 142.

[20] Not qualifying for the derogation in the second subpara. of Art. 28a(1)(a).

[21] Above, p. 192.

[22] Art. 25(6), now contained in the transitional provision in Art. 28j(2) of the 6th Directive, inserted by Directive 91/680.

[23] Art. 25(8).

Member States applying the flat-rate scheme must ensure that supplies falling within the scope of the distance sales mechanism in Article 28b(B)(1)[24] are treated in the same way regardless of whether they are made by flat-rate farmers or by a normal taxable person.[25] Member States may release flat-rate farmers from the administrative obligations imposed on taxable persons by Article 22.[26] If they do so, however, they are obliged to take the measures necessary for the correct application of the transitional arrangements for the taxation of intra-Community transactions.[27] Member States may exclude from the flat-rate scheme certain categories of farmers and farmers for whom the normal scheme or the simplified scheme in Article 24(1) would not give rise to administrative difficulties.[28] Flat-rate farmers always have the right to opt for the application of the normal scheme or, where applicable, for the simplified scheme provided for in Article 24(1).[29] Member States applying the flat-rate scheme must fix the uniform basis of assessment for the purposes of own resources using the common method of calculation in Annex C to the Directive.[30]

TRAVEL AGENTS

Article 26 of the Sixth Directive makes special arrangements for travel agents or tour operators who deal with customers in their own name[31] and use the supplies and services of other taxable persons in the provision of travel facilities. The legislative history of the provision, which did not appear in the Commission's Proposal, provides no guidance regarding the thinking behind it. It appears, however, to be intended to resolve the practical difficulties and complexities which would result under the general rules of the Directive from the use and provision by the travel agent of services in different Member States[32]; at the same time it ensures that tax accrues to the Member State where the travel services are performed. All transactions performed by the travel agent in respect of a journey are treated as a single service supplied by the travel agent to the traveller at the place where the agent is established, and the charge to tax is based on the agent's margin, i.e., the difference between the price paid by the traveller (exclusive of VAT) and the actual cost to the agent of supplies and services provided by other taxable persons where those transactions are for the direct benefit of the traveller. The tax on such

[24] Above, p. 139.
[25] Art. 25(9), inserted by the transitional provision in Art. 28j(3).
[26] Art. 22(4).
[27] Second subpara. of Art. 25(4), contained in Art. 28j inserted by Directive 91/680.
[28] Art. 25(9).
[29] Art. 25(10).
[30] Art. 25(12).
[31] Travel agents acting as intermediaries and accounting for tax in accordance with Art. 11A(3)(c) are excluded from the scope of the special arrangements.
[32] See Case C–163/91, *Van Ginkel BV* v. *Inspecteur der Omzetbelasting, Utrecht* [1992] ECR I–5723, paras. 13 and 14.

transactions is non-deductible by (or non-refundable to) the agent. The effect of these arrangements is that the travel agent acts as a collection point for the (mainly foreign) tax charged by the various suppliers to whom he entrusts elements of the travel package. He bears definitively the tax chargeable on their services in the various Member States concerned and incorporates it as hidden tax in the total price of the travel package. At the same time he invoices to the customer the tax on his own margin payable in the Member State in which he is established.

In keeping with the general principle underlying the Directive, the arrangements provide for taxation of services performed within the Community while allowing exemption with refund of input tax in respect of services performed outside the Community. Thus, where the transactions entrusted by the travel agent to other taxable persons are performed outside the Community, his service is treated as an exempted intermediary service under Article 15(4) of the Directive. Where the transactions are performed both inside and outside the Community, only that part of the travel agent's service relating to transactions outside the Community is exempt.

In its Second Report[33] the Commission took the view that an agent was to be regarded as acting in his own name where the traveller dealt solely with the agent and the latter made out the bill or invoice in his own name, regardless of who ultimately assumed the risk of the contract being improperly executed.

In *Van Ginkel BV*[34] the Court held that the fact that a travel agent merely provided accommodation for the traveller, who arranged his own transport, did not remove the service from the scope of Article 26. Travel agents offered a variety of formulas to fit in with the needs of customers, and the exclusion of services on the ground that only accommodation was offered would lead to complex rules which would depend on the constituent elements of the service offered to the particular traveller.[35]

The supplies received by a travel agent taken into account for the purpose of calculating the margin and not giving rise to deduction or refund are those which are 'for the direct benefit of the traveller'. This includes items such as transport, hotel costs, cost of trips, and so forth but presumably excludes indirect costs such as the travel agent's general overheads.

The transitional provision in Article 28(3)(a), in conjunction with Annex E, Point 15, allows Member States to continue to tax the services of travel agents referred to in Article 26, and those of travel agents acting in the name and on the account of the traveller, for journeys outside the Community. Article 28(3)(b), in conjunction with Annex F, Point 27, allows Member States

[33] At 42.

[34] Above, note 32.

[35] The decision is in accordance with the conclusion of the VAT Committee that it is sufficient, for the operation of Art. 26, that the travel agent makes use of the services of one other taxable person: see the Commission's 2nd Report 43.

to continue to exempt such services in respect of journeys within the Community.[36]

SECOND-HAND GOODS, WORKS OF ART, ANTIQUES, AND COLLECTORS' ITEMS

In the Proposal for the Sixth Directive the Commission recognized the need for special rules on second-hand goods. Goods which leave commercial channels as the result of being supplied to a final consumer bear tax definitively. Where the final consumer subsequently resells the goods to a taxable person (a dealer for example), the latter is not entitled to deduct the VAT remaining in their value. None the less when the taxable person resells the goods he is liable to account for tax in full on the goods. The application of the normal rules thus gives rise to double taxation, discouraging the use of commercial channels for the resale of goods. The Commission proposed that, by way of derogation from the normal rules of the Directive, taxable persons purchasing goods for resale should be allowed to deduct a certain amount deemed to correspond to input tax.[37] At the instigation of the European Parliament the proposed arrangements were extended to works of art, antiques, and collectors' items. The proposed scheme was not however adopted by the Council. Instead Article 32 of the Sixth Directive merely envisaged the adoption, before 31 December 1977, of a Community system of taxation to be applied to such goods and provided that, pending the entry into force of the Community system, Member States applying special schemes to such items were entitled to retain them.[38]

[36] See however the judgment in Case C–74/91, *Commission* v. *Germany* [1992] ECR I–5437, in which it was held that Annex F, Point 27, applied solely to the single service provided by the travel agent and not the various constituent services provided by other taxable persons. The Court held further that, since Germany had opted for taxation under the special scheme provided for in Art. 26, it was not entitled to rely on the transitional exemption for passenger transport in Annex F, Point 17, to exclude certain intra-Community transport services from the taxable amount for the services of travel agents under Art. 26.

[37] See Art. 26 of the Proposal. See also the Explanatory Memorandum.

[38] See in this regard Case 165/88, *ORO Amsterdam Beheer BV and Concerto* v. *Inspecteur der Omzetbelasting* [1989] ECR 4081, where the Court held that pending the introduction of a Community system Member States were under no obligation to make special arrangements to avoid double taxation of second-hand goods. See also Case 17/84, *Commission* v *Ireland* [1985] ECR 2375, in which the Commission contended that Ireland could not rely on Art. 32 to retain its rules on the trading in of second-hand goods. The Irish arrangements led in fact to the same result (in terms of total tax payable to the State and resale price of the trade-in) as the methods contemplated by the Commission in its Proposal for a 7th Directive; however, the Commission objected that they entailed a reduction of the taxable amount on the sale of the new car contrary to Art. ll of the 6th Directive. The Court dismissed the Commission's application, holding that the object and effect of the Irish system was to offset the residual part of the VAT already borne by the second-hand goods traded in, so that on resale the normal VAT rules could be applied to those goods. The Irish system therefore fell within Art. 32 and did not infringe Art. 11. See also the judgment in the parallel case brought against the Netherlands (Case 16/84 [1985] ECR 2355).

Pursuant to Article 32 the Commission submitted to the Council on 11 January 1978 a Proposal for a Seventh Directive.[39] Following disagreement in the Council concerning both the scope and terms of the special arrangements the Commission withdrew the Proposal. The Commission published a further Proposal for a directive amending the Sixth Directive in 1988[40] and in revised form in early 1989.[41] The proposal was finally adopted on 14 February 1994 as Directive 94/5.[42]

The Directive, which inserts a new Article 26a into the Sixth Directive, applies to works of art,[43] collectors' items,[44] antiques,[45] and second-hand goods.[46] Under Article 26a(B) special arrangements apply to the supply of such goods by taxable dealers[47] where they have been supplied to him within the Community by a non-taxable person, by another taxable person in so far as the supply was exempt under Article 13(B)(c)[48] or qualified for exemption under Article 24 (small undertakings) and involved capital assets or by another taxable dealer covered by the special arrangements.[49] The common feature of all of those cases is that the dealer is unable to deduct VAT on the acquisition of the goods. The Directive does not use the technique of an input tax deduction originally proposed by the Commission; instead it limits the taxable amount to the dealer's profit margin, i.e., the difference between his selling and purchase prices, less the VAT relating to the margin.[50] Taxable persons may opt to extend the arrangements to supplies of works of art, collectors' items, or antiques which they have imported themselves, works of art supplied to them by their creators or their successors in title, and works of art supplied to them by a taxable person other than a taxable dealer where the supply was subject to the reduced rate under Article 12(3)(c). Member States are to determine the detailed rules for exercising this option, which must in any event cover a period equal to at least two calendar years. For supplies of works of art, collectors' items, or antiques imported by the taxable dealer himself, the purchase price used for calculating the margin is the taxable amount on importation, plus the import VAT paid.[51]

Taxable persons purchasing goods from a taxable dealer under the special arrangements are not entitled to a deduction,[52] and taxable dealers are not permitted to mention separately the VAT paid on the margin on their invoices for such goods.[53] Taxable dealers are not entitled to deduct the VAT

[39] OJ 1978, C26, amended on 14 May 1979, OJ 1979, C136.

[40] COM(88)846.

[41] 11 January 1989, OJ 1989, C76/10.

[42] Council Directive 94/5 supplementing the common system of VAT and amending Directive 77/388—special arrangements applicable to second-hand goods, works of art, collectors' items, and antiques, OJ 1994, L60/16.

[43] As defined in Art. 26a(A)(a), in conjunction with Annex I(a).

[44] Defined in Annex I(b).

[45] Defined in Annex I(c).

[46] Defined in Art. 26A(d).

[47] Defined in Art. 26a(A)(e).

[48] Above, p. 185.

[49] Art. 26a(B)(2).

[50] Art. 26a(B)(3).

[51] Art. 26a(B)(4).

[52] Art. 26a(B)(6).

[53] Art. 26a(B)(9).

which they have paid on works of art, collectors' items, or antiques imported by them, the VAT on works of art supplied to them by their creators or their successors in title, or the VAT on works of art supplied to them by a taxable person other than a taxable dealer.[54] A taxable dealer may, however, choose to apply the normal arrangements to any supply, in which case he may deduct the VAT incurred on the transactions described above. The right of deduction arises at the moment when the tax on the supply covered by the option becomes chargeable.[55] Where a taxable dealer applies both the normal and the special arrangements, he must account for the two sets of transactions separately.

Supplies of goods covered by the special arrangements made under the conditions laid down in Article 15 are exempt.[56]

Article 26a(C) lays down a set of rules which Member States may apply, in derogation from the arrangements in Article 26a(B), to sales by public auction. In particular, the taxable amount is the total amount invoiced to the purchaser by the organizer (including (i) the auction price; (ii) taxes, dues, levies, and charges; and (iii) incidental expenses such as commission, packing, transport, and insurance costs) less (i) the net amount paid by the organizer to his principal; and (ii) the VAT due by the organizer in respect of the supply. The net amount paid to the principal is equal to the difference between the auction price and the organizer's commission.

The special arrangements apply in the same way regardless of whether the taxable dealer and his supplier are in the same or in different Member States. Article 26a(D) prevents any overlap between the special arrangements and the transitional arrangements for intra-Community trade. Goods supplied subject to the special arrangements are excluded from taxation under the intra-Community acquisition mechanism in Article 28a(1)(a).[57] The intra-Community exemptions in Article 28c(A) and the distance sales mechanism in Article 28b(B) are also inapplicable.[58] It may be noted that intra-Community supplies of new[59] means of transport under the conditions laid down in Article 28c(A) are excluded from the special arrangements.[60]

Directive 94/5 also contains a number of transitional provisions. In particular Article 28o(1) allows Member States which on 31 December 1992[61] applied special arrangements other than those provided for in Article 26a(B) to supplies of second-hand means of transport effected by taxable dealers to continue to apply those arrangements during the period referred to in Article 28l,[62] subject

[54] Art. 26a(B)(7). [55] Art. 26a(B)(11). [56] Art. 26a(B)(5).
[57] Art. 26a(D)(b). [58] Art. 26a(D)(c).
[59] For the purposes of the transitional arrangements 'new means of transport' cover nearly new, and hence certain second-hand, goods.
[60] Art. 26a(D)(a).
[61] In addition, Denmark is permitted to introduce such arrangements: Art. 28o(2).
[62] Above, p. 136.

to their being adjusted to comply with a number of conditions. Article 28o(4) contains transitional provisions applicable solely to Germany.

The Directive gives Member States the general power to take measures concerning the right of deduction in order to prevent taxable dealers from enjoying unjustified advantages or sustaining unjustified loss.[63] In addition, the Council may, on a proposal from the Commission, authorize a Member State to introduce particular measures for the purpose of combatting fraud by providing that the tax due under the special arrangements for taxing the profit margin cannot be less than the amount of tax which would be due if the margin were equal to a certain percentage of the selling price, fixed by reference to the normal profit margins of economic operators in the sector concerned.

SIMPLIFICATION AND ANTI-AVOIDANCE MEASURES

Article 27(1) of the Sixth Directive allows the Council, acting unanimously on a proposal from the Commission, to authorize any Member State to introduce derogating provisions in order to simplify the procedure for charging the tax or to prevent certain types of tax evasion or avoidance. Measures intended to simplify the procedure for charging the tax, except to a negligible extent, may not affect the amount of tax due at the final consumption stage. Article 27(2) to (4) lays down the procedure by which such authorization is granted. Following notification of the Commission, which in turn is responsible for notifying the other Member States, authorization is deemed to have been granted by the Council unless the Commission or a Member State requests the Council to raise the matter within two months of notification of the Member States. Many individual authorizations of this kind have been granted over the years. Initially they were not published in the Official Journal. However, since the fifth such authorization[64] a formal decision of the Council has been published in the interests of transparency. It is unclear whether a Member State may rely against a taxable person on a rule based on an unpublished authorization, although arguably it would be precluded from doing so by the principle of legal certainty.[65]

Article 27(5) allowed Member States which on 1 January 1977 applied special measures of the type referred to in Article 27(1) to retain them providing that they notified them to the Commission before 1 January 1978 and that where such derogations were designed to simplify the procedure for charging the tax they conformed with the abovementioned requirement in Article 27(1). The special measures notified to the Commission are listed as Annex I to the Commission's First Report.

[63] Art. 2.

[64] OJ 1983, L181/25.

[65] This question was put to the Court in Case C-340/92, *Finanzamt Mainz* v. *Boesenberg*, but the case was subsequently withdrawn. The UK derogations are published in the Orange Tax Handbook, issued annually by Butterworths, London.

In Case C–97/90, *Lennartz*[66] Advocate General Jacobs explained the rationale of Article 27(1) in the following terms:

The general rules of the Sixth Directive . . . are intended to reconcile the interests of administrative simplicity with the objectives of the common VAT system, in particular that of neutrality. It would clearly have been difficult, if not impossible, to envisage all the technical difficulties or forms of avoidance or evasion which the tax authorities throughout the Community might encounter. Moreover, a Community approach may not be appropriate if the commercial practice in question is producing significant distortions in one Member State only. It was therefore appropriate to allow Member States to seek individual authorization for measures dealing with particular problems.[67]

A taxable person may resist the application of a national measure purportedly adopted under Article 27 if a Member State fails to observe the procedural requirements of Article 27[68] or the terms of the authorization granted or if the authorization itself infringes the procedural or substantive requirements of Article 27.

Article 27 was first considered by the Court in Case 324/82, *Commission* v. *Belgium*,[69] where it held in relation to Article 27(5):

the measures notified must be of such a nature as to prevent tax evasion or avoidance and . . . in principle they may not derogate from the basis for charging VAT laid down in Article 11, except within the limits strictly necessary for achieving that aim.[70]

The Court held that, although Article 27 could in some circumstances provide the basis for the application of standard amounts, Belgium had gone beyond what was necessary by systematically taxing new cars on the basis of their catalogue prices.

In Case 5/84, *Direct Cosmetics* v. *Commissioners of Customs and Excise*[71] the Court held that an amendment to an anti-avoidance measure retained by the United Kingdom under Article 27(5), consisting in the deletion of the condition that the measure must be necessary 'for the protection of the revenue', constituted a 'special measure' requiring authorization under Article 27(1). The Court noted that the VAT Tribunal had found that the amendment was one of substance; moreover, the deletion of the words in question, which were the equivalent of the words 'to prevent certain types of tax evasion or avoidance' in Article 27(1), severed any apparent link with the Directive, so that notification was necessary to allow the legality of the new measure to be appraised. The United Kingdom subsequently notified and obtained authorization for the

[66] *Lennartz* v. *Finanzamt München III* [1991] ECR I–3795, at para. 71 ff.

[67] The Advocate General took the view that a measure subjecting the right of deduction to a threshold of 10% business use did not on the face of it seem unreasonable or disproportionate to the aims in view.

[68] See in particular para. 37 of the first *Direct Cosmetics* case: note 71, below.

[69] [1984] ECR 1861.

[70] Para. 29.

[71] [1985] ECR 617.

amended provision under Article 27(1). The measure[72] allowed Customs and Excise to issue directions to 'direct sales' companies selling goods to retail customers through non-taxable agents, requiring them account for tax not on the wholesale price to the agent but on the open-market value on a sale by retail. In Joined Cases 138 and 139/86, the second *Direct Cosmetics* case,[73] it was argued that such legislation went beyond the scope of Article 27(1) because it caught taxable persons who adopted such sales methods for commercial reasons and not just to avoid tax. However, the Court held that, unlike tax evasion, which involved an element of intent, intent to avoid tax on the part of the taxpayer was not an essential element of tax avoidance. Its ruling was based on a teleological interpretation of the Directive:

> That interpretation is in conformity with the principle governing the system of Value Added Tax according to which the factors which may lead to distortions of competition at national and Community level are to be eliminated and a tax which is as neutral as possible and covers all the stages of production and distribution is to be imposed. . . . It follows that the system of Value Added Tax is concerned principally with objective effects, whatever the intentions of the taxable person may be.[74]

[72] Para. 3 of Sched. 4 to the Value Added Tax Act 1983, authorized by Council Decision 85/369, OJ 1985, L199/60. The authorization was later removed by Council Decision 89/534, OJ 1989, L280/54.

[73] *Direct Cosmetics Ltd and Laughtons Photographs Ltd* v. *Commissioners of Customs and Excise* [1988] ECR 3937.

[74] Para. 23 of the judgment. The Court also rejected a number of other arguments alleging procedural and substantive defects in the national measure and the authorization granted.

10

Excise Duties and Similar Taxes

Excise duties are most frequently taxes on the production or sale of specific goods, often luxury or non-essential goods. They may be levied on the value of the goods (*ad valorem* duties) or—more usually—on the basis of some other characteristic, such as volume or weight (specific duties). The special taxes on the purchase of motor cars in Denmark or the Netherlands may be classed as excise duties. Excise duties represent one of the most ancient forms of taxation, perhaps because of the relative ease of assessment and collection. In the past they have been levied on a great variety of products, but the main modern excise duties are those on alcoholic drinks, tobacco products, motor fuels, and motor vehicles.

Excise duties may also be levied on the use of certain goods or on the provision of certain services. In the United Kingdom these are often called excise licence duties in order to distinguish them from excise duties in the usual sense; examples are road tax and television licences. With the exception of road tax on commercial vehicles, most such taxes are of little importance from the point of view of economic integration since they have little cross-border impact or effect on the competitive situation of businesses.

High levels of excise duties discourage sales and hence imports of the product concerned; differences in the level of taxation of substitutable products or in the way in which they are taxed distort competition between them. The need for border tax adjustments where states apply different systems and rates of tax requires the retention of tax frontiers, making importation and exportation more complicated and expensive. Accordingly, large variations in duties are inconsistent with a single market. However, differences in rates reflect different choices by governments; excise duties are used by some governments not only as a means of gathering revenue but also to influence their citizens' behaviour, often on grounds of health or energy policy. Harmonization is thus a difficult and sensitive matter. Moreover, there can be no harmonization or indeed comparison of rates without harmonization of the structures of taxation—the manner in which goods are classified and defined for tax purposes, the basis of assessment, and the type of tax. Harmonization of structures is important in itself, since differences in tax structures have significant effects on conditions of competition.

The six original Member States levied excise duties on a variety of products, including matches, sewing thread, playing cards, and sugar, and the rates and bases of taxation were equally diverse. Many of these taxes were historical curiosities and raised insignificant amounts of revenue; indeed, some Member States were beginning to rationalize their systems even before the Community began to work towards harmonization. The move to restrict excise duties to a small core group of products was thus facilitated.

As was seen in Chapter 2, the harmonization of excise duties, along with other indirect taxes on goods, was given high priority at an early stage in the development of the Community. Initial proposals for the harmonization of duties on tobacco and liquid hydrocarbon fuels were followed in 1972 by a comprehensive package comprising a series of draft directives on alcoholic drinks and on the coverage of excise duties in general (all based on Article 99 of the Treaty and submitted as part of the first, abortive programme of measures intended to achieve Economic and Monetary Union following the Werner Report). With the partial exception of tobacco, none of those proposals met with any success in the Council; the Member States were unable to agree to substantial changes in their existing systems.[1] However, although the 1972 package, in particular the proposal for a framework directive, remained a dead letter for some twenty years, the efforts of the Member States to improve the coherence and neutrality of their own systems resulted in the abolition of the more obscure and unproductive duties and thus a degree of *de facto* harmonization.

The harmonization of excise duties was one of the main objectives of the 1985 White Paper on the completion of the single market, and new packages of proposals on rates (1987) and structures (1990) were put forward. The 1987 rates package called for harmonized rates and was criticized for its inflexibility, in view of the great differences in existing rates and the varying importance of excise duties for national treasuries. A second package put forward in 1989 proposed a set of minimum and target rates. The proposals were limited in their scope to what was thought to be necessary for the elimination of tax frontiers; even so, the measures ultimately adopted by the Council were still less ambitious, so that considerable divergence and potential discrimination remains.

GENERAL PROVISIONS

The 1972 draft framework directive on excise duties and indirect taxes other than Value Added Tax levied directly or indirectly on the consumption of products[2] envisaged the progressive harmonization of excise duties and taxes

[1] Beginning in 1968, however, several measures were adopted providing tax and duty exemptions for travellers and for small non-commercial consignments. In so far as relations between Member States are concerned these provisions are now of purely historical interest following the passage of the 1992 measures, and it is not proposed to discuss them.

[2] OJ 1972, C43/23; Bull. Supp. 3–72, 6.

on goods. With effect from 1 January 1974 the Member States were to apply a harmonized system of excise duties to mineral oils (petroleum products), manufactured tobacco, alcohol, beer, and wine. All other duties and taxes on goods other than turnover tax were to be discontinued, with the exception of those which did not require border controls or tax adjustments. Any proposed changes in the rates of existing duties were to be subject to a consultation procedure. The Council was to retain the power to introduce harmonized taxes on other products. A further draft decision[3] called for the establishment of an excise committee which was to be consulted by the Commission before the adoption of implementing measures in relation to the harmonization of excise duties.

In the wake of the 1985 White Paper, the Commission put forward a new proposal for a framework directive in 1990, along with its proposals on structures of duty on the main dutiable products;[4] it was intended in particular to permit the abolition of frontier controls on the completion of the Single Market. The proposal was adopted, with the addition of some details, as Council Directive 92/12 on the general arrangements for products subject to excise duty and on the holding, movement, and monitoring of such products.[5] The 'products subject to excise duty' referred to in the title are mineral oils, alcoholic beverages, and manufactured tobacco. Member States may levy indirect taxes other than VAT on other products only if these taxes give rise to no need for frontier tax adjustments. Products become subject to duty on their manufacture or their importation into the Community; duty becomes chargeable on their release for consumption. Where goods which have already been released for consumption are then held for commercial purposes in another Member State they are subject to duty in the second Member State, and the duty paid in the first state is to be refunded (a destination system of taxation is thus retained). However, products acquired by individuals for their own use are taxed in the country of purchase, and no duty is chargeable on their subsequent importation into another Member State; fairly generous minimum guide levels are laid down for the quantities of goods which may be regarded as being intended for private use. Goods dispatched by mail order or similar means to a consumer in another Member State are subject to duty in the state of destination; the vendor may be required to appoint a tax representative in that state.

Dutiable products are to be produced, processed, and held in a system of authorized tax warehouses until their release for consumption. This system, and the concomitant suspension of duty, extends to the stage of receipt of such goods by traders, so that products can be dispatched under suspension of duty from a warehouse in one Member State to a trader in another.

[3] Proposal for a Council Decision establishing a Committee on Excise Duties, OJ 1972, C43/42; Bull. Supp. 3–72, 80.

[4] OJ 1990, C322/1.

[5] OJ 1992, L76/1.

Authorized warehouse-keepers may appoint tax representatives in other Member States. Goods are moved between states on the basis of an administrative or commercial document, at the option of the consignor. The document is in quadruplicate at least: one copy to be retained by the consignor, one for the consignee, one for the tax authorities of the state of destination, and one to be returned to the consignor for discharge; the authorities of the state of departure may require a further copy. Member States retain considerable liberty in determining the necessary verification measures, including the possible use of tax labels. Uniform exemptions are provided for, and the relevant provisions of the directives on imports of goods by individuals are repealed.[6] A Committee on Excise Duties is established, composed of representatives of the Member States, to assist in the drafting of implementing measures and generally to examine the application of the excise duty rules. The mutual assistance provisions of Directive 77/799[7] are extended to the harmonized excise duties. Despite the anachronism of their retention in a single market, duty-free sales in intra-Community travel at airports and ports (and at the terminals of the Channel tunnel) may be continued until 30 June 1999.

Some amendments to the new system, mainly of a technical nature, were made by Directive 92/108.[8] Provision was made in particular for computerized procedures and for transit arrangements where goods are shipped between Member States through EFTA countries. Claims for the recovery of excise duties on tobacco, alcohol, and petroleum products were also brought within the scope of the mutual assistance provisions of Directive 76/308.[9]

TOBACCO

The 1967 proposal for a regulation and a resolution on excise duties applicable to manufactured tobacco[10] was part of a package including measures on

[6] That is to say, Directive 74/651 of 19 December 1974 on the tax reliefs to be allowed on the importation of goods in small consignments of a non-commercial character within the Community, OJ 1974, L354/57; Directive 83/183 of 28 March 1983 on tax exemptions applicable to permanent imports from a Member State of the personal property of individuals, OJ 1983, L105/64; Directive 68/297 of 19 July 1968 on the standardization of provisions regarding the duty-free admission of fuel contained in the fuel tanks of commercial motor vehicles, OJ 1968, L175/15 (English Spec. Ed. 1968 (II), 313); and, in so far as it applies to movements between Member States, Directive 69/169 of 28 May 1969 on the harmonization of provisions laid down by law, regulation, or administrative action relating to exemption from turnover tax and excise duty on imports in international travel, JO 1969, L133/6 (English Spec. Ed. 1969 (I), 232).

[7] OJ 1977, L336/15, as amended by Directive 79/1070, OJ 1979, L331/8.

[8] Council Directive 92/108 of 14 December 1992 amending Directive 92/12 on the general arrangements for products subject to excise duty and on the holding, movement and monitoring of such products and amending Directive 92/81, OJ 1992, L390/124.

[9] OJ 1976, L73/18, as amended by Directive 79/1071, OJ 1979, L331/10.

[10] OJ 1967, 198/12.

the establishment of a common organization of the market in raw tobacco and the regulation of state tobacco monopolies. This combination in itself gives some indication of the complexity of the problem: it was necessary not only to consider purely fiscal problems concerning the level of rates and the amount of revenue gathered by duties on tobacco in each Member State but also to reconcile the conflicting interests of the states which were producers of tobacco and those which were not. Broadly speaking, the tobacco-producing states in the south of the Community produced dark tobacco of relatively low quality; their duties on cigarettes were proportional, so that cheaper brands containing home-produced tobacco were taxed less heavily than more expensive brands made from light Virginia tobacco, mainly imported from the United States. The other Member States applied mainly specific taxation, that is to say, duties based on the number of cigarettes or quantity of tobacco. In the former states the tax-induced price differential at the level of the consumer between cheaper and more expensive brands was thus much wider than in the latter, giving cigarettes made from home-grown tobacco a competitive advantage. There was thus a fundamental obstacle to harmonization of the tax structure, and this conflict between specific and proportional tax has not been resolved.

The draft regulation sought to eliminate distortions of competition and obstacles to trade caused by national excise duties; it called for a uniform structure of proportional duties calculated on the retail price, with an element of degressivity on higher-priced products. There was to be a standard basic amount of tax for all cigarettes whose price was under a certain minimum. All that the Council could agree upon initially was a resolution calling for the adoption of a directive on the introduction in stages of a harmonized system of excise duties on manufactured tobacco.[11] In the case of cigarettes, the system was to involve a combination of proportional and specific taxation, and in the final stage of harmonization there was to be a fixed relationship between the proportional and specific elements such as to allow the range of retail prices to reflect fairly the range of manufacturers' prices. How that was to be done was naturally left unsaid.

In 1970 the Commission submitted an amended proposal for a directive, corresponding to the system outlined in the Council Resolution. It provided for harmonization in stages, the move from one stage to the next to be decided upon by the Council in the light of the experience of Member States with each stage. During the first stage cigarettes were to be subject to proportional and specific duty; the specific duty was to be between 5 and 75 per cent of the aggregate excise duty on the most popular price class. This

[11] Council Resolution of 21 April 1970 on taxes other than turnover taxes on the consumption of manufactured tobacco, OJ 1970, C50/1 (English Spec. Ed., Second Series (IX), 35).

proposal was adopted with little change by the Council in December 1972, with the first stage to run from 1 July 1973 to 30 June 1975.[12]

A second directive defining the various groups of manufactured tobacco other than cigarettes was adopted in December 1978.[13] Meanwhile the first stage was extended several times because of the inability of the Council to agree on the ratio between proportional and specific taxation on cigarettes; it ended on 30 June 1978. In the second stage, originally intended to run from 1 July 1978 to 31 December 1980, the specific duty on cigarettes was to be between 5 and 55 per cent of the aggregate amount of excise duty and turnover tax on the most popular price category.[14] The United Kingdom was permitted for a limited period to levy additional duty on cigarettes of a high tar content, in accordance with its health policy.

Like the first, the second stage was extended several times, ultimately to run indefinitely.[15] The Commission initially submitted a proposal for a third stage running from 1 January 1981 to 31 December 1986 during which the possible range of specific duties would gradually be narrowed further (to between 10 and 35 per cent of aggregate tax),[16] with a view to arriving in a final stage at a fixed proportion of 20 per cent, but the proposal found no agreement in the Council.

In the 1987 package the Commission submitted a new proposal on the harmonization of rates, intended to come into effect by 1 January 1993.[17] It proposed a uniform specific excise duty (initially ECU 19.5 per 1,000 cigarettes) and a proportional duty at a harmonized rate: the sum of excise duty and VAT was to be between 52 and 54 per cent of the retail price including tax. Under a separate proposal other types of manufactured tobacco were to be subject to *ad valorem* tax at harmonized rates, again taking into account the incidence of VAT.[18] Following criticism of the inflexibility of the 1987 proposals, in the 1989 package[19] the Commission adopted a new approach: instead of harmonized rates of specific and proportional duty it put forward target rates to be achieved 'in the longer term', with minimum rates applicable from 1 January 1993.

[12] Council Directive 72/464 of 19 December 1972 on taxes other than turnover taxes which affect the consumption of manufactured tobacco, OJ 1972, L303/1 (English Spec. Ed. 1972 (31 December), 3).

[13] 2nd Council Directive 79/32 of 18 December 1978 on taxes other than turnover taxes which affect the consumption of manufactured tobacco, OJ 1979, L10/8.

[14] Council Directive 77/805 of 19 December 1977 amending Directive 72/464 on taxes, other than turnover taxes, which affect the consumption of manufactured tobacco, OJ 1977, L338/22. The Commission had proposed a range from 15% to 50%, with a possible minimum duty (OJ 1976, C45/4).

[15] Council Directive 86/246 of 16 June 1986, OJ 1986, L164/26.

[16] OJ 1980, C264/6.

[17] Proposal for a Council Directive on the approximation of taxes on cigarettes, OJ 1987, C251/3.

[18] Proposal for a Council Directive on the approximation of taxes on manufactured tobacco other than cigarettes, OJ 1987, C251/4.

[19] OJ 1990, C12/4 and 8; amendments OJ 1992, C268/7.

Two directives were adopted on 19 October 1992. Council Directive 92/79 on the approximation of taxes on cigarettes[20] requires Member States to apply minimum consumption taxes, to comprise a specific duty per unit, a proportional duty (calculated on the maximum retail price), and VAT. The minimum total excise duty (specific and *ad valorem* duty excluding VAT) is set at 57 per cent of the retail price (including all taxes) of cigarettes in the price category most in demand. This criterion applies in addition to the existing rule on the relationship between specific and proportional duty laid down by Directive 72/464 as amended. Council Directive 92/80 on the approximation of taxes on manufactured tobacco other than cigarettes[21] lays down minimum rates of duty for cigars and cigarillos, fine-cut tobacco intended for the rolling of cigarettes, and other smoking tobacco (snuff and chewing tobacco, which are said to account for 0.8 per cent of tobacco consumption, are omitted). Member States retain broad discretion, however, since a high degree of harmonization is less important for these products than it is for cigarettes; they may apply specific or *ad valorem* taxes or a mixture of both. The minima are expressed both as percentages and as minimum amounts. For cigars and cigarillos the minimum duty is 5 per cent of the retail price including taxes or ECU 7 per 1,000 units or per kilogramme, for fine-cut tobacco intended for rolling cigarettes it is 30 per cent or ECU 20 per kilogramme and for other smoking tobacco it is 20 per cent or ECU 15 per kilogramme. Under both Directives the minimum duty is to be reviewed from time to time; neither makes any mention of longer-term targets.

The Commission also proposed some largely technical modifications of the existing legislation to provide for the abolition of tax frontiers.[22] The proposal was enacted as Directive 92/78 of 19 October 1992.[23] It draws a distinction between fine-cut loose tobacco intended for the rolling of cigarettes and other tobacco, and establishes common exemptions.

ALCOHOL AND ALCOHOLIC DRINKS

The taxation of alcoholic drinks raises a number of issues. Large differences in rates make it difficult to abolish frontier barriers without a risk of diversion of trade, at least in the form of cross-border shopping, yet attitudes to the proper level of rates vary. Rates are high in the northern countries of the Community, at least partly on health grounds, and duties are a significant source of revenue, while many southern countries charge very low rates of duty. The manner in which tax is charged and monitored may differ; most

[20] OJ 1992, L316/8.

[21] OJ 1992, L316/10.

[22] Proposal for a Council Directive amending Council Directives 72/464 and 79/32, OJ 1990, C322/16; amended proposal, OJ 1992, C268/5.

[23] OJ 1992, L316/5.

countries have a system of bonded warehouses, and some use tax labels as proof of payment of tax on goods released for circulation. The structure of taxation and the relationship between the rates charged on different types of drink or drinks of different alcoholic strength may vary, affecting the conditions of competition in relation to the products concerned. The simplest solution would no doubt be to charge a single rate of tax on the alcohol content of all alcoholic drinks, perhaps with a higher rate for spirits, as suggested by the European Parliament in its opinion on the Commission's 1989 rates proposal.[24]

There has been a general tendency for states to charge higher rates on drinks which are usually imported than on drinks which are characteristic of domestic production. This tendency has given rise to a number of cases under Article 95 of the Treaty.[25] It is also partly responsible for a long-standing problem which still has not been resolved: the relative weight of tax on wine and beer. There is a considerable degree of competition between wine and beer, and probably some competition between wine and spirits, so that tax neutrality demands some degree of proportionality between the levels of tax on each. However, many Member States impose little or no tax on wine but a relatively significant amount of tax on beer (until recently the United Kingdom did the opposite, charging a disproportionately high level of tax on wine). Indeed, the harmonization of excise duties on wine was opposed by some Member States and by the European Parliament, which argued that duty on wine should be abolished (one argument was that a difference in treatment was justified by the fact that wine is an agricultural product while beer is an industrial product). The distinction between beer and wine is not the only persistent anomaly; the justification for the different treatment in most Member States of sparkling and still wine is hard to discern.

The Commission's 1972 excise duty package contained four draft directives on the harmonization of structures of excise duty on alcohol (i.e., potable spirits and ethyl alcohol used for industrial purposes), wine, beer, and mixed beverages.[26] It was envisaged that existing duties on other alcoholic drinks such as mead, cider, or perry could be retained until border tax adjustments were abolished, at which time they would themselves be abolished unless they did not give rise to any need for such adjustments.

There was considerable divergence in the approaches of the Member States to the taxation of spirits. All of them taxed ethyl alcohol, and applied the highest rates to spirits intended for drinking. Industrial uses of alcohol were usually exempt, and alcohol used in perfume was subject to a reduced rate. In

[24] OJ 1992, C94/41. In its resolution on the 1985 proposals on alcoholic drinks (OJ 1986, C36/64) the European Parliament advocated the outright abolition of duties on alcohol on the ground that they were 'a relic of an undemocratic mentality'.

[25] See Ch. 3.

[26] OJ 1972, C43/25, 32, 37, and 41; Bull. Supp. 3–72, 24, 46, 62, and 74.

most Member States other forms of alcohol such as methyl or propyl alcohol were subject to tax when they were put to uses for which ethyl alcohol would be taxable. In some cases such substitution was prohibited. In Italy, for reasons of agricultural policy, synthetic ethyl alcohol was subject to a high rate of tax.[27] In some Member States different rates were applied according to whether the alcohol was produced from grain, sugar cane, or grapes. France applied a higher rate of duty to spirits normally drunk before a meal than to those usually drunk afterwards. There were also differences in the manner in which the production and possession of untaxed alcohol was supervised, the point at which the tax was applied and the periods for payment.

The draft directive on duties on alcohol covered all ethyl alcohol other than that contained in beer, wine, and certain other drinks. Since it was proposed that only alcohol for human consumption should be taxed there was no need to refer to other forms of alcohol. A single rate of duty was to be applied to all ethyl alcohol, subject to a reduced rate for alcohol contained in fortified wine, certain wine with a natural alcohol content of more than 15 per cent by volume, and alcohol made from grape must. Duty was payable on production, but payment could be deferred until release of the alcohol for consumption. The production, use, and possession of untaxed alcohol was to be supervised by means of 'real and fictitious warehouse systems'. The real warehouse system involved the physical presence of excise officials or the use of equipment such as meters which offered equivalent safeguards, while the fictitious system was based simply on accounts. The real warehouse system was compulsory at the production stage, and either system could be used at subsequent stages. A tax document was to be required for any movement of untaxed alcohol.

As has been pointed out, harmonization of duty on wine required a preliminary decision on the question whether or not there should be any duty at all. The Commission proposed that duty should be levied in all Member States since the absence of duty on wine would place it at a competitive advantage. This would be particularly undesirable in the northern countries of the Community, where the result would be a tax advantage for an imported product over the domestic product. As in the case of alcohol, in the Member States which taxed wine there were considerable differences in the tax structure and differences in the manner in which duty was levied.

The draft directive on a harmonized excise duty on wine used a definition of wine similar to that used in the common organization of the market in wine under the common agricultural policy; it covered all grape wine with an alcohol content of 15 per cent by volume or less and certain non-fortified wines with a higher alcohol content. Exported wine, wine used in the production of products subject to the draft directive on alcohol, and wine used to

[27] See Case 140/79, *Chemial* [1981] ECR 1 and Case 46/80, *Vinal* v. *Orbat* [1981] ECR 77; above, Ch. 3.

make vinegar were to be exempt from duty, and Member States were permitted to exempt wine consumed by growers and producers, their employees, and families. Two categories of wine were established, sparkling wine and non-sparkling wine, and Member States were to apply the same rate of duty to all wine in each category; they were permitted, however, to apply a higher rate to quality wines psr ('produced in specified regions') than to other wines. The duty was to be payable on production or importation, but once again payment could be deferred until the release of the wine for consumption. Specific supervisory measures for producers were considered unnecessary, since there were already fairly strict controls under the applicable agricultural regulations; in other respects wine was to be held under a 'fictitious warehouse' system and tax documents were required for any movements.

The main problem to be overcome in harmonizing the taxation of beer was the basis of assessment. While Germany and France taxed the quantity of beer produced, Italy and the Benelux countries based their calculation on the worts. In Italy production losses were taken into account to a large extent, so that the tax paid corresponded broadly to the amount of final product, but in the Benelux countries they were not.[28] The Commission proposed taxation of the final product in order to avoid arbitrary differences between breweries (production losses can vary widely) and discrimination between domestic and imported beer.

In the proposal for a directive beers were divided into four categories according to their alcohol content (their 'original extract' under the Plato method), and the same rate of duty was to be applied to all beer in the same category; the reduced rates applied to products of small breweries in Germany and the Benelux countries were to be phased out. Duty was to be payable when beer left the brewery premises, was consumed there, or was imported. Supervision was to be on the basis of accounts.

Finally, the Commission submitted a proposal for a directive on the system of excise duties to be applied to mixed drinks in order to provide for mixtures of dutiable drinks which might not be covered by any one of the other proposals (for example, a mixture of beer and sparkling wine, apparently a popular drink in Germany, or a mixture of wine and fruit juice). In such cases duty was to be calculated separately on the dutiable components; mixtures of alcohol and other substances were in any event covered by the alcohol directive.

In response to the European Parliament's opinions on its proposals the Commission withdrew its proposal on mixed beverages and amended the proposal on alcohol. There matters stood for several years. In 1979 the

[28] For the difficulties to which this gave rise in calculating border tax adjustments see Cases C–152/89, *Commission* v. *Luxembourg* and C–153/89 *Commission* v. *Belgium* [1991] ECR I–3141 and I–3171, in which the Court held that the resulting favourable treatment for domestic beer was contrary to Arts. 95 and 96.

Commission made compromise proposals involving the taxation of spirits at a single rate in each Member State calculated on the volume of pure alcohol, the taxation of beer on the basis of the final product, the taxation of intermediate products (fortified wine and similar products) at a reduced rate, and a Community ceiling for the ratio between the rates of tax on wine and beer, but there was still no agreement in the Council. In 1985, after the adoption of the White Paper but not as part of the 1992 programme, the Commission submitted two further proposals supplementing the 1972 package.[29] The first called for the rates of duty on wine and beer to reflect the difference in their alcohol content and required Member States to apply the same rate of VAT to all products within each category of alcoholic drink. The second called for a single rate structure to be applied in each Member State to all fortified wine and similar products. The duty was to be specific and was to be based on the volume of the product or its alcoholic strength by volume; a derogation would have permitted France to retain its reduced rate of tax for certain liqueur wines so long as it treated imports the same way.[30]

In the 1987 package the Commission then put forward a draft directive laying down common rates of duty for each category of alcoholic drink and for alcohol used in perfume and cosmetics.[31] The considerable divergences in rates in the different Member States, particularly in relation to spirits, made this a difficult exercise. Rather than taking an arithmetic or weighted average of the rates currently applied, it made a rough assessment of an appropriate mid-range rate for each category; the rates ranged from ECU 1,271 per hectolitre of pure alcohol for spirits to ECU 1.32 per degree Plato per hectolitre of finished product for beer. The result would have been a considerable increase in revenue (and of course consumer prices) for certain southern Member States, a considerable reduction for Denmark, Ireland, and the United Kingdom and moderate changes for the others.

In accordance with its new approach announced in May 1989, in October 1989 the Commission put forward a new proposal setting minimum rates of duty, accompanied by target rates to be achieved through a further process of convergence.[32] The proposed minimum rates were in fact lower than the existing rates in most Member States, and ranged from ECU 1,118.5 for spirits to ECU 0.748 per degree Plato per hectolitre of product for beer. The target rates were twice the minimum rates for wine and beer and 25 per cent higher than the minimum rates for spirits and intermediate products.

In September 1990 the Commission submitted a new proposal for

[29] Proposal for a Council Directive laying down certain rules on indirect taxes which affect the consumption of alcoholic drinks; proposal for a Council Directive concerning the harmonization of excise duties on fortified wine and similar products, OJ 1985, C114/6 and 7.

[30] Cf. Case 196/85, *France*.

[31] Proposal for a Council Directive on approximation of the rates of excise duty on alcoholic beverages and on the alcohol contained in other product, OJ 1987, C250/4.

[32] OJ 1990, C12/12; amendment OJ 1992, C268/6.

harmonization of excise duty structures on all types of alcoholic drinks.[33] It was adopted, with some minor additions and changes, as Council Directive 92/83 of 19 October 1992 on the harmonization of the structures of excise duties on alcohol and alcoholic beverages.[34] The Directive defines several categories of drinks—beer, still and sparkling wine, other fermented beverages (still and sparkling), intermediate products, and ethyl alcohol—according to their classification in the Community's customs and statistical nomenclature.[35] The beer category includes mixtures of beer with non-alcoholic drinks, so long as the alcoholic strength by volume is greater than 0.5 per cent. Still wine is defined as grape wine with an alcoholic strength by volume greater than 1.2 per cent but not greater than 15 per cent in which all the alcohol is of fermented origin; it also covers wine of an alcoholic strength up to 18 per cent in which all the alcohol is of fermented origin and there has been no enrichment of the must. Sparkling wine covers grape wine of an alcoholic strength greater than 1.2 per cent but not greater than 15 per cent in which all the alcohol is of fermented origin, in bottles with 'mushroom stoppers' fastened in place or containing a high level of carbon dioxide. The category 'other fermented beverages' includes drinks such as cider, perry, mead, and fruit wines to a maximum alcoholic strength of 15 per cent, where all the alcohol is of fermented origin, and drinks such as grape must mixed with alcohol up to an alcoholic strength of 10 per cent in the case of still drinks and 13 per cent in the case of sparkling drinks. The category of intermediate products covers fortified wines and similar products with an alcoholic strength not greater than 22 per cent by volume. Finally, ethyl alcohol includes spirits, ethyl alcohol and alcohol preparations, and other drinks with an alcoholic strength in excess of 22 per cent.

Member States must apply excise duty to each of the categories of products, normally at a uniform rate for each category. They may apply reduced rates to beer and ethyl alcohol produced by small independent firms, to beer, wine, and other fermented beverages with a low alcohol content, to intermediate products with an alcoholic strength not exceeding 15 per cent, and certain natural sweet wines, and to ethyl alcohol products with an alcohol content not exceeding 10 per cent. They may exempt from duty persons who produce beer, wine, or other fermented beverages for their own use and do not sell their products. For beer they may choose one of two methods: a rate per hectolitre per degree Plato or a rate per hectolitre per degree (percentage point) of alcoholic strength by volume. States which apply the Plato method may establish categories of beer comprising up to four degrees Plato, with a

[33] OJ 1990, C322/11; amendment OJ 1992, C268/6.

[34] OJ 1992, L316/21.

[35] The combined nomenclature, published annually. Under Article 26 of the Directive, references to CN codes are to those of the version in force when the Directive was adopted: Commission Regulation 2587/91, amending Annex I to Council Regulation 2658/87 on the tariff and statistical nomenclature and on the Common Customs Tariff, OJ 1991, L259/1.

separate rate for each category. The Member States may apply separate rates or a single rate to still and sparkling wine and to the still and sparkling subcategories of other fermented beverages. Denatured alcohol and alcohol used in the production of vinegar, medicines, and foodstuffs are exempted from duty; Member States may exempt alcohol used for scientific or medical purposes or in manufacturing processes.

The rates proposal became Council Directive 92/84 of 19 October 1992 on the approximation of rates of excise duty on alcoholic beverages.[36] The Directive sets minimum rates for beer, wine, intermediate products, and alcohol and alcoholic beverages (the residual category); there is no mention of target rates. The minimum rate for beer is ECU 0.748 per hectolitre per degree Plato or ECU 1.87 per hectolitre per degree of alcohol of the finished product, the rate proposed by the Commission, while the minimum rate for both still and sparkling wine is ECU 0 (the Commission had proposed ECU 9.35 per hectolitre for still wine and ECU 16.5 for sparkling wine). The minimum rate for wine also applies to the category 'other fermented beverages' (see Article 15 of Directive 92/83). Discriminatory taxation of beer and wine thus remains a matter for Article 95 of the Treaty; it may be added that to refer to a minimum rate of 0 as 'harmonization' is curious terminology. Although the Economic and Social Committee and the European Parliament have consistently displayed a more favourable attitude towards wine than towards beer, in their opinions on the rates proposal they both recognized the need to treat the two products equitably. Indeed, the European Parliament proposed the insertion of a provision stating that 'there should be an equivalent level of excise duty attached to beer and wine to prevent a distortion in patterns of consumption based on economic criteria'.[37] The failure to resolve this issue may be attributed in part to the fact that the purpose of the Directive was to achieve the minimum degree of harmonization necessary for the removal of frontier controls, not to eliminate discriminatory taxation within individual Member States.

The minimum rate for intermediate products is ECU 45 per hectolitre of product. The minimum rate for alcohol and alcoholic drinks is ECU 550 per hectolitre of pure alcohol content; however, Member States whose existing rate of duty does not exceed ECU 1,000 may not reduce it, and Member States whose existing rate is more than ECU 1,000 may not reduce it below that figure. The Directive permits temporary derogations in relation to the taxation of alcoholic beverages in Denmark and Italy, and reduced rates for certain regions of Greece, Italy, and Portugal. The rates are to be reviewed every two years, taking into account the functioning of the internal market, competition between different categories of alcoholic drinks, and the wider objectives of the Treaty.

[36] OJ 1992, L316/29. [37] OJ 1992, C94 at 45.

MINERAL OILS (PETROLEUM PRODUCTS)

In all Member States excise duties on petroleum products bear most heavily on those used as motor fuel. There is generally some link, though not a precise or explicit one, between those taxes and investment in transport infrastructure. Their harmonization thus raises issues different from those raised by harmonization of duties on tobacco or alcoholic drinks. Whereas taxes on those products fall almost solely on the consumer, taxes on fuel affect inputs; they have considerable impact on industry and commerce, whether in the form of transport costs or of production costs. Accordingly, harmonization must take into account not only the possible deflection of trade in a frontier-free market where there are significant variations in consumption taxes, but also the possible effects on the conditions of competition for businesses in different States. Varying levels of taxation also affect choices between energy sources; there are thus repercussions for energy and environmental policy, whether these are desired or not. For example, there is a contradiction between the desire to use tax to discourage consumption of petroleum products and the desire to apply a neutral system of taxation to all energy sources.

The first Commission proposal on petroleum products was submitted in December 1970.[38] It simply laid down maximum rates of tax to be applied to certain fuels (diesel and heavy fuel oils). In 1973 the Commission then submitted a draft framework directive harmonizing structures of taxation of mineral oils,[39] which defined the products to be covered, the chargeable event (release of products from the place of production or from a bonded warehouse, importation, sale for use as motor fuel of products other than those normally covered by the Directive), common exemptions (including use in manufacturing processes and as industrial heating fuel), controls, and collection methods. Member States were to remain free to set their own rates of tax, subject to a consultation procedure in relation to special rates for certain users. Like the 1972 package on excise duty structures for alcoholic drinks, the proposal met with no success.

The set of rates proposals submitted by the Commission in August 1987 following the Single European Act included a draft directive on the approximation of the rates of duty on mineral oils,[40] which provided for common rates of duty on the main motor fuels and heating oils. It met the same objections of rigidity as the other proposals in that package; in accordance with the

[38] Proposal for a Council Directive on the approximation of specific consumption taxes on liquid hydrocarbons intended for use as fuel, OJ 1971, C14/25.

[39] Proposal for a Council Directive on the harmonization of excise duties on mineral oils, OJ 1973, C92/36.

[40] OJ 1987, C262/8.

change of approach adopted in relation to other products subject to excise duty, an amended proposal submitted in November 1989[41] called for minimum rates of duty on leaded and unleaded petrol, on liquid petroleum gas and methane used as road fuel, and on kerosene used as a propellant, and rate bands (minimum and maximum rates) for other products; these minimum rates and rate bands differed little from the common rates in the earlier proposal. The Commission undertook to submit a further proposal on target rates towards which the rates applied in Member States were to converge. A proposal setting target rates for petrol and for kerosene used as a propellant and a new rate band for diesel was submitted in February 1991.[42] The new rate band for diesel was said to include a 'CO_2 supplement'. While the European Parliament approved the proposal, the Economic and Social Committee expressed reservations, suggesting that the Commission was missing its chance to propose a thorough and rational harmonization of the taxation of all energy sources.

In September 1990, meanwhile, the Commission submitted a draft directive on excise duty structures.[43] It required the imposition of duties at harmonized rates on a series of products (heating oil, motor fuels and additives, substitutable products) defined by reference, once again, to the customs and statistical nomenclature. It laid down the taxable event (in addition to the general rule laid down in the framework directive, Directive 92/12) and common exemptions (non-fuel uses, rail, air, and water transport). Member States were to be at liberty to grant exemptions or reduced rates for products used, under fiscal control, in the generation of electricity by public utilities, in agriculture and fisheries, and in local public transport.

The structures draft became Council Directive 92/81 of 19 October 1992 on the harmonization of the structures of duty on mineral oils.[44] Its scope is at first sight broad, covering a range of products identified by their codes in the combined nomenclature. However, products other than those for which a rate is set in the Rates Directive, Directive 92/82, are taxable only where they are intended for use as heating fuel or motor fuel; in such cases the rate of duty is to be that applicable to the corresponding fuel specifically referred to in the Rates Directive. Any other product intended for use as motor fuel or as an additive to motor fuels is to be taxed as motor fuel. Other hydrocarbons intended for use as heating fuel are taxable at the rate for the equivalent oil. Coal, peat, and similar solid fuels, and natural gas are exempted from the

[41] Amended proposal for a Council Directive on the approximation of the rates of excise duty on mineral oils, OJ 1990, C16/10. Amended and consolidated proposal (including target rates), OJ 1992, C48/13.

[42] Proposal for a Council Directive fixing certain rates and target rates of excise duty on mineral oils, OJ 1991, C66/14.

[43] Proposal for a Council Directive on the harmonization of the structures of excise duties on mineral oils, OJ 1990, C322/18; amended proposal, OJ 1992, C45/3.

[44] OJ 1992, L316/12.

latter rule, but they may be taxed by the Member States where no border formalities result (see Article 3(3) of Directive 92/12, the General Arrangements Directive).

Specific exemptions are laid down for products used for purposes other than locomotion or heating and those used in commercial aviation and in shipping or fishing in Community waters. Member States may establish exemptions or reduced rates in particular for products used in electricity generation or in combined heat and power plants, commercial navigation on inland waterways, rail transport, the development of 'environmentally friendly' products, agriculture, and fisheries. The Council may, by unanimous decision, authorize individual Member States to establish other derogations on specific public policy grounds. A proposal for a directive on the colouring or marking of gas oil benefiting from an exemption or a reduced rate of duty was submitted in December 1993[45]; it is expected to be adopted by Summer 1994.

At the same time the Council adopted a decision pursuant to Article 8(4) of the Directive, the provision on additional derogations: Decision 92/510 authorizing Member States to continue to apply to certain mineral oils when used for specific purposes existing reduced rates of excise duty or exemptions from excise duty.[46] It authorized exemptions or reductions of one kind or another for all Member States. The most widespread are in favour of local public transport, air navigation not already exempted by Article 8(1) of the Directive, LPG, natural gas and methane, navigation in private pleasure craft, and fuel used by the armed forces.

Council Directive 92/82 of 19 October 1992 on the approximation of the rates of excise duties on mineral oils[47] lays down minimum rates for leaded and unleaded petrol, diesel, heating oil, heavy fuel oil, liquid petroleum gas and methane, and kerosene. Different rates are set for diesel, LPG and methane, and kerosene depending on the use to which they are put, with a particularly low rate for use as heating fuel (ECU 0 in the case of LPG and methane, and kerosene). Once again, there is no mention of target rates, and even the rate bands for certain products, which were said by the Commission to be essential in order to avoid distortions of competition, have been deleted. The minimum rates for the main motor fuels, however, correspond to those proposed by the Commission. During a transitional period of two years Luxembourg, whose rates were particularly low, enjoys a derogation in respect of petrol and diesel, and Greece has a derogation in respect of diesel. Portugal and Greece also enjoy permanent derogations in respect of fuel consumed in the Azores and on certain Aegean islands respectively. The rates are to be reviewed every two years, having regard to the functioning of the internal market, the real value of the rates, and the wider objectives of the Treaty.

In March 1992, as a supplement to its proposals on structures and rates of

[45] OJ 1994, C15/18. [46] OJ 1992, L316/16. [47] OJ 1992, L316/19.

duty, the Commission submitted a draft directive on excise duties on motor fuels from agricultural sources ('biofuels'—ethanol, methanol, and certain vegetable oils).[48] The proposal was intended to achieve policy objectives in the fields of energy, agriculture, and the environment; it will, according to the Commission, increase security of supply and allow the use of 'set-aside' land. Its main provision is that the rate of duty on such fuel should be no more than 10 per cent of the rate of duty on the fuel for which it is a substitute. The proposal is now before the Council.

ROAD TAX

The harmonization of duties on motor fuels cannot be viewed in isolation, since there is a close relationship between those duties and national systems of road tax. That is to say, transport infrastructure is typically funded by a combination of tax on motor fuel and tax on vehicles; the ratio between the two, between the different kinds of fuel and between private cars, lorries, and buses varies. Some Member States also charge tolls on motorways and other works such as bridges and tunnels. Varying levels of road tax are perceived to cause distortions in the conditions of competition for road haulage, although the relative importance of road tax diminishes in relation to that of fuel tax the more the vehicle is driven. Nevertheless it has long been considered that excise duties on fuel, road tax, and tolls should be treated together for the purposes of harmonization.

A first proposal concerning road tax was in fact made in 1963, well before the first proposals on excise duties. This draft decision on the harmonization of certain provisions affecting competition in transport by road, rail, and inland waterway was based on Article 75 of the Treaty, on the common transport policy, and was not directly concerned with tax harmonization; it was part of a broader effort to lay down common rules on international transport in order to avoid distortions of competition both between carriers from different Member States and between different modes of transport. The proposal was adopted as Council Decision 65/271 of 13 May 1965.[49] It envisaged the elimination of double taxation of vehicles used for transport in a Member State other than the state of registration, a uniform basis of assessment for the taxation of goods vehicles and of canal barges, and the application to goods transport of the common system of VAT, once it was adopted. In view of the inclusion of tax provisions Article 99 was added as a legal basis for the decision; a proposed provision calling for the adjustment of systems of

[48] Proposal for a Council Directive on excise duties on motor fuels from agricultural sources, OJ 1992, C73/6.

[49] OJ 1965,1500 (OJ, English Spec. Ed. 1965–1966, 67).

tax on transport (including taxes on fuel) in such a way as to charge users the costs of transport infrastructure was omitted.

However, the Commission's 1964 proposal for a draft implementing regulation on the elimination of double taxation in relation to road tax in international transport[50] was not accepted, and was withdrawn several years later. A further proposal for an implementing directive[51] submitted in 1968 provided for the adjustment of national systems of tax on commercial vehicles. Under the proposal Member States were to replace their existing taxes with a tax on the use of transport infrastructure, according to a common basis of assessment (maximum gross weight, in a number of categories). They remained free to set their own rates, on the basis of the difference between the marginal cost of road use and the revenue from excise duties on motor fuel used by commercial vehicles. Although it received the agreement in principle of the Council in June 1978,[52] the proposal met opposition from one Member State and was not ultimately adopted.

In 1971 the Commission also submitted a draft decision[53] on the introduction of a common system of charges for the use of transport infrastructure (roads, railways, and inland waterways), to reflect the marginal social cost of that use. Its objective was to promote optimal use of infrastructure and charge users the cost of its construction and operation (thus ensuring fair conditions of competition between modes of transport). In relation to roads such charges were to take the form of vehicle taxes, fuel taxes, and direct charges for use. This last type of charge was not further specified, although the Commission, in its accompanying memorandum, referred to the possibility of special charges for traffic in cities with a view to relieving congestion.

There matters stood, once again, for several years, until the renewal of activity following the 1985 White Paper. In late 1986 the Commission submitted to the Council a communication on vehicle taxation[54] in which it identified the main policy aims to be taken into account in relation to the taxation of commercial vehicles (harmonization of conditions of competition within and between modes of transport, allocation of transport infrastructure costs to users, revenue, freedom of movement within the Community). It set out three possible approaches: harmonization of tax structures in accordance with the 1968 Proposal, approximation of rates, and a move from taxation on the basis of nationality to territorial taxation (that is to say, according to the dis-

[50] Text published with the opinion of the Economic and Social Committee, OJ 1965, 145.

[51] OJ 1968, C95/41.

[52] See the replies to Written Questions 164/79, OJ 1979, C178/13, and 410/79, OJ 1979, C275/10.

[53] OJ 1971, C62/15.

[54] Communication from the Commission to the Council on elimination of distortions of competition of a fiscal nature in the transport of goods by road: Study of vehicle taxes, fuel taxes, and road tolls: COM(86)750. See also the European Parliament Resolution on payment for the use of transport infrastructure in the framework of the common transport policy and elimination of distortions of competition by vehicle taxes, fuel taxes and road tolls, OJ 1987, C281/83.

tance covered in any given country). In January 1988 it went on to submit a draft directive on the charging of transport infrastructure costs to heavy goods vehicles,[55] under which diesel-powered heavy goods vehicles were to be taxed according to their maximum gross weight, in categories defined by reference to the number and configuration of axles. They were to be subject to road tax only in their home country, and could not be given any exemption from tax on account of periods spent in other Member States. Road tolls remained permissible so long as they were not discriminatory. In the longer term it envisaged the recovery of infrastructure costs by means of taxation on a territorial basis, taking into account the harmonization of excise duties on diesel. A modified proposal submitted in November 1990[56] provided for standard minimum tax rates to be calculated annually by the Commission on the basis of average road infrastructure costs for each vehicle category.

In the meantime Germany had introduced legislation providing for a road use levy on heavy goods vehicles, accompanied by a reduction in its road tax on such vehicles. The levy was intended, according to the German government, to create fairer conditions of competition between German and foreign transporters by maintaining the contribution of German lorries to road costs while increasing that of foreign lorries. The Commission challenged the legislation before the Court of Justice on the ground that it changed the existing situation to the detriment of transporters from other Member States and discriminated against them, contrary to Article 76 of the Treaty. In its judgment[57] the Court upheld that view; the new tax was payable by all transporters, but its impact was offset by a reduction in tax for German transporters alone. Following the judgment of the Court of Justice the Commission made further changes to its proposal for a directive.[58] The minimum rates were reduced, but were made subject to review by the Council every two years, and Member States were to be authorized to impose user charges in respect of their entire motorway network or specific motorways, bridges, tunnels, or mountain passes.

On the basis of the amended proposal, in October 1993 the Council adopted Directive 93/89 on the application by Member States of taxes on certain vehicles used for the carriage of goods by road and tolls and charges for the use of certain infrastructures.[59] The Directive, based on Articles 75

[55] OJ 1988, C79/8.

[56] OJ 1991, C75/1. See also the resolutions of the European Parliament of 17 November 1988, 23 November 1989, and 6 April 1990 on taxation of goods vehicles, OJ 1988, C326/215, OJ 1989, C323/97, and OJ 1990, C113/205 respectively. In its opinion on the September 1990 proposal for a directive on excise duty structures the European Parliament suggested an excise duty surcharge to be allocated to a Community infrastructure fund (see OJ 1991, C183/286).

[57] Case C–195/90, *Commission* v. *Germany* [1992] ECR I–3141.

[58] OJ 1992, C311/63.

[59] OJ 1993, L279/32. The Directive formed part of a package with a measure on 'road cabotage', Regulation 3118/93 laying down the conditions under which non-resident carriers may operate national road haulage services within a Member State (OJ 1993, L279/1), which was dependent on agreement on taxation of heavy goods vehicles.

and 99, establishes minimum rates of road tax for categories of heavy goods vehicles with a permissible gross weight of not less than twelve tonnes. Road tax may be charged solely by the Member State of registration. During a transitional period certain Member States may charge lower rates, and derogations are permitted in respect of small vehicles engaged exclusively in local transport within one country. Member States may be authorized to apply additional reductions or exemptions for vehicles operated within part of their territory, in furtherance of socio-economic policies or for reasons linked to their infrastructure. Although the Commission's proposal included a provision similar to Article 33 of the Sixth VAT Directive, prohibiting Member States from applying taxes on the use or possession of heavy goods vehicles other than the enumerated road taxes, that provision does not appear in the Directive.

Tolls or user charges may be charged in respect of motorways and other similar multi-lane roads, bridges, tunnels, and mountain passes; Member States without a general system of motorways or dual carriageways may charge tolls or user charges for the use of the highest category of road. Subject to consultation with the Commission, tolls or user charges may also be made payable for other sections of the road network where that is justified in particular on grounds of safety. There may be no discrimination on grounds of nationality. A ceiling is set for user charges, which are to be proportionate to the duration of the use of the roads or structures concerned. Two or more Member States may co-operate in a common system of user charges, and five Member States—Belgium, Denmark, Germany, Luxembourg, and the Netherlands—signed an agreement to that effect in February 1994. Tolls are to be calculated on the basis of the cost of construction, operation, and development of the roads or structures concerned. The Directive does not prevent Member States from imposing taxes on the registration of vehicles, special taxes for particularly heavy or over-sized vehicles, or charges aimed at reducing congestion in specific areas at specific times.

THE PROPOSAL FOR A CARBON TAX

The proposal for a Council Directive introducing a tax on carbon dioxide emissions and energy[60] is primarily aimed at the phenomenon of global warming; it seeks to combat the 'greenhouse effect' by limiting emissions of carbon dioxide from the burning of fossil fuels. A simple carbon tax was, however, politically unacceptable since it would have a great impact on predominantly coal-burning countries such as the United Kingdom and Germany while France, which produces most of its electricity in nuclear plants, would escape lightly. It seemed anomalous to favour nuclear over fossil fuel sources of

[60] OJ 1992, C196/1.

energy, although that is the obvious result of any effort to curb carbon emissions by means of fiscal measures. Accordingly, the draft cites as a secondary goal the efficient use of energy. It calls for a combined tax on all non-renewable energy sources, half of it on carbon content and half based on energy content. The tax is to be levied on coal, lignite, peat, and their derivatives, natural gas, petroleum products, ethanol and methanol where they are used as heating or motor fuels, and electricity. The provisions governing the manner in which the tax is to be levied are similar to those laid down for products subject to excise duty in Directive 92/12. A fixed amount of tax per quantity of product is laid down for certain categories of petroleum products. Otherwise, the products subject to the tax are to be taxed at ECU 2.81 per tonne of carbon dioxide emitted in their combustion and ECU 0.21 per gigajoule of energy content. Electricity is to be taxed at ECU 2.1 per megawatt hour, with a reduced rate for hydroelectric plants. Provision is made for derogations in favour of firms with high energy consumption which are placed at a disadvantage by an increase in imports from non-OECD countries which do not have similar tax measures. The Directive is intended to be revenue-neutral; increases in revenue resulting from the tax are to be offset by reductions in other taxes.

Because of concern about the effect of such a tax on the competitiveness of industry, the application of the proposed directive is to be conditional on the introduction in other OECD countries (in particular the United States) of similar tax measures. The reception given to the US administration's proposal for an energy tax makes that an unlikely prospect for the time being. This could be viewed as a lesson in the benefits of international harmonization: assuming measures on taxation of hydrocarbons to be desirable, if the United States and the Community could have found a way of agreeing on the measures to be taken both could have benefited.

Direct Taxation and Company Taxation

11

Introduction to Company Taxation

The Community law on company taxation has developed differently from the Community law on Value Added Tax. From the very beginning, the First and Second Directives on Value Added Tax established the foundations of a common system of taxation applicable both domestically and in intra-Community trade, later directives further developing and refining the system already in existence. Notwithstanding the early endeavours of the Commission[1] and the strong economic case for harmonizing, or at least co-ordinating, company taxes,[2] it is only comparatively recently that limited progress has been made.

The three instruments adopted, namely two directives based on Article 100 of the EC Treaty and a convention concluded by the Member States under Article 220 of the Treaty, are not directed at comprehensive harmonization of the Member States' diverse systems of company taxation. They do not attempt to eliminate the differences in returns on cross-border investment resulting from the lack of uniformity in rates of tax, tax systems, and the basis of assessment. Instead, they have the more limited aim of eliminating specific obstacles to cross-border co-operation between companies established in the Community. Those obstacles fall into two categories:

(1) obstacles to the *setting up* of transnational companies and groups;
(2) obstacles to the *functioning* of such companies and groups.

The Merger Directive[3] of 23 July 1990 is directed towards the first type of obstacle. It seeks to reduce the tax disincentives associated with the grouping and restructuring of companies from different Member States. It is concerned essentially with the regrouping or restructuring operation itself. The Parent–Subsidiary Directive[4] of the same date is directed at the second type of problem. It eliminates in part the tax obstacles to dividend flows between subsidiary and parent companies in different Member States. On 6 December 1990 the Commission tabled two further proposals complementing the

[1] For a historical account of the Commission's initiatives in this field, see Ch. 2.

[2] See, e.g., Devereux and Pearson, *Corporate tax harmonization and economic efficiency*, Institute for Fiscal Studies, Report Series No. 35.

[3] Council Directive 90/434 on the common system of taxation applicable to mergers, divisions, transfers of assets, and exchanges of shares concerning companies of different Member States, OJ 1990, L225/1.

[4] Council Directive 90/435 on the common system of taxation applicable in the case of parent companies and subsidiaries of different Member States, OJ 1990, L225/6.

Parent–Subsidiary Directive, namely a proposal on the deduction of losses of permanent establishments and subsidiaries in other Member States[5] and a proposal on intra-Community interest and royalty payments between parent and subsidiary companies.[6]

The Arbitration Convention,[7] which was originally submitted to the Council in the form of a directive, is also concerned with obstacles of the second type. It introduces an arbitration procedure designed to eliminate double taxation occurring in connection with the adjustment of profits of associated enterprises in different Member States when an upward adjustment in an enterprise's profits in one Member State is not accompanied by a corresponding adjustment in the results of the other enterprise. The Convention is not yet in force since it has not been ratified by all the Contracting Parties. It should be noted that it confers no interpretative jurisdiction on the Court.

Although the Merger and Parent–Subsidiary Directives establish a 'common system of taxation', they do so in limited areas. Their scope and effect can be understood only in the light of the national systems of company taxation which they partly harmonize. For readers who are not familiar with the international aspects of those systems, some explanation of the basic concepts and principles is necessary at this juncture. It should be noted that the comparative information given in this chapter to illustrate the differences in tax systems is based mainly on the Ruding Committee Report[8] and that there may have been changes in particular systems since the Report was written.

BASIC PRINCIPLES OF INTERNATIONAL COMPANY TAXATION

Tax Jurisdiction

Most countries base their tax systems on two criteria, namely residence and source: they tax income received by individuals or companies resident within their territory and also tax income of non-residents arising from sources there. Most EC Member States accordingly claim the right to tax companies resident within their territory on both their domestic and their foreign income (including foreign-branch profits and dividends paid by foreign subsidiaries)[9];

[5] Proposal for a Council Directive concerning arrangements for the taking into account by enterprises of the losses of their permanent establishments and subsidiaries situated in other Member States, OJ 1991, C53/30.

[6] Proposal for a Council Directive on a common system of taxation applicable to interest and royalty payments made between parent companies and subsidiaries in different Member States, OJ 1991, C53/26, amended on 10 June 1993, OJ 1993, L178/18.

[7] Convention of 23 July 1990 on the elimination of double taxation in connection with the adjustment of profits of associated enterprises, OJ 1990, L225/10.

[8] *Report of the Committee of Independent Experts on Company Taxation*, generally known as the 'Ruding Committee' after its chairman Onno Ruding (Brussels: E.C. Commission, 1992).

[9] An important exception is France, whose company tax system is based on the territoriality principle—French companies are in principle not subject to French company tax on profits from

they also tax the profits made by the permanent establishments of non-resident companies situated within their territory. When a parent company receives dividend income from a foreign subsidiary, the income has usually already been subject to two sets of foreign taxation, namely the foreign company tax on the profits of the subsidiary out of which the dividend is paid and foreign withholding tax[10] on the dividend itself. Any company taxation imposed by the parent company's State of residence would therefore constitute a third layer of taxation.[11]

Relief for Foreign Tax

In order to reduce the double taxation of profits of companies and groups of companies operating in more than one country, most countries grant relief from tax either on a unilateral basis under domestic legislation or under bilateral taxation treaties negotiated with other countries. Normally it is the country of residence which grants the greater relief, the source country merely reducing the level of withholding tax payable on distributions of profits.[12]

The two mechanisms for granting relief most widely used by countries of residence are the credit method and the exemption method.[13]

Under the credit method a country continues to tax the foreign income but permits certain foreign taxes paid on the income to be set off against the domestic liability. The United Kingdom, for example, uses the credit method for granting both unilateral relief and relief under its double taxation treaties. The unilateral relief extends to foreign company tax paid on branch profits and withholding taxes paid on dividends from foreign companies; in the case of dividends, if the company receiving the dividend controls, directly or indirectly, at least 10 per cent of the voting rights in the foreign company, relief is also given for the underlying company tax on the profits out of which the dividend is paid. Other Member States using the credit method for granting relief in respect of dividend income are, as regards treaty relief, Greece, Spain, Ireland, and Portugal and, as regards unilateral relief, Denmark, Germany, Greece, Spain, and Italy.[14]

Member States using the credit method restrict relief for foreign tax to the domestic tax that would be paid on the foreign income. States use different

a trade or business carried on outside France (although they are subject to tax on passive income such as dividends from a foreign subsidiary).

[10] See below, p. 261.

[11] It will seen later that the company tax systems operated by some Member States ('imputation systems') discriminate in particular against cross-border dividends: see below, p. 250 ff.

[12] In addition, countries operating imputation systems of company taxation sometimes allow a partial refund of imputation tax credits: see below, p. 252.

[13] Art. 23A and 23B of the 1977 OECD Model Income Tax Convention, unamended by the 1992 Model, envisage the use of either method.

[14] Source: Ruding Committee Report, note 8 above, Tables 3A.22 and 3A.23, at 266–7.

methods of calculating this restriction, which may work on a source-by-source or country-by-country basis. Consequently, companies receiving dividends from countries with different levels of taxation, some higher and some lower than the level in their country of residence, cannot set off unused credit attaching to income from a high-tax country against their remaining domestic liability on income from a lower-tax country.[15] A further restriction is that relief for underlying company tax often extends only to the tax paid by the immediate subsidiary paying the dividend—no relief is given for tax paid by lower-tier subsidiaries.[16]

The exemption method completely exempts qualifying foreign income from domestic corporate tax. No question therefore arises of setting off foreign tax against domestic liability or of distinguishing between withholding tax and underlying company tax. The Member States using the exemption method for granting relief in respect of dividend income received by companies are Belgium, Denmark, Germany, Greece, France, Italy, Luxembourg, and the Netherlands in the case of treaty relief, and Belgium, France, Luxembourg, and the Netherlands in the case of unilateral relief.[17] The exemption of foreign income is sometimes linked to holding company rules designed to eliminate multiple taxation of income passing through several companies within a group. Such rules, which apply to both domestic and foreign income, generally specify a minimum holding in the subsidiary for exemption of dividend income. Thus, for example, under the Netherlands participation exemption (*deelnemingsvrijstelling*) dividends and profits on the sale of shares received by Dutch companies or Dutch permanent establishments of foreign companies from holdings in domestic or foreign companies are exempted provided generally that at least 5 per cent of the nominal paid-up capital is held and certain other conditions are met.[18]

Depending on the levels of taxation in the residence or source country, the credit and exemption methods may lead to quite different results. A company resident in a country applying the exemption method is always taxed on its foreign income at the rate applicable in the source country. A company resident in a country applying the credit method, on the other hand, is taxed at

[15] This problem has, e.g., led many UK companies investing abroad to establish a foreign intermediary holding company, often in the Netherlands, whose function is to collect dividends from group subsidiaries in countries with different levels of taxation and then to pay a single dividend to the UK parent company; this allows the level of taxation on dividends from the subsidiaries to be averaged out and avoids loss of tax credit.

[16] The UK and Germany extend relief to lower-tier subsidiaries under certain conditions. For a summary of the rules in the Member States, see de Hosson and van Noordenne, 'Current status of the implementation of the direct tax directives', [1992–3] *EC Tax Review*, 158–9.

[17] Source: Ruding Committee Report, note 8 above, Tables 3A.22 and 3A.23 at 266–7.

[18] See Shelton and de Petter, 'Holding Companies: A Review of the New Luxembourg Rules and Six Other Countries', [1991] *European Taxation* 63 and 107. See also de Hosson and van Noordenne, 'Current status', 159–60. France and Luxembourg require a 10% holding. Belgium has no minimum holding requirement.

the higher of the rates applicable in its country of residence and the source country.

A majority of the members of the Ruding Committee[19] favoured the use of the exemption method in the Community because it promotes 'capital import neutrality'.[20] This term is used by economists to denote the situation where taxation is neutral with respect to the importation of capital because domestic and foreign suppliers of capital to any national market obtain the same after-tax rate of return from similar investments in that market.[21] The exemption method is consistent with that objective because foreign investors all bear the source-country rate of taxation on the income from their investment rather than the different rates applicable in their countries of residence. It should be noted, however, that some Member States using the exemption method have rules refusing or limiting relief where the profits out of which a foreign dividend is paid were subject to an abnormally low level of taxation.[22]

Company Tax Systems

Ultimately it is only natural persons (i.e., the shareholders of companies) who suffer taxation, the companies themselves merely constituting an intermediate vehicle which may be used for collection of tax. Classical systems of taxation do not make any allowance for the fact that the same profits of a company are taxed twice, first in the hands of the company and secondly as dividends in the hands of its shareholders. Dividends are taxable in full regardless of the company tax borne on the profits out of which they are they paid. Classical systems are applied by Luxembourg and the Netherlands although, as already noted, both countries have special arrangements for holding companies designed to prevent multiple taxation of income passing through several companies.

The double taxation of distributed profits under classical systems discriminates in favour of retained profits and is thus thought to distort financing decisions. In order to overcome this problem some countries have adopted 'imputation systems' under which shareholders are granted a tax credit representing all or part of the company tax paid on the dividend. The tax credit is set against the shareholders' personal income tax liability on the dividend, thus eliminating or reducing the double taxation of the income. Imputation systems are applied in France, Germany, Ireland, Italy and the United Kingdom.[23]

19 Above, note 8.

20 See the Ruding Committee Report, 377.

21 See the Ruding Committee Report, 17.

22 See below, p. 261. By contrast, the credit method automatically takes account of lower levels of foreign taxation by topping up any foreign tax paid to the domestic level.

23 Belgium, Denmark, and Portugal operate modified classical systems under which shareholder relief is granted for personal tax on dividends, but the relief is unconnected with the company tax paid on the distribution. Spain, Greece, and Germany operate systems providing relief

In a domestic context imputation systems are an effective means of integrating company and personal income taxes in order to reduce double taxation. In an international context they usually discriminate between domestic and foreign shareholders and between companies with domestic sources of profits and those with predominantly foreign income.

Disadvantages for Companies with Predominantly Foreign Income

Member States granting tax credits to shareholders in respect of dividends wish to be sure that company tax has been paid on the profits out of which the dividends are paid. Imputation systems therefore provide for the imposition of a tax on companies paying dividends to shareholders designed to compensate for the tax credit. The disadvantage of this mechanism for a company with predominantly foreign income may be illustrated by reference to the United Kingdom system. The United Kingdom imposes an imputation tax on dividends called 'Advance Corporation Tax' (ACT). Normally a company is entitled to deduct any ACT paid on distributions from its corporation tax liability on its profits. Consequently, for a company making a distribution out of domestic profits fully subject to United Kingdom corporation tax ACT does not constitute an additional tax cost. However, where a United Kingdom company has mainly foreign income, its domestic corporation tax liability is likely to be small owing to the relief granted by the United Kingdom for foreign company taxes and withholding taxes. Consequently, it has insufficient liability against which to set the ACT which it has paid. Any unrelieved ACT becomes an additional tax cost, with the result that distributed foreign income suffers a higher level of taxation at the company level than domestic income.[24]

This disadvantage is not specific to the United Kingdom imputation system. Although not operating in quite the same way, the French, German, and Italian systems provide for the imposition of imputation taxes[25] whose function is similarly to ensure that domestic company tax has actually been paid whenever dividends carry a tax credit for shareholders. In France, for example, the imputation tax (the *précompte*) is not, in the manner of ACT, paid systematically on all distributions; however, where a company distributes income

at the company level: Spain operates a system under which a deduction is made from the tax base for distributed profits; Greece does not impose company tax on distributed profits; Germany, in addition to offering relief at the shareholder level under its imputation system, applies a lower rate of tax to distributed profits: see the Ruding Committee Report, in particular Table 3.2 at 65.

[24] For a discussion of the UK ACT problem and the Inland Revenue proposals for reform, see Freeman and Griffith, 'Surplus ACT—A solution in sight?'; Lewis, 'Surplus ACT'; and Troup, 'Surplus ACT—a practitioner's comment on the consultative document', *Fiscal Studies*, November 1993, published by the Institute for Fiscal Studies.

[25] The *précompte* in France, *imposta di congualio* in Italy and *Ausschüttungsbelastung* in Germany. Ireland has a similar system to the UK.

that has not borne French company tax, the company must pay an imputation tax equal to the tax credit received by the shareholder.

Imputation taxes are generally payable on distributions without regard to foreign taxes already paid.[26] Member States are unwilling to countenance the revenue loss involved in extending tax credits to domestic shareholders without a corresponding payment of domestic company tax. To that extent, therefore, foreign income is denied the benefit of the imputation system and is subject to double taxation as under a classical system.[27]

Disadvantages of Imputation Systems for Foreign Shareholders

Under domestic legislation foreign shareholders are generally denied the tax credits granted to resident shareholders. Some Member States adopt more liberal arrangements under double taxation treaties. The United Kingdom has done so under a number of its double tax treaties with EC and non-EC countries.[28] Its treaties normally allow a full refund of the tax credit to foreign individual shareholders and corporate portfolio shareholders (i.e., those possessing no more than 10 per cent of the voting power of the paying company), subject to a withholding tax (known as an 'abatement') on the total of the dividend and the credit. In some treaties half credits are allowed for corporate shareholders with more substantial holdings.

France refunds tax credits (subject to a withholding tax) to individual and corporate portfolio shareholders (i.e., those having a 5 to 25 per cent holding depending on the treaty) under bilateral treaties with some Member States.[29] Italy refunds the tax credit only under its treaty with the United Kingdom. Ireland extends tax credits to foreign shareholders under its treaties with the United Kingdom and a number of non-EC countries. Germany has traditionally reserved the tax credit for residents (including permanent establishments in Germany) although recent treaties with the USA and Switzerland provide for a 10 per cent refund.[30]

[26] There are limited exceptions. For example, the French system gives some relief for foreign tax inasmuch as, where a parent company receives income from a subsidiary in a country having a tax treaty with France, foreign withholding tax (only) on the income may be set off against the *précompte* payable on the distribution of the income—for further details see M. A. Bouzoraa, 'Implementation of the Parent–Subsidiary Directive: France', *European Taxation*, April/May 1992.

[27] For the comments of the Ruding Committee on this issue, see 54–5 and 195 of the Report.

[28] Although not under those with Belgium, Germany, Greece, and Portugal.

[29] It also refunds (subject to withholding tax) the imputation tax to individual shareholders under treaties not providing for the refund of the tax credit and to all non-portfolio corporate shareholders (who never receive tax credits) under any treaty. Since such shareholders do not receive a refund of the tax credit, imposition of the imputation tax (the function of which is to ensure that corporate tax has been paid on dividends carrying a tax credit) is not justified.

[30] For further details see Table 3A.15 at 257 of the Ruding Committee Report.

Withholding Taxes

Withholding taxes on dividends perform two basic functions:

(1) they are the means by which a state taxes shareholders whom it cannot reach by direct assessment;
(2) they ensure compliance with tax obligations by shareholders whom a state is able to tax by direct assessment.[31]

Withholding taxes on domestic dividend payments perform the second function and are generally creditable against or take the place of the shareholder's liability.[32] All the Member States except France, Ireland, and the United Kingdom levy withholding taxes ranging from 15 to 50 per cent on domestic payments.

Withholding taxes on cross-frontier dividend payments perform the first function, representing an actual revenue gain to the source country. In effect they constitute taxation at source of dividend income of the foreign shareholders. All Member States except the United Kingdom levy withholding taxes on some or all cross-border dividend payments. The normal withholding tax rates applicable under legislation are generally reduced under bilateral tax treaties.[33]

The Netherlands and Luxembourg have comparatively low withholding tax rates under their tax treaties, and as both countries exempt income from foreign subsidiaries and operate classical corporate tax systems which do not impose an imputation tax on the distribution of exempt foreign income, they are popular choices for the location of intermediate holding companies by both EC and non-EC groups.[34]

The denial of tax credits to foreign investors and the levying of withholding taxes clearly have a distortive effect on returns from equity investment. A report published by the Institute for Fiscal Studies in October 1989 concluded that the relatively simple expedient of extending imputation tax credits to foreign shareholders and abolishing withholding taxes would lead to a significant improvement in the efficiency of the European economy.[35]

[31] For a succinct, but lucid, explanation of the different functions of withholding taxes, see Gammie, 'The Harmonization of Corporate Income Taxes in Europe: The Ruding Committee Report', (1992) 13 *Fiscal Studies* 110 ff.

[32] For a country-by-country analysis of the treatment of resident investors, see Table 3A.34 of the Ruding Committee Report.

[33] For a summary of the withholding tax rates applicable to dividend payments made by subsidiary companies to their parent companies, see Table 3A.18 at 261 of the Ruding Committee Report.

[34] For a summary of holding company rules see Shelton and De Petter, 'Holding Companies', note 18 above.

[35] Devereux and Pearson, 'Corporate Tax Harmonization and Economic Efficiency', *IFS Report Series*, No. 35.

12

The Parent–Subsidiary Directive

AIMS AND SCOPE OF THE DIRECTIVE

The Directive, which was adopted on 23 July 1990 and was to be implemented in national law by 1 January 1992, was based on a Commission proposal originally submitted to the Council in 1969.[1] It was adopted under Article 100 of the EC Treaty, which provides for the approximation of national provisions directly affecting the establishment or functioning of the Common Market. The preamble to the Directive refers to the need to introduce tax rules which are neutral from the point of view of competition 'in order to allow enterprises to adapt to the requirements of the common market, to increase their productivity and to improve their competitive strength at the international level'.[2] Specifically, the Directive seeks to eliminate the tax disadvantage suffered by companies from different Member States, by comparison with companies of the same Member State, where they seek to co-operate by forming groups of parent companies and subsidiaries.[3]

The Directive requires Member States:

(a) to refrain, subject to limited exceptions, from imposing withholding taxes on distributions of profits made by subsidiary companies to their parent companies (defined as companies possessing a 25 per cent equity holding or share of the voting rights) in other Member States; and
(b) to grant parent companies double tax relief in respect of such income by the exemption or credit method. Member States choosing the credit method are obliged to grant relief for the underlying company tax on the profits out of which the distribution is made and for any withholding taxes that are exceptionally still permitted by the Directive.

Thus, in keeping with the stated aim of facilitating the grouping of Community companies, the scope of the Directive is limited to profit distributions between associated companies, and does not extend to payments to individual shareholders or companies holding shares as a portfolio investment.[4] Since prior to the adoption of the Directive most Member States already granted relief to parent companies on the terms specified, its main impact was to require Member States to abolish the withholding taxes applicable under domestic legislation or bilateral treaties with other Member States.

[1] OJ 1969, C39/7. [2] 1st recital of the preamble.
[3] 2nd and 3rd recitals of the preamble.

The Directive is more restricted in certain respects than the original 1969 proposal. In particular, under the proposal the threshold for parent-company status was a 20 per cent holding; moreover, a company qualified as a parent company if its holding resulted from a transfer of assets, regardless of the size of the holding.[5] The proposal also provided for a system of consolidated profits where the parent company had a minimum holding of 50 per cent of the capital of the subsidiary.[6] The system was intended in particular to allow losses incurred by subsidiaries to be taken into account in calculating the parent company's taxable profits[7] and could be extended, at the option of the parent company, to subsidiaries situated in non-member countries.

IMPACT OF THE DIRECTIVE ON IMPUTATION SYSTEMS

The Directive does not address the disadvantages for foreign shareholders and companies with foreign income inherent in imputation systems.[8] The term 'withholding tax' is expressly stated not to cover any advance payment or prepayment (*précompte*) of corporation tax to the Member State of the subsidiary made in connection with a distribution of profits to its parent company.[9] In that connection the Ruding Committee made two recommendations for future legislation[10]: First, Member States applying imputation taxes should be required, on a reciprocal basis, to allow such taxes to be reduced by corporate income tax paid in another Member State in respect of dividends remitted by a subsidiary or profits earned by a permanent establishment. The effect of this would be to eliminate, at the expense of the country of the parent company or head office, the double taxation occurring upon the distribution of foreign income to the company's shareholders. Secondly, Member States granting tax relief for dividends received by domestic shareholders from domestic companies should be obliged, on a reciprocal basis, to provide equivalent relief for dividends received by domestic shareholders from companies in other Member States. This recommendation, designed to address the disadvantages of imputation systems for foreign shareholders, embodies a different solution from the one adopted by the United Kingdom and France

[4] It is worth noting that the Ruding Committee, pointing out that some Member States have stipulated a lower threshold than the 25% holding prescribed by the Directive, recommended that there should be a substantial reduction in the holding requirement before the end of 1994: see the Ruding Committee Report (Brussels: E.C. Commission, 1992), 203. A substantial reduction in the 25% threshold seems desirable in so far as it would facilitate the raising of equity capital from other Member States. Moreover, the threshold is possibly too high, or at least over-simplistic, even when measured against the more limited aim of promoting grouping of companies.

[5] Art. 3 of the Proposal.

[6] Art. 7 of the Proposal.

[7] 6th recital in the preamble to the Proposal. At the suggestion of the European Parliament the matter of relief for foreign losses became the subject of a separate proposal: see Ch. 14.

[8] See above, pp. 251–2.

[9] Art. 7(1).

[10] Ruding Committee Report, note 4 above, p. 208.

under their tax treaties, namely extension of tax credits by the source country to foreign shareholders;[11] instead the shareholder's country of residence would grant tax credits in respect of foreign corporate taxes paid.[12]

INDIVIDUAL PROVISIONS OF THE DIRECTIVE

Article 1

1. Each Member State shall apply this Directive:
   —to distributions of profit received by companies of that State which come from their subsidiaries of other Member States,
   —to distributions of profits by companies of that State to companies of other Member States of which they are subsidiaries.
2. This Directive shall not preclude the application of domestic or agreement-based provisions required for the prevention of fraud or abuse.

The common system of taxation established by the Directive applies only to distributions of profits between companies of different Member States. The factor connecting a company to a particular State is discussed under Article 2.

Commentators in the Netherlands[13] have raised the question whether a Member State may 'compartmentalize' the profit distributions which a parent company receives from its subsidiary company, that is to say, limit exemption to the portion of the distributed profits corresponding to the period for which the parent company possessed the required holding in the subsidiary. This question has arisen as a result of rulings of the Dutch Supreme Court[14] requiring capital gains on the disposal of shares to be apportioned where the parent company did not qualify for the Dutch participation exemption throughout the period for which the shares were held. However, in the absence of an express derogation in the Directive there seems to be no basis for such a rule. If the Community legislature had intended to place such a restriction on the application of the Directive it would surely have included a further derogation in Article 3(2).

Unlike the Sixth VAT Directive, the Parent–Subsidiary Directive makes no provision concerning administrative arrangements for implementing the Directive. It must, however, be presumed that the Member States are entitled to introduce arrangements to ensure that the benefit of the Directive is claimed only in respect of qualifying transactions. It is not clear that the fraud proviso in Article 1(2) adds much to that general power. It is submitted that,

[11] Above, p. 252.

[12] For the difficulties which the recommendation is likely to present for the UK, see Gammie, 'The Harmonisation of Corporate Income Taxes in Europe: The Ruding Committee Report', [1992] 13 *Fiscal Studies*, 115, published by the Institute for Fiscal Studies.

[13] See, e.g., Jan A.G. van der Geld, 'Some general problems in the implementation of the Parent–Subsidiary Directive', [1992–4] *EC Tax Review* 227.

[14] Published in [1986] BNB 305, [1991] BNB 268, and [1992] BNB 195.

by virtue of the principle of proportionality, any arrangements must stay within the limits of what is necessary and appropriate to ensure the requisite administrative control or to combat fraud. Thus, for example, it would not, on the one hand, seem unreasonable for a Member State to require that an application be made to the tax authorities for recognition as a qualifying parent company. On the other hand, legislation which granted exemption from withholding tax only by way of a refund upon application to the authorities, involving delay and administrative costs for taxpayers, would seem unnecessary.

The scope of the abuse proviso is unclear, the Directive offering no definition of what constitutes an 'abuse'. On the assumption that 'fraud' and 'abuse' have separate meanings, it seems that 'abuse' must be intended to cover forms of tax avoidance which fall short of fraud but are none the less considered illegitimate, even if in some cases strictly legal. There is however no generally accepted definition of illegitimate tax avoidance. Countries have different ideas of what practices are illegitimate; moreover, they have traditionally dealt with them in different ways. Some Member States have general anti-abuse provisions; for example, Paragraph 42 of the German *Abgabenordnung* 1977 provides for taxation on the basis of a legal arrangement consistent with the true economic situation where an artificial legal structure is adopted.[15] Other Member States have specific legislative or treaty provisions aimed at particular practices. Of particular relevance here are two types of practice:

(1) the use of tax havens or low-tax jurisdictions: this generally involves the use of companies in countries where there is no or little tax[16] or where special privileges are granted to certain types of company or activity.[17] The precise arrangements vary, but generally the tax-haven company is used merely as a conduit for transferring profits earned from economic activity elsewhere;[18]
(2) treaty-shopping: this term is used to denote the situation where a person resident in country A seeks to take advantage of a tax treaty between

[15] See also Art. L64 of the French *Livre de Procédures Fiscales*, as amended by Act 87–502. See also Isabel Verlinden, 'Belgium: Anti-avoidance measures and rulings', *European Taxation*, February 1993, 57, where the author examines Belgian abuse rulings and provisions and compares them with the position in the Netherlands, the UK, and the US.

[16] e.g., the Bahamas, Bermuda, the Cayman Isles, the Channel Isles, Isle of Man, Hong Kong, Lichtenstein, and the Dutch Antilles.

[17] e.g., Luxembourg holding companies exempted under the Act of 1929, Belgian co-ordination centres, Dutch and German investment companies, Irish companies qualifying under the Irish financial centre arrangements.

[18] For a summary of the main types of tax-haven operation, see Davies, *Principles of International Double Taxation Relief*, (London: Sweet and Maxwell, 1985), p. 10 ff. See also Andrea Manganelli, 'Italy: New rules on international tax avoidance', *European Taxation*, October 1992, 347, where the author summarizes the main types of rules enacted by countries to combat abuse involving tax havens and looks in detail at the Italian provisions.

countries B and C. For example, it may be that country B has a treaty with country A whereas country C does not, and that by routing its investment through a company in country B a company in country A can reduce the withholding taxes levied on dividends or obtain payment of tax credits. Treaty-shopping is often combined with the use of companies in tax-haven countries, particularly those such as the Dutch Antilles and former British colonies which have tax treaties with major countries.[19]

The Parent–Subsidiary Directive establishes favourable arrangements for cross-border dividend payments between Member States, and it was evidently felt necessary to allow Member States to apply provisions to combat practices which improperly exploit the benefits of the Directive. Since prior to the implementation of the Directive most Member States already granted unilateral parent-company relief and treaty reductions in withholding taxes, they have simply modified or extended their existing provisions. The question arises as to the nature of the practices which Member States are permitted to restrict and the permitted scope of anti-abuse provisions. Some commentators[20] have suggested that the abuse proviso permits different implementation of the Directive in the Member States. However, the Court seems more likely to seek a uniform application of the Directive by laying down criteria defined by reference to the aims and scheme of the Directive. The effectiveness of the Directive would be seriously undermined if Member States were permitted to limit its application by reference to their own notions of abuse. It is not possible here to consider the merits of all the various anti-abuse provisions applied by the Member States.[21] We restrict ourselves to considering what criteria might be appropriate for the purpose of defining the limits of such provisions. Before we do so, it may be useful to identify several practices which might be perceived to constitute abuse in the context of the Directive:

(1) A non-EC company might artificially route its investment into a Member State via an intermediate holding company in another Member State in order to gain the benefit of the latter's tax treaty and minimize withholding taxes. In order to combat such a practice a Member State might refuse the withholding tax exemption where the parent company is controlled by non-EC interests unless it can show that the arrangement is not an artificial arrangement designed to take advantage of the withholding tax exemption.[22]

[19] For a discussion of modern treaty-shopping structures, see Felix J. Wurm, 'Treaty shopping in the 1992 OECD Model Convention', [1992] 12 *Intertax* 658.

[20] See, e.g., Jan A. G. van der Geld, 'Some General Problems', 225 and 226.

[21] For an overview of the anti-abuse provisions applied by the Member States in connection with the Directive, see de Hosson and van Noordenne, 'Current status of the implementation of the direct tax directives', [1992] 3 *EC Tax Review* 162 and 163.

[22] France has provisions of this type: see M. A. Bouzoraa, 'Implementation in France', *European Taxation*, April/May 1992, 136 at 142.

(2) A parent company in a Member State might repatriate profits from tax havens through intermediary holding companies in other Member States or from subsidiaries in other Member States having low tax rates or offering special privileges for certain companies or activities. In response a Member State might apply rules denying the parent company exemption of the income.[23]

Those examples raise two basic questions:

(1) What importance is to be attached to the fact that a group is ultimately owned by non-EC residents?
(2) To what extent may a Member State deny companies subject to its jurisdiction the ability to take advantage of lower tax levels elsewhere in the Community?

As suggested earlier, the permissible limits of anti-abuse provisions must be determined in the light of the objectives of the Directive. Such provisions must not, it is submitted, detract from those objectives by restricting the application of the Directive in cases which properly fall within its scope. The specific objective of the Directive is to eliminate certain tax disadvantages associated with the functioning of transnational groups within the Community. That objective is to be seen against the broader aim of strengthening Community undertakings and making them more competitive by allowing cross-border co-operation.[24]

Non-EC Groups

It must be clear that, at one extreme, the mere fact that a group of companies operating within the EC is ultimately owned wholly or in part by non-EC residents cannot of itself be a reason for denying it the benefits of the Directive. Where a non-EC group comprises companies carrying on business in several Member States, the grant of relief in respect of dividend flows between those companies must fall within the aims of the Directive.

Where, however, at the other extreme a non-EC group adopts a structure with no commercial purpose purely to avoid withholding taxes or imputation

[23] Belgium, e.g., excludes from relief dividends from companies established in a tax haven, holding or finance companies established abroad which enjoy a favourable regime, certain investment companies, and intermediary holding companies distributing dividends from income that would not qualify for relief. A list of tax havens and companies enjoying a favourable regime is published in the Official Gazette. Distributions from such sources are presumed not to be from profits subject to a profits tax similar to the Belgian tax and hence are excluded from parent-company relief. In the case of dividends from holding or finance companies and investment companies, the presumption may be rebutted by the recipient of the dividend: see Francis Vanderhoydonck and Patrick Verjans, 'Implementation of the Parent–Subsidiary Directive: Belgium', *European Taxation*, April/May 1992, 132.

[24] 1st, 2nd, and 3rd recitals of the preamble.

taxes on profits distributed to a non-EC resident (for example a brass-plate intermediary holding company in a Member State with a favourable treaty with the non-member country in which the ultimate holding company is resident), it would not serve the aims of the Directive to allow the benefit of the Directive to be used in that way. This would probably be an instance of 'abuse' for the purposes of Article 1(2).

The real difficulty lies in determining where to draw the line between those two extremes. Naturally, commercial considerations permitting, companies adopt structures which are the most tax efficient. It would be to construe the concept of abuse too widely to regard as abusive any structure which allowed an investment to be made in a Member State by a non-EC resident at a lower tax cost than if the investment were made directly. As an exception to the general scheme of the Directive, the abuse proviso surely falls to be construed narrowly. It would seem appropriate to restrict its application to artificial arrangements. In this connection some guidance may be derived from Article 11(1) of the Merger Directive, which permits Member States to deny the benefit of that Directive where the transaction 'has as its principal objective or as one of its principal objectives tax evasion or tax avoidance; the fact that one of the operations referred to in Article 1 is not carried out for valid commercial reasons . . . may constitute a presumption that the operation has tax evasion or tax avoidance as its principal objective or as one of its principal objectives.' It may be equally relevant here to inquire into the reasons why subsidiaries are owned in one form of group structure rather than another. The absence of valid commercial reasons for a structure would cast doubt on whether granting the benefit of the Directive would further the aim of promoting cross-frontier co-operation. A commercial-purpose test is possibly easier to apply to reorganizations etc. comprising specific transactions with specific objectives. However, it would perhaps not be unreasonable for a Member State to demand that a parent company controlled by non-EC interests should demonstrate some commercial substance by performing substantial head office or co-ordination functions. Whether a requirement of business activities going beyond such functions would be justified is unclear.

Distributions from other Member States

It is perhaps worth making first of all the seemingly obvious remark that a Member State need not rely on the proviso in Article 1 if the distribution does not fall within the scope of the Directive. That remark is prompted by a tendency in tax literature to use the term 'anti-abuse provision' in a broader sense than it has in the Directive. Thus, for example, the refusal of parent-company relief for distributions made by companies, such as Luxembourg holding companies, not qualifying as a 'company of a Member State' under Article 2 is not an anti-abuse provision for the purposes of Article 1.

To what extent may a Member State refuse parent-company relief in respect of a qualifying distribution from a subsidiary company in another Member State? It is clear, on the one hand, that if a Member State were permitted to refuse exemption to parent companies in respect of dividend income paid from profits subject to a low level of taxation in another Member State, this would be liable to interfere with the aim of eliminating obstacles to cross-frontier co-operation. The income would be subject to double taxation to an extent which depended on the respective levels of taxation in the Member States concerned. On the other hand, the Directive does not guarantee capital import neutrality (i.e., restriction of tax to the level applicable in the country of investment) since Article 4(1) offers Member States the choice of the exemption or credit method for granting relief to the parent company. The credit method automatically tops up low taxation in the country of investment to the domestic level. Member States applying the exemption method would argue that exemption is justified only if the income out of which the dividend is paid has been subject to a level of company taxation comparable to the domestic level.

It has already been suggested that a Member State may rely upon the anti-abuse proviso only to combat artificial arrangements. Arguably, however, there is nothing in Article 4 of the Directive to prevent a Member State which applies the exemption method from using the credit method in cases where exemption is not justified because the distribution is made out of income that has been subject to abnormally low levels of taxation in another Member State.[25] The contrary view would be unfortunate since it might lead certain States to opt entirely for the credit method.

The Abuse Proviso and the Principle of Proportionality

It seems clear that anti-abuse legislation must go no further than is necessary and appropriate to serve the permitted purpose of such legislation. For example, certain commentators[26] raise the question whether, in a case where a parent company receives, from an intermediary holding company in another Member State, dividends derived partly from trading income subject to tax in that State and partly from a holding held in a tax haven, the entire dividend may be excluded from relief or only the proportion relating to the tax-haven profit. It is submitted that, while the denial of exemption in respect of the tax-haven profit is justifiable, anti-abuse legislation refusing exemption in respect of the entire dividend would be disproportionate to its permitted purpose.

[25] Denmark has retained provisions permitting the use of the credit method in exceptional cases. See Overgaard, Koch-Nielsen & Gronborg, 'Legislation: Denmark', [1992] 4 *EC Tax Review*, 256. See also B. P. Dik, 'Implementation of the Parent–Subsidiary Directive in Denmark', *European Taxation*, April/May 1992, 134 ff.

[26] Vanderhoydonck and Verjans 'Implementation in Belgium', *European Taxation*, April/May 1992, p. 133.

Article 2

For the purposes of this Directive 'company of a Member State' shall mean any company which:

(a) takes one of the forms listed in the Annex hereto;

(b) according to the tax laws of a Member State is considered to be resident in that State for tax purposes and, under the terms of a double taxation agreement concluded with a third State, is not considered to be resident for tax purposes outside the Community;

(c) moreover, is subject to one of the following taxes, without the possibility of an option or of being exempt:

—impôt des sociétés/vennootschapsbelasting in Belgium,
—selskabsskat in Denmark,
—Körperschaftsteuer in the Federal Republic of Germany,
—*φόρος εισοδήματος νομικών προσώπων κερδοσκοπικού χαρακτήρα* in Greece,
—impuesto sobre sociedades in Spain,
—impôt sur les sociétés in France,
—corporation tax in Ireland,
—imposta sul reddito delle persone giuridiche in Italy,
—impôt sur le revenu des collectivités in Luxembourg,
—vennootschapsbelasting in the Netherlands,
—imposto sobre o rendimento das pessoas colectivas in Portugal,
—corporation tax in the United Kingdom,

or to any other tax which may be substituted for any of the above taxes.

Thus, by virtue of Article 2(a) the term 'company' is exhaustively defined in the Annex to the Directive by reference to concepts of national law. The Annex reads as follows:

List of companies referred to in Article 2(a)

(a) companies under Belgian law known as 'société anonyme'/'naamloze vennootschap', 'société en commandite par actions'/'commanditaire vennootschap op aandelen', 'société privée à responsabilité limitée'/'besloten vennootschap met beperkte aansprakelijkheid' and those public law bodies that operate under private law;

(b) companies under Danish law known as: 'aktieselskab', 'anpartsselskab';

(c) companies under German law known as: 'Aktiengesellschaft', Kommanditgesellschaft auf Aktien', 'Gesellschaft mit beschränkter Haftung', 'bergrechtliche Gewerkschaft';

(d) companies under Greek law known as: '*ανώνυμη εταιρία*';

(e) companies under Spanish law known as: 'sociedad anónima', 'sociedad comanditaria por acciones', 'sociedad de responsabilidad limitada' and those public law bodies which operate under private law;

(f) companies under French law known as 'société anonyme', société en commandite par actions', 'société à responsabilité limitée' and industrial and commercial public establishments and undertakings;

(g) the companies in Irish law known as public companies limited by shares or by guarantee, private companies limited by shares or by guarantee, bodies registered under the Industrial and Provident Societies Acts or building societies registered under the Building Societies Acts;

(h) companies under Italian Law known as 'società per azioni', 'società in accomandita per azioni', 'società a responsabilità limitata', and public and private entities carrying on industrial and commercial activities;

(i) companies under Luxembourg law known as 'société anonyme', 'société en commandite par actions', 'société à responsabilité limitée';

(j) companies under Dutch law known as: 'naamloze vennootschap', 'besloten vennootschap met beperkte aansprakelijkheid';

(k) commercial companies or civil law companies having a commercial form, cooperatives and public undertakings incorporated in accordance with Portuguese law;

(l) companies incorporated under the law of the United Kingdom.

It will be noted that in a number of cases the continental concept of a partnership limited by shares (société en commandite par actions, Kommanditgesellschaft auf Aktien, etc.) qualifies as a company for these purposes. These entities must be distinguished from ordinary limited partnerships (société en commandite, Kommanditgesellschaft, etc.), which are not capital companies and do not qualify as companies under the Directive.

On 26 July 1993 the Commission submitted to the Council a proposal[27] for an amendment under which the scope of the Directive would be extended to any entity subject to corporate tax.

The Directive refers to national law for the purposes of defining fiscal residence (Article 2(b)). Although not defined, 'residence' must be presumed to mean full liability to tax in the state concerned rather than partial liability, for example in respect of the profits of a permanent establishment in that state. Such is the normal understanding of the term, and the one which corresponds to the definition in the OECD Model Convention. Article 4(1) of that Convention provides:

> For the purposes of this Convention, the term 'resident of a Contracting State' means any person who, under the laws of that State, is liable to tax therein by reason of his domicile, residence, place of management or any other criterion of a similar nature. But this term does not include any person who is liable to tax in that State in respect only of income from sources in that State or capital situated therein.

The Commentary to Article 4(1) explains that that definition is intended to cover the various forms of personal attachment to a State which under domestic law form the basis for comprehensive taxation.[28]

The second part of Article 2(b) envisages the case where a company is resident for tax purposes both in a Member State and in a third country by reason of different connecting factors. Where a tax treaty exists between the two

[27] COM(93)293 final, OJ 1993, C225/5. [28] Para. 8.

countries, the tax residence of the company will normally be resolved in favour of one of the countries. Article 4(3) of the OECD Model Convention provides:

> Where by reason of the provisions of paragraph 1 a person other than an individual is a resident of both Contracting States, then it shall be deemed to be a resident of the State in which its effective management is situated.

To qualify under the Directive a company must, first, meet the criteria for tax residence laid down by the law of the Member State concerned and, secondly, not be deemed resident in a non-member country under a treaty clause similar to Article 4(3) of the OECD Model. Thus, where a company is resident for tax purposes in a Member State by virtue of being incorporated there but is deemed under a tax treaty to be resident in a non-member country because its place of effective management is in that country, it is excluded from the scope of the Directive even if it has a permanent establishment subject to tax in that or any other Member State. On the other hand, the fact that a company resident for tax purposes in a Member State has a permanent establishment in a non-EC country subject to tax in that country under a tax treaty does not exclude it from the scope of the Directive. Moreover, it seems that a company which is dual resident according to the laws of a Member State and a non-member country not linked by any tax treaty would none the less satisfy Article 2(b)—the absence of a treaty would mean that the company remained subject to comprehensive taxation in a Member State.

The company, in addition to being incorporated and resident for tax purposes in the Community, must be 'subject to one of' the various national corporate taxes mentioned 'without the possibility of an option or of being exempt'. The wording of Article 2(c) suggests that the relevant test is whether the company, as an entity, is one which is subject to company tax. The possibility of the option or exemption concerns the entity itself rather than particular categories of income. Statements in the Council minutes bear this out. According to de Hosson,[29] the minutes specifically mention as being excluded from the Directive Luxembourg holding companies covered by the Act of 31 July 1929,[30] Dutch investment companies covered by Article 28 of the 1969 Dutch Corporation Tax Act,[31] German investment companies covered by the

[29] *The Direct Investment Tax Initiatives of the European Community* (Deventer, The Netherlands: Kluwer, 1990), 35. Although Council minutes are not published, de Hosson appears to have knowledge of them.

[30] Under that law companies whose activity is limited to the holding of shares in other companies or certain other securities or rights may be exempt from Luxembourg tax, apart from the annual subscription tax of 0.2% on share capital and capital duty of 1%. See further Edward Bruin, 'Implementation of the Parent–Subsidiary Directive: Luxembourg', *European Taxation*, April/May 1992, 161.

[31] See however the comments of Smit and van Weeghel, 'Implementation of the Parent–Subsidiary Directive: Netherlands, *European Taxation*, April/May 1992, 166 at 170, who question whether such companies are excluded from the scope of the Directive according to the

Act on *Kapitalanlagegesellschaften*, and Spanish and Portuguese companies which are fiscally transparent, that is to say, whose income is exempt in so far as their profits are taxed in the hands of shareholders. De Hosson states that the reference to the possibility of an option concerns the arrangements which used to apply in Belgium whereby private limited companies could opt for fiscal transparency. While in the light of the Court's previous practice it would be wise to attach only limited importance to statements in the minutes regarding particular types of company, the minutes as a whole seem to confirm that the purpose of the provision is to exclude certain categories of companies subject to special regimes removing them from the scope of company taxes. Thus, the fact that the income of a subsidiary paying a dividend is wholly exempt, for example because it is derived from subsidiaries or permanent establishments in other Member States or non-member countries, does not remove it from the scope of the Directive. The requirements of Article 2 do not therefore guarantee that a distribution by a qualifying subsidiary is made out of profits that have actually been subject to company taxation in a Member State. As already suggested, Member States may, however, rely on the abuse proviso in Article 1 to limit parent-company relief where the distribution forms part of an artificial arrangement, for example a device to repatriate profits from a tax haven via another Member State with a liberal regime.

Company of which Member State?

The three conditions laid down by Article 2 need not necessarily be met in a single Member State. It seems, for instance, that a company incorporated in one Member State but resident for tax purposes in a second Member State satisfies the requirements of Article 2. This raises the question of which Member State a company belongs to where it does not satisfy all the criteria in the same Member State. Under Article 1 a Member State is required to apply the Directive solely to companies 'of that State' in respect of profits distributed by or to companies 'of other Member States'. This issue has been the subject of some discussion amongst commentators,[32] who focus on the following type of situation:

> A company incorporated in the Netherlands has its principal business establishment and place of management in Belgium and has a German permanent establishment subject to German company tax. The company

literal wording of Art. 2. It seems that such companies, although subject to corporate tax, benefit from a zero rate if certain conditions concerning the distribution of investment income to shareholders are met. De Hosson concludes that the exclusion of such companies must be on the basis that they are granted effective exemption.

[32] See, e.g., Schonewille, 'Some Questions on the Parent–Subsidiary Directive and the Merger Directive', [1992] 1 *Intertax* 13, in which the author reviews the opinions expressed by several commentators and adds his own views.

receives dividends from subsidiaries in Germany and France which are effectively connected with the German permanent establishment and hence are taxable in Germany. Is Germany required by the Directive to refrain from taxing the dividends?

If, as some commentators suggest, a company is taken to belong to the Member State in which it is resident for tax purposes, then only the Netherlands is obliged by the Directive to grant relief to the parent company. In order to overcome this problem Schonewille argues that each of the three criteria in Article 2 might constitute an independent test of where a company belongs, so that a company belongs to all the Member States in which it fulfils any of the three criteria. In the above example the company would therefore be a Dutch company by virtue of the criteria in Article 2(a) and (b),[33] a Belgian company by virtue of the criteria in (b) and (c), and a German company by virtue of criterion in (c). Schonewille would thus reject the view that Germany, not being the State of the parent company for the purposes of Article 4(1), is under no obligation to grant relief in respect of the dividends received from the French subsidiary.

Schonewille's imaginative solution is attractive at first sight: Article 4 of the Directive would then be interpreted as applying to a Member State which claims the right to tax the dividend income of the permanent establishment of a non-resident company covered by the Directive. However, a more normal understanding of the term 'State of the parent company' would be the State in which the company is resident for tax purposes. Indeed the wording of Article 4 seems to envisage one rather than several States. Moreover, Schonewille's view is difficult to reconcile with the provisions of the Merger Directive, which contains an identical definition of 'company of a Member State' and whose application likewise depends on identifying the State to which the companies concerned belong. It seems clear, for example, that the 'State of the transferring company' for the purposes of that Directive is the State in which the company is resident for tax purposes.[34]

It is moreover doubtful whether the perceived problem actually exists. In the above example Germany would be in breach of Article 52 of the EC Treaty[35] if it were to refuse to extend to permanent establishments of companies resident in other Member States the relief which it is obliged to grant under the Directive to companies resident for tax purposes in Germany: the rationale for the relief, namely the tax already borne on the income, is valid regardless of the difference in the positions of a resident company and a permanent establishment. As far as dividends received by the non-resident company's German permanent establishment from German subsidiaries are

[33] The Netherlands bases tax residence on the criterion of incorporation.

[34] See below, p. 280.

[35] For a more detailed discussion of the implications of Art. 52 in the tax sphere, see Ch. 16.

concerned, Germany would be obliged by Article 52 to extend to the permanent establishment whatever arrangements it chose to apply to resident companies. This is surely an appropriate result.

Article 3

1. For the purposes of applying this Directive,
   (a) the status of parent company shall be attributed at least to any company of a Member State which fulfils the conditions set out in Article 2 and has a minimum holding of 25% in the capital of a company of another Member State fulfilling the same conditions;
   (b) 'subsidiary' shall mean that company the capital of which includes the holding referred to in (a).
2. By way of derogation from paragraph 1, Member States shall have the option of:
   —replacing, by means of bilateral agreement, the criterion of a holding in the capital by that of a holding of voting rights,
   —not applying this Directive to companies of that Member State which do not maintain for an uninterrupted period of at least two years holdings qualifying them as parent companies or to those of their companies in which a company of another Member State does not maintain such a holding for an uninterrupted period of at least two years.

The 25 per cent holding criterion corresponds to the one used in Article 10(2) of the OECD Model Convention. The Convention expressly requires the holding to be held 'directly'. The same probably applies to the Directive, although the latter is silent on this point. On a literal reading, capital is not expressly limited to voting capital and extends to, for example, non-voting preference shares. That view is arguably supported by the option granted to Member States in Article 3(2) to adopt the criterion of voting rights. Moreover, it is entirely conceivable that a holding of non-voting shares might be acquired in the framework of cross-frontier co-operation between companies rather than as a mere portfolio investment.

The use and position of the words 'at least' confirm that a Member State may adopt more liberal arrangements as regards both the conditions set out in Article 2 and the holding requirement. Numerous Member States have retained the significantly lower holding requirements for parent-company relief which they already applied; most have chosen not to adopt a more liberal requirement for the withholding tax exemption.[36]

Article 3(2) allows Member States to replace by bilateral agreement the criterion of capital holding by that of voting rights. The use of such a criterion is also envisaged by the Commentary to the OECD Model Convention and has traditionally been favoured by the United Kingdom in its double taxation agreements. Member States opting for the voting rights criterion must presumably likewise set the minimum at no more than 25 per cent of voting rights.

[36] See de Hosson and van Noordenne, 'Current status', 159–60.

The second proviso in Article 3(2) concerning a minimum holding period seems to have been inserted to respond to the fear that there might be abuse through the quick resale of shares.[37] De Hosson questions whether the provision is necessary, given that Article 1(2) allows Member States to apply provisions to combat fraud or abuse. The explanation may be that the provision survives from the original 1969 proposal, which did not contain the general abuse proviso. Moreover, a two-year holding requirement may have been considered too long or too absolute to be caught by Article 1(2), since an acquisition and sale of shares might conceivably take place within a shorter period for valid commercial reasons. The provision's lack of precision is likely to give rise to litigation. On one view it allows a Member State to suspend the grant of relief for up to two years before granting relief retrospectively; a contrary view is that it is sufficient for a Member State to require a guarantee that the tax will be paid in the event of the holding not being retained for the minimum period. That the provision constitutes an exception to the general scheme of the Directive speaks in favour of the narrower construction. Support for the practicality of that view is provided by the Dutch rules, which allow the minimum one-year holding period required for the purposes of the withholding tax exemption to be fulfilled after the distribution is made, provided that a guarantee is given by the subsidiary.[38]

Article 4

1. Where a parent company, by virtue of its association with its subsidiary, receives distributed profits, the State of the parent company shall, except when the latter is liquidated, either:

—refrain from taxing such profits, or

—tax such profits while authorizing the parent company to deduct from the amount of tax due that fraction of the corporation tax paid by the subsidiary which relates to those profits and, if appropriate, the amount of the withholding tax levied by the Member State in which the subsidiary is resident, pursuant to the derogations provided for in Article 5, up to the limit of the amount of the corresponding domestic tax.

2. However, each Member State shall retain the option of providing that any charges relating to the holding and any losses resulting from the distribution of the profits of the subsidiary may not be deducted from the taxable profits of the parent company. Where the management costs relating to the holding in such a case are fixed as a flat rate, the fixed amount may not exceed 5% of the profits distributed by the subsidiary.

[37] Explanatory Memorandum to the 1969 Proposal.

[38] See van der Geld, 'Some general problems', 226. For a summary of the minimum holding periods laid down by Member States for the purposes of parent-company relief and the withholding tax exemption, see de Hosson and van Noordenne, 'Current status', 161–2. For further discussion of the holding requirement, see Vanistendael, 'The Implementation of the Parent–Subsidiary Directive in the EC—Comments on some unresolved questions', *Tax Notes International*, 21 September 1992.

3. Paragraph 1 shall apply until the date of effective entry into force of a common system of company taxation.

The Council shall at the appropriate time adopt the rules to apply after the date referred to in the first subparagraph.

For the purpose of granting relief under Article 4 Member States may therefore choose between the exemption method and the credit method. Member States opting for the credit method are required only to give relief for the relevant portion of underlying company tax paid by the subsidiary distributing the profit—they are not obliged to give relief for tax paid by lower-tier Community subsidiaries. In its proposal of 26 July 1993 for an amending directive[39] the Commission sought to extend the relief to tax paid by such subsidiaries. The words 'up to the limit of the amount of the corresponding domestic tax' make it clear that Member States may restrict the foreign tax credit to the domestic liability on the specific income. A Member State applying a lower rate of tax than the Member State of the subsidiary is therefore not obliged to allow surplus foreign tax credit to be relieved against domestic tax on other income.

Denmark, although applying the exemption method in most cases, applies the credit method where the income out of which the dividend is paid is subject to company taxation deviating significantly from the Danish tax. The legality of such rules is discussed under Article 1.[40]

The meaning of the term 'distributed profits' and the words 'by virtue of its association with its subsidiary' are examined under Article 5.[41]

Unlike the proposal, Article 4 of the Directive does not apply to liquidation profits. The possible reasons for this are discussed below.[42] In the interests of certainty it may be preferable to interpret the phrase 'except when the latter is liquidated' (German: '*anläßlich der Liquidation*'; French: 'à l'occasion de la liquidation') as referring to cases where formal liquidation proceedings have been commenced pursuant to the applicable national law.

Article 4(2) allows Member States to refuse deduction of charges relating to the holding from the taxable profits of the parent company. The term 'charges' is sufficiently broad to cover not only management costs but also loan interest and other costs incurred in connection with the acquisition of the holding. In the Netherlands, for example, costs incurred by the parent company in connection with a holding are deductible only if they contribute to income that is taxable in the Netherlands; costs connected with foreign holdings are therefore not tax deductible.[43] Germany, on the other hand, permits the deduction of such costs, unless they qualify as acquisition costs and

[39] Note 27, above. [40] Above, p. 261. [41] Below, p. 271 ff. [42] Below, p. 273.

[43] See the section on the Netherlands in Van der Lande and Bellingwout, *The EEC Merger and Parent–Subsidiary Directives of 23 July 1990 in Practice* (Bruylant, Brussels: 1992), at 157. *Direct Investment Initiatives*, at 40.

have to be capitalized.[44] Some Member States have tended to specify a fixed percentage for management costs. The Directive allows this practice to continue, limiting the non-deductible amount to 5 per cent of the profits distributed. Belgium, France, and Portugal have taken advantage of this option.[45] According to De Hosson,[46] the Council minutes indicate that the option concerning deduction of losses refers to the case where there is a reduction in the value of a subsidiary's shares following a distribution. A commentary on the German legislation suggests that it covers legislation such as section 26(8) of the German *Körperschaftsteuergesetz*, which provides that losses arising *inter alia* from a write-down of the going concern value of a holding in a foreign subsidiary or from the sale of the holding are not taken into account in determining the taxable income of the parent company where the losses result from the distribution of dividends and the dividends are exempt or lead to a tax credit.[47]

Article 5

1. Profits which a subsidiary distributed to its parent company shall, at least where the latter holds a minimum of 25% of the capital of the subsidiary, be exempt from withholding tax.

2. Notwithstanding paragraph 1, the Hellenic Republic may, for so long as it does not charge corporation tax on distributed profits, levy a withholding tax on profits distributed to parent companies of other Member States. However, the rate of that withholding tax must not exceed the rate provided for in bilateral double-taxation agreements.

3. Notwithstanding paragraph 1, the Federal Republic of Germany may, for as long as it charges corporation tax at a rate at least 11 points lower than the rate applicable to retained profits, and at the latest until mid-1996, impose a compensatory withholding tax of 5% on profits distributed by its subsidiary companies.

4. Notwithstanding paragraph 1, the Portuguese Republic may levy a withholding tax on profits distributed by its subsidiaries to parent companies of other Member States until a date not later than the end of the eighth year following the date of application of this Directive.

Subject to the existing bilateral agreements concluded between Portugal and a Member State, the rate of this withholding tax may not exceed 15% during the first five years and 10% during the last three years of that period.

Before the end of the eighth year the Council shall decide unanimously, on a proposal from the Commission, on a possible extension of the provisions of this paragraph.

'Distributed Profits'

Two basic questions arise with respect to the term 'distributed profits' in

44 Ibid., section on Germany, Rieger and Fueger at 135.

45 See de Hosson and van Noordenne, 'Current status', 158.

46 Ibid., at 40.

47 See Rieger and Fueger in *EEC Directives in Practice*, 135–6.

Articles 4 and 5: first, in the absence of a common definition, is the term to be defined exclusively by national law? Secondly, does the term have an identical meaning in both Articles?

It may be noted that Article 10(3) of the OECD Model Convention defines the term 'dividend' broadly as 'income from shares, *jouissance* shares or *jouissance* rights, mining shares, founders' shares or other rights, not being debt-claims, participating in profits, as well as income from other corporate rights which is subjected to the same taxation treatment as income from shares by the laws of the State of which the company making the distribution is a resident'. The Commentary to the Convention states that payments regarded as dividends may include not only distributions of profits decided by annual general meetings, but also other benefits in money or money's worth, such as bonus shares, bonuses, profits on liquidation, and disguised distributions of profits.[48]

There is in practice little uniformity in national law with respect to the definition of distributed profits, particularly disguised distributions. The lack of uniformity may be illustrated by the position in France. The latter has traditionally applied a broad concept of distributed profits under domestic law, including excess directors' fees, interest on loans from shareholders, advances or loans to shareholders, under-declarations of profits resulting from excessively low prices charged to associated companies, etc. According to Bouzoraa,[49] however, the French tax authorities, on the premise that Articles 4 and 5 leave the definition of 'distributed profits' to be determined by national law, propose to limit the scope of the Directive to dividends in the narrow sense. This represents a complete reversal of their previous attitude when they sought to include the widest possible range of distributions under the dividend Article of tax treaties in order to be able to impose withholding tax on the deemed dividends.[50]

An issue of particular importance is the treatment of excessive debt interest. Normally a company may deduct any debt interest paid from its taxable profits even if it is paid to a shareholder of the company. Article 11(6) of the OECD Model Convention provides, however, that, where interest is paid between persons between whom there is a special relationship, Article 11 (i.e., the Article on interest) does not apply to any amount which is excessive in relation to the debt. The state of the borrower may therefore deny the normal relief on the excess interest. Article 11(6) has been expanded by further provisions in some double taxation conventions so as to allow the benefits of

[48] Para. 28, as renumbered on 23 July 1992.

[49] 'Implementation of the Parent–Subsidiary Directive: France', *European Taxation*, April/May 1992, 136 ff., in particular at 141.

[50] See also van Waardenburg, '*France: Tax treaties and constructive dividend distributions—Ruling No. 4J–2–91*', European Taxation, October 1992, 330. The author undertakes a detailed review of the divergent interpretations of the French double taxation treaties with respect to the imposition of withholding taxes on constructive profit distributions.

the convention to be denied by the state of the borrower in so far as the amount of the loan itself is considered excessive having regard to the debt to equity ratio of the borrower. Disallowance of deduction of interest on the latter ground (often referred to as 'thin capitalization') may also be based on Article 9 (adjustment of profits of associated enterprises). The rationale for denying deduction is that the excess interest must be regarded as a distribution of profit, and indeed some countries actually treat it as such. Oliver[51] argues that, since the reason for the disallowance is that the borrowing is being assimilated to equity capital and the excess interest to a dividend (irrespective of whether that is the machinery by which domestic law provides for the disallowance) it would be preferable for the interest to be classified as a dividend and for parent-company relief to be given on that basis rather than leaving the matter to the vagaries of the non-mandatory mutual agreement procedure[52]; however, the 1992 Model and commentaries do not resolve this problem.

Vanistendael[53] contends that, in the context of the Directive, a distinction should be made between the positions of the parent and subsidiary companies. The extension of parent-company relief for underlying corporate tax under Article 4 to constructive distributions would presuppose matching definitions in the source state and state of residence, which is invariably not the case. Double taxation arising from thin capitalization rules should be eliminated as a transfer pricing issue under the Arbitration Convention, which would allow a fair allocation of profits between the two states rather than requiring the state of residence to provide all the relief. He also points out that under Article 4 the parent company must receive the distribution 'by virtue of its association with its subsidiary' (French: 'à titre d'associée'; German: 'als Teilhaberin'); a parent company does not receive constructive dividends in its capacity as shareholder of the subsidiary. He takes a different view with respect to the withholding tax exemption under Article 5, arguing that, if interest charges or transfer prices are reclassified as distributed profits, relief should be granted under the Directive. The problem of divergent interpretations of anti-abuse clauses in different Member States does not arise because the withholding tax is applied solely in the source State.

Vanistendael's view seems convincing. A preliminary point is that there is no reason to suppose that the definition of 'distributed profits' should be left wholly to national law. It would surely be preferable for the Court to lay down certain criteria which may be applied by national authorities in the framework of their national systems of company taxation. Thus, it is not

[51] 'Interest, dividends and the elimination of double taxation (Articles 10, 11 and 23)' [1992] 12 *Intertax* 680.

[52] See Art. 25 of the OECD Model.

[53] 'The implementation of the Parent/Subsidiary Directive in the EC—Comments on some unresolved questions', *Tax Notes International*, 21 September 1992.

inconceivable that 'distributed profits' might be interpreted for the purposes of Article 5 as extending to all payments made out of post-tax profits which are in substance treated as distributions to the parent company by the law of the state of the subsidiary. An analogy may perhaps be drawn with the Court's approach in relation to VAT. In Case 320/88, *Shipping and Forwarding Enterprise SAFE*,[54] for example, it laid down an independent definition of the 'supply of goods' for the purposes of Article 5 of the Sixth Directive which the national authorities could apply by reference to their national law on immoveable property. Secondly, while the state of the subsidiary may, in the absence of common rules, choose to apply anti-abuse provisions reclassifying certain payments as distributions, there seems to be no good reason why it should be allowed to have the best of both worlds by not so classifying them for the purposes of the Directive. Inclusion of constructive dividends within the scope of Article 5 would serve the aim of the Directive of avoiding double taxation without in any way undermining the effectiveness of the anti-abuse measures of the source state. Moreover, the absence in Article 5 of any reference to the capacity in which the parent company receives the dividend means that there is no textual bar to inclusion of reclassified interest payments within its scope.

As Vanistendael points out, an equally broad interpretation of Article 4 is problematic. First, there is the textual problem mentioned above. It is questionable whether the term 'by virtue of its association with its subsidiary' can be interpreted as covering payments which are not received by the parent company in its capacity as shareholder. Secondly, it is doubtful whether the intention can have been to require the state of the parent company to extend exemption to any payments, even those not received by the parent company as shareholder, which the source state chooses to classify as distributions.

There is thus certainly some force in the argument that the term 'distributed profits' should be considered from different perspectives for the purposes of Articles 4 and 5. Moreover, in addition to the textual difference already noted, there is the further difference that liquidation profits are expressly excluded from the scope of Article 4 whereas, in the absence of any reference, they are presumably covered by Article 5. Vanistendael[55] argues that this again reflects a difference in perspective between the two provisions. For the subsidiary company the distribution of liquidation profits is a distribution of retained earnings, so that the same rule should apply as applied to distributions during the life of the company. However, when the parent company at the time of the liquidation is a company which acquired the shares during the life of the company, the liquidating distribution must be considered to be a payment for the surrender of the shares upon liquidation, entailing a possible capital gain.

[54] [1990] ECR I–285. [55] 'Implementation', at 605.

Withholding Tax

The term 'withholding tax' is not defined in the Directive and, although commonly used in international tax literature to cover the deduction of tax at source on cross-border payments by the source country, has no precise meaning. Article 10 of the OECD Model Income Tax Convention merely speaks of taxation of dividends by the country of residence of the company paying the dividends. It seems clear that for the purposes of Article 5 'withholding tax' should be interpreted broadly as extending in principle to any taxation levied by the country of the subsidiary by reason of the distribution of profits regardless of the mechanism used for charging the tax. If the term were limited to taxes actually imposed by deduction at source, the Directive could be circumvented by, for example, taxing distributions by direct assessment. Support for a broad view is also to be derived from Article 7 of the Directive, where it was evidently thought necessary specifically to exclude imputation taxes paid by a company in connection with a distribution.[56] Arguably a higher company tax rate for distributed profits would also be contrary to Article 5(1), since the marginal rate would effectively be a deduction of tax at source and would not serve the same function as an imputation tax.[57]

The provisions concerning Greece and Germany take account of the special features of their company tax systems. Since Greece taxes distributed profits only at the shareholder level, exemption of profits distributed to foreign shareholders from withholding tax would deprive it of any tax revenue from the business activity producing those profits. Germany similarly applies a significantly lower rate to distributed profits.[58] The Greek withholding tax may not exceed the rate 'provided for in bilateral double-taxation agreements'. At 1 January 1991 Greece applied withholding tax rates varying from 25 per cent (Belgium, Germany, and Italy) to 50 per cent for certain shares[59]; Greece may therefore continue to impose withholding tax at 25 per cent on dividend payments to other Member States, or such lower rate as may subsequently be provided for in any bilateral agreement. As is apparent from the Preamble,[60] the Portuguese derogation is prompted by budgetary considerations rather than special characteristics of its tax system. The literal meaning of the phrase 'Subject to existing bilateral agreements' is unclear. Does it mean that Article 5(4) is without prejudice to all existing agreements, regardless of whether they provide for a rate of withholding tax higher or lower than 15 per cent, or does it merely mean that it is without prejudice to

[56] Below, p. 275.

[57] It may be noted that until 1 January 1992 France imposed a higher rate of tax (42%) on distributed profits. From that date the rate became the same as for retained profits (34%). Source: *Ruding Committee Report*, 64.

[58] Retained profits: 50%; distributed profits: 36%, at 1 January 1991. Source: *Ruding Committee Report*, 64.

[59] See *Ruding Committee Report*, 263.

[60] 5th Recital.

Portugal's bilateral agreements providing for a lower rate? De Hosson's view[61] that the latter is the correct interpretation seems convincing. As an exception the provision falls to be construed narrowly. Moreover, the broader interpretation would produce curious results. Portugal has no existing treaty with a Member State providing for a rate exceeding 15 per cent.[62] In practice, therefore, precedence could be given to a higher treaty rate only during the last three years of the eight-year period when the general rate was reduced to 10 per cent. This would lead to the absurd position where it would be able to apply a 15 per cent withholding tax under its agreements with a number of Member States, but would be restricted to a rate of 10 per cent in the case of States with which it had no treaties!

Article 6

The Member State of a parent company may not charge withholding tax on the profits which such a company receives from a subsidiary.

This provision appears to be of limited significance. According to De Hosson,[63] it was prompted by Belgian rules under which a withholding tax of 10 per cent was imposed on dividends received by Belgian companies from abroad.

Article 7

1. The term 'withholding tax' as used in this Directive shall not cover an advance payment or prepayment (précompte) of corporation tax to the Member State of the subsidiary which is made in connection with a distribution of profits to its parent company.

2. This Directive shall not affect the application of domestic or agreement-based provisions designed to eliminate or lessen economic double taxation of dividends, in particular provisions relating to the payment of tax credits to the recipients of dividends.

Member States thus retain the right to impose imputation taxes[64] on the distribution of dividends to foreign parent companies notwithstanding the denial of tax credits to the latter. The Directive does not therefore attempt to remedy the disadvantages of such systems for foreign shareholders.[65]

The wording of paragraph 2 is peculiar at first sight since it might be wondered why, but for this paragraph, the Directive might preclude the application of provisions reducing double taxation, in particular refunds of tax credits. However, the scope of the provision becomes clearer when it is remembered that refunds of tax credits or imputation taxes to foreign shareholders are liable to be reduced by withholding taxes.[66] Some commentators

[61] *Direct Investment Initiatives*, note 29 above, at 44.

[62] At 1 January 1991 Portugal's withholding tax rates were as follows: UK, Spain, and Denmark: 10%; Belgium,Germany, France, Italy: 15%; Luxembourg, the Netherlands, Ireland, Greece: 25% (no treaty): *Ruding Committee Report*, 263.

[63] *Direct Investment Initiatives*, note 29 above, at 44.

[64] Above, p. 250 ff.

[65] Above, p. 252.

[66] Above, p. 252.

have argued that on its wording the provision cannot be used as a basis for withholding tax on refunds of tax credits since it only permits measures which reduce double taxation. However, that view would make the provision redundant. The provision is presumably intended to authorize measures which, although in themselves imposing a charge, form part of arrangements designed to reduce double taxation. In refunding tax credits the United Kingdom applies the withholding tax to both the dividend and the tax credit. This has led some commentators[67] to suggest that only the withholding tax on the tax credit can be justified on the basis of Article 7(2). It is unclear whether that view is tenable if the withholding tax is imposed in the context of a measure which leads to an overall reduction of economic double taxation.

[67] See, e.g., Vanistendael, '*Implementation*'.

13

The Merger Directive

INTRODUCTION

In so far as they involve the disposal or cancellation of shareholdings and the transfer of assets from one company to another, corporate grouping or restructuring operations are liable under most tax systems to give rise to taxable gains at the shareholder or company level. For example, a restructuring operation involving the transfer by a company of all or part of its business to another company in exchange for shares in the acquiring company typically gives rise to a tax charge on the transfer of the business assets based on the difference between the value of the shares received and the book value of the assets transferred. Most Member States traditionally granted relief for gains realized in connection with such grouping or restructuring operations, normally in the form of a temporary deferral of taxation. However, the arrangements varied in their scope and terms and often did not extend to cross-border operations.[1]

On 23 July 1990 the Council adopted Council Directive 90/434 on the common system of taxation applicable to mergers, divisions, transfers of assets, and exchanges of shares concerning companies from different Member States.[2] The Directive, which was based on a proposal originally submitted to the Council in 1969, was adopted pursuant to Article 100 of the Treaty, which provides for the approximation of national provisions directly affecting the establishment or functioning of the Common Market. According to the preamble to the Directive, the disadvantages which existed for cross-border grouping and restructuring operations, by comparison with domestic operations, constituted a disincentive to transnational co-operation between Community companies. It was not possible to remove those disadvantages by extending at the Community level the systems in force in the Member States

[1] See the discussion of the existing situations in Belgium, France, Germany, the Netherlands, and the UK in Cougnon and others, *The EEC Merger and Parent–Subsidiary Directives of 23 July 1990 in Practice* (Bruylant, Brussels: 1992). See also the following articles in *European Taxation* concerning individual Member States: Noel, 'France: Implementation of the EC Merger Directive', July 1992, 230, Koester, 'Germany: Implementation of the EC Merger Directive', June 1992, 196, Betten, 'Netherlands: Implementation of the Merger Directive', February 1993, 42, Clayson, 'United Kingdom: Government Implements the Merger Directive (or some of it anyway)', November 1992 370. See also, more generally, Thömmes and Tomsett, 'Issues in the implementation of the Merger Directive in the EC Member States', [1992] 4 *EC Tax Review*, 228.

[2] OJ 1990, L225/1.

because the differences between those systems tended to produce distortions.[3] Consequently, it was necessary to introduce common tax rules which would be neutral from the point of view of competition.[4]

Specifically the Directive has the dual aim of avoiding:

> the imposition of tax in connection with mergers, divisions, transfers of assets or exchanges of shares, while at the same time safeguarding the financial interests of the State of the transferring or acquired company.[5]

Those four types of operations are considered individually below. At this juncture it is sufficient to note that mergers and divisions are liable to give rise to taxable gains at both the company and the shareholder levels, transfers of assets (solely) at the company level, and exchanges of shares (solely) at the shareholder level. The apparent conflict between the aims of avoiding taxation of such operations while preserving Member States' financial interests is resolved by providing for temporary deferral of taxation at the company and shareholder levels. At the company level this is achieved by recourse to the concept of the 'permanent establishment'. Article 5(1) of the OECD Model Tax Convention defines a 'permanent establishment' as 'a fixed place of business through which the business of an enterprise is wholly or partly carried on'. By virtue of Article 5(2) the term includes in particular a place of management, a branch, an office, a factory, a workshop, and also a mine, oil or gas well, quarry, or other place of extraction of mineral resources.

In the case of most cross-border mergers, divisions, or transfers of assets the acquiring company intends to carry on the business of the transferring company using the transferred assets. In doing so it usually acquires a permanent establishment in the country of the transferring company. This is important because under most double taxation treaties the right of a country to tax profits of a non-resident depends on the company having a permanent establishment within its territory. Thus, Article 7(1) of the OECD Model Convention provides:

> The profits of an enterprise of a Contracting State shall be taxable only in that State unless the enterprise carries on business in the other Contracting State through a permanent establishment situated therein. If the enterprise carries on business as aforesaid, the profits of the enterprise may be taxed in the other State but only so much of them as is attributable to that permanent establishment.

Consequently, even after a merger, division, or transfer of assets the State of the transferring company normally retains the right to tax the profits of the new permanent establishment and, more significantly, any gains arising on the subsequent disposal of its assets by the acquiring company. The Directive exploits this by requiring Member States to defer taxation of any gains arising

[3] 2nd and 3rd recitals. [4] 1st and 3rd recitals. [5] 4th recital in the preamble.

in connection with the operation until the assets are ultimately disposed of by the acquiring company.

It may be noted that the Directive departed from the 1969 proposal, which expressly conferred upon Member States the right to tax the profits of permanent establishments situated within their territory[6] and contained a definition of a 'permanent establishment' based largely on the 1963 OECD Model Convention.[7]

Mergers and divisions, like share exchanges, are also liable to give rise to taxation of gains made by shareholders of the transferring or acquired company on the cancellation of their shareholdings in that company. The Directive reconciles the aim of avoiding immediate taxation of such gains with the need to preserve Member States' financial interests by requiring Member States to exempt from immediate taxation the gains made by the shareholders, while allowing them to tax gains made on any subsequent disposal of the new shares received in exchange on the basis of the tax value of the old shares. Thus, as in the case of gains at the company level, the principle is essentially one of deferral of taxation rather than permanent exemption.

THE PROVISIONS OF THE DIRECTIVE

Article 1

Each Member State shall apply this Directive to mergers, divisions, transfers of assets and exchanges of shares in which companies from two or more Member States are involved.

The Directive does not apply to purely domestic transactions involving solely companies from the same Member State. The term 'company from a Member State' is defined in Article 3 of the Directive, in conjunction with the Annex thereto, in identical terms to those used in the Parent–Subsidiary Directive.[8] Thus, a company qualifies for the purposes of the Directive if it takes one of a number of specified forms under national law, is resident for tax purposes in a Member State and is subject to one of the national corporate taxes listed. On 23 July 1993 the Commission submitted a proposal[9] to the Council seeking the extension of the scope of the Directive to all entities subject to corporate tax.

Since under Article 1 the Directive applies only where companies from two or more Member States are involved, it is important to determine the Member State to which a company belongs. Since there seems to be no reason why a company should not qualify for the purposes of the Directive by

[6] Art. 12(1) of the Proposal.

[7] Annex to the Proposal.

[8] Art. 2 of the Parent–Subsidiary Directive, in conjunction with the Annex thereto, above, at p. 262 ff.

[9] COM(93)293 final, OJ 1993, C225/3.

fulfilling the three criteria in Article 3 in different Member States, the question arises as to which of those criteria determines the Member State to which a company belongs. It has already been suggested in relation to the Parent–Subsidiary Directive[10] that the most convincing view is that a company belongs to the Member State in which it is resident for tax purposes. The relevant connecting factor for the purposes of directives harmonizing rules on company taxation must surely be a company's fiscal residence rather than its place of incorporation. Textual support for that view is to be found in Article 10 of the Merger Directive. In particular, when Article 10(2) speaks of the State of the transferring company applying a system of taxing world-wide profits, it can only be referring to the company's state of fiscal residence. On that view the Directive would apply, for example, to a merger between two companies incorporated in the same Member State where one of the companies was resident for tax purposes in that state and the other in another Member State. It would not, on the other hand, apply to the transfer, between two companies incorporated and resident for tax purposes in the same Member State, of a permanent establishment subject to tax in another Member State, since a company resident in one state does not belong to another state merely by virtue of having a permanent establishment there. That view finds support in Article 10 of the Directive, which expressly envisages that a transferring company may have a permanent establishment in a Member State other than that to which it belongs.[11]

A further question is whether a purely domestic transaction which forms part of a larger cross-frontier merger or reorganization is covered by the Directive. An affirmative answer would be consistent with the wording of Article 1 and would undoubtedly serve the aims of the Directive since the absence of relief for part of an operation might constitute an impediment to the operation as a whole or compel the parties to structure the operation differently. The point is perhaps academic since Member States are unlikely to apply less favourable arrangements to purely domestic transactions.

Article 2

For the purposes of this Directive:

(a) 'merger' shall mean an operation whereby:

—one or more companies, on being dissolved without going into liquidation, transfer all their assets and liabilities to another existing company in exchange for the issue to their shareholders of securities representing the

[10] Above, p. 266.

[11] However, in such a case it would surely constitute a restriction of a company's freedom of establishment contrary to Art. 52 of the EC Treaty for the company's State of fiscal residence to refuse to grant, in respect of the transfer of a foreign permanent establishment to another company resident for tax purposes within its territory, relief equivalent to that available for a purely domestic transfer. Equally, the Member State in which the permanent establishment is situated would, it is submitted, contravene Art. 52 if it refused to grant relief equivalent to that available for domestic companies.

capital of that other company, and, if applicable, a cash payment not exceeding 10% of the nominal value, or, in the absence of a nominal value, of the accounting par value of those securities,

—two or more companies, on being dissolved without going into liquidation, transfer all their assets and liabilities to a company that they form, in exchange for the issue to their shareholders of securities representing the capital of that new company, and, if applicable, a cash payment not exceeding 10% of the nominal value, or in the absence of a nominal value, of the accounting par value of those securities,

—a company, on being dissolved without going into liquidation, transfers all its assets and liabilities to the company holding all the securities representing its capital;

(b) 'division' shall mean an operation whereby a company, on being dissolved without going into liquidation, transfers all its assets and liabilities to two or more existing or new companies, in exchange for the *pro rata* issue to its shareholders of securities representing the capital of the companies receiving the assets and liabilities, and, if applicable, a cash payment not exceeding 10% of the nominal value or, in the absence of a nominal value, of the accounting par value of those securities;

(c) 'transfer of assets' shall mean an operation whereby a company transfers without being dissolved all or one or more branches of its activity to another company in exchange for the transfer of securities representing the capital of the company receiving the transfer;

(d) 'exchange of shares' shall mean an operation whereby a company acquires a holding in the capital of another company such that it obtains a majority of the voting rights in that company in exchange for the issue to the shareholders of the latter company, in exchange for their securities, of securities representing the capital of the former company, and, if applicable, a cash payment not exceeding 10% of the nominal value or, in the absence of a nominal value, of the accounting par value of the securities issued in exchange;

(e) 'transferring company' shall mean the company transferring its assets and liabilities or transferring all or one or more branches of its activity;

(f) 'receiving company' shall mean the company receiving the assets and liabilities or all or one or more branches of the activity of the transferring company;

(g) 'acquired company' shall mean the company in which a holding is acquired by another company by means of an exchange of securities;

(h) 'acquiring company' shall mean the company which acquires a holding by means of an exchange of securities;

(i) 'branch of activity' shall mean all the assets and liabilities of a division of a company which from an organizational point of view constitute an independent business, that is to say an entity capable of functioning by its own means.

Mergers

A 'merger' thus includes three types of operation, involving the transfer of all the assets and liabilities of a company (or more than one company) to, respectively, (1) another existing company, (2) a newly formed company or (3) the transferring company's parent company. In the first two cases the shareholders of the transferring company receive shares[12] in the acquiring company (plus in some cases a limited cash payment). The three operations may be represented diagrammatically as follows:

(1) Transfer to an existing company

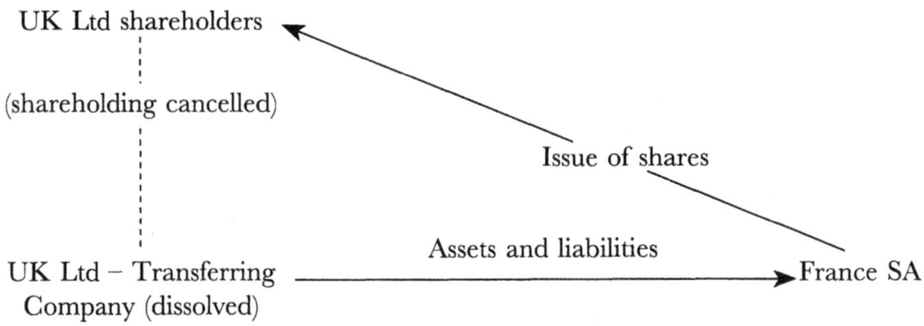

UK Ltd transfers all its assets and liabilities to France SA and is dissolved. The UK Ltd shareholders receive shares in France SA in exchange for their holdings in UK Ltd, which are cancelled.

(2) Transfer to a newly formed company

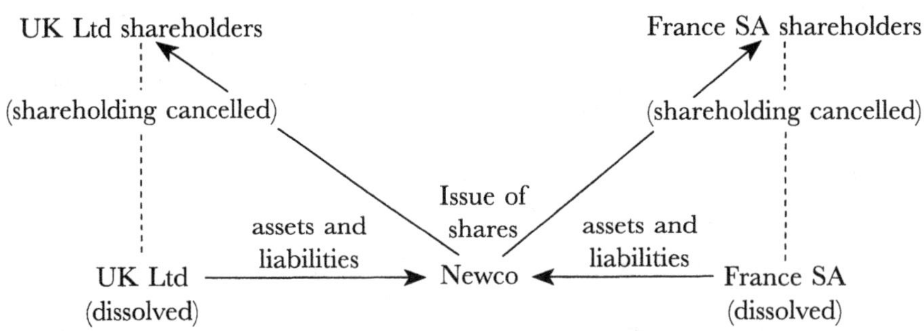

[12] In the absence of any express indication it would seem that the term 'securities representing the capital' does not cover debt instruments. That view is supported by the terms used in the French ('titres représentatifs du capital social de la société') and German ('Anteilen am Gesellschaftskapital') versions. It should be noted, however, that the UK has taken the view that this is unnecessarily restrictive and has decided to extend relief to such instruments.

Both UK Ltd and France SA transfer all their assets and liabilities to Newco and are dissolved. The UK Ltd and France SA shareholders receive shares in Newco in exchange for their holdings in the dissolved company, which are cancelled.

(3) Transfer to a parent company

UK Parent Ltd

↑

assets and liabilities

|

French Subsidiary SA
(dissolved)

The French subsidiary transfers all its assets and liabilities to its UK parent company and is dissolved. The parent company's shareholding is cancelled.

In all three cases the transferring company is dissolved following the transfer of its assets and liabilities without being formally liquidated. This form of merger, based on French, German, and Italian law and formerly unknown in English law, was introduced by the Third Council Directive on Company Law,[13] but only with respect to *domestic* mergers of public limited companies.[14] The draft Tenth Directive on Company Law provides for the extension of the arrangements to cross-border mergers of public limited companies. However, adoption of this Directive has been hampered in particular by disagreement over the question of employee participation, an issue of particular concern to the German Government.[15] In addition, the Proposal for a Regulation on the Statute for a European Company contains provisions governing the formation of a European Company based on the Third Directive and draft Tenth Directive.[16] Given the company law vacuum resulting from the non-adoption of the Tenth Directive and, to a lesser extent, the Regulation on the

[13] 3rd Council Directive of 9 October 1978 based on Art. 54(3)(g) of the Treaty concerning mergers of public limited liability companies, OJ 1978, L295/36. Even after the implementation of the Directive, take-overs and share exchanges remain the more common form of merger in some Member States, in particular the UK and the Netherlands: see Wooldridge, *Company Law in the United Kingdom and the European Community* (Athlone Press, 1991).

[14] See in particular Arts. 3 (merger by acquisition), 4 (merger by the formation of a new company), and 24 (acquisition by parent company).

[15] See Wooldridge, '*Company Law*'.

[16] Amended Proposal of 16 May 1991, OJ C176/1. See Art. 17 ff.

European Company Statute, most Member States have postponed implementation of the provisions governing taxation of these types of transaction pending the necessary company law changes.[17] The Member States' reluctance to draft tax legislation without the relevant company law framework is understandable, although they must be assumed to have considered this problem before they agreed to the adoption of the Directive. The non-implementation of the Directive might be an issue if either of two companies incorporated in a single state engaging in a domestic merger under the company law of that state, or incorporated in two states permitting cross-border mergers, were resident for tax purposes in another Member State whose tax law did not provide for such a merger. If it is correct that the connecting factor for the purposes of the Directive is fiscal residence, the state of fiscal residence would be obliged to apply the Directive notwithstanding the absence of domestic provisions permitting cross-border mergers.

Divisions

An illustration of this type of operation would be where a United Kingdom company, on being dissolved without going into liquidation, divided its assets and liabilities between another United Kingdom company and a French company (which may or may not be newly formed), its shareholders receiving shares (and possibly a limited cash payment) in the two acquiring companies.

The division operations described in Article 2(b) are based on the Sixth Council Directive on Company Law.[18] However, the latter, like its counterpart, the Third Directive, applies only to domestic operations. Once again, therefore, the company law framework is lacking.

Transfers of Assets

A 'transfer of assets' is not as broad as the term suggests, but must entail the transfer of a 'branch of [the transferring company's] activity' as defined in Article 2(i). Although the Court has not yet had occasion to interpret this term, it may be noted that Advocate General Jacobs, in his Opinion in Case C–164/90, *Muwi Bouwgroep* v. *Staatssecretaris van Financiën*,[19] took the view it has the same meaning as the equivalent term in Directive 69/335[20] on capital duty. Article 7(1)(b) of that Directive provides for a reduction in the rate of capital duty where 'one or more capital companies transfer all their assets and

[17] See de Hosson and van Noordenne, 'Current status of the implementation of the direct tax directives' [1992] 3 *EC Tax Review*, 165.

[18] 6th Council Directive of 17 December 1982 based on Art. 54(3)(g) of the Treaty, concerning the division of public limited companies, OJ 1982, L378/47.

[19] [1991] ECR I–6049.

[20] OJ English Spec. Ed. 1989 (II), 412.

liabilities, or one or more parts of their business[21] to one or more capital companies which are in the process of being formed or which are already in existence'. Although not expressly endorsing the link with the Merger Directive made by the Advocate General, the Court seems to have been partly influenced by the definition in Article 2(i) of that Directive when it held that, for the purposes of Directive 69/335, the transfer must consist of elements which, whether they constitute all the company's assets or only part thereof, constitute a whole capable of autonomous functioning. Case law on Article 7(1)(b) of Directive 69/335 may therefore have some relevance here. Of particular note is the Court's judgment in Case 50/91, *Commerz-Credit-Bank AG-Europartner* v. *Finanzamt Saarbrücken*,[22] where the Court rejected the German tax authorities' view that the transfer of a branch (of a bank) could not qualify under Article 7(1)(b) if it did not form a distinct area of business activity, shared certain central resources and was subject to instructions from head office.

Exchanges of Shares

This type of operation may be illustrated diagrammatically as follows:

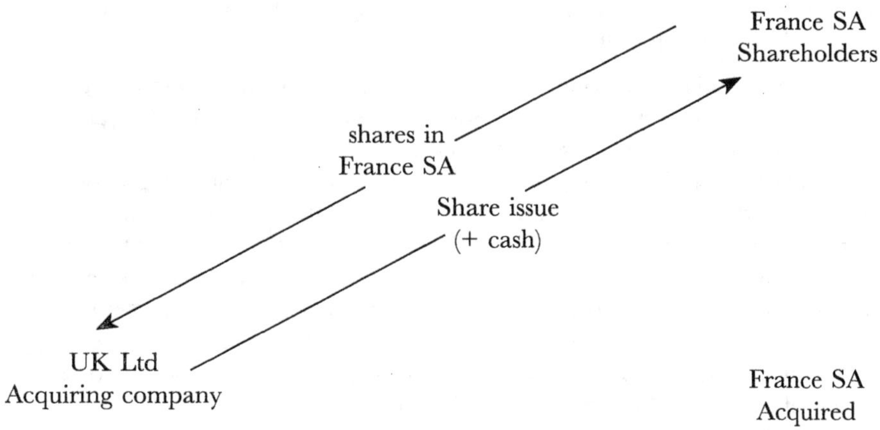

As a result of the operation UK Ltd obtains a holding representing a majority of the voting rights in France SA, thus becoming the latter's parent company. France SA's shareholders become shareholders in the parent company, UK Ltd.

[21] It may be noted that the French text of Directive 69/335 uses the same term as in the Merger Directive, namely 'branche de leur activité' (branch of their activity).

[22] Judgment of 13 October 1992 [1992] ECR I–5225.

Article 4

1. A merger or division shall not give rise to any taxation of capital gains calculated by reference to the difference between the real values of the assets and liabilities transferred and their values for tax purposes. The following expressions shall have the meanings assigned to them:

—value for tax purposes: the value on the basis of which any gain or loss would have been computed for the purposes of tax upon the income, profits or capital gains of the transferring company if such assets or liabilities had been sold at the time of the merger or division but independently of it,

—transferred assets and liabilities: those assets and liabilities of the transferring company which, in consequence of the merger or division, are effectively connected with a permanent establishment of the receiving company in the Member State of the transferring company and play a part in generating the profits or losses taken into account for tax purposes.

2. The Member States shall make the application of paragraph 1 conditional upon the receiving company's computing any new depreciation and any gains or losses in respect of the assets and liabilities transferred according to the rules that would have applied to the transferring company or companies if the merger or division had not taken place.

3. Where, under the laws of the Member State of the transferring company, the receiving company is entitled to have any new depreciation or any gains or losses in respect of the assets and liabilities transferred computed on a basis different from that set out in paragraph 2, paragraph 1 shall not apply to the assets and liabilities in respect of which that option is exercised.

Article 4 therefore provides relief from taxation of gains arising at the company level in connection with a merger or division. By virtue of Article 9 it also applies to transfers of assets. The effect of Article 4 is not to provide for a permanent exemption from taxation but for a deferral of the taxation of gains which would otherwise occur immediately on the disposal of assets in connection with such operations. The financial interests of the Member State of the transferring company are preserved in two ways. First, the 'transferred assets and liabilities' are limited to those which, in consequence of the operation, become effectively connected with a permanent establishment of the receiving company within the territory of the transferring company. In other words, by virtue of its right to tax profits or gains of the permanent establishment, the Member State of the transferring company retains the right to tax any gain when the assets are ultimately disposed of by the permanent establishment of the foreign receiving company. Gains in respect of any assets which do not remain connected with a permanent establishment in the state of the transferring company (e.g. because they are transferred to the main establishment of the acquiring company or are and remain connected with a permanent establishment of the transferring company in another Member State[23] or outside

[23] See however Art. 10 below.

the Community) may be taxed. Apportionment may be necessary where the tax values of individual assets cannot be determined. Secondly, by virtue of Article 4(2) the exemption from taxation is conditional upon the receiving company's computing any new depreciation and any gains or losses on the assets and liabilities transferred on the same basis as that applied by the transferring company. The tax history of the assets and liabilities therefore remains unaltered by the transfer. The transfer cannot result in increased depreciation allowances or a step-up in the base value used for the purposes of calculating any subsequent taxable gain.

The capital gain is computed by reference to the difference between the real values of the assets and liabilities and their values for tax purposes, that is to say the values which would normally have been used for calculating any gain or loss for the purposes of tax on income, profits or capital gains. The broad wording of Article 4(1) suggests that Member States may be required to defer taxation not only of gains resulting from an actual appreciation in the value of the assets concerned but also purely 'tax gains', that is to say differences between the cost of an asset and its value as depreciated for corporate income tax purposes.[24] This view is consistent with the purpose of the Directive, which is to allow the unhindered passage of assets, complete with their tax history, from one company to another.

The scope of Article 4(1) is limited to taxation of capital gains and does not extend to other taxes such as capital duties or transfer taxes. However, it should be noted that Directive 69/335 provides for reductions in the capital duty payable on contributions made in connection with corporate reorganizations and the like.

Article 4(3) allows Member States to permit companies to opt out of the arrangements under the Directive. Thus, a Member State might for example permit a company with accumulated losses to opt for immediate taxation of any gains and to offer the acquiring company a step-up in the tax value of its assets. Presumably, however, the transferring company should benefit from a partial exemption in respect of any assets and liabilities not subject to the option.

Article 5

The Member States shall take the necessary measures to ensure that, where provisions or reserves properly constituted by the transferring company are partly or wholly exempt from tax and are not derived from permanent establishments abroad, such provisions or reserves may be carried over, with the same tax exemption, by the permanent establishments of the receiving company which are situated in the Member State of the transferring company, the receiving company thereby assuming the rights and obligations of the transferring company.

[24] Thus, with reference to the UK, Art. 4(1) seems broad enough to include capital allowance balancing charges. It should be noted however that in its consultative document on the EC direct tax measures the Inland Revenue took the contrary view.

Most countries allow companies to constitute various tax-free reserves by making provision against taxable profits. Tax-deductible provisions include bad debts, staff commitments such as bonus, vacation, retirement and redundancy payments, depreciation of assets, and probable commitments such as warranty claims, guarantees, or legal costs.

Article 5 requires Member States to allow such tax-free reserves to be included among the assets and liabilities transferred to the permanent establishment of the receiving company situated within their territory. That obligation extends only to reserves deriving from domestic establishments which remain within the tax jurisdiction of the state of the transferring company after the transfer. The further safeguard is added that the receiving company must assume the rights and obligations of the transferring company. Thus, for example, a receiving company acquiring tax-free reserves designed to cover staff commitments would be required to honour those commitments.

By virtue of Article 9, Article 5 also applies to transfers of assets.

Article 6

To the extent that, if the operations referred to in Article 1 were effected between companies from the Member State of the transferring company, the Member State would apply provisions allowing the receiving company to take over the losses of the transferring company which had not yet been exhausted for tax purposes, it shall extend those provisions to cover the take-over of such losses by the receiving company's permanent establishments situated within its territory.

Member States are thus required to allow carry-over of losses in cross-border operations on the same terms as are applicable to domestic operations. By virtue of Article 9, Article 6 also applies to transfers of assets. Where a company transfers only part of its assets and liabilities to another company, it is presumably necessary to arrive at an appropriate allocation of losses to the part of the business transferred. This may prove difficult in practice.

Article 7

1. Where the receiving company has a holding in the capital of the transferring company, any gains accruing to the receiving company on the cancellation of its holding shall not be liable to any taxation.

2. The Member States may derogate from paragraph 1 where the receiving company's holding in the capital of the transferring company does not exceed 25%.[25]

Article 7 covers the situation where, in the event of a merger or division, the receiving company already has a substantial shareholding in the transferring company. For example, suppose that a United Kingdom company, owned partly by a French company and partly by other shareholders, merges with the French company, the latter issuing shares to the United Kingdom com-

[25] In its amending Proposal submitted on 23 July 1993 (note 9, above) the Commission suggests that holding company status for the purposes of Art. 7(2) be defined by direct reference to Art. 3(1)(a) of the Parent–Subsidiary Directive.

pany's other shareholders in exchange for their shares in that company. The French company's shareholding in the absorbed United Kingdom company is cancelled. Provided that its holding exceeds 25 per cent, the French company's gains arising on the cancellation of the holding qualify for a permanent exemption from tax. France of course retains the right to tax the French company on any gains arising at the company level upon the ultimate disposal of the United Kingdom company's assets.

Article 8

1. On a merger, division or exchange of shares, the allotment of securities representing the capital of the receiving or acquiring company to a shareholder of the transferring or acquired company in exchange for securities representing the capital of the latter company shall not, of itself, give rise to any taxation of the income, profits or capital gains of that shareholder.

2. The Member States shall make the application of paragraph 1 conditional upon the shareholder's not attributing to the securities received a value for tax purposes higher than the securities exchanged had immediately before the merger, division or exchange.

The application of paragraph 1 shall not prevent the Member States from taxing the gain arising out of the subsequent transfer of securities received in the same way as the gain arising out of the transfer of securities existing before the acquisition.

In this paragraph the expression 'value for tax purposes' means the amount on the basis of which any gain or loss would be computed for the purposes of tax upon the income, profits or capital gains of a shareholder of the company.

3. Where, under the law of the Member State in which he is resident, a shareholder may opt for tax treatment different from that set out in paragraph 2, paragraph 1 shall not apply to the securities in respect of which such an option is exercised.

4. Paragraphs 1, 2 and 3 shall not prevent a Member State from taking into account when taxing shareholders any cash payment that may be made on the merger, division or exchange.

Mergers, divisions, and share exchanges are all liable to give rise to taxation of gains realized by shareholders of the transferring or acquired company on the disposal or cancellation of their shareholdings. Article 8 exempts such gains from immediate taxation, but preserves the right of Member States to tax any gains arising on the ultimate disposal of the new shares as if they had been the old shares. Thus, any gain arising on the ultimate disposal of the new shares is to be calculated by reference to the value which would have been used for calculating the gain on the cancellation of the old shares but for the Directive. The underlying principle is therefore the same as that applicable, by virtue of Article 4, to gains realized at the corporate level on the disposal of assets in connection with a merger, division or transfer of assets.

Like Article 4(3), Article 8(3) allows Member States to grant shareholders the right to opt for different treatment. It may be to the shareholder's advantage to do so where the cancellation of the shareholding produces a loss or he has other losses against which to set any gains.

Article 8(4) allows Member States to tax any cash consideration received in connection with the merger, division, or share exchange. It is unclear from the wording of the provision how the taxable proportion of any gain is to be calculated. It would seem that the most appropriate solution would be the following:

$$\frac{\text{Cash consideration}}{\text{Market value of new shares plus cash consideration}} \times \text{Gain}$$

Member States would thus be permitted to tax the proportion of the gain which the cash consideration represents to the total consideration received for the shares disposed of.

Article 10

1. Where the assets transferred in a merger, a division or a transfer of assets include a permanent establishment of the transferring company which is situated in a Member State other than that of the transferring company, the latter State shall renounce any right to tax that permanent establishment. However, the State of the transferring company may reinstate in the taxable profits of that company such losses of the permanent establishment as may previously have been set off against the taxable profits of the company in that State and which have not been recovered. The State in which the permanent establishment is situated and the State of the receiving company shall apply the provisions of this Directive to such a transfer as if the former State were the State of the transferring company.

2. By way of derogation from paragraph 1, where the Member State of the transferring company applies a system of taxing world-wide profits, that Member State shall have the right to tax any profits or capital gains of the permanent establishment resulting from the merger, division or transfer of assets, on condition that it gives relief for the tax that, but for the provisions of this Directive, would have been charged on those profits or capital gains in the Member State in which that permanent establishment is situated, in the same way and in the same amount as it would have done if that tax had actually been charged and paid.

The application of Article 10(1) and (2) may be illustrated by the example of a United Kingdom company transferring its permanent establishment in France to a German company. The consequences of that operation are as follows:

(i) The United Kingdom[26] must henceforth renounce any right to tax the permanent establishment, but may reinstate losses of the foreign establishment previously set off against the company's taxable profits in so far as they have not been recovered. The latter option is evidently inspired by the legislation of certain Member States which, while generally

[26] The German text of Art. 10 confirms that 'the latter State' refers to the State of the transferring company.

[27] Below, p. 296.

exempting profits from foreign establishments, tax them to the extent necessary to recover losses which have been relieved against the company's domestic profits.[27] Since the right to tax future profits is renounced, recovery of losses in this manner is no longer possible; the option is therefore given to reinstate the losses in the transferring company's results.

(ii) France is treated as the State of the transferring company for the purposes of the Directive. It is therefore obliged to defer taxation of any gains arising from the transfer. Its financial interests are preserved by its continuing right to tax the permanent establishment

(iii) Under Article 10(2) the United Kingdom may tax any profits or capital gains resulting from the transfer provided that it gives relief for the tax that France would have charged on the transfer but for the Directive. The United Kingdom therefore preserves its normal share of tax revenue from the transfer of the permanent establishment (i.e. any additional tax imposed after granting foreign tax relief) but may not profit from the deferral of taxation required of France. The exercise of this option therefore necessitates a calculation of the notional French tax payable.

Article 11

1. A Member State may refuse to apply or withdraw the benefit of all or any part of the provisions of Titles II, III and IV where it appears that the merger, division, transfer of assets or exchange of shares:

(a) has as its principal objective or as one of its principal objectives tax evasion or tax avoidance; the fact that one of the operations referred to in Article 1 is not carried out for valid commercial reasons such as the restructuring or rationalization of the activities of the companies participating in the operation may constitute a presumption that the operation has tax evasion or tax avoidance as its principal objective or as one of its principal objectives;

(b) results in a company, whether participating in the operation or not, no longer fulfilling the necessary conditions for the representation of employees on company organs according to the arrangements which were in force prior to that operation.

2. Paragraph 1(b) shall apply as long as and to the extent that no Community law provisions containing equivalent rules on representation of employees on company organs are applicable to the companies covered by this Directive.

Although not defining 'tax evasion or avoidance' the Merger Directive offers rather more guidance on the meaning of those terms than does the Parent–Subsidiary Directive on the meaning of 'abuse'. The intention was evidently to allow Member States to limit the benefit of the Directive to operations which are genuine vehicles for cross-frontier grouping or reorganization falling within the aims of the Directive. The express inclusion of a commercial-purpose test is consistent with that view. It is submitted that 'tax evasion or avoidance' should be given a special meaning for the purposes of the Merger Directive covering the securing, even by lawful means, of any tax advantage not warranted by the aims of the Directive. The principle of proportionality presumably demands that national provisions should not go further than is necessary to eliminate the unwarranted advantage and have the effect of denying the benefit of the Directive in cases of genuine cross-border co-operation. Whether an operation has as its 'principal objective' or as 'one of its principal objectives' tax avoidance or evasion and whether there are 'valid commercial reasons' for an operation seem to be questions for the opinion of the national courts, having considered all the facts of the case.

Two particular questions arising from the implementing rules adopted by Member States are worth mentioning here. First, is a Member State entitled to require advance clearance of an operation? Noel[28] suggests that such a requirement is not in itself contrary to the Directive, since Article 11 does not specify how Member States are to verify the purpose of an operation. However, while a procedure for obtaining an advance ruling unquestionably serves the interests of legal certainty, it is unclear whether it is so essential as to justify denying the benefit of the Directive in the case of an unnotified, but legitimate, operation. Secondly, may a Member State specify a minimum period for which assets or shares must be held after an operation and, if so, how long may that period be?[29] While the period for which assets or shares are held may certainly be a relevant factor for the purpose of determining the legitimacy of a transaction, it is questionable whether a Member State may lay down an irrebuttable presumption that a failure to hold assets or shares for a minimum period after an operation constitutes tax avoidance. This may lead to the benefit of the Directive being withheld in genuine cases, particularly if the holding period is relatively long.

The proviso concerning employee representation responds to the German preoccupation that cross-frontier mergers and reorganizations may lead to national legislation on this matter being circumvented. However, it seems that ultimately no such proviso was included in the German implementing legislation.[30]

[28] Noel in *European Taxation*, July 1992, considers this issue with reference to the French rules, under which the application of the 'régime de faveur' is subject to prior approval by the Ministry of Finance.

[29] e.g., para. 25(4) of the *Umwandlungsteuergesetz* prevents the tax-free transfer of assets of a permanent establishment by a non-resident company if the company sells the newly issued shares within seven years of the transfer: see Koester, 'Germany: Implementation of the EC Merger Directive', *European Taxation*, June 1992, 196 at p. 201. Minimum holding requirements have also been laid down in certain cases by France and the Netherlands: see de Hosson and van Noordenne, 'Current status', at p. 169.

[30] See Koester, 'Germany: Implementation', at p. 201.

14

Proposals for Further Legislation on Company Taxation and the Report of the Ruding Committee

INTEREST AND ROYALTY PAYMENTS

Unlike dividends, which are paid out of post-tax profits, interest on business loans and royalties is generally deductible in computing a company's taxable profits even when paid to a shareholder.[1] A number of Member States levy withholding taxes on payments to non-residents,[2] although numerous reductions and exceptions are provided for under bilateral tax treaties.[3] Companies receiving such payments are generally granted tax relief by the credit method rather than the exemption method, thus ensuring that the payments are taxed in the state of the recipient.

On 6 December 1990[4] the Commission submitted to the Council a Proposal for a Council Directive on a common system of taxation applicable to interest and royalty payments made between parent companies and subsidiaries in different Member States. The Proposal requires Member States to exempt such payments from withholding tax.[5] It thus envisages that interest and royalty payments between associated companies should be taxable solely in the Member State of the recipient.

In its Explanatory Memorandum[6] the Commission explained the reasoning behind the Proposal in the following terms:

> While the unilateral measures taken by Member States to eliminate the double taxation of such income and bilateral tax agreements have gone some way towards overcoming this obstacle, they are not a satisfactory solution and do not fully meet the requirements of the internal market.
>
> Such unilateral measures and bilateral agreements generally allow withholding taxes, often levied at reduced rates, to be set against the tax payable by the recipient companies. However, double taxation occurs wherever it is not stipulated that withholding taxes are deductible from the taxable profits of the recipient company or where that

[1] See, however, the discussion at p. 271 ff., above.

[2] Withholding tax is also frequently levied on payments to residents. In such cases, however, it merely fulfils a compliance function.

[3] See Tables 3A.19 and 3A.20 at 263–5 of the Ruding Committee Report (Brussels: E.C. Commission, 1992).

[4] OJ 1991, C53/26, amended on 10 June 1993, COM(93)196 final, OJ 1993, C178/18.

[5] Art. 1.

[6] *Bulletin of the European Communities*, Supplement 4/91, 51.

company cannot use or can only partially use the tax credit because the amount of tax payable by it is insufficient or nil.

What is more, bilateral agreements generally make the reduction or abolition of the withholding tax conditional on completion of administrative formalities. Application of withholding taxes may also give rise to cash-position problems, since some time will elapse between receipt of the income from which the withholding tax has been deducted and the setting-off of the tax credit against payment of tax.

The most sensible solution is therefore to abolish these withholding taxes altogether.

Both interest and royalties are defined broadly in the Proposal. Interest means 'income from debt-claims of every kind, whether or not carrying a right to participate in the debtor's profits, including premiums and prizes attaching to bonds or debentures'.[7] Royalties are defined as 'payments of any kind received as a consideration for the use of, or the right to use, any copyright of literary, artistic, or scientific work including cinematographic films, any patent, trade mark, design, or model, plan, secret formula or process, or for the use of, or the right to use, industrial, commercial, or scientific equipment, or for information concerning industrial, commercial or scientific experience'.[8] Both definitions are based on those in Articles 11 and 12 of the 1977 OECD Model Income Tax Convention. Also covered are any other payments regarded as interest or royalty payments either under a double taxation convention or under the tax laws of the Member State of the debtor.[9]

A number of important provisions or definitions in the Proposal are borrowed from the Parent–Subsidiary Directive. Thus, the definition of 'company of a Member State' is the same,[10] as are the definitions of parent and subsidiary companies.[11] Also based on the Parent–Subsidiary Directive are the options to use the criterion of voting rights for the purpose of defining parent and subsidiary companies and to impose a two-year minimum holding requirement.[12]

Transitional provisions are included for Greece and Portugal, which, as net importers of capital and technology, are permitted to levy withholding taxes within certain limits for a period of seven years, subject to possible extension.[13] Like the Parent–Subsidiary Directive, the Proposal also contains a provision to the effect that Member States are not precluded from applying domestic or agreement-based provisions required for the prevention of fraud or abuse[14]; this proviso assumes particular importance in this context because interest and royalty payments are generally deductible in the State of the debtor.[15] The Proposal provides that the Directive is to apply to payments

[7] Proposed Art. 2(1)(a).

[8] Proposed Art. 2(1)(b).

[9] Art. 2(2), inserted by the amending proposal of 10 June 1993.

[10] Art. 3 of the Proposed Directive; Art. 2 of the Parent–Subsidiary Directive.

[11] Art. 4 of the Proposed Directive; Art. 3 of the Parent–Subsidiary Directive.

[12] Art. 4(2) of the Proposed Directive; Art. 3(2) of the Parent–Subsidiary Directive.

[13] Art. 5.

[14] Art. 7.

[15] See Explanatory Memorandum, Note on Art. 7, *Bulletin of the European Communities*, Supplement 4/91.

made to a permanent establishment of the recipient company located in the Member State of the debtor company only if that Member State does not apply withholding tax to payments made between resident parent companies and subsidiaries[16]; this provision is intended to relieve Member States from the obligation to treat payments to permanent establishments of foreign companies more favourably than payments to resident companies.[17]

The prospects for the eventual adoption of the proposal are reasonable. The main stumbling block is the Member States' concern about possible abuse; none the less, the scope of the proposal has been considerably widened during the discussions in the Council so as to cover all interest and royalty payments between enterprises rather than just those between subsidiaries and parents.

LOSSES

In considering the Parent–Subsidiary Directive we were concerned with the repatriation by companies of foreign profits. It is also possible for a foreign subsidiary or permanent establishment to make losses. The possibility of obtaining relief for losses is a factor to be considered by any potential investor. Losses of domestic branches of a company are automatically relieved by inclusion in the company's total taxable results. Moreover, in most Member States losses of subsidiaries in which there is a substantial group holding may be relieved either by consolidation of the group's results (Denmark, Germany, Spain, France, Luxembourg, the Netherlands and Portugal) or tax arrangements for losses (UK and Ireland)[18]; the terms on which such relief is granted , however, vary considerably.

Treatment of foreign losses is generally less favourable. Subject to certain exceptions,[19] the Member States do not allow losses incurred by foreign subsidiaries to be set off against the profits of resident parent companies. Most Member States do, however, allow relief for foreign branch losses. Member States applying the credit method generally allow the foreign establishment's results, whether positive or negative, to be incorporated in the company's

[16] Art. 6.

[17] See the Explanatory Memorandum, general comments, para. 9; also the specific comments on Art. 6.

[18] For further details see Table 3A.25 of the Ruding Committee Report. See also the Annex to the Commission's Proposal for a directive on losses, *Bulletin of the European Communities*, Supplement 4/91, 58. Notable exceptions are Belgium, Greece, and Italy, whose legislation provides neither for consolidation of results nor loss arrangements for resident or foreign subsidiaries.

[19] Denmark allows consolidation of wholly-owned foreign subsidiaries. France has a system of consolidation applicable in certain limited cases, and also allows deduction of losses of foreign subsidiaries incurred in the first 5 years of investment in the EC, subject to reincorporation of the losses once profits are made. The Netherlands allows relief, under certain conditions, for losses arising in connection with the winding up of a subsidiary. Source: Ruding Committee Report and Annex to the Commission Proposal on losses.

results. Member States exempting foreign branch income under domestic or treaty provisions are generally more reluctant to allow relief for losses. However, Belgium, Germany, and the Netherlands compromise by allowing losses of foreign permanent establishments to be deducted and later recovering them by incorporating subsequent profits made by the permanent establishment in the company's taxable profits.[20]

The inadequacy of existing relief, particularly as regards losses of foreign subsidiaries, is manifest. In view of the considerable disparities between the arrangements in force in the various Member States the Commission chose to propose a common system of relief for losses of permanent establishments and subsidiaries in other Member States.[21] Its Proposal for a Directive, submitted to the Council on 6 December 1990, draws on existing arrangements by offering, for the purpose of setting off losses of permanent establishments in other Member States, the choice of the credit method or the method of allowing deduction of losses and taxing subsequent profits.[22] The Proposal requires the latter method to be used for the purpose of relieving losses of subsidiaries.[23]

Member States are required to grant relief to 'enterprises' which are resident within their territory for tax purposes.[24] Both 'permanent establishment' and 'subsidiary' are defined, the latter as 'any company in the capital of which an enterprise of a Member State has a minimum holding of 75%, giving it a majority of voting rights'.[25] An enterprise, permanent establishment, or subsidiary falls within the scope of the Directive only if it is subject to one of the specified income or corporate taxes.[26] Member States are permitted to extend the application of the Directive to permanent establishments and subsidiaries situated outside the Community, provided that they do so on terms no more favourable than those applicable to Community losses.[27]

The proposal has made some progress in the Council. However, some Member States would prefer to deal first with losses of permanent establishments and only later with those of subsidiaries since this would involve little immediate change for many Member States.

THE RUDING COMMITTEE

In late 1990 the Commission appointed a committee under the chairmanship of Mr Onno Ruding to study the impact of taxation on the location of invest-

[20] For the tax arrangements applicable to profits from foreign permanent establishments, see Table 3A.27 at 271 of the Ruding Committee Report. See also the Annex to the Commission's Proposal on losses.

[21] Proposal for a Council Directive concerning arrangements for the taking into account by enterprises of the losses of their permanent establishments and subsidiaries situated in other Member States, OJ 1991, C53/30.

[22] Arts. 5 to 7. [23] Arts. 9 and 10. [24] Arts. 1 and 2. [25] Art. 2.

[26] Art. 3. [27] Art. 4.

ment and the allocation of profits between businesses in different countries. It was asked to investigate whether differences in corporate taxation led to distortions affecting the common market, particularly in relation to investment decisions and competition, and to make proposals for remedial action by the Community should it consider them necessary. The committee found that there were considerable differences in the systems of corporation tax applied in the Member States, in tax rates, and in the tax base.[28] There were also differences in the tax treatment of cross-border dividend, interest, and royalty payments. Differences in tax rates and double taxation relief, the levying of withholding tax, and unrelieved imputation taxes were particularly significant causes of differences in the cost of capital, and thus distortion of capital flows and of competition, although there had been some convergence of tax systems in recent years.

The committee set three main priorities for remedial action: the elimination of corporation tax obstacles to cross-border investment, the establishment of minimum corporation tax rates and a minimum common tax base, and transparency of tax incentives for industry. While total harmonization was not an immediate priority, the committee was of the view that a common system of corporation tax should ultimately be adopted.

The committee's specific recommendations fell under two main headings: (a) elimination of double taxation of cross-border income flows; and (b) harmonization of the three components of corporate taxes, namely rates, base, and systems. It indicated a rough schedule for implementation of its proposals—a first phase to be completed by the end of 1994, a second phase to run concurrently with the second phase of economic and monetary union, and a third phase to coincide with full economic and monetary union. It also recommended that local business taxes levied on a composite base be replaced by a profits tax levied on the same basis as national corporation tax.

Its proposals concerning the elimination of double taxation focused on the abolition of withholding taxes, the regulation of transfer pricing, the treatment of foreign losses, and completion of the network of bilateral tax treaties. The scope of the Parent–Subsidiary Directive should be extended to all taxable businesses and the participation threshold should be reduced substantially (Phases I and II). The proposed Interest and Royalties Directive should be adopted, again extended in its scope and with measures to counter tax evasion (Phase I). The Arbitration Convention should be ratified by all Member States as soon as possible, and rules and procedures for transfer-pricing adjustments should be agreed, possibly obviating the need for recourse to the Convention (Phase I). The Transfer of Losses Directive (concerning permanent establishments and subsidiaries) should be adopted (Phase I); there should be provision for both vertical and horizontal offsetting of losses within

[28] *Report of the Committee of Independent Experts on Company Taxation* (Brussels: E.C. Commission, 1992).

groups of companies at the national level (Phase II) and in the longer term throughout the Community (Phase III). The network of bilateral income tax treaties should be completed, and a common policy agreed on such treaties both within the Community and in relations with non-member countries (Phase I). In the absence for the foreseeable future of a common non-discriminatory corporation tax system, Member States applying imputation taxes on the distribution of profits earned in another Member State should be obliged to allow such tax to be reduced by corporate income tax paid by a subsidiary or permanent establishment in another Member State; in addition, states granting tax relief on dividends received from domestic companies should extend that relief to dividends received from companies in other Member States (Phase I).

As regards tax rates, base, and system, the committee proposed that a directive should lay down a minimum corporation tax rate of 30 per cent on both retained and distributed income (Phase I), followed by a maximum rate of 40 per cent (Phase II), and that there should be only a single tax on corporate income or, failing which, local income taxes should be taken into account when fixing the statutory corporation tax rate. Minimum standards should be set for a number of components of the tax base for which harmonization through market forces is unlikely to be effective. While making a general recommendation that the Commission establish an independent group of experts to examine the various aspects of the tax base, it specifically identified the following components as requiring attention: depreciation of assets including goodwill, leasing, stock valuation, provisions, pension deductions, business expenses, headquarters costs, thin capitalization, carry-forward and carry-back of losses, and roll-over of capital gains on reinvestment (Phases I and II). Action should also be taken to harmonize the dates of payment of tax and to allow unincorporated businesses to be taxed as if they were companies (Phase II).

As regards the form which the common corporation tax system should take, there was considerable disagreement in the committee.[29] The latter merely recommended that the Commission and the Member States examine in the course of Phase I alternative approaches to determine the most appropriate system for the Community (to be implemented in Phase III).

The Commission reacted cautiously to the report.[30] In general it endorsed the recommendations on the elimination of double taxation, which broadly corresponded to its own plans. It declared its intention in particular to propose an extended scope for the Parent–Subsidiary and Merger Directives, and

[29] See Professor Rädler's proposals in Annex 10A of the Report, together with the dissenting view of K. Messere in Annex 10B; a corrected text of the latter is set out in *European Taxation*, January 1993, 13.

[30] Communication to the Council and the European Parliament of 26 June 1992, SEC (92)1118; Economic and Social Committee opinion (on both the Report and the Commission's communication) OJ 1993, C19/65.

called for further discussion on aspects such as transfer pricing and thin capitalization. It was more reserved in its attitude towards the recommendations on corporate tax harmonization. Although the introduction of a minimum tax rate might be feasible, many of the recommendations on harmonization of rates, the tax base and, ultimately, tax systems were very far-reaching, and further study would be necessary before any concrete proposals could be made.[31]

[31] For further discussion of the Ruding Committee Report and the Commission's reaction to it, see Vanistendael, 'Comments on the Ruding Report', *EC Tax Review*, January 1992, and 'The Ruding Committee Report: a personal view', Institute for Fiscal Studies, *Fiscal Studies*, May 1992; de Buitleir, 'The Ruding Committee Report and the EC Commission's Response', *European Taxation*, January 1993, 15; Messere, 'A personal view on certain aspects of the Ruding Committee Report and the EC Commission's reaction to it', *European Taxation*, January 1993, 2.

15

The Arbitration Convention

The Convention on the elimination of double taxation in connection with the adjustment of profits of associated enterprises[1] is intended to resolve the problem of double taxation which may arise where financial or other transfers between related companies and businesses in different Member States are considered by the tax authorities of one of those states to result in the transfer of profits away from the country in which they are earned and ought therefore to be taxed.

Related companies or businesses may be able to define their own financial relationships and thus the price and other conditions of transactions between them. Indeed, where goods or services pass between related firms it may not be easy to determine the price that should be paid, particularly in the case of inter-company loans or licences for the use of intellectual property such as patents. The greater the degree of integration the more difficult the matter becomes. In the case of wholly-owned subsidiaries or branches, especially the latter, it may be virtually impossible to assess with any accuracy the value that has been transferred, and there is not generally any commercial need to do so. Only where parent and subsidiary, or head office and branch, are in different countries does it become necessary to separate their earnings, and then only for tax purposes. Such a separation is largely artificial. However, differences in structures and rates of tax in the different States in which the firms concerned operate may mean that the allocation of earnings between them affects the total amount of taxation borne by the corporate group. Firms may thus assess the value of their transfers in such a way as to allocate revenue in the most convenient manner, for example to a group company in a country with low tax rates or other favourable tax treatment.

Most countries have measures for dealing with this where the result is thought to deprive the Treasury of money to which it considers itself entitled. Normally they apply some version of an arm's length principle; related firms are to be taxed as if they were entirely independent and dealt with each other at arm's length. That is to say, firms' revenues are assessed as if, in respect of each transaction with a related firm, they had paid the price which would have been charged by an unrelated company in the market-place. In the special case of thin capitalization the tax authorities may also characterize a loan as a capital contribution and apply the rules on taxation of dividends.

[1] OJ 1990, L225/10. The Convention is not yet in force, but ratification is likely to be completed soon. For a thorough analysis, see L. Hinnekens, 'The Tax Arbitration Convention', [1992] *EC Tax Review*, 70.

In the United Kingdom, for example, section 770 of the Income and Corporation Taxes Act 1988 provides that where property is sold by one body of persons to another which it controls or which is under the same control, and the price differs from the price which might have been expected in a transaction between independent persons dealing at arm's length, the financial results of the buyer and seller are computed on the basis of the arm's length price. Section 773(4) extends that rule to lettings and hirings of property, transfers of rights, interests and licences, and the provision of business facilities; the rule is also applied by the Inland Revenue to loan interest.

Where the tax authorities of one state make such an adjustment there is no obligation on the authorities of the state in which the related company or business unit is taxed to make a corresponding adjustment. In the absence of any corresponding adjustment the result is double taxation, since the same earnings are taxed in both countries. Even where a corresponding adjustment is made, through reassessment by the competent tax authority or by application of a bilateral double tax treaty, the result may not be satisfactory. Under Article 9(1) of the OECD Model Double Taxation Convention,[2] tax authorities may make an adjustment where trading conditions between related firms are different from those which would obtain between independent firms. Where one state makes such an adjustment, Article 9(2) requires the other State to make a corresponding adjustment. Article 7(2) of the Model Convention lays down a similar provision for the taxation of foreign permanent establishments.

However, even if both authorities apply an arm's length principle, they may not arrive at the same calculation of the appropriate transfer price. There are different versions of the arm's length principle—for example, open market price, cost plus expenses and an arbitrary profit margin, resale price minus expenses and a profit margin—and tax authorities choose between them according to the circumstances. Furthermore, two authorities applying the same version of the principle may arrive at a different conclusion on the facts. The OECD Model Double Tax Convention provides for negotiation between the tax authorities in order to establish a single arm's length price, but it does not provide any guarantee of a result for the companies concerned; nor is there any time limit for these negotiations. Moreover, even today there is not a complete network of double taxation treaties between the Member States of the Community. It was in order to seek to resolve that problem that in 1976 the Commission submitted to the Council a draft directive,[3] based on Article 100 of the Treaty, intended to ensure that where the

[2] *Model Double Taxation Convention on Income and Capital; Report of the OECD Committee on Fiscal Affairs* (Paris: OECD, 1977).

[3] Proposal for a Council Directive on the elimination of double taxation in connection with the adjustment of transfers of profits between associated enterprises (arbitration procedure), OJ 1976, C301/4.

adjustment of profits by a Member State resulted in double taxation the firms concerned were able to obtain redress. The draft eliminated double taxation by a procedure under which the tax authorities of both Member States whose revenue was affected were obliged, in the absence of a satisfactory solution arrived at by one authority acting unilaterally or by mutual agreement, to submit the matter to binding arbitration. The draft was associated with the proposal for a directive on mutual assistance in matters of direct taxation.[4] However, unlike the directive on mutual assistance but like the other early proposals on company taxation submitted to the Council by the Commission, the draft directive did not receive a favourable response, in part because recourse to binding arbitration impinged on the fiscal sovereignty of the Member States. It was also thought that the existence of a provision in the Treaty which specifically envisaged the conclusion of conventions aimed at the elimination of double taxation (Article 220) meant that that legal basis should be preferred over the general harmonization provision of Article 100. When, therefore, the renewed drive towards completion of the single market revived interest in efforts at harmonization of aspects of direct taxation, the substance of the transfer pricing proposal was taken up in the form of a multilateral convention, much of the wording of which is taken directly from the OECD Double Taxation Convention. The choice of this form has a number of disadvantages, which will be discussed below.

The Convention was signed on 23 July 1990, the day on which the Parent–Subsidiary and Merger Directives were adopted. It was concluded for a period of five years, and comes into force on the first day of the third month following its ratification by the last signatory State. By June 1994 the Convention had been ratified by eleven Contracting States, with only Portugal yet to complete the ratification process. It may be supposed that the five-year period is intended to begin on the date of the Convention's entry into force, although that is nowhere stated; the alternative would be to deprive of all practical significance a measure the duration of which may already be considered exiguous, in view of the possible length of the procedure envisaged. At the end of the five-year period the Contracting States are to discuss the extension of the Convention or any other measures; a Contracting State may also call for a revision of the Convention at any time. No provision is made in the Convention for the accession to the Community of new Member States. Any accession will therefore require the negotiation of accession conventions, as in the case of the Brussels Convention on jurisdiction and the enforcement of judgments in civil and commercial matters,[5] which was also concluded pursuant to Article 220 of the Treaty.

[4] Proposal for a Council Directive concerning mutual assistance by the competent authorities of the Member States in the field of direct taxation, OJ 1976, C94/2; adopted as Directive 77/799, OJ 1977, L336/15.

[5] Consolidated version: OJ 1990, C189/1.

The Convention applies to all forms of tax on the income of individuals and corporations, in particular those listed in Article 2(2)—in the United Kingdom and in Ireland, income tax and corporation tax. The general principle governing the adjustment of profits[6] (Article 4) is the arm's length principle. Under Article 4(1), where the financial arrangements made between associated enterprises in different Contracting States have the result that profits accrue to a firm other than the one to which they would have accrued had the firms been independent, the sums concerned may be included in the profits of the firm to which they would normally have accrued, and taxed in its hands. Enterprises are associated where one participates directly or indirectly in the management, control, or capital of the other or where the same persons participate in the management, control, or capital of both. According to a joint declaration on Article 4(1) annexed to the Convention, the rule applies not only to direct transactions between associated enterprises but also to transactions between one associated enterprise and a permanent establishment of the other in a third Contracting State.[7] Under Article 4(2) the profits of a foreign branch (permanent establishment) are to be assessed as if it were a separate business dealing independently with the firm to which it belongs. This provision on branches is arguably redundant in view of Article 1(2) of the Convention, under which a permanent establishment is deemed to be an enterprise of the state in which it is situated. Article 4 repeats Articles 9(1) and 7(2) of the OECD Model Convention almost word for word.

The Convention comes into operation where that principle is not observed, so that the same profits are included in the results of two or more firms in different Contracting States. It lays down a procedure for the resolution of disputes between a firm which considers that an adjustment has been made which results in double taxation and the tax authorities of its Contracting State (or the authorities of the state in which its branch is situated, in the case of relations between head office and branch) which allows the other firm concerned and the tax authorities of the latter's Contracting State to become involved. Although the Convention (like the original proposal for a directive) appears generally to assume that only two firms and two Contracting States will be concerned by any given case, more complex situations may be imagined. A firm may, for example, provide goods or services at what is regarded as an under-valued price to more than one related firm (it will be recalled that the definition of a related firm is a broad one, covering any shareholding), or there may be a chain of operations involving firms in several Contracting States. While it is no doubt possible to regard the relations between each pair of firms as a separate case to be dealt with bilaterally under the Convention, it

[6] It might be better to speak of 'results', since according to Art. 1(3) the Convention also applies where any of the firms concerned have made losses.

[7] Although the English text uses the phrase 'third country', implying that transfers via a non-member country could be caught, all the other language versions have 'third Contracting State'.

would seem more satisfactory to treat the entire configuration in a single procedure, so that all the issues can be dealt with in their context and the rights and interests of all the parties can be taken into account.

Where the tax authorities of a Contracting State intend to adjust the results of a firm on the ground that part of its profits have been transferred to a related firm contrary to the arm's length principle they must first inform the firm, so that it can inform the related firm, and the latter can inform the authorities of its Contracting State (Article 5). The authorities are not prevented from proceeding immediately to make the adjustment. Where both firms and the tax authorities of the other Contracting State agree to the adjustment (which will presumably entail a corresponding adjustment in the second Contracting State, although that is nowhere made explicit) the matter goes no further; the Convention procedure is not initiated. No form is prescribed, but some concrete expression of agreement seems necessary.

Where a firm considers that its results or those of a related firm have been adjusted in a manner inconsistent with the arm's length principle as defined in Article 4 of the Convention it may, within three years of the first notification of the action resulting in double taxation, submit its case to the competent authority of its state (in the United Kingdom, the Commissioners of Inland Revenue; in Ireland, the Revenue Commissioners) (Article 6(1)). The notification referred to is probably the notice provided for in Article 5, that is to say the date on which one of the firms was first given notice of the intention of the tax authorities to make an adjustment. In the case of a branch, the head office of the company may submit the case to the authorities of the state where the branch is situated. The firm must inform the competent authority if other Contracting States may be concerned, and that authority must inform the competent authorities of those other states; it is hard to imagine a case covered by the Convention in which other Contracting States would not be concerned. If no satisfactory unilateral solution is found, the competent authority of the first state must attempt to reach an agreement eliminating double taxation, on the basis of the arm's length principle, with the competent authority of any other state concerned (Article 6(2)). The wording of these provisions appears to contemplate a situation where more than two firms and states may be involved.

If no such agreement is reached within two years of the date on which the case was submitted, the competent authorities concerned must appoint an advisory committee to give an opinion on the elimination of the double taxation in issue (Article 7(1)). The two-year time limit is extended where one of the firms has also submitted the case to a national court or tribunal under the appeal provisions of national law; it may also be waived with the consent of the firms concerned. The committee must give its opinion, based on the arm's length principle set out in Article 4, within six months of the date on which the case was referred to it.

The advisory committee is composed of two representatives of each competent authority concerned (or one, if the authorities so agree) and an even number of independent persons of standing chosen from a permanent list composed of five nominees of each Contracting State. The members of the committee then choose a chairman from the same list of independent persons; the chairman must possess the qualifications required for appointment to the highest judicial offices in his country or be a jurisconsult of recognized competence (the qualifications required for appointment to the Court of Justice of the European Communities). The firms concerned in the procedure may submit to the committee any documents or other evidence which they consider useful, and both they and the tax authorities concerned must comply with any request for documents or evidence made by the committee. The authorities are not, however, required to take administrative measures contrary to their national law or usual administrative practice, provide information which is not obtainable under their national law or administrative practice, reveal business secrets, or provide information whose disclosure is contrary to the public interest (Article 10(1)). In so far as the second exception simply means that the tax authorities are not obliged by the Convention to obtain information which they cannot obtain under national law it is a necessary proviso, but it should not be interpreted as permitting them to withhold information which is in fact in their possession. Moreover, a blanket exception in relation to business secrets and other sensitive information does not seem necessary, since the members of the committee are bound by an obligation of secrecy (Article 9(6)). The firms concerned are entitled to appear before the committee, and may be summoned to do so (Article 10(2)). The committee adopts its opinion by a simple majority of its members (Article 11(2)).

The opinion of the advisory committee is simply that, an opinion which is not automatically binding on the tax authorities. It is the authorities themselves who must, acting by common consent within six months of the delivery of the opinion, adopt a decision eliminating the double taxation (Article 12(1)). In their decision they may disregard the opinion, although the decision must in any event comply with the arm's length principle laid down in Article 4; however, if they fail to agree on an alternative solution, they must act in accordance with the opinion. This procedure meets the objection that the binding arbitration envisaged by the Commission's 1976 proposal impinged upon the fiscal sovereignty of the Member States.

Double taxation is deemed to be eliminated if the profits are included in the taxable profits of one firm only or the tax chargeable in one state is reduced by the amount of the tax chargeable on them in the other (Article 14). The latter solution may not be satisfactory for companies in so far as it may not enable them to carry over losses to another tax year; it also penalizes companies situated in Contracting States with high tax rates since they continue to pay more tax than they would have done had the original division of revenue between the firms concerned corresponded to that now considered correct by the tax authorities.

The procedure laid down in the Convention thus provides a certain protection for taxpayers. However, the obligation on the tax authorities to initiate the Convention procedure is not absolute, and there is some scope for obstruction. First of all, the tax authority to which a case is submitted pursuant to Article 6 is required to take the matter further only if 'the complaint appears to it to be well-founded'. Although that phrase appears to imply a preliminary assessment by the tax authority, it cannot mean that the initiation of the procedure is subject to its unilateral and uncontrolled discretion. It should be interpreted as a filter for manifestly unfounded submissions.

Secondly, pursuant to Article 7(3) of the Convention, where the law of a Contracting State does not permit the tax authorities to derogate from decisions of judicial bodies there is no obligation on the part of the tax authorities to proceed to arbitration unless and until the firm situated in that state has allowed the time for an internal appeal to expire or, where it has submitted an appeal, it has withdrawn it before delivery of a decision. France and the United Kingdom have stated that they will apply this provision (in their unilateral declarations on Article 7 annexed to the Convention). It places before taxpayers an invidious choice at an early stage in the procedure; they are forced to opt for a national remedy or for arbitration, although the Convention is intended to provide an additional remedy. In its opinion on the Commission's 1976 proposal, which contained a similar provision, the European Parliament called for harmonization of legislation in order to eliminate this problem.[8]

Finally, under Article 8(1) the tax authorities need not initiate the mutual agreeement procedure at all where legal or administrative proceedings have resulted in a finding that, by virtue of actions giving rise to the adjustment of profits by the authorities, one of the firms concerned is liable to a serious penalty. This provision is open to objection on two counts. First of all, its result is that firms which are fined for action regarded as an attempt to evade taxation will in addition be subject to double taxation. It is not clear that double taxation should be used as an additional sanction in this way. Secondly, the individual declarations of the Contracting States on Article 8 annexed to the Convention reveal a very broad view of what constitutes a serious penalty. In Germany, for example, it includes any administrative fine for an infringement of tax legislation; in France, penalties for 'lack of good faith'; in the United Kingdom, administrative sanctions for the negligent delivery of incorrect claims or returns. Luxembourg states that it will apply a rule of reciprocity: a serious penalty is anything regarded as such by the other Contracting State concerned. In many states, therefore, virtually any infringement of tax

[8] OJ 1977, C163/24.

legislation will deprive firms of any right to protection against double taxation.

A further likely source of difficulty is the lack of any provision for the interpretation of the terms used in the Convention. The only term defined in the Convention is the expression 'competent authority'; for the rest, reference is to be made to the double taxation convention between the states concerned. That is of little help where there is no such convention, or where more than two states are concerned. Moreover, where the convention in question is based on the OECD Model, it will itself contain few definitions and will instead refer to the national legislation of the state applying the convention. The likely inconsistency resulting from such an approach may be acceptable in bilateral relations but seems less appropriate in a multilateral system which is intended to produce a uniform result, particularly where the terms which remain undefined include expressions fundamental to the application of the Convention such as 'enterprise' and 'profits'.

While the Convention is far from providing an entirely satisfactory solution to the problem of double taxation in the context of transfer pricing disputes, it nevertheless represents an advance over classical double taxation treaties. Its great merit is that, unlike internal appeal procedures or bilateral negotiations between tax authorities, it directly involves all the parties affected—that is to say not only the tax authorities but also the firms which are called upon to pay the tax—and provides for impartial arbitration culminating in the elimination of the double taxation, a means of recourse which does not depend on the discretion of the tax authorities. The introduction of a time limit is also important for taxpayers.

The type of instrument chosen is also open to objection. The Commission's 1976 proposal was for a directive based on Article 100 of the Treaty, on the ground that the problem of transfer price adjustments affected 'the establishment or functioning of the common market'. While the Commission therefore disagreed with the conclusion of the Council that a multilateral convention under Article 220 was the appropriate way of proceeding, and has never withdrawn its proposal, it did not challenge the decision of the Member States to conclude a convention, perhaps on the basis that an imperfect solution was better than none at all. However, the choice of a convention rather than a directive has a number of drawbacks from the point of view of taxpayers. Unlike a directive, a convention does not form part of the corpus of Community law which is enforced by the Commission (by proceedings under Article 169 of the Treaty), and whose consistency is ensured by the Court of Justice. A directive would have come into force automatically after a specific period (like the Parent–Subsidiary and Merger Directives), and would not have been dependent on ratification by all Member States. It would have applied immediately to new Member States without requiring further negotiation. In so far as its provisions were sufficiently clear and precise it could have had direct effect, enabling taxpayers to enforce its principles directly in the national courts; the latter would have been able to refer questions of interpretation to the Court of Justice for a preliminary ruling under Article 177 of the Treaty. While the law of some Member States does give the provisions of self-executing international treaties precedence over contrary national law, even in those countries the rules laid down in the Convention can be enforced only by the national courts, and there is no mechanism for ensuring consistency and uniformity in their application. In the context of the Brussels Convention on jurisdiction and the enforcement of judgments, referred to above, consistency is ensured by the Court of Justice by virtue of a separate protocol giving it jurisdiction to deliver preliminary interpretative rulings in a procedure similar to that of Article 177. No such protocol has been envisaged for the application of the Arbitration Convention.

One of the possible reasons for the choice of a convention rather than a directive is the perception that a procedure of binding arbitration represents a considerable incursion on the fiscal sovereignty of Member States. That concern could perhaps have been met by the adoption of a directive harmonizing transfer pricing rules. That would not, however, have provided an entirely satisfactory solution, since there would still have been scope for divergent calculations on the basis of the same facts; a uniform adjustment in both countries would not have been guaranteed.

More generally, even the Commission's 1976 draft directive was a palliative rather than a solution, as was recognized at the time. In its opinion on the proposal the European Parliament stated that a general solution to tax distortions could be found only in 'a gradual harmonization of taxation'; that remark is even more appropriate today. The solution to disputes over alleged double taxation probably lies not in *ad hoc* measures but in the creation of a common tax court for such litigation—a solution advocated in the Neumark Report in 1962.[9] Indeed, in so far as the underlying problem in this area is not so much double taxation as the correct allocation of revenue between national treasuries, its solution is to be found in a more general harmonization of the taxation of business.

[9] See p. 15 above.

16

The Prohibition of Discrimination and the Fundamental Freedoms: Their Impact in the Sphere of Direct Taxation

INTRODUCTION

Apart from Article 220, which requires the Member States to enter into negotiations with a view to abolishing double taxation within the Community, the Treaty contains no specific provisions on direct taxation. The Treaty basis for the limited harmonization achieved in the sphere of company taxation is the general provision on harmonization of laws in Article 100, a provision requiring unanimity in the Council. At present policy in matters of direct taxation thus remains almost exclusively a matter for the Member States. Even in this sphere, however, the Member States must observe the general constraints imposed by the Treaty with respect to restrictions on the free movement of goods, services, persons, and capital. In considering the compatibility of national tax provisions with the Treaty the Court therefore faces the difficult task of weighing the jealously guarded prerogatives of the Member States against the fundamental freedoms guaranteed by the Treaty. That task can be particularly difficult where a Member State pleads that a restriction is necessary in order to meet imperative requirements connected with the functioning of its tax system. A further problem for the Court is the particular danger in the tax field of ruling on one aspect of a complex problem which would be better resolved by legislation or convention than by interpretation of the Treaty.

The purpose of this chapter is to consider, in the light of the Court's case law, the consequences in the sphere of direct taxation of the following provisions of the Treaty: *Article 6*,[1] laying down the general prohibition of discrimination on grounds of nationality; *Article 48* on the free movement of workers within the Community; *Article 52*, which confers on nationals of a Member State the right of establishment in other Member States; *Article 59* on the free movement of services; and, finally, *Article 73b*, inserted by the Treaty of Maastricht, removing restrictions on the movement of capital and payments.

[1] As renumbered by the Treaty of Maastricht. The prohibition of discrimination was formerly contained in Art. 7.

RELATIONSHIP BETWEEN ARTICLE 6 AND THE FREEDOMS

Article 6 of the Treaty, as amended by the Maastricht Treaty, provides that:

> Within the scope of application of this Treaty, and without prejudice to any special provisions contained therein, any discrimination on grounds of nationality shall be prohibited.
>
> The Council, acting in accordance with the procedure referred to in Article 189c, may adopt rules designed to prohibit such discrimination.

The relationship between Article 6, on the one hand, and Articles 48, 52, and 59, on the other, was explained in the following terms in Case 305/87, *Commission* v. *Greece*[2]:

> the general prohibition on grounds of nationality laid down in Article [6] of the Treaty has been implemented, in regard to their several domains, by Articles 48, 52 and 59 of the Treaty. Consequently, any rules incompatible with those provisions are also incompatible with Article [6] . . .
>
> Article [6] of the Treaty . . . applies independently only to situations governed by Community law in regard to which the Treaty lays down no specific prohibition of discrimination.

Since in their respective spheres Articles 48, 52, and 59 give specific expression to Article 6, it follows that direct recourse by a taxpayer to Article 6 would be necessary only in the case of discrimination caught by the Treaty but not restricting any of the freedoms. It is hard to imagine a situation where this would be the case since restrictions on cross-border investment not caught by Article 48, 52, or 59 are likely to be covered by the new Article 73b.[3]

The Treaty limits the grounds on which discriminatory measures falling within the scope of Articles 48, 52, and 59 may be justified to ones of public policy, public security, and public health.[4] The Court has, however, gradually broadened its interpretation of Article 59, in line with its case law on goods under Article 30, so as to bring within its scope non-discriminatory restrictions on the free movement of services arising from differing national rules. That broader interpretation has been accompanied by a *Cassis de Dijon*-style[5]

[2] [1989] ECR 1461.

[3] Unless discrimination between two foreign nationals falls outside the scope of Art. 52 but is caught by the general prohibition of discrimination in Art. 6: see below, p. 318.

[4] See Articles 48(3), 56(1), and 66.

[5] Case 120/78, *Rewe-Zentrale* v. *Bundesmonopolverwaltung für Branntwein* [1979] ECR 649. 'Cassis de Dijon' was the product in issue in the case. The Court held (para. 8) that obstacles to the movement of goods resulting from the disparities between national laws on marketing were to be accepted in so far as they were necessary to satisfy mandatory requirements relating in particular to fiscal supervision, the protection of public health, the fairness of commercial transactions, and the defence of the consumer. The list of mandatory requirements has been extended by the Court in later cases. (It may be noted that the term 'mandatory requirements', which is a

approach whereby restrictions which do not discriminate on grounds of nationality or origin may be justified by the need to protect public interests recognized by Community law.[6] More recently a similar trend has been discernible in relation to Article 52 and even Article 48.[7] The possible consequences in the tax sphere of these general developments in the case law are discussed below.[8] At this juncture it need merely be noted that the identification of discrimination remains an important part of any analysis.

FREEDOM OF ESTABLISHMENT

Article 52 provides that:

> Within the framework of the provisions set out below, restrictions on the freedom of establishment of nationals of a Member State in the territory of another Member State shall be abolished by progressive stages in the course of the transitional period. Such progressive abolition shall also apply to restrictions on the setting up of agencies, branches or subsidiaries by nationals of any Member State established in the territory of any Member State.
>
> Freedom of establishment shall include the right to take up and pursue activities as self-employed persons and to set up and manage undertakings, in particular companies or firms within the meaning of the second paragraph of Article 58, under the conditions laid down for its own nationals by the law of the country where such establishment is effected, subject to the provisions of the Chapter relating to capital.

Article 58 provides that:

> Companies or firms formed in accordance with the law of a Member State and having their registered office, central administration or principal place of business within the Community shall, for the purposes of this Chapter, be treated in the same way as natural persons who are nationals of Member States.
>
> 'Companies or firms' means companies or firms constituted under civil or commercial law, including cooperative societies, and other legal persons governed by public or private law, save for those which are non-profit-making.

tautology, would have been better translated as 'imperative requirements', as used in later translations, or even 'overriding requirements').

[6] The origins of this approach may be traced back to Case 33/74, *Van Binsbergen* v. *Bestuur van de Bedrijfsvereniging voor de Metaalnijverheid* [1974] ECR 1299. For more recent examples, see Case 205/84, *Commission* v. *Germany* [1986] ECR 3755, and Case C–76/90, *Säger*, below, note 72.

[7] See, in relation to both Arts. 52 and 48, *Kraus* v. *Land Baden-Württemberg*, below, p. 326. See also, in relation to Art. 52, the Opinion of Advocate General Jacobs in Case C–168/91, *Konstantinidis* v. *Stadt Altensteig and Others*, [1993] ECR I–1191, para. 48, where he referred to Advocate General Lenz's Opinion in Case 221/85, *Commission* v. *Belgium* [1987] ECR 719, at 730 ff., and to Advocate General Van Gerven's Opinion in Case C–340/89, *Vlassopoulou* [1991] ECR I–2357, at 2370, para. 10. See also the judgment in Case C–351/90, *Commission* v. *Luxembourg* [1992] ECR I–3945, in particular at para. 14.

[8] Below, p. 328 ff.

Article 52 confers the right of primary and secondary establishment in other Member States, although the right of companies to move their primary establishment from one Member State to another must be read subject to the Court's decision in Case 81/87, *Daily Mail.*[9] Secondary establishments include not only agencies and branches but also subsidiaries. Article 52 is thus based partly on an economic concept of establishment in so far as it allows the right to be exercised through a separate legal entity. The Treaty does not indicate what degree of ownership is required for a company to qualify as a subsidiary for this purpose. It is submitted that an appropriate criterion would be one of effective control by the investing company.[10]

Article 52 is mainly concerned with ensuring that foreign nationals are treated in the host state in the same way as a national of that state, although it also prohibits a state from hindering the establishment of one of its own nationals in another state.[11]

Corporate Nationality, Seat, and Fiscal Residence

Unlike natural persons, companies are of course creatures of the law. Their connection with a particular state arises from their being incorporated under the law of that state, having their central administration or principal place of business there, or being controlled by shareholders who are themselves connected with the state. Article 58 of the Treaty disregards the latter criterion, often used in tax treaties, and focuses on the company's seat, that is its registered office, central administration, or principal place of business.[12] In Case 270/83, *Commission* v. *France*[13] the Court held that it was the company's seat[14] that 'serves as the connecting factor with the legal system of a particular State, like nationality in the case of natural persons'.

Most States however base their tax systems on residence rather than nationality. It is a person's residence which generally determines the strength of his economic and financial ties with a state; moreover, residents are generally the main beneficiaries of the public facilities and services financed from tax revenues.

[9] *The Queen* v. *HM Treasury and Commissioners of Inland Revenue, ex parte Daily Mail and General Trust plc* [1988] ECR 5483, discussed below, at p. 319 ff.

[10] See, e.g., the definition of effective control in Art. 3(3) of the Merger Regulation, Regulation 4064/89. Such a criterion seems preferable to an arbitrary threshold such as the 25% holding provided for by the Parent–Subsidiary Directive.

[11] See *Daily Mail*, para. 16.

[12] See also Judge David Edward, *Corporations and the Court, Corporate Law—The European Dimension* (Butterworths, London: 1991), at 149.

[13] [1986] ECR 273, para 18.

[14] Although the English translation of the judgment uses the term 'registered office', it is clear from the context and from other language versions that the Court intended to refer to all three connecting factors in Art. 58: see in particular the French text, where the more general term 'siège' is used.

It is well established that discrimination on grounds of nationality covers both overt and covert discrimination. For example in Case C-3/88, *Commission* v. *Italy*[15] the Court stated:

> The principle of equal treatment, of which Articles 52 and 59 of the Treaty embody specific instances, prohibits not only overt discrimination by reason of nationality but also all covert forms of discrimination which, by the application of other criteria of differentiation, lead in fact to the same result.

Different treatment on grounds of residence may, in principle, constitute covert discrimination on grounds of nationality contrary to Article 52 of the Treaty, since the majority of nationals of a state will satisfy a residence condition whereas most nationals of other Member States will not.[16] In Case C–330/91, *Commerzbank*[17] the Court extended that principle to fiscal residence. In any event, since the fiscal residence of a company is normally based either on its place of incorporation or on the place where its central management and control is located, its fiscal residence will in fact generally coincide with its 'nationality' for the purposes of the provisions on freedom of establishment.

Different treatment of nationals of other Member States is, however, only discriminatory if they are, in all material respects, in the same position as a Member State's own nationals. There is of course a basic distinction in international tax law between tax residents and tax non-residents inasmuch as residents are in principle fully liable to tax in a Member State, usually on their worldwide income, whereas non-residents are generally subject to tax only in respect of income arising in the Member State concerned. That distinction may not however always be relevant; it is necessary to examine carefully in each case whether the different treatment accorded to non-residents is justified by the difference in their tax position.

Discrimination against Non-resident Companies

In Case 270/83, *Commission* v. *France*[18] the French legislation restricted shareholders' tax credits in respect of dividends received from French companies to persons having their habitual residence or registered office in France. The Commission contended that France had infringed Article 52 by not granting to the French branches and agencies of insurance companies of other

[15] [1989] ECR 4035, para. 8. See also Case 22/80, *Boussac* v. *Gerstenmeier* [1980] ECR 3427 and Case 152/73, *Sotgiu* v. *Deutsche Bundespost* [1974] ECR 153.

[16] Case C–221/89, *The Queen* v. *The Secretary of State for Transport, Ex parte Factortame Limited* [1991] ECR I–3905, para. 32.

[17] Judgment in *The Queen* v. *Inland Revenue Commissioners, ex parte Commerzbank* [1993] ECR I–4017, at para. 15.

[18] [1986] ECR 273.

Member States, on the same terms as applied to French insurance companies, shareholders' tax credits in respect of dividends paid to such branches or agencies by French companies. Its case was based on two main submissions: (a) discrimination against insurance companies registered in other Member States; (b) an indirect restriction of the freedom of such companies to establish themselves either through a subsidiary or through a branch or agency. The arguments put forward by France in its defence may be grouped under two heads: (a) there were objective differences between the situations of secondary establishments and companies incorporated in France; (b) the difference in treatment was due to the particular characteristics of, and the differences between, the tax systems of the Member States and to double taxation agreements, and the rules were necessary to prevent tax avoidance.

The Court upheld the Commission's application. Dealing first with the contention that there were objective differences between the situations of the two types of taxpayer, the Court stated:[19]

> Even if the possibility cannot altogether be excluded that a distinction based on the location of the registered office[20] of a company or the place of residence of a natural person may, under certain conditions, be justified in an area such as tax law, it must be observed in this case that French tax law does not distinguish, for the purpose of determining the income liable to corporation tax, between companies having their registered office in France and branches and agencies situated in France of companies whose registered office is abroad. By virtue of Article 209 of the Code Général des Impôts, both are liable to taxation on profits made in undertakings carried on in France, to the exclusion of profits which are made abroad or which France is entitled to tax under the terms of a double-taxation agreement.
>
> Since the rules at issue place the companies whose registered office is in France and branches and agencies situated in France of companies whose registered office is abroad on the same footing for the purposes of taxing their profits, those rules cannot, without giving rise to discrimination, treat them differently in regard to the grant of an advantage related to taxation, such as shareholders' tax credits. By treating the two forms of establishment in the same way for the purposes of taxing their profits, the French legislature has in fact admitted that there is no objective difference between their positions in regard to the detailed rules and conditions relating to that taxation which could justify different treatment.

Following closely the Opinion of Advocate General Mancini,[21] the Court thus focused on the fact that under the principle of territoriality permanent establishments and resident companies were subject to the same rules for the purposes of the annual taxation of their profits. It was no defence for France to plead that the discrimination was balanced out by other tax and financial advantages enjoyed by a permanent establishment by comparison with a company incorporated under French law.[22] Nor could France plead that compa-

[19] At paras. 19 and 20 of the judgment.

[20] See note 14 above.

[21] See point 10 of the Opinion.

nies of other Member States could obtain the benefit of the tax credit by setting up subsidiaries in France, since 'Article 52 expressly leaves traders free to choose the appropriate legal form in which to pursue their activities in another Member State'[23]; this statement is discussed further below.[24]

As regards France's second group of arguments, the Court made the obvious point that the absence of harmonization did not preclude the application of Article 52. It then added that 'the risk of tax avoidance cannot be relied upon in this context. Article 52 of the EEC Treaty does not permit any derogation from the fundamental principle of freedom of establishment on such a ground'. The French Government had claimed that, since neither French domestic law nor its double tax agreements granted tax credits to foreign companies with major holdings in French companies, foreign companies might be induced to place their French shares in the hands of a permanent establishment in order to gain the benefit of the tax credit. Although the dividend income would then be subject to French corporation tax, there might be an overall saving of tax depending partly on the level of taxation in the investor's country of residence. This issue is considered further below.[25]

It is important to appreciate that the Court's decision was based on the fact that *under French tax law* the positions of the two types of taxpayer were substantially the same. The Court expressly left open the possibility that distinctions based on residence might in some cases be justified. That would, for example, probably apply to a refusal to grant tax credits on dividends paid by a resident subsidiary to its parent company resident in another Member State since the non-residence of the parent company would place it in a different tax position from a domestic parent company: the dividend income of the foreign parent company would not be taxable in the Member State of the subsidiary.[26] The principle of non-discrimination, on which the judgment in *Commission* v. *France* is based, does not oblige a Member State to take account of the fact that a non-resident company may be subject to further taxation on certain income in its state of residence or elsewhere; double taxation arising from conflicts of tax jurisdiction must be resolved by convention or harmonization.[27]

[22] See para. 21 of the judgment. The advantages in question are set out in more detail in the Report for the Hearing.

[23] Para. 22 of the judgment.

[24] See below, p. 330.

[25] See below, pp. 331–2.

[26] As already noted, in *Commission* v. *France* the French Government based its argument concerning tax avoidance on its refusal to grant tax credits to major corporate shareholders in other Member States.

[27] For further discussion of the judgment in *Commission* v. *France*, see Wouters, 'The case-law of the European Court of Justice on direct taxes: Theme and Variations', *Maastricht Journal of European and Comparative Law*, 1994, I, No. 2.

Relationship between Article 52 and the Community Legislation on Company Taxation

From the above discussion it also follows that the relief from withholding tax which Member States are required to grant under the Parent–Subsidiary Directive[28] in respect of profit distributions made by subsidiaries to non-resident parent companies is probably not required by Article 52 itself: withholding taxes generally represent only partial taxation of the dividend income of non-residents. Similarly, the tax relief granted by the Directive to parent companies in respect of distributions of profits received from their subsidiaries in other Member States goes further than Article 52 by requiring the Member State of the parent company to take account of tax paid in another Member State.

The same does not always seem to be true of the situations covered by the Merger Directive.[29] Let us suppose, for example, that a United Kingdom company transfers a branch of its business to a French company in exchange for shares in the French company, the branch becoming a United Kingdom permanent establishment of the French company. Such an operation would constitute a 'transfer of assets' falling within the scope of the Merger Directive. Under the Directive the United Kingdom would be required to defer taxation of the gains arising on the disposal of the assets. Since the permanent establishment would remain subject to United Kingdom corporation tax, the United Kingdom would be able to tax the ultimate disposal of the assets by the French company. Arguably, even in the absence of the Merger Directive, Article 52 of the Treaty would itself impose an obligation on the United Kingdom, if it granted similar relief in respect of purely domestic transactions, to extend such relief to a transaction of the type described above. The purchase by the French company of the United Kingdom establishment would constitute an exercise of its right of establishment under Article 52. Given that the corporation-tax position of the United Kingdom establishment would in all material respects remain unaltered following its acquisition by the non-resident company, it is difficult, in the light of the principle laid down in *Commission* v. *France*, to see how a refusal to extend the relief to such a transaction would be justified.

Further Examples of Discriminatory Tax Rules

In Case C–330/91, *Commerzbank*[30] a German bank made a number of loans to United States companies through its United Kingdom branch. It initially paid United Kingdom corporation tax on the interest received on the loans, but subsequently obtained a ruling that the interest was exempt under the

[28] See Ch. 12. [29] See Ch. 13. [30] Note 17, above.

1946 Anglo–American double taxation convention. The Inland Revenue refunded the overpaid tax but refused to grant repayment supplement (i.e. statutory interest) on the repayment on the ground that the relevant rules did not permit the supplement to be paid to tax non-residents. The United Kingdom argued that there was no infringement of Article 52 because Commerzbank's position had to be compared with that of a resident company under the relevant scheme of taxation *viewed as a whole*: a resident company would be liable for tax on such income and would not therefore be entitled to a refund of tax or, therefore, repayment supplement; the denial of repayment supplement did not discriminate against Commerzbank but merely prevented it from being placed at an even greater advantage over a resident company. However, Advocate General Darmon[31] noted that that was a false comparison. The proper comparison was between a resident company and a non-resident company which had overpaid tax *for whatever reason.*[32] The Court, following the Advocate General, held that the United Kingdom rule entailed unequal treatment and that the fact that only non-residents qualified for the exemption from tax did not justify a rule of a general nature withholding the supplement.

Case C–1/93, *Halliburton Services BV* v. *Staatssecretaris van Financiën*[33] concerned a provision of the Dutch legislation imposing a tax on transfers of immovable property. The legislation granted exemption from the tax where the transfer formed part of an internal reorganization within a group of public or private limited liability companies incorporated under Dutch law. As part of an internal restructuring Halliburton Co. Germany GmbH, a wholly owned subsidiary of the United States company Halliburton Inc., transferred its Dutch permanent establishment to Halliburton Inc.'s Dutch subsidiary, Halliburton Services BV. The transaction was refused exemption by the Dutch tax authorities on the ground that the transferor was not a Dutch private or public limited liability company. The Court held the Dutch rule to be discriminatory and contrary to Articles 52 and 58. It rejected the Dutch Government's argument that, since it was the Dutch company that was liable for payment of the tax, the situation was purely internal to the Netherlands; the tax none the less affected the terms of sale and had an impact on the vendor's position. It also rejected the argument that the restriction was justified because the Dutch tax authorities could not verify whether legal forms in other Member States were equivalent to the relevant Dutch entities; in that connection it pointed to the framework for co-operation between tax authorities provided by the mutual assistance directives, namely Council Directive 77/799,[34] as amended by Council Directives 79/1070[35] and 92/12.[36]

In his Opinion Advocate General Lenz made two further points which, although not expressly taken up by the Court, merit attention. First, he

[31] Opinion of 17 March 1993.
[32] Para. 11.
[33] [1994] ECR I–1137.
[34] OJ 1977, L336/15.
[35] OJ 1979, L331/8.
[36] OJ 1992, L76/1.

made the comment—which any prudent tax planner would endorse—that in establishing himself in another Member State a trader will wish to take account of the costs and risks attached to unravelling his investment should the need arise; such costs and risks therefore have an indirect impact on the trader's freedom of establishment.[37] Secondly, he noted that in several other cases on Articles 52[38] and 59[39] the Court had established the principle that the host state could not simply plead difficulties of verification where the exercise of the fundamental freedoms depended on a comparison of its legislation with that of the State of origin and was obliged to undertake such verification.

Double-taxation Conventions

Member States may not rely on a double-taxation convention concluded with another Member State in order to restrict the application of Article 52. In responding to the French government's contention in *Commission* v. *France*[40] that the different treatment of permanent establishments was attributable to double-taxation conventions, the Court held[41]:

> The rights conferred by Article 52 of the Treaty are unconditional and a Member State cannot make respect for them subject to the contents of an agreement concluded with another Member State. In particular, that article does not permit those rights to be made subject to a condition of reciprocity imposed for the purpose of obtaining corresponding advantages in other Member States.

The benefits which Member States confer on residents of other Member States under bilateral conventions vary from one convention to another.[42] The question arises whether a Member State may distinguish between residents of other Member States with respect to the grant of such benefits or whether Article 52 embodies a 'most favoured nation' clause requiring the most favourable treatment to be extended to residents of all Member States. For example, would it be lawful for the United Kingdom to grant a partial tax credit on a dividend paid by a United Kingdom subsidiary to a French parent company but not to grant the same tax credit in respect of a payment to a German parent company? The position is far from clear. It is uncertain first whether the scope of Article 52 extends beyond discrimination in favour of a Member State's own nationals to discrimination between nationals of other Member States. If not, then the question arises whether such discrimination would be caught directly by Article 6 and, if so, whether the prohibition of discrimination contained therein applies to legal persons, since Article 58 assimilates legal persons to natural persons only for the purposes of the right of establishment. If Article 52 or 6 does apply, the further question

[37] Point 18 of the Opinion.
[38] e.g *Vlassopoulou*, note 7, above.
[39] e.g. *Commission* v. *Germany*, note 6 above.
[40] Note 18 above.
[41] Para. 26.
[42] See above, p. 252.

arises whether persons who are tax resident in two other Member States must be regarded as being in the same position. There is some force in the argument that, in the absence of harmonization of corporate tax systems, Member States must be allowed, in reaching agreements under Article 220 of the Treaty, to take account of the particular features and interaction of their respective systems. However, it is unclear whether such considerations can justify different treatment of two foreign residents who are in an identical position for the purposes of domestic taxation in the host state.

A Member State may not rely on a convention concluded with a non-member country after the entry into force of the Treaty[43] in order to justify a national rule contravening the Treaty. A particular question which arises here is the legality of the 'limitation of benefits' clauses commonly contained in tax conventions. For example, Article 26 of the recent United States–Netherlands treaty contains an extremely detailed set of rules designed to limit the benefits of the treaty to companies having a real connection with the Netherlands. At the insistence of the Dutch Government, some account has been taken in the treaty of the Netherlands' EC membership by, for example, allowing certain EC residents to be considered 'good' owners of Dutch companies.[44] While it is difficult to see how a Member State can be seen to have infringed the EC Treaty Articles on the freedoms, or even its duty of co-operation under Article 5, by failing to ensure that its tax treaty partner extends the benefits of the treaty to residents of other Member States, it must clearly take care not to discriminate itself with respect to benefits which it grants under the tax treaty.

Primary Establishment of Companies

In *Daily Mail*[45] a company registered and resident for tax purposes in the United Kingdom sought to rely on Article 52 to defeat a national rule requiring Treasury consent in order to move its central management and control, and hence under United Kingdom law its tax residence, to the Netherlands. The Treasury was prepared to give its consent to the company only if it first disposed of certain assets and paid Capital Gains Tax on the disposal. This would have defeated the principal purpose of the transfer, which was to allow

[43] The first para. of Art. 234 provides that the Treaty is not to affect rights and obligations arising from agreements concluded with non-member countries before the Treaty entered into force. See in this regard the judgment of 2 August 1993 in Case C–158/91, *Ministère Public and Direction du Travail et de l'Emploi* v. *Levy* [1993] ECR I–4287; also the judgment of 3 February 1994 and Opinion of Advocate General Tesauro of 19 December 1993 in Case C–13/93, *Office National de l'Emploi* v. *Minne* [1994] ECR I–376. While the second para. of Art. 234 requires Member States to take steps to eliminate incompatibilities between such agreements and the Treaty, a failure to do so could presumably at most lead to an action by the Commission under Art. 169 based on Art. 5.

[44] For a detailed analysis of the treaty, see 'A Commentary to the United States–Netherlands Tax Convention' by various authors in [1993] 4–5 *Intertax* 165 ff.

[45] Above, note 9.

the company to avoid United Kingdom Capital Gains Tax on the disposal of a significant part of its non-permanent assets. The Court held that Articles 52 and 58 conferred no right on a company incorporated under the legislation of a Member State to transfer its central management and control to another Member State. In arriving at that conclusion it emphasized that companies were creatures of national law and existed only by virtue of the varying national legislation determining their incorporation and functioning. It described the divergence in such legislation in the following terms:

> The legislation of the various Member States varies widely in regard to both the factor providing a connection to the national territory required for the incorporation of a company and the question whether a company incorporated under the legislation of a Member State may subsequently modify that connecting factor. Certain States require that not merely the registered office but also the real head office, that is to say the central administration of the company, should be situated on their territory, and the removal of the central administration from that territory thus presupposes the winding-up of the company with all the consequences that winding-up entails in company law and tax law. The legislation of other States permits companies to transfer their central administration to a foreign country but certain of them, such as the United Kingdom, make that right subject to certain restrictions, and the legal consequences of a transfer, particularly in regard to taxation, vary from one Member State to another.

The Court observed that Article 58 took account of the differences in national legislation by placing on the same footing the registered office, central administration, and principal place of business. It added that no convention had yet come into force under Article 220, which provides for agreements with a view to securing the retention of legal personality in the event of transfer of the seat of companies from one country to another. Moreover, none of the company law directives adopted under Article 54(3)(g) of the Treaty dealt with the differences in question. It concluded that the differences in national legislation could be resolved only by future legislation or conventions.

By thus restricting a company's right of primary establishment the Court adopted a different approach from Advocate General Darmon, who considered that the question whether the transfer of central management and control amounted to establishment depended on whether the transfer reflected genuine integration of the company into the economic life of the host State.

It must be clear that a rule barring a company from transferring its central administration to another Member State cannot be justified purely on tax grounds: a Member State cannot object to the loss of revenue from taxes which would have been payable in respect of the company's activity subsequent to the transfer of tax residence[46]; the revenue accruing to it in respect of the period preceding the transfer may be preserved by taxing, on the occasion of the change of fiscal residence, any unrealized gains, tax-free reserves,

[46] See the Opinion of Advocate General Darmon at para. 12.

etc. in so far as the assets concerned do not remain subject to the Member State's tax jurisdiction by reason of their connection with a permanent establishment within its territory.[47] However, the tax rules applied by the Member States have their roots in company law. Some states, for example the United Kingdom and the Netherlands, allow companies to be incorporated under their law even if their centre of activities is elsewhere (the 'incorporation doctrine'). Other states, like Germany, apply the doctrine of 'the real seat' according to which a company must have its central administration in the state of incorporation. Thus, under German law the transfer by a company to another Member State of its central administration not merely gives rise to tax consequences similar to those of a winding-up but entails the actual winding-up of a company. Equally, German law does not recognize the corporate status of a company carrying on business exclusively within German territory but formed under the law of another state, and the shareholders of such a company become personally liable for its debts. Given the differences in national legislation the Court adopted a reactive approach and declined to embrace the incorporation doctrine. Its decision has been defended on the ground that rejection of the real-seat doctrine would lead companies to incorporate in the state whose company law has the lowest requirements with respect to capitalization, financial disclosure, creditor protection, or employee representation.[48]

It is, however, unclear why the Court rejected the Commission's view that, where a company has the right to transfer its central management and control under mutually compatible legislation of the state of incorporation and the host state, the genuine exercise of that right should be protected by Article 52 of the Treaty. The Court could have protected genuine movement where it was permitted by national company law without opening the door to abuse. Moreover, as already noted, the state of incorporation would not be placed at a financial disadvantage on account of its liberal company law rules since it would be entitled to tax the transfer of tax residence.

In 1993 the Commission published a study[49] on whether Member States' rules of company and private international law should be harmonized so as to

[47] See the Opinion of Advocate General Darmon at para. 13, where he concluded that the national authorities were entitled to attach to the transfer of a company's central administration fiscal consequences similar to those of a winding-up. It may be noted that by s. 158 of the Finance Act 1988 the UK introduced a provision whereby a company ceasing to be resident in the UK is deemed to dispose, at market value, of all its assets other than those which remain within the charge to capital gains tax by virtue of being connected with a UK branch.

[48] For a summary of the various issues raised, see Ebke and Gockel, 'European Corporate Law', *The International Lawyer*, Spring 1990, 239 ff.; see also the case note by Lever in (1989) 26 *CML Rev.* 327–34. For a more critical review, see van Thiel, 'Daily Mail Case, Tax Planning and the European Right of establishment—A Setback', *European Taxation*, November 1988, 357; and Schmitthoff, 'Tax and company migration', *Business Law Brief*, December 1988.

[49] *Etude sur le transfert de siège d'une société d'un Etat Membre à un autre* (Luxembourg: EC Commission, 1993).

enable a company to transfer its real seat to another Member State without dissolution. The study examines the academic and pragmatic arguments in favour of a harmonized framework for the transfer of a company's real seat, considers a number of practical problems[50] which would need to be resolved by harmonization, discusses the possibility of providing for the transfer of a company's registered office,[51] and reviews the provisions of existing Community legislation governing analogous transfers in the context of European Economic Interest Groupings,[52] Societates Europeae,[53] and cross-border mergers.[54] The study concludes by proposing two possible solutions, reflecting first the incorporation doctrine and second the real-seat doctrine without dissolution. Draft directives on the transfer of the real seat from one Member State to another Member State without dissolution (the company remaining subject to the law of the state of incorporation) and on the transfer of the registered office from one Member State to another Member State without dissolution (with change of applicable law) are annexed to the study.[55] It should be noted in particular that one of the public policy provisions included in the draft directive on real-seat transfers, to the effect that the host state is not required to apply the directive where there is evidence that the principal purpose of the choice of the state of incorporation and the host state is to elude provisions of the law of the host state which would apply had it been incorporated there ('forum-shopping'),[56] is inspired partly by the concern expressed by Advocate General Darmon in *Daily Mail* that, in order to amount to establishment, the transfer of a company's real seat should reflect genuine integration into the economic life of the host state.[57]

Taxation of Cross-frontier Traders

In Case C–112/91, *Werner* v. *Finanzamt Aachen-Innenstadt*,[58] the taxpayer, a German national, resided in the Netherlands but carried on business as a dentist ten kilometres away in Germany. His wife, a Dutch national, worked

[50] Protection of shareholders, unsecured and secured creditors, employees, and debenture-holders, forum-shopping, tax, and legal certainty (in particular, how to ensure a simple mechanism for recognizing when a company's real seat has in fact been transferred).

[51] *Siège social.*

[52] Council Regulation 2137/85 of 25 July 1985 on the European Economic Interest Grouping (EEIG) (OJ 1985, L199/1).

[53] Amended proposal for a Council Regulation on the Statute for a European Company (COM(91)174 final–SYN 218) (OJ 1991, C176/1).

[54] Proposal for a Tenth Council Directive based on Art. 54(3)(g) of the Treaty concerning cross-border mergers of public limited companies (COM(84)727 final) (OJ 1985, C23/11).

[55] Although it should be noted that the study is expressed not to constitute an official position taken by the Commission.

[56] Art. 3(5).

[57] See the comments on Art. 3(5) in the 'Exposé des motifs' of the draft directive on real-seat transfers, at p. 35 of the study.

[58] Judgment of 26 January 1993, [1993] ECR I–429.

as an employee in his dental practice. The couple's sole income was derived from the practice. The German tax authorities applied to the taxpayer the German rules for non-residents. Unlike a resident taxpayer, he was therefore subject to taxation only on his income arising in Germany. On the other hand, he did not qualify for various reliefs granted to resident taxpayers: in particular, married resident taxpayers were entitled to a preferential rate for married couples known as 'the splitting tariff' and to certain reliefs based on the personal situation of the taxpayer, such as dependent child allowance, household allowance, handicapped person's allowance, allowance for insurance contributions, etc. Because the taxpayer had no other income, it would have been more advantageous for him to be treated as a resident taxpayer. He argued that the German rules preventing this were contrary to Article 52 of the Treaty. The Court held that Article 52 did not preclude a Member State from taxing its nationals who carry on business within its territory more heavily when they are not resident in its territory than when they are resident. However, its decision was not based on the absence of discrimination but on the lack of any relevant intra-Community element. It reasoned that Mr Werner was a German national who had qualified as a dentist in Germany and had always carried on business in Germany. The only element that was not purely internal was that he resided in another Member State. The Court distinguished *Commission* v. *France*[59] and *Biehl*,[60] which were cases involving foreign nationals whose right of establishment or free movement was restricted by discriminatory national rules. It also distinguished Case 115/78, *Knoors*,[61] where a Dutch national sought to establish himself in the Netherlands on the basis of professional qualifications acquired in another Member State. Mr Werner, the Court pointed out, was a German national establishing himself in his state of origin on the basis of a qualification and experience acquired in Germany. The solution arrived at by the Court corresponded to that proposed by Advocate General Darmon, who pointed out that Mr Werner had not exercised any rights under Article 48, 52, or 59 of the Treaty to reside in the Netherlands. That being so, he could not rely in his country of origin, where he was established, on rights recognized by Community law.[62]

A discussion of the reverse-discrimination issues raised by the case would go beyond the limits of this study. We would merely note that the Court's conclusion that there was no Community dimension seems curious given that the cross-frontier element, his non-residence, was the sole cause of the alleged discriminatory restriction on his self-employed activity in Germany. This was surely not an internal situation but a problem the solution of which falls squarely within the objectives of the single Community market. In holding in

[59] Above, note 13. [60] Case 175/88 [1990] ECR I-1779.

[61] *Knoors* v. *Secretary of State for Economic Affairs* [1979] ECR 399.

[62] See in particular para. 44 of the Opinion.

effect that no Treaty freedom was in issue the Court adopted a rather narrow approach to the Treaty.[63]

For tax lawyers the case was a disappointment because neither the Court nor the Advocate General found it necessary to consider the issue of whether a Member State may, without being guilty of discrimination, tax a non-resident carrying on an activity exclusively within its territory, and deriving all or nearly all his income from that activity, more heavily than a resident. This question seems likely, however, to be considered in a further case referred by the German courts, Case C–279/93, *Finanzamt Köln-Altstadt* v. *Roland Schumacker*. The Court has been asked, *inter alia*, whether Article 48 allows Germany to impose a higher level of income tax on a Belgian national residing in Belgium and working in Germany than on a comparable German resident where the former derives almost all his income from Germany.[64]

FREE MOVEMENT OF SERVICES AND WORKERS

The discussion so far has been concerned with the freedom of establishment. National tax rules may also restrict the free movement of workers and services. It is convenient here to take the unusual step of dealing with those two freedoms together.

Workers

Article 48(1) and (2) of the Treaty provide that:

> 1. Freedom of movement for workers shall be secured within the Community by the end of the transitional period at the latest.
> 2. Such freedom of movement shall entail the abolition of any discrimination based on nationality between workers of the Member States as regards employment, remuneration and other conditions of work and employment.

By virtue of Article 48(2) freedom of movement entails the abolition of all discrimination based on nationality between workers of the Member States with respect to remuneration, thus precluding discriminatory national provisions on income tax.[65] That principle finds specific expression in Article 7 of Council Regulation 1612/68 on freedom of movement for workers within the

[63] See also Wouters, 'Theme and Variations'.

[64] See also the Commission Recommendation of 21 December 1993 (94/79), OJ 1994, L39/22, in which the Commission recommends that a Member State should refrain from subjecting various forms of income of non-resident taxpayers to heavier personal taxation than if the taxpayer, his spouse and children were resident in the Member State, where the non-resident can show that the income taxable in the Member State constitutes at least 75% of his total taxable income during the tax year.

[65] *Biehl* v. *Administrations des Contributions de Luxembourg*, note 60 above, para. 11.

Community,[66] which provides that workers who are nationals of a Member State are to enjoy, in the territory of another Member State, the same tax advantages as national workers.

Like Article 52, Article 48 prohibits covert discrimination taking the form of discrimination by reference to residence.[67] In *Biehl* the Luxembourg government sought to justify a rule preventing workers who ceased to be resident in Luxembourg during a tax year from receiving a repayment of overpaid income tax on the ground that the rule was necessary to preserve the system of progressive taxation. It argued that a person who was able to spread his income between two states might be taxed at a lower average rate than persons resident in a single state throughout the tax year. The Court rejected that argument on the ground that the rule was none the less liable to infringe the principle of equal treatment in a number of circumstances, for example where the migrant worker had no income in the country which he left or to which he went during the year of assessment.[68] As Wouters[69] points out, the Court curiously based its finding of discrimination on a hypothetical situation which evidently was not the one in the main proceedings. The explanation for this is that the Luxembourg court's question was framed in such a way that it was sufficient for the Court to rule in the abstract on the legality of a national rule totally precluding refunds of tax to workers leaving the country. The judgment cannot be taken to support the proposition that a worker can resist the non-discriminatory application of a national rule simply by showing that it is potentially discriminatory.

Services

The first paragraph of Article 59 provides:

> Within the framework of the provisions set out below, restrictions on freedom to provide services within the Community shall be progressively abolished during the transitional period in respect of nationals of Member States who are established in a State of the Community other than that of the person for whom the services are intended.

A tax provision might restrict cross-border services provided by traders established in other Member States by, for example, imposing discriminatory taxation on the consideration for the services (e.g. on debt interest or royalties) or by refusing to allow taxpayers to deduct the cost of the services for income tax purposes.[70]

It has already been noted[71] that in recent years there has been a general tendency in the case law to move away from a discrimination-based approach

[66] OJ, [1968] English Spec. Ed. (II), 475.
[67] *Biehl*, paras. 13 and 14.
[68] Paras. 15 and 16 of the judgment.
[69] 'Theme and Variations'.
[70] See Case C–204/90, *Bachmann* v. *Belgian State* [1992] ECR I–249.
[71] Above, p. 310.

towards an interpretation analogous to that given to Article 30. The process has been gradual and was noticeable first in relation to Article 59. In Case C–76/90, *Säger* v. *Dennemeyer*,[72] the Court confirmed suggestions in earlier cases[73] by holding that the scope of Article 59 extended to 'any restriction, even if it applies without distinction to national providers of services and to those of other Member States, when it is liable to prohibit or otherwise impede the activities of a provider of services established in another Member State where he lawfully provides similar services'. More recently a similar trend has been discernible in relation to Articles 48 and 52. Perhaps the clearest expression of this is to be found in the judgment of 31 March 1993 in Case C–19/92, *Kraus* v. *Land Baden-Württemberg*,[74] in which a German national challenged a German rule requiring him to obtain administrative authorization before he could use his L.L.M. from Edinburgh university. The Court held:

> Articles 48 and 52 preclude any national measure concerning the conditions governing the use of a further university degree acquired in another Member State which, even if applicable without discrimination on grounds of nationality, is liable to impede, or make less attractive, the exercise by Community nationals, including those of the Member State which adopted the measure, of fundamental freedoms guaranteed by the Treaty. The position would be otherwise only if such a measure pursued a legitimate objective compatible with the Treaty and was justified by imperative reasons relating to the public interest.[75]

It will be noted that the foregoing passage also embodies a rule of reason similar to that developed by the Court in the 'Cassis de Dijon' line of cases. It has similarly been held that restrictions on the free movement of services which are not discriminatory can be justified by imperative requirements relating to the public interest in so far as that interest is not safeguarded by the legislation in the State of establishment of the person providing the services.[76] As in the case of Article 30, discriminatory measures can in principle be justified only on the grounds expressly provided for by the Treaty.[77] However, as Wouters[78] points out, the recent judgment in Case C–2/90, *Commission* v. *Belgium*[79] suggests that the gap between the two types of justification is not unbridgeable. In that case the Court upheld a Walloon decree

[72] [1991] ECR I–4221, para. 12. See also the earlier decision in *Commission* v. *Germany*, above, note 6.

[73] See note 6 above.

[74] [1993] ECRI–1663, Para. 32, authors' own translation.

[75] Para. 32, authors' own translation. See also Case C–340/89, *Vlassopoulou* v. *Ministerium für Justiz, Bundes- und Europaangelegenheiten Baden-Württemberg* [1991] ECR I–2357.

[76] See *Commission* v. *Germany*, note 6 above, at paras. 27 and 29; see also *Säger*, note 72 above, para. 15.

[77] See, e.g., Case 352/85, *Bond van Adverteerders* v. *Netherlands* [1988] ECR 2085, at paras. 32–3; Case C–353/89 *Commission* v. *Netherlands* [1991] ECR I–4069, para. 15; Case C–288/89, *Stichting Collectieve Antennevoorziening Gouda* v. *Commissariaat voor de Media* [1991] ECR I–4007, at para. 11.

[78] 'Theme and Variations'.

[79] [1992] ECR I–4431.

overtly discriminating[80] against foreign waste on the ground of environmental protection, a ground not listed in the Treaty.

It was during this recent period of evolution of the case law that the Court was asked, in *Bachmann*,[81] to examine the legality of a national tax rule in the light of both Article 48 and 59. The taxpayer, a German national working in Belgium, challenged the refusal by the Belgian authorities to allow him to deduct for tax purposes sickness and invalidity insurance and life assurance premiums paid to a German company under policies which he had taken out before moving to Belgium. Belgian law allowed deduction of sickness and invalidity insurance premiums only if paid to a mutual insurance company recognized by Belgian law and deduction of private pension contributions and life assurance premiums only if paid in Belgium.

In relation to Article 48, the Court held that persons who worked successively in two Member States normally concluded insurance contracts in the first state. Rules such as the Belgian ones were liable to work to the particular disadvantage of such workers, who as a general rule were nationals of other Member States.[82] The Court rejected arguments to the effect that pensions and life assurance benefits were non-taxable where premiums were not deductible,[83] that a migrant could terminate his invalidity or sickness insurance contract and conclude a new one in Belgium,[84] that the restriction was justified on grounds of public interest relating to insurance,[85] and that verification of payments by the tax authorities was difficult, if not impossible.[86] However, in relation to life assurance and private pensions the Court accepted the Belgian Government's argument that the restriction was justified on public-interest grounds consisting in the need to preserve the cohesion of its tax rules. There was a link in the Belgian system between deduction of the premiums or contributions and taxation of the subsequent insurance benefits—one was the corollary of the other. The cohesion of the system demanded that, where the authorities granted a deduction, they should be able to tax the subsequent benefits paid.[87] The Court considered that an undertaking given by the insurer to pay the tax was not a sufficient guarantee because of the difficulties of enforcing the undertaking where the insurer was established in another Member State.[88] Although such an undertaking could be supported by a guarantee this would involve additional costs for the

[80] The Court's remark, at para. 36 of the judgment, that the measure in question was not discriminatory owing to the differences between waste produced in different places and its link to its place of production is unconvincing. For a more thorough analysis of the judgment, see Judge David Edward and William Robinson, 'The Court of Justice and Environmental Protection', in *European Community Energy Law: Selected Topics*, Graham and Trotman.

[81] Judgment of 28 January 1992 in *Bachmann*, note 70 above. See also the judgment of the same date in the parallel proceedings in C–300/90, *Commission* v. *Belgium* [1992] ECR I–305.

[82] Para. 9.

[83] Paras. 10 and 11.

[84] Paras. 12 and 13.

[85] Paras. 15 and 16.

[86] Paras. 17–20.

[87] Paras. 21–23.

[88] Para. 24.

insurer which would have to be passed on in the premiums, so that insured persons, who might in addition be subject to double taxation on benefits paid out, would no longer have any interest in maintaining their policies. While it was true that bilateral conventions between some Member States allowed the deduction of premiums paid in a Contracting State and conferred on one state alone the right to tax the subsequent benefits, such a solution was possible only by means of conventions or harmonizing measures. The Court concluded that the cohesion of a scheme such as the Belgian one could not be preserved by less restrictive measures and that any other measures would have consequences similar to those resulting from the non-deductibility of contributions.[89] In relation to sickness and invalidity insurance, the Court held that it was for the national court to assess whether the Belgian provisions were necessary to meet the public-interest objective.

Similarly, in relation to Article 59 the Court held that provisions which required an insurer to be established in a Member State in order for insured persons to qualify in that State for certain tax deductions discouraged insured persons from using insurers established in another Member State and hence constituted an obstacle to the latter's freedom to provide services.[90] However, for the reasons given in relation to Article 48, it took the view that the restriction concerning life assurance and pensions was justified on public-interest grounds. It again left the national court to assess whether the provisions concerning sickness and invalidity insurance were necessary.

The *Bachmann* case is considered further in the more general discussion below.

TAX AND THE FREEDOMS IN THE LIGHT OF THE RECENT DEVELOPMENTS IN THE CASE LAW

The foregoing discussion of the Treaty Articles and case law prompts a number of basic questions regarding the scope of Articles 48, 52, and 59 and the circumstances in which a Member State may rely on public interest grounds in defence of tax rules. It should be emphasized that the conclusions which follow are necessarily highly speculative.

The Scope of Articles 48, 52, and 59

Taken to its logical conclusion, an approach focusing on the existence of a restriction rather than on discrimination would bring all charging provisions in national tax legislation within the scope of the Treaty Articles on the freedoms. It seems however that, at most, tax rules imposing a general tax would

[89] Paras. 21 to 28. [90] Para. 31.

be caught only if they were so burdensome as to constitute a barrier to free movement, and it is even possible that, by analogy with its recent judgment on Article 30 in Case C–*Keck*,[91] the Court would be unwilling to extend the scope of the freedoms to tax rules which affect all relevant taxpayers in the same manner in law and in fact.[92]

If a parallel were to be drawn with Article 30, then Articles 48, 52 and 59 would none the less extend beyond indirectly discriminatory rules, such as the one in *Bachmann*, to restrictions arising simply because of disparities in national legislation. Of particular interest to taxpayers are the limits to Article 52. Let us suppose, for example, that by historical accident the tax legislation of a Member State granted particularly favourable tax treatment to a legal form which existed in some, but not all, Member States; let us suppose further that, in contrast to the Dutch rule in *Halliburton*,[93] the legislation extended the same treatment to equivalent legal forms in other Member States and hence was non-discriminatory. An undertaking from a Member State with no equivalent legal form would be compelled, if it wished to establish itself in the Member State, either to adopt the relevant legal form in that state or to suffer a tax penalty. Alternatively, let us suppose that for historical reasons a particular legal form was commonly used by traders in a number of Member States but was subject to heavier taxation than other legal forms in the host state, where for that reason it was seldom used. In both cases the tax rules of the host state could be said to impede the freedom of establishment of traders of other Member States.

Would either of these cases fall within the scope of Article 52? It may be noted that in *Säger*[94] Advocate General Jacobs suggested that the case for drawing a direct parallel with Article 30 was stronger for Article 59 than for Article 52, particularly where the nature of the service was not such as to involve the provider of the service moving physically between Member States. He considered that as a general rule it was not unreasonable to expect a person establishing himself in a Member State to comply with the law of that state in all respects.[95]

While there may be a case, particularly in the light of new provisions on capital movements and payments discussed below, for a broader view of Article 52 with respect to fiscal restrictions on cross-border payments (such as the imposition of withholding taxes on payments to non-resident parent companies), the two examples given above may illustrate problems for which

[91] Judgment of 24 November 1993 in *Keck and Mithouard*, [1993] ECR I–6097.

[92] See para. 16 of the judgment in *Keck*. The Court, modifying its previous case law, held that rules prohibiting certain sales arrangements fell outside the scope of Art. 30 provided that the rules applied to all relevant traders operating within national territory and affected in the same manner, in law and in fact, the marketing of domestic products and those from other Member States.

[93] See above, note 33.

[94] Note 72 above. See point 22 ff. of the Opinion.

[95] At para. 23.

legislative solutions would be more appropriate. The impediment to establishment in those examples is in any event less serious than in the case of taxation of payments to non-residents in so far as the trader is free to arrange his affairs to take advantage of the tax laws of the host state by adopting a different legal form there. But what then of the Court's statement in *Commission* v. *France* that 'Article 52 expressly leaves traders free to choose the appropriate legal form in which to pursue their activities in another Member State'?[96] The apparent conflict between this statement and Advocate General Mancini's view in that case that Article 52 was not to be interpreted as requiring the three forms of secondary establishment to be subject to identical taxation rules[97] has attracted some comment, but the two may be reconciled. The Advocate General treated the Commission's proposition that restricting the choice of secondary establishment indirectly restricted the freedom of establishment as a separate contention from its argument based on discrimination against foreign insurers, expressly stating that 'discrimination and restrictions on establishment are different phenomena and it does not necessarily follow that a measure likely to give rise to the one will also contribute to the other'. While accepting that 'the discouragement of agencies and branches may be an aspect of the discriminatory treatment of foreign companies', Advocate General Mancini considered that such discouragement 'does not affect their *right* to establish themselves in France'.[98] The Court, however, expressly linked the two contentions[99] and dealt with them together. That the Court's statement was directed at *discriminatory* restrictions of the choice of secondary establishment is made clear if it is considered in context, for the Court continued 'and that freedom of choice must not be limited by discriminatory tax provisions'.

The Scope of the Public Interest Defence

The first question here is what type of national rule can be justified by the need to preserve the cohesion of a Member State's tax system or to prevent tax avoidance. We have seen that the Court has traditionally distinguished between measures discriminating on grounds of nationality or origin and measures which apply without distinction. The former may in principle be justified only on the grounds listed in the Treaty whereas the latter may on certain conditions also be justified by imperative requirements recognized by Community law. The judgment in *Bachmann* indicates that covertly discriminatory tax rules can sometimes be justified by imperative requirements. Referring to the Belgian provisions, the Court observed that there was a risk that they might 'operate to the particular detriment of those workers who are,

96 At para. 22 of the judgment.

97 At para. 11 of the Opinion.

98 Para. 11 of the Opinion; emphasis added.

99 See para. 15 of the judgment.

as a general rule, nationals of other Member States'.[100] In his Opinion Advocate General Mischo expressly described the provisions as discriminatory[101] and pointed out that the restrictions in question did not arise from disparities in national legislation.[102] From the viewpoint of foreign insurers, the discriminatory nature of the Belgian provisions was even clearer. A requirement that an insurer be established in Belgium in order for premiums paid to it to qualify for tax deduction could work to the disadvantage only of insurers established in other Member States. None the less the Court, referring to the judgment in Case 205/84, *Commission* v. *Germany*,[103] accepted that an establishment requirement for foreign providers of services could be justified on public interest grounds.

In *Commission* v. *France*[104] the Court held that in the context of that case the risk of tax avoidance could not justify a derogation from Article 52. In *Bachmann* the Commission referred to that passage in support of the view that the risk of tax avoidance could not justify a derogation from the principle of the free movement of workers. However, Advocate General Mischo distinguished the *Bachmann* rule from the French legislation on the ground that the latter entailed direct discrimination by reference to the location of a company's seat.

It is clear that in the EC there can be no place for fiscal discrimination directly on the basis of nationality. Other types of restriction cover a whole spectrum ranging from rules discriminating by reference to fiscal residence and place of establishment, at one extreme, to genuinely even-handed rules, at the other. In the case of companies discrimination on grounds of fiscal residence, although technically covert, coincides to a very large extent with discrimination on grounds of the company's 'nationality' for the purposes of Articles 52 and 58. Indeed in *Commission* v. *France* the French rules could probably have been formulated just as easily in terms of the fiscal residence of the insurers. Establishment requirements also impose an extremely severe restriction on the free movement of services and are in some cases indistinguishable from direct discrimination on grounds of nationality. It is submitted that the Court should adopt a stringent approach to discrimination of this kind. More generally it would be preferable for the Court, rather than making rigid and possibly fragile distinctions, to weigh up in each case the severity of the restriction and the importance of the national interest at stake.

A further question arising more specifically from the *Bachmann* case concerns the nature of the fiscal interests which merit protection. In most cases it seems that a Member State should be able to preserve the cohesion of its tax system and overcome risks of tax avoidance by non-discriminatory means. For example, as noted in relation to the *Daily Mail* case, a Member State can

[100] Para. 9 of the judgment.
[101] e.g. at para. 12.
[102] See para. 11.
[103] [1986] ECR 3755.
[104] Note 13 above, at para. 25.

protect itself from tax avoidance in the event of a transfer of fiscal residence of a company by recovering any deferred or uncrystallized tax on the occasion of the transfer of residence. The particular problem in *Bachmann* was how Belgium should recover tax deferred pursuant to its policy on pensions and insurance where neither the taxpayer nor the paying insurer was resident in Belgium. Belgium's difficulty in recovering tax foregone stands in sharp contrast to the risk of tax avoidance pleaded by the French government in *Commission* v. *France*. France's plea was actually no more than a statement of the obvious, namely that if the discrimination against foreign branches were eliminated, this might lead to greater use of branches, depending on the levels of corporate taxation in the state of origin and in France and on whether France continued its policy of refusing to grant tax credits to foreign companies with major shareholdings in French subsidiaries. Possible distortions in investment decisions arising from interaction of tax systems, levels of taxation, and the extent of double taxation reliefs surely cannot justify discriminatory taxation.

In *Bachmann* the Court indicated that the formulation of fiscal policy was a matter for the discretion of the Member States. The absence of any qualification of that statement is surprising. While it may be accepted that it is not for the Court to appraise the underlying economic, social, or other aims pursued by a Member State, or even its decision to use tax as the instrument for attaining those aims, there seems to be no reason in principle why it should not consider whether a tax policy is suited to the aim in view and whether the Member State might just as easily have chosen a tax policy less restrictive of the Community freedoms. Certainly, the Belgian policy of allowing deduction from tax of insurance and pension contributions, a device commonly employed in systems of income tax, must be considered an appropriate and convenient way of achieving the social aim of promoting the conclusion of insurance and pension contracts by taxpayers. Suppose, however, that a Member State seeking to assist small and medium-sized undertakings applied a policy of granting accelerated capital allowances to undertakings having a single establishment. Such a policy, although not directly discriminatory, would work to the disadvantage of medium-sized foreign undertakings establishing themselves within the Member State. Could not the same aim be better implemented by a policy based on turnover involving no restriction on freedom of movement?

Proportionality

Where a Member State is entitled to rely on an imperative requirement recognized by Community law, it remains to be considered whether the rules which it applies are appropriate and necessary for that purpose, that is whether they comply with the principle of proportionality. In *Bachmann* the

Court seems to have accepted a surprisingly low standard of justification given the severity of the restriction which an establishment requirement imposes on cross-border services. In particular, it is questionable, first, whether a guarantee of payment on the part of foreign insurers was actually necessary, given that the penalty of immediate suspension of deductions in respect of further premiums paid to defaulting or slow-paying insurers would in itself constitute a substantial incentive for compliance. Insurance companies are, after all, generally undertakings of some standing and permanence closely supervized by their State of establishment. In order to allow its tax authorities to monitor compliance, Belgium could have introduced an authorization procedure obliging foreign insurers to submit regular reports on contributions received and payments made, duly certified by the insurer's state of establishment.[105] Secondly, if a guarantee was necessary, should the appraisal of whether this was an economic proposition not have been left to the insurers? The use of tax representatives to assume the obligations of non-resident taxpayers is after all an extremely common device and indeed one expressly provided for by the Sixth VAT Directive.[106]

FREE MOVEMENT OF CAPITAL AND PAYMENTS

Article 73b, inserted by the Treaty of Maastricht, provides that:

> 1. Within the framework of the provisions set out in this Chapter, all restrictions on the movement of capital between Member States and between Member States and third countries shall be prohibited.
>
> 2. Within the framework of the provisions set out in this Chapter, all restrictions on payments between Member States and between Member States and third countries shall be prohibited.

However, Article 73d provides:

> 1. The provisions of Article 73b shall be without prejudice to the right of Member States:
>
> (a) to apply the relevant provisions of their tax law which distinguish between taxpayers who are not in the same situation with regard to their place of residence or with regard to the place where their capital is invested;
>
> (b) to take all requisite measures to prevent infringements of national law and regulations, in particular in the field of taxation and the prudential supervision of financial institutions, or to lay down procedures for the declaration of capital movements for purposes of administrative or statistical information, or to take measures which are justified on grounds of public policy or public security.

[105] See the Opinion of Advocate General Mischo, in particular at point 22, where he referred in this connection to *Commission* v. *Germany*, above.

[106] For further analysis of the *Bachmann* case, see the case note by Professor Roth, (1993) 30 *CML Rev.* 387–95. See also the case note by Hinnekens and Schelpe in [1992] 1 *EC Tax Review*, 58.

2. The provisions of this Chapter shall be without prejudice to the applicability of restrictions on the right of establishment which are compatible with this Treaty.

3. The measures and procedures referred to paragraphs 1 and 2 shall not constitute a means of arbitrary discrimination or a disguised restriction on the free movement of capital and payments as defined in Article 73b.

The following declaration was annexed to the Maastricht Treaty:

The conference affirms that the right of Member States to apply the relevant provisions of their tax law as referred to in Article 73d(1)(a) of this Treaty will apply only with respect to the relevant provisions which exist at the end of 1993. However, this declaration shall apply only to capital movements between Member States and to payments effected between Member States.

But for Article 73d, the broad wording of Article 73b might have been construed as prohibiting the application of any tax rules placing at a disadvantage inward investment from, or outward investment to, other Member States or non-member countries, even those which are non-discriminatory. Article 73b would thus have rendered illegal many of the restrictions inherent in the existing company and income tax systems of the Member States, including the remaining withholding taxes on intra-Community dividends, interest, and royalty payments, the refusal of tax credits to foreign shareholders under imputation tax systems, and the imputation taxes suffered on the distribution of foreign-source income.[107] We have seen that under the existing case law restrictions of this type on movements of capital and payments between subsidiary and parent companies are probably not precluded by Article 52 and therefore fail to be removed by harmonization of legislation.[108] The proviso in Article 73d, combined with the declaration annexed to the Treaty,[109] appears to be intended to allow Member States to retain non-discriminatory restrictions existing at the end of 1993. However, Article 73d(3) makes it clear that Article 73d provides no defence for discriminatory rules or disguised restrictions on movements of capital or payments. Thus, it seems that the fact that two taxpayers are in different situations with regard to their place of residence or place of investment would not justify different domestic tax burdens or differences with respect to, for example, refunds of overpaid tax or payment of interest on such refunds.

Subject to existing restrictions, the wording of the Treaty and the declaration annexed to it appear to justify a broad view of the freedom. Hitherto the Court's approach in tax cases relating to Article 52 has been based firmly on discrimination. For the future, a parallel development of the case law on

[107] See Ch. 11.

[108] Above, pp. 315–16.

[109] It seems that the restriction of the scope of the declaration to movements of capital and payments between Member States is explained by the fact that Art. 73c contains a general provision allowing Member States to retain restrictions existing at 31 December 1993 in relation to non-member countries.

Articles 52 and 73b in this sphere seems essential if arbitrary distinctions between different categories of cross-border investment are to be avoided. Support for the principle of parallelism is to be found in Article 73d(2), which makes it clear that Article 73b does not eliminate restrictions which in principle fall within the scope of Article 52 but are compatible with it.

Conclusion

17

Conclusions and Prospects

In Chapter 1 the principal aim of tax harmonization in the Community was described as the elimination of fiscal obstacles to economic integration. As was emphasized there, harmonization is not an end in itself but an instrument in the construction of a single market for goods, services, labour, and capital. Any assessment of the progress made must therefore reflect that broader purpose. It is clear from the legislation and case law discussed in preceding chapters that considerable progress has been made, particularly in the sphere of indirect taxation. Nevertheless, the fact that important fiscal barriers to free movement continue to exist after more than three decades of work suggests that a sense of satisfaction would be misplaced.

The early studies, in particular the Neumark Report, were works of great vision, and many of their conclusions remain valid today. They clearly identified the fiscal obstacles to trade and free movement, and made suggestions for their elimination. The Community institutions and the Member States, however, have not always kept sight of the objectives of harmonization.

The Commission itself, in its pursuit of full harmonization in the unfavourable climate of the 1970s and early 1980s, did not always display political sensitivity; moreover, not all of its proposals were well conceived. While the Council has for the most part been receptive to indirect tax reform, it has acted as a brake on moves towards direct tax harmonization. National governments have not felt the same need for sweeping reform in the company and income tax fields as was felt in the case of turnover tax, where an additional incentive for harmonization of the VAT base was provided by the need to ensure uniform collection of own resources. There has been a tendency for representatives of national treasuries, meeting in the Council, to focus on possible losses of revenue in the short term and to place less weight on the increase in efficiency which integration should bring.

For much of the 1970s and early 1980s it was above all the Court that ensured the advancement of the basic principles of the common market, particularly in the field of indirect taxation. It is likely to be called upon to play a similar role in relation to many aspects of direct taxation if legislative solutions are not found for many important obstacles to trans-frontier business. In doing so it will face difficult and sensitive issues as classical notions of domestic and treaty law come under scrutiny. One example, and the source of some concern, is the impact of the fiscal cohesion criterion developed in the recent *Bachmann* decision. While there may be cases in which limits must be placed on the freedoms in order to take account of the fiscal autonomy of the Member States, such limits should be narrowly drawn. The recent company tax legislation will also constitute an important area for the Court over the next few years. It will in particular fall to the Court to step in to remedy the legislature's failure to define key terms, such as withholding tax, distributions of profits, and abuse.

TAX HARMONIZATION AND THE SINGLE MARKET

In indirect tax the 1992 harmonization was minimalist—limited to what was necessary to allow open frontiers without too much diversion of trade. The Community must consider what further harmonization, especially of VAT, is necessary or desirable in order to create a common market. A system based on collection of tax in the country of origin would have the advantage of theoretical purity and hence be less complex in practice than the present arrangements. It would eliminate the need for the cumbersome control mechanism introduced in order to police the present arrangements and ease the burden on business. However, unless the Commission can find a workable solution for redistributing revenue between the Member States in accordance with existing patterns, it is unlikely to secure the requisite unanimous agreement in the Council. The Commission's report on the operation of the transitional VAT arrangements has yet to be published. However, it seems to be generally accepted that, after an initial period of settling down, the system is now for the most part working reasonably well. The problems reported mainly concern either specific categories of transaction, such as chain transactions and cross-border processing, or the special schemes, in particular the distance sales mechanism. If the present arrangements are to be retained for any length of time, priority must be given to resolving such problems. The need for the special schemes, which are both complicated and burdensome for business, flows not from the transitional arrangements themselves but from the lack of uniformity of rates and rate structures. In particular the distance sales mechanism, which requires traders to have multiple registrations in the Community, could be abolished if there were closer alignment of rates. Further harmonization of rates must therefore be a priority.

The codification of the VAT legislation promised by the Commission is highly desirable. In its original form the Sixth Directive disguised its imprecision by a semblance of clarity. Even that has now been removed by the complex drafting of the transitional provisions and their insertion as a single Article partitioned off from the remainder of the Directive.

It is only recently that progress has been made in the direct tax sphere. By focusing its approach on specific obstacles to integration the Commission was able to take advantage of the impetus generated by the single market programme and secure the adoption of a number of longstanding proposals on company taxation. There are also reasonable prospects for the adoption of the remaining proposals, those extending the scope of the Parent–Subsidiary and Merger Directives and the proposals on interest and royalties and losses. In the case of the interest and royalties proposal the stumbling block is the Member States' concern about possible abuse; none the less, the scope of the proposal has been considerably widened during the discussions in the Council so as to cover all interest and royalty payments between enterprises rather than just those between subsidiaries and parents. The losses proposal has made less progress, some Member States preferring to deal first with losses of permanent establishments and only later with those of subsidiaries, since this would involve little immediate change for many Member States. The early adoption of both proposals is highly desirable.

In view of the principle of subsidiarity and the importance attached by Member States to fiscal sovereignty, the Commission is unlikely to propose substantial harmonization of corporate taxes for the foreseeable future. The obstacles to economic integration posed by the differences in corporate tax systems and base are none the less undeniable. The case for harmonization of the corporate tax base is in fact far stronger than it was for harmonization of the VAT base prior to the elimination of tax frontiers. Fiscal neutrality and transparency, two characteristics which might be thought essential in a market striving to resemble an internal market, are wholly lacking. The post-tax return on cross-border investment varies significantly according to the place of investment and the place of residence of the shareholder. Those differences stem from a variety of factors, including differences in rates and tax base, special incentives offered in specific sectors, the discriminatory effects of imputation systems, limits on double taxation and loss relief, and the impact of rules on thin capitalization. Moreover, the complexity of the situation is such that a company thinking of investing in other Member States can determine the likely return on its investment only after obtaining costly advice on the impact of each state's tax rules on its business and on tax planning opportunities. Its tax burden may vary significantly according to the legal form chosen in a particular State or the method by which its investment is financed. Cross-border mergers and acquisitions often entail the use of complex tax planning structures, such as stapled stock or dividend access plans designed to overcome differences in tax systems. Harmonization of tax systems and base would simplify the tax issues in cross-border investment and provide the basis for fair fiscal competition between states. Subject possibly to a minimum rate, rate harmonization is less essential. Member States could retain their budgetary freedom within the limits possible in a transparent competitive environment. Moreover, incentives could still be offered to particular sectors as a matter of economic or social policy, within limits consistent with avoidance of abuse and with fair fiscal competition and subject to notification in the interests of transparency.

For the present, however, complete harmonization of tax systems and base is not a realistic prospect. It is true that significant improvements in tax neutrality may be achieved by more modest measures. The abolition of withholding taxes on intra-group dividends was a major step in that direction. Priority should also be given to remedying the discriminatory effects of imputation systems on foreign income and distributions to foreign shareholders, the adoption of a uniform definition of headquarters costs and co-ordination of thin capitalization rules. Moreover, fairer fiscal competition between states could be ensured by restricting, and making more transparent, the special tax incentives offered to holding companies and companies in the financial sector. On a less formal level, Community co-operation with respect to tax treaty negotiation seems essential, if only to avoid possible conflicts between EC law and tax treaty law. Completion of the treaty network between Member States is also necessary.

Ultimately, however, many of the above measures would be no more than a palliative, addressing the symptoms rather than the cause. Moreover, far from simplifying cross-border tax planning, a series of individual instruments regulating specific problems would be more likely to add an extra layer of complication. It is perhaps regrettable that the Community should have devoted so much energy to facilitating cross-border trade and investment but have failed to make significant progress in the vital area of direct taxation.

Further Reading

This list is intended simply to provide a few suggestions for further reading in the fields touched on in this book.

General

BERLIN, D., *Droit Fiscal Communautaire* (Paris: Presses Universitaires de France, 1988).

—— 'L'Élimination des frontières fiscales dans la CEE' (1989) 15 *Droit Pratique du Commerce International* 35.

BIEBER, R. (ed.), *1992: One European Market?* (Baden-Baden: Nomos, 1988).

BOS, M., and NELSON, H., 'Indirect Taxation and the Completion of the Internal Market of the EC' (1988) 27 *Journal of Common Market Studies* 27.

CARTOU, L., *Droit Fiscal International et Européen*, 2nd edn. (Paris: Dalloz, 1986).

CNOSSEN, S. (ed.), *Tax Coordination in the European Community* (Deventer: Kluwer, 1987).

EASSON, A. J., *Taxation in the European Community* (London: Athlone Press, 1993).

—— *Tax Law and Policy in the EEC* (London: Sweet & Maxwell, 1980).

LEE, C., PEARSON, M., and SMITH, S., *Fiscal Harmonisation: An Analysis of the European Commission's Proposals* (IFS Report Series, No. 28) (London: Institute for Fiscal Studies, 1988).

Commentaire Mégret, *Le Droit de la CEE* (2nd edn., vol. 5, pt. 1) 'Dispositions fiscales' by D. Calleja and R. Wägenbauer (Brussels: Éditions de l'Université de Bruxelles, 1993).

SHOUP, C. (ed.), *Fiscal Harmonization in Common Markets* (New York: Columbia University Press, 1967).

VANISTENDAEL, F., 'The Limits to the New Community Tax Order', [1994] CMLR 293.

WESTAWAY, T., 'The Fiscal Dimension of 1992' in D. Swann (ed.), *The Single European Market and Beyond* (London: Routledge, 1992).

VAT

Coopers & Lybrand, *A Guide to VAT in the EC–the 1993 Changes* (Deventer: Kluwer, 1993).

TERRA, B. J. M., and KAJUS, J., *A Guide to the European VAT Directives* (Amsterdam: IBFD, 1993).

Other Indirect Taxation

DANUSSO, M., and DENTON, R., 'Does the European Court look for a Protectionist Motive under Article 95?' [1990] *Legal Issues of European Integration* 67.

PEARSON, M., and SMITH, S., *The European Carbon Tax: An Assessment of the European Commission's Proposals* (London: Institute for Fiscal Studies, 1991).

SMITH, S., 'Excise Duties and the Internal Market' (1988) 27 *Journal of Common Market Studies* 147.

Company Taxation

CHOWN, J., and HOPPER, W., 'Company Tax Harmonization in the European Economic Community' [1992] *Intertax* 275.

Coopers & Lybrand, *EC Initiatives in Direct Taxation and the National Responses* (Deventer: Kluwer, 1993).

COUGNON, J. M., and others, *The EEC Merger and Parent-Subsidiary Directives of 23 July 1990 in Practice* (Brussels: Bruylant, 1992).

DEVEREUX, M., and PEARSON, M., *Corporate Tax Harmonization and Economic Efficiency* (IFS Report Series, No. 28) (London: Institute for Fiscal Studies, 1989).

DE HOSSON, F., *Direct Investment Tax Initiatives of the European Community* (Deventer: Kluwer, 1990).

Hinnekens, L., 'The Tax Arbitration Convention', [1992] *EC Tax Review* 70.

Report of the Committee of Independent Experts on Company Taxation (Ruding Committee) (Brussels and Luxembourg: Commission of the European Communities, 1992).

THÖMMES, O., 'Harmonization of Enterprise Taxation in the EC' [1990] *Intertax* 208.

—— and BETTEN, R., *EC Corporate Tax Law* (Amsterdam: IBFD, 1992).

Index

accounting requirements
  common VAT system, 207–8
accounting services
  VAT, 186
Action Programme for Taxation (1975), 24, 25
acts preparatory to trading, 112
administrative charges, 46
Advance Corporation Tax, 251
advertising services
  place of supply, 155–56
Advisory Committee on VAT, 212–13
Agreement on the European Economic Area, 8
agricultural activities, 108
  petroleum products used in, 239, 240
agricultural alcohol, 74
agricultural outputs
  reduced rates of VAT, 203
agricultural products
  motor fuels derived from, 11, 241
  VAT, 18
agricultural undertakings
  VAT flat-rate scheme, 18, 215–17
air navigation, 240
aircraft
  intra-Community acquisitions
    common VAT system, 137–38, 144–45
  State institutions, used by, 189
airports
  duty-free sales, 228
alcohol and alcoholic drinks
  agricultural alcohol, 74
  beer, 232, 234, 235, 236–37
  classification, 236
  ethyl alcohol products, 232–33, 236
  excise duties, 51–52. *see also* excise duties
    anomalies, 232
    approximation of rates, 237
    harmonization of rates, 23, 231–37
    harmonization of structures, 236
    minimum rates, 237
  mixed drinks, 234
  spirits, 232–33, 235, 236
  wine, 23, 232, 233–34, 235, 236–37
Algeria, 91
ambulance services
  VAT exemption, 180
amusement machines
  taxation, 47
amusements
  VAT not deductible on, 194
anti-avoidance measures
  common VAT system, 222–24
antiques, VAT on, 29, 89
  reduced rates of tax, 202, 203
  special rules, 219–22
Arbitration Convention, 6, 247, 300–8
  adjustment of profits, 303, 304
  advantages of, 307
  advisory committee, 304–5
  application, 303
  arm's length principle, 303, 304
  decisions, 305
  disadvantages of convention instrument, 307–8
  enforcement, 307, 308
  entry into force, 302
  infringements of tax legislation, 306–7
  initiation of procedure, 304, 306
  interpretation, lack of provision for, 307
  legal status, 307, 308
  operation of, 303–4
  procedure, 304–6
  Ruding Committee recommendations, 297
  signing and ratification, 302
  time limits, 304, 307
armed forces
  fuel used by, 240
art works. *see* works of art
Article 95, EC Treaty, 6, 8, 27, 34–77
  beneficiaries, 51–56
  differential taxation, 69–76
  direct effect, 36–37
  exports, applicability to, 52–56
  indirect protection, 66–68
  'other' products, 56–57, 65–77
  recovery of unlawfully charged tax, 76–77
  relationship with other Articles, 37–46
    Articles 12 and 13 (customs duties), 38–42
    Article 30 (quantitative restrictions), 42–44
    Article 37 (State monopolies of a commercial character), 44–45
    Articles 92 and 93 (State aid), 45–46
  scope, 46
    internal taxation, 46
    products of other Member States, 49–51
    taxes imposed directly or indirectly on products, 47–48
  similar products, 56–57, 57–59
    equal treatment, 59–65

Article 96, EC Treaty, 6, 77–78
  application, 78
  direct effect, 78
Article 97, EC Treaty, 79–81
  application, 79–81
  direct effect, 80
Article 98, EC Treaty, 6, 81–82
Article 99, EC Treaty, 6, 82–84
Article 220, EC Treaty, 6
artistic services, 189
  place of supply, 154
assembled goods
  VAT transitional arrangements, 138
assimilated persons
  VAT transitional arrangements, 139–40
associated companies
  transfers of profits between, 27, *see also* Arbitration Convention
  VAT, 117–18
authors
  copyright royalties, *see* royalty payments
  supplies of services by, 189

banking services, 186–88
banking transactions
  place of supply, 155
beer
  harmonization of excise duties, 232, 234, 235, 236–37
Belgium
  direct taxes, 5
betting taxes, 132
  VAT exemption, 188–89
biofuels
  excise duties, 11, 241
blind persons
  transactions carried out by, 189
  workshops for, 189
boats
  intra-Community trade
    VAT arrangements, 137–38, 144–45
border tax adjustments, *see* frontier tax adjustments
bridges, tolls on, 241
Brussels Convention, 302
building land
  supply of, 108, 182, 183
buildings, 182–84
  letting of, 182, 184
business activity, *see also* economic activity
  what constitutes, 111n
business promotion schemes, 122–25

calculation of taxable profits
  harmonization of rules, 27
camping sites, 182
capital duty, 6, 19, 20
capital gains tax, 3
  harmonization, 16
  Merger Directive provisions, 285–87
capital goods
  deduction of input VAT, 196–97
capital import neutrality, 250
capital movements, *see* free movement of capital
capital transactions
  harmonization of taxes, 17, 19
carbon tax
  proposal for, 6, 12, 244–45
carriage of goods by road, 47
cars, *see* motor vehicles
cascade turnover taxes, *see* turnover taxes
Cassis de Dijon case-law, 42–43, 70, 310–11, 326
cemeteries
  supply of goods and services to bodies responsible for, 189
central banks
  gold imports, 167
cessation of trading
  VAT provisions, 106–8
chain transactions, 337
Channel Islands, 92
chargeability of tax (common VAT system), 199–200
chargeable event (common VAT system), 199–200
charitable organisations
  welfare and social security work, 177
charitable purposes
  VAT provisions, 109
cheque transactions, 186
children and young persons
  education of, 177
  protection of 177
    supply of services and goods linked to, 177
children's clothing, 204
children's footwear, 204
cigarettes, *see* tobacco
co-operation between tax authorities
  common VAT system, 211–12
coal, 239–40
  carbon tax proposal, 244–45
coins, 186, 188
collectors' items, VAT on, 89, 186, 188
  reduced rates of tax, 202, 203
  special rules, 219–22
commercial navigation
  petroleum products used in, 240
commercial property rights
  transfers and assignments
    place of supply, 155
commercial vehicles
  taxation of, 242–43

commission, 127, 128
Committee on Excise Duties, 228
Common Customs Tariff, 130, 165
common system of value added tax, *see* VAT common system
Community Customs Code, 49, 129
Community tax, 11
Community VAT Directives, *see* VAT legislation
company administration services, 186
company taxation, 3, 21, 246–47, 338
  associated enterprises, *see* Arbitration Convention
  basic principles of international taxation, 247–53
  classical system of taxation, 21, 250
  common system, 246–47
    Ruding Committee recommendations, 297, 298
  conventions, *see* Arbitration Convention
  corporate income tax, 3, 4
  definition of 'company', 262–67
  development of Community law on, 246
  discriminatory tax rules, 312–24
    company's seat, discrimination by reference to, 312, 313–15
    freedom of establishment and, 311, 312–24
    primary establishment, transfer of, 319–22
    residence, discrimination on grounds of, 312–13, 331
  divisions, 278, 284; *see also* Merger Directive
  double taxation, 247, 250, 297
    relief, 254
  European Company Statute, 22
  exchanges of shares, 278, 285, *see also* Merger Directive
  fiscal residence, 263–64, 312–13, 331
  fraud, 257
  grouping or restructuring operations, *see* Merger Directive
  harmonization, 2, 10, 16, 19, 21–22, 22, 23–24, 26–27, 31, 246–47, 297
    development of, 30–31
    future developments, 338–39
    need for, 10
    plans for Economic and Monetary Union, 23–24
  illegitimate tax avoidance, 257
  imputation systems, 21, 250–52
    disadvantages of, 251–52, 339
    impact of Parent-Subsidiary Directive, 255–56
    Parent-Subsidiary Directive provision, 275–76
    Ruding Committee recommendations, 298
  interest and royalty payments, 293–95
  losses, relief for, 295–96
  mergers, 278, 282–84; *see also* Merger Directive
  obstacles to economic integration, 10
  parent company relief, *see* Parent-Subsidiary Directive
  pre-existing systems in Member States, 5, 6
  proposals for further legislation, 293–99
  related firms in different Member States. *see* Arbitration Convention
  relief for foreign tax, 248–50
    credit method, 248–50, 254
    exemption method, 249–50, 254
    Parent-Subsidiary Directive provisions, 254, 268–70
  Ruding Committee Report, 247, 250, 255, 296–97
    recommendations, 297–99
  systems of taxation, 21, 250–52
    Ruding Committee investigation, 297
  tax base, 298
  tax credits, 250–52
  tax evasion, 24
  tax-free reserves, 287–88
  tax havens, 19, 24, 257
  tax jurisdiction, 247–48
  tax rates
    minimum tax rate recommendation, 298
  Transfer of Losses Directive, 297
  transfers of assets, 278, 284–85, *see also* Merger Directive
  treaty-shopping, 257–58
  witholding taxes. *see* witholding taxes
competition, 2, 8
  distortion, 7, 15–16, 66
  equal conditions. *see* free competition
competitive neutrality, 14, 15, 99, 110
composite supplies, 97–99
conditional sale agreements, 95n
consideration (common VAT system), 119
  business promotion schemes, 122–25
  criteria, 120
  mandatory charges, 125–26
  meaning of, 119–26
  non-monetary, 121–26
  statutory levies, 125
  supplies and intra-Community acquisitions, 119–26
  taxable amount, 126–30
construction works
  handing over of, 96–97
consultancy services
  place of supply, 155
consumer expenditure
  common VAT system, *see* VAT system

consumption taxes, 3, 47
  compatibility with VAT, 132–34
contract work, delivery of
  definition, 145
  intra-Community trade, 145–46
copyright royalties
  legislative proposals, 293–95
corporate tax, *see* company taxation
cost-sharing arrangements, 177
counterfeit currency, 131
countervailing duties, 48
Court of Justice, 6, 336
  discriminatory taxation
    application of Article 95, 6, 27
  VAT legislation, interpretation of, 89–90
    domestic exemptions, 172–73
credit card transactions, 127, 187–88
credit control, 186
credit sale agreements, 95
credit transactions
  VAT exemption, 186–88
cremation services, 189
cross-border business activities
  elimination of tax barriers to, 30
cross-border dividend payments, 253, 258
  parent company relief, *see* Parent-Subsidiary Directive
cross-border investment, 2
  harmonization of tax systems and base, 338
  obstacles to, 10
cross-border mergers and acquisitions, 10, 20, 21, 338, *see also* Merger Directive
  tax obstacles, 19, 21
cross-border movement
  discriminatory restrictions on, 9
cross-border services
  common VAT system, 87, 88, *see also* supplies of services; VAT common system
    place of supply, 154–60
  taxation of
    discriminatory tax rules, 325
    freedom of establishment and, 322–24
cross-border shopping, 2, 10
  special arrangements to prevent, 88, 137–38, 139–40
cross-border tax planning, 339
cultural services
  place of supply, 154
  VAT exemption, 180
currency transactions, 186
current accounts, 186
customers' materials
  production of goods from, 96
customs duties
  exports, 38, 41–42, 55
  illegal transactions, 130–31
  imports, 38–41
  internal taxation and, distinction between, 38–42, 78
  prohibition, 35, 38
  refund of, 78
Customs Union, 35
Cyprus, 92

data processing
  place of supply, 155
De Hosson, F., 264–65, 268, 270, 275
debenture issue, 99–100
debenture transactions, 186
debt collection, 186
debt interest, 271–72
deduction of input tax
  common VAT system, 190–98
  private use of goods and, 101–4
deliveries of contract work
  intra-Community trade, 145–46
Denmark, 5
dental services
  VAT exemption, 176
deposit accounts, 186
destination system of taxation, 3, 6, 13, 16, 36, 77, 135, 136
  retention of, in VAT common system, 87–88, 91, *see also* VAT transitional arrangements
diesel, 239, 240
differential taxation
  discrimination against imports, 69–76
  luxury products, 72–73
  social considerations, 75
direct effect
  Article 95, 36–37
  Article 96, 78
  Article 97, 80
  domestic exemptions, 173–74
direct taxes, 2, 3, 309
  companies, *see* company taxation; Merger Directive; Parent-Subsidiary Directive
  compatibility with EC Treaty, 309–35
  discriminatory tax rules
    companies, 312–15
    free movement of capital and, 333–35
    free movement of services and, 309
    free movement of workers and, 309
    freedom of establishment and, 309, 311–24
  general prohibition on discrimination, 310
  harmonization moves, 10, 14, 16, 309, 336, 339, *see also* company taxation
    early moves, 19–22
    Neumark Report, 16
    single market and, 337–38
  pre-existing systems in Member States, 3, 5

discounts, 128
discriminatory restrictions
  cross-border movement, on, 9
discriminatory taxation, 2, 6, 7, 8–9, 27
  average rates of tax, 79–81
  companies, 312–24
  concealed subsidisation of exports, 77–78
  covert discrimination, 313, 325
  direct taxes, 81–82, 309, 312–15
    free movement of capital and, 333–35
    free movement of services and, 325–28, 328–30
    free movement of workers and, 324–25, 328–30
    nationals of other Member States, discrimination between, 318
    overt and covert discrimination, 313, 325
  exports, against, 52–56
  'four freedoms' and, 310–35
  general prohibition, 7, 310–11
  imperative requirements, 309, 330, 332–33
  imports, 6, 7, 8, *see also* Article 95
    beneficiaries of Article 95, 51–56
    customs duties provisions and, 38–41
    differential taxation, 69–76
    indirect protection, 66–68
    internal taxation, 34–77; *see also* Article 95
    'other' products, 56–57, 65–77
    progressive taxation, 70, 72, 73
    quantitative restrictions provisions and, 42–44
    scope of Article 95, 46–51
    similar products, 56, 57–65
    State aid provisions and, 45–46
    State monopolies provisions and, 44–45
  internal taxation on products, 34–77; *see also* Article 95
  luxury products, 69, 72–73
  married women, 33
  public interest defence, 310, 328, 330–32
  recovery of unlawfully charged tax, 76–77
  repayments of tax on exports, 77–78, 79
  reverse discrimination, 35, 49, 323
  social considerations, 75
distance sales to individuals, 88, 137, 139–40, 337
distortion of competition, 7, 15
  indirect protection, 66
  Neumark Committee, 15–16
distributed profits, 19, *see also* company taxation
  definition, 271–74
  liquidation profits, 269, 273–74
  Parent-Subsidiary Directive provisions, 268–69, 270, 271–74
  witholding tax, *see* witholding taxes
dividends, 99. *see also* company taxation
  definition (OECD Model Convention), 271
  double taxation, 20, 21, 23, 250
  imputation tax credits, 20, 250–52, 298
  parent company relief, *see* Parent-Subsidiary Directive
  relief for foreign tax, 248–50
  witholding taxes, 9, 10, 16, 17, 31, 253
domestic exemptions (common VAT system), 89, 170–72
  abuse of, 172
  ambulance services, 180
  banking and finance, 186–88
  betting and gambling, 188–89
  cultural services, 180
  direct effect, 173–74
  education, 177–78
  fund-raising, 180
  independent groups of persons, 177
  insurance transactions, 181–82
  judicial interpretation, 172–73, 174
  land transactions, 182–85
  medical exemptions, 176
  non-profit-making organizations, 178–79
  physical education, services closely linked to, 179–80
  postage stamps, 188
  public postal services, 175
  radio and television, 180–81
  sport, services closely linked to, 179–80
  technical exemption, 185
  telecommunications services supplied by public postal services, 175
  transitional exemptions, 174, 189
  uniform rules, 170
  welfare, 177–78
double taxation, 6, 19
  associated enterprises, *see* Arbitration Convention
  companies, 247, 250
  distributed profits, 250
  dividends and interest payments, 20, 21, 23, 250
  harmonization of arrangements, 16, 17
  imports, 26
  investments, 20
  related companies, *see* Arbitration Convention
  road tax, 241, 242
  second-hand goods, 219
double taxation conventions
  freedom of establishment and, 318–19
  limitation of benefits clauses, 319
double taxation treaties, 5, 301
drugs
  illegal importation, 130, 131

duty-free allowances
  harmonization, 18–19
duty-free sales
  intra-Community travel, 228

EC Treaty
  approximation of provisions of national laws, 7
  customs duties (Articles 12 and 13), 38–42
  direct taxes, compatibility of, 309–35
  discrimination on grounds of nationality
    prohibition of, 7, 310–11; *see also* discriminatory taxation
  equal treatment of foreign investors, 7
  'four freedoms', 7, 8
    discriminatory tax rules, and, 310–35
  primary objectives, 8
  quantitative restrictions, prohibition of, 42–44
  State aid provisions, 7, 45–46
  State monopolies, 44–45
  tax provisions, 6–8, 34
    Article 95, 34–77; *see also* Article 95
    Article 96, 77–78
    Article 97, 79–81
    Article 98, 81–82
    Article 99, 82–84
    Maastricht Treaty amendments, 8
economic activity (common VAT system)
  acquisition of goods for purposes of, 112
  acts preparatory to trading, 112
  conflicting considerations, 110–11
  definition, 108–11
  'in any place', 109
  independent activity, 114–15
  letting of immovable property, 110
  occasional transactions, 108, 109
  provision of services for no remuneration, 109–10
  purpose or results, 109
  trade promotion services, 109–10
economic and monetary union, 22–24, 25
economic conveyances, 93
economic integration
  tax obstacles, 10, 11
economic utilization, right of, 96
education, 111
  services connected with
    place of supply, 154
  VAT exemptions, 177–78
EFTA countries, 5, 8
electric current, 95
electricity
  carbon tax proposal, 244–45
  petroleum products used in generation, 239, 240
  reduced VAT rates, 202
emphyteusis, 96
employed persons, 114
employers' organizations, 179
employment levy, 133–34
employment relationship, 114–15
energy, 12
  carbon tax proposal, 244–45
  mineral oils (petroleum products), 238–41
entertainment
  services connected with
    place of supply, 154
  VAT not deductible on, 194
environmental protection, 11, 12
  carbon tax proposal, 244–45
equal conditions of competition, *see* free competition
equal treatment, *see also* discriminatory taxation
  direct investors, 27
  foreign investors, 7
  imports, taxation of, *see* Article 95; discriminatory taxation
  income taxation, 33
  men and women, 33
equipment leasing, 186
establishment
  fixed establishment (common VAT system), 158–60
  freedom of, *see* freedom of establishment
  permanent, 278, 279, 290–91
ethanol, 241, 245
ethyl alcohol products
  excise duties, 232–33, 236
European Company Statute, 22
European Economic Area Agreement, 8
excess tax, recovery of, 76–77
exchange of information, 1
  intra-Community transactions, 29, 211
exchange restrictions, 19
excise duties, 47, 132, 225–26
  ad valorem duties, 225
  authorized warehouses, 227–28
  claims for recovery, 228
  Committee on, 228
  duty-free allowances, 19, 228
  goods subject to
    intra-Community trade in, 138, 143–44
    VAT arrangements, 138, 143–44
  harmonization, 9–10, 11, 13–14, 22, 25, 28, 29
    alcohol and alcoholic drinks, 23, 231–37
    development of, 17, 18, 30, 225
    EC Treaty provisions, 6, 82–84
    general provisions, 225–28
    mineral oils (petroleum products), 11, 238–41
    motor fuels, 17, 238–41
    mutual assistance provisions applicable to, 228

rates, 9–10, 23
road tax, 225, 241–44
tobacco, 23, 228–31
licences, 225
pre-existing systems in Member States, 4, 6
provision of services, 225
specific duties, 225
television licences, 225
transit arrangements, 228
use of certain goods, 225
executor services, 186
exemptions from VAT
domestic, *see* domestic exemptions
exports from the Community, 167–69
imports, *see* import exemptions
exploitation of property, 108–9
exports
concealed subsidisation (Article 96), 77–78
customs duties and charges having equivalent effect, 38, 41–42, 55
discriminatory taxation, 41–42
applicability of Article 95, 52–56
from the Community
VAT exemptions, 167–69
repayment of input tax, 77–78, 79

factoring, 186
farmers
flat-rate schemes, 215–17
Faroe Islands, 92
final importation of certain goods
VAT exemptions, 164–66
financial advice, 186
financial products, 48
financial rationality, 14
financial services, 186–88
financial transactions
place of supply, 155
fiscal control
common VAT system, 138, 211–12
fiscal discrimination, *see* discriminatory taxation
fiscal frontiers, *see* tax frontiers
fiscal groups, 117–18
fiscal harmonization, *see* harmonization of taxes
fiscal neutrality, 20, 35, 134, 338
fiscal policy, 11, 332
fiscal residence, 263–64
discrimination on grounds of, 312–13, 331
transfer of
anti-avoidance measures, 331–32
fiscal sovereignty, 10, 36, 338
fiscal stamps, 188
fiscal transparency, 20
fisheries
petroleum products used in, 239, 240
fishery undertakings
VAT flat-rate scheme, 215–17
fixed establishment (common VAT system)
concept of, 158–60
flat-rate schemes
farmers, 215–17
small undertakings, 214–15
foreign currency transactions
VAT valuation, 129
foreign dividend income, 247–48
imputation tax credits, 20, 250–52
relief for foreign tax, 248–50
witholding taxes, 253
foreign goods, 91
foreign income
corporate tax, *see* company taxation
foreign investors
equal treatment, 7
foreign losses
relief for, 295–96
foreign products, *see* imports
foreign shareholders
imputation taxes, 252, 255, 275–76, 339
witholding taxes, 253, 254
foreign taxable persons
refunds for, 26
forestry undertakings
flat-rate scheme, 215–17
fossil fuels
carbon tax proposal, 244–45
France, 92
company taxation system, 251–52
direct taxes, 5
indirect taxes, 4, 14
fraud, 257
Fredersdorf Report, 25
free competition, 2, 8, 10, 35, 36, *see also* discriminatory taxation
State aid, 7, 45–46
free movement of capital, 2, 8, 48, 333
abolition of restrictions on, 31
discriminatory tax rules, and, 20, 333–35
economic and monetary union, plans for, 22
exchange restrictions, abolition of, 19
harmonization of capital gains tax, 16
tax obstacles, 19–20
free movement of goods, 2, 8, 13, 35, 49
obstacles to, 14, 15
tax frontiers and, 14
free movement of persons, 8
free movement of services, 2, 7, 8, 48
discriminatory tax rules, and, 325–28, 328–30
non-discriminatory restrictions, 310–11, 326
scope, 328–30
free movement of workers, 2, 7
discriminatory tax rules, and, 32, 324–25, 328–30
frontier workers, taxation of, 16, 32
scope, 328–30

free of charge services, 109–10
freedom of establishment, 7, 311–12
  Community company tax legislation, and, 316
  companies or firms, 311, 312
  corporate nationality, 312
  cross-frontier traders, taxation of, 322–24
  discriminatory tax rules, and, 309, 312–24, 328–30
    company's seat, reference to, 312, 313–15
    discrimination between nationals of other Member States, 318
  double taxation conventions, and, 318–19
  non-discriminatory tax rules, and, 329–30
  primary establishment of companies, 312, 319–22
  scope of, 328–30
  secondary establishments, 312
French overseas departments, 91
frontier tax adjustments, 1, 2, 6, 9, 14, 34, 79
frontier taxes, 9
  abolition, 16, 17, 18
frontier workers, taxation of, 16, 32
fuels (petroleum products)
  harmonization of excise duties, 238–41
fund-raising events
  VAT exemption, 180

gambling
  taxation of, 132
  VAT exemption, 188–89
gaming machines
  taxation, 47
gas, 95
gas oil, 240
GATT, 3
Germany
  company taxation, 252
  witholding tax on dividend payments, 270, 274
Gibraltar, 92
global warming
  carbon tax proposal, 244–45
gold
  coins, 186, 188
  held for investment purposes, 30
  importation by central banks VAT exemption, 167
'good tax'
  criteria for, 2
goods, 3
  common VAT system, *see* VAT system
  exports, *see* exports
  free movement of, *see* free movement of goods
  frontier taxes, 9
  in transit, 163–64
  imports, *see* imports
  intra-Community acquisitions, *see* intra-Community acquisitions
  private use of, 100–104
  self-supplies, 106–8
  supply of, *see* supplies of goods
  transfer to non-business use, 100–101
  value added tax, *see* supplies of goods; VAT common system
government departments
  intra-Community acquisitions, 137–38, 140–42
graduated schemes of taxation, *see* differential taxation
graves
  supplies to bodies responsible for, 189
Greece, 5
  witholding tax on dividend payments, 270, 274–75

harmonization of taxes, 1–2
  Action Programme for Taxation (1975), 24, 25
  aim of, 8, 336
  capital gains tax, 16
  capital transactions, taxes on, 17, 19
  company taxes, *see* company taxation
  development of, 13–33
    economic and monetary union, plan for, 22–24
    stagnation in the 1970s, 24–27
    towards a single market, 24–32
  direct taxes, *see* direct taxes
  double taxation arrangements, 16, 17
  duty-free allowances, 18–19
  EC Treaty provisions, 6–8
  environmental concerns, 11, 12
  excise duties, *see* excise duties
  'four freedoms' and, 8
  Fredersdorf Report, 25
  full harmonization of national systems, 10
  income tax, 16, 32–33
  indirect taxes, *see* indirect taxes
  individuals, taxation of, 32–33
  insurance contracts, taxation of, 19
  need for, 8, 10
  Neumark Committee report, 15–16
  policy considerations, 11–12
  purpose of, 8–10
  road tax, 18
  single market, and, 337–39
  stock exchange transactions, 19
  transport taxes, 17
  turnover taxes, 2, 9, 13–14, 14, 17, 82–84
  VAT, *see* VAT common system; VAT harmonization
  wealth tax, 33

White Paper (1985), 27–28
witholding taxes, 16, 17, 21, 23–24, 31
health inspections, 42
fees for, 47
heat, 95
heat and power plants
petroleum products used in, 240
heating oil, 239, 240
heavy goods vehicles
road tax, 6, 243, 244
tax on, 47–48
hire of goods
movable tangible property, 26
place of supply, 155
safes, 182
hire-purchase transactions, 95
finance element, 127–28
holding companies, 24
taxable persons, whether, 112–14
holiday camps, 182
hospital care, 111
private hospitals, 109
VAT exemption, 176
hospitals
intra-Community acquisitions, 139
hotel accommodation, provision of, 182
housing, 204
hydrocarbons, *see also* mineral oils
carbon tax proposals, 244–45

identification numbers (VAT system), 207
illegal transactions (common VAT system), 130–32
immovable property
interests in, 95–96
letting and leasing of, 94, 110, 182, 184
rights of ownership or possession, 95–96
rights of user over, 95–96
services connected with
place of supply, 154
transfer of title, 95–96
immovable property societies, 96
import exemptions (common VAT system), 162–63
final importation, 164–66
goods in transit, 163–64
individual exemptions, 163–67
re-importation of goods, 166
temporary imports, 164
import licences
charge on issue of, 39
imports
common VAT system, 90–91; *see also* VAT common system
chargeable event, 200
reimportation of goods, 129, 166
taxable amount, 129
counterfeit currency, 131
customs duties
internal taxation and, distinction between, 38–41
discrimination against
internal taxes, 34–77; *see also* Article 95
State monopolies, 44–45
elimination of double taxation, 26
illegal transactions, 130–32
intra-Community acquisitions. *see* intra-Community acquisitions; VAT transitional arrangements
narcotic drugs, 130, 131
non-member countries, from
common VAT system, 91, 93, 161–67, *see further* VAT common system
'other' products, 65–77
products imported from other Member States, 49–51
quantitative restrictions (Article 30), 42–44
similar products, 56, 57–65
imputation taxes, *see* company taxation
incidental expenses, 127–28
income tax, 3, 21
equal treatment for men and women, 33
harmonization, 16, 32–33
non-residents, 32–33
pre-existing systems in Member States, 5
independent activity, 114–15
independent groups of persons
services supplied by
VAT exemption, 177
indirect discrimination, 313
indirect protection, 66–68
indirect taxes, 2, 3
capital transactions, 19
destination system, *see* destination system of taxation
discriminatory, *see* discriminatory taxation
EC Treaty provisions, 6–8; *see also* EC Treaty
frontier tax adjustments, 2
harmonization, 13–14, 25–27, 28, 336, 337
development of, 17–19
draft framework directive (1972), 226–27
EC Treaty, Article 99, 6, 82–84
excise duties, *see* excise duties general provisions, 226–28
legislative power, 82–84
Neumark Report, 15–17
transitional arrangements, 29 VAT, *see* VAT common system; VAT harmonization
White Paper (1985), 28, 226
origin system, 3, 16
pre-existing systems in Member States, 3–4, 13

individuals
  cross-border shopping, 88, 137–38
  distance sales to, 137
  intra-Community acquisitions
    VAT transitional arrangements, 88, 137–38, 139–40
  taxation of
    harmonization of national laws, 32–33
information, supply of
  place of supply, 155
input tax
  Article 97, 79–81
  deduction
    holding companies, 113–14
    private use of goods and, 101–4
    VAT, 190–98
installed goods
  VAT transitional arrangements, 138
Institute for Fiscal Studies, 253
institutional purchasers
  cross-border purchases, 88, 137
insurance companies
  intra-Community acquisitions, 139
insurance costs, 127, 128
insurance transactions
  place of supply, 155
  taxation of, 19, 132
  VAT exemption, 181–82
intangible property
  assignments of, 99
  exploitation of, 108
intellectual property rights
  transfers and assignments, 155
interest on credit, 128
interest payments
  common system of taxation, proposals for, 293–95
  definition, 294
  double taxation, 20, 21, 23
  witholding taxes, 9, 16, 17, 31, 292
interim payments, 209
internal charges or expenses, 48
internal levy, 42
internal market, *see* single market
internal taxation, 40, 46
  customs duties and, 38–41, 78
  discriminatory taxation of foreign products, prohibition of, 34–36, 46; *see also* Article 95; discriminatory taxation
  indirect protection, 66–68
  neutrality, 35
  recovery of unlawfully charged tax, 76–77
  repayment of tax on exported products, 77–78
international goods traffic
  VAT export exemptions, 167–69
intra-Community acquisitions of goods
  common VAT system
    transitional provisions, 90–91; *see also* VAT transitional arrangements
  definition, 141
  place of supply, 150–52
intra-Community transactions
  exchange of information, 29, 211
  VAT reporting requirements, 209–10
intra-Community transport of goods
  transitional arrangements, 156–57
intra-Community travel
  duty-free sales, 228
intrastat, 212
investment
  advice, 186
  double taxation, 20
  fund management, 186
  preliminary expenditure, 112
invoicing requirements (common VAT system), 207–8
Ireland, 5, 204
Isle of Man, 92
Italy, 4, 5

Kajus, J. 99
kerosene, 239, 240

land and buildings
  transfer of title, 95
land transactions
  VAT exemptions, 182–85
land vehicles
  intra-Community trade in new vehicles, 137–38, 144–45
lawyers, 189
leaded petrol, 240
leasing transactions, 94–95, 182, 184
  immovable property, 110
lending transactions, 186–88
liability for payment (common VAT system), 205–6
  intra-Community acquisitions, 206
  obligations of person liable, 207–12
  supplies of goods and services, 206
lignite, 245
liquid petroleum gas, 239, 240
liquidation profits, 269, 273
local authorities
  intra-Community acquisitions
    VAT transitional arrangements, 137–38, 140–42
  taxable persons, whether, 115–17
local public transport
  petroleum products used in, 239, 240
local tax collectors
  taxable persons, whether, 115
loss-making activities, 109
losses, relief for

legislative proposals, 295–96, 338
lotteries
VAT exemption, 188–89
luxury products
taxation of, 69, 72–73, 225
VAT not deductible on, 194

Maastricht Treaty on European Union
free movement of capital, 8, 334
mail-order sales, 88, 137
mandatory charges, 125–26
manufactured tobacco, *see* tobacco
married women
tax discrimination, 33
medical care
VAT exemption, 176
medical professions
supplies of services by, 189
Member States
discriminatory tax rules, *see* discriminatory taxation
pre-existing systems of taxation, 3–6
Merger Directive, 7, 10, 31, 246, 247, 277–79, 298
advance clearance requirements, 292
aims, 278
application, 279–80
cancellation of holdings, 288–89
capital gains taxation, 285–87
carry-over of losses, 288
divisions, 284
employee representation proviso, 291, 292
exchanges of shares, 285
extension of scope of, 338
freedom of establishment and, 316
individual provisions
Article 1, 279–80
Article 2, 280–85
Article 4, 285–87
Article 5, 287–88
Article 6, 288
Article 7, 288–89
Article 8, 289–90
Article 10, 290–91
Article 11, 291–92
mergers, 282–84
permanent establishment, 278, 279, 290–91
tax evasion or avoidance, 291–92
tax-free reserves, 287–88
transfers of assets, 284–85, 316
transfers of securities
taxation of gains arising out of, 289–90
merger proposals, 31
methane, 239, 240
methanol, 241, 245
mineral oils (petroleum products)
harmonization of excise duties, 11, 238–41
approximation of rates, 240
biofuels, 241
derogations, 239–40
exemptions, 239–40
minimum rates, 240
structures of duty, 239
mining activities, 108
mixed or composite supplies
VAT common system, 97–99
Monaco, 92
monetary compensation amounts
dismantling of, 26
monopolies, 5; *see also* State monopolies
monuments commemorating war dead
supplies to bodies responsible for, 189
'Morton's fork', 3
motor fuels
agricultural products, derived from, 11, 241
excise duties
harmonization, 17, 238–41
road tax and, 241
motor vehicles
intra-Community acquisitions, 137–38, 144–45
registration tax, 47
road tax, 241–44
motorway tolls, 241, 243, 244
movable property
customers' materials, produced from, 96
hiring out of, 26
place of supply, 155
leases of, 94
services connected with
place of supply, 154
mutual assistance charge, 132
mutual assistance directive, 24

narcotic drugs
illegal importation, 130, 131
national industries
subsidies to, 7
nationality, discrimination on grounds of, *see* discriminatory taxation
natural gas, 239–40, 240
carbon tax proposal, 244–45
reduced rates of VAT, 202
Netherlands
pre-existing tax system, 4
Neumark, Fritz, 15
Neumark Committee, 11, 15–17, 33, 308, 336
new buildings, 183
letting of, 184
supply of, 108
new means of transport
definition, 144–45
intra-Community acquisitions
VAT reporting requirements, 210, 211

new means of transport (*cont.*):
VAT transitional arrangements, 137–38, 144–45
taxable persons, 145
Noel, O. 292
nominee services, 186
non-business activity
supplies made in course of, 111
non-business purposes
transfer of goods to, 100–101
use of goods for, *see* private use of goods
non-discrimination, principle of, 7, 309, *see also* discriminatory taxation
fundamental freedoms, relationship with, 310–11
non-discriminatory restrictions, 9, 334
non-fiscal barriers to trade
quantitative restrictions, 42–44
non-fiscal burdens, 48
non-member countries
imports from, 91, 93, 161–67
non-monetary consideration, 121–26
non-profit-making organizations
charities, 109
VAT exemption, 178–79
non-residents
discriminatory taxation of, *see* discriminatory taxation
income tax, 32–33
shareholders, *see* foreign shareholders
non-taxable intra-Community acquisitions, 142–43
non-taxable legal persons
cross-border shopping, 88, 137–38
intra-Community acquisitions
VAT reporting requirements, 210
VAT transitional arrangements, 88, 137–38, 139, 140–42
non-taxation of acquisitions
from certain suppliers, 141–42
notaries and bailiffs
taxable persons, whether, 108, 114–15

occasional transactions, 108, 109
OECD Model Convention
'dividend', definition of, 271
parent company holding criterion, 267, 268
'permanent establishment', definition of, 278
'resident of a contracting State', 263–64
OECD Model Double Taxation Convention, 301, 302
OECD Model Income Tax Convention
taxation of dividends, 274
old people's homes, 177
Oliver, D. 272
origin system of taxation, 3, 13, 16, 30, 135, 136
'other' products, import of
tax treatment, 65–77
overseas countries and territories, 91–92

packing expenses, 127, 128
Parent-Subsidiary Directive, 7, 10, 31, 246, 247, 294, 295
abuse proviso, 257, 258–59
distributions from other Member States, 260–61
non-EC groups, 259–60
permissible limits of anti-abuse provisions, 258, 259
principle of proportionality, and, 261–62
administrative arrangements, 256–57
aims and scope of, 254–55
application
distributions from other Member States, 260–61
non-EC groups, 259–60
cross-border dividend payments, 258
definition of 'company', 262–65
company of which Member State?, 265–67
fiscal residence, 263–64
'distributed profits', 270, 271–74
excessive debt interest, 271–72
extension of scope of, 338
fraud, 256, 257
freedom of establishment and, 316
illegitimate tax avoidance, 257
impact on imputation systems, 255–56
individual provisions, 256
Article 1, 256–62
Article 2, 262–67
Article 3, 267–68
Article 4, 268–70
Article 5, 270–75
Article 6, 275
Article 7, 275–76
liquidation profits, distribution of, 269, 273–74
relief for tax, 268–70
Ruding Committee recommendations, 297, 298
status of parent company, 267
holding criterion, 267–68
tax havens, 257
treaty-shopping, 257–58
witholding tax relief, 270, 274–75, 316
meaning of 'witholding tax', 274
parking vehicles
letting of premises and sites for, 182, 185
passenger transport, 30
payment cards, 187–88
payment of tax (common VAT system)
person liable for, 205–6
obligations of, 207–12

payment requirements
VAT system, 208–10
peat, 239–40
carbon tax proposal, 244–45
performers
supplies of services by, 189
petroleum products
carbon tax proposal, 244–45
harmonization of excise duties, 238–41
pharmaceutical products
registration fees, 47
philanthropic purposes
activities carried out for, 109
philosophical institutions
supplies of staff by, 178
physical education
VAT exemption, 179–80
place of import
imports from non-Member countries, 161
place of supply (common VAT system), 135
intra-Community acquisitions of goods, 150–52, *see also* VAT transitional arrangements
services, 154–56
application of the rules, 157–58
concept of a fixed establishment, 158–60
intra-Community transport of goods, 156–57
transitional arrangements, 156–57
policy considerations, 11
influence in harmonization process, 11–12
ports
duty-free sales, 228
Portugal, 5
witholding tax on dividend payments, 270, 275
postage stamps
VAT exemption, 188
postal services
VAT exemption, 175
power plants
petroleum products used in, 240
pre-existing systems of taxation, 3–6, 13
preliminary investment expenditure, 112
private hospitals, 109
private individuals, *see* individuals
private pleasure craft, 240
private tuition, 177–78
private use of goods, 100–104
deduction of input tax, and, 101–4
private use of services, 100–101, 104–6
professional organizations
VAT exemption, 178–79
professional services
place of supply, 155
supply of, 189
professions, 108
progressive taxation, 69, 70, 72, 73
proportionality, principle of, 291
imperative requirements and, 332–33
Parent-Subsidiary Directive abuse proviso and, 261–62
protection, indirect, 66–68
public authorities
intra-Community acquisitions
VAT transitional arrangements, 88, 137, 140–42
order of
performance of services in pursuance of, 99
taxable persons, whether, 115–17
water supply, 189
public interest defence
scope of, 330–32
public postal services
VAT exemption, 175
public radio and television
exempted activities, 180–81
taxable commercial activities, 181
public transport
petroleum products used in, 239, 240

qualified majority voting, 7
quantitative restrictions, prohibition of
discriminatory internal taxation and, 35, 42–44
State monopolies, 44

radio and television
VAT exemption, 180–81
rail transport
petroleum products used in, 240
rates of tax
turnover taxes
average rates, 79–81
VAT, 200–205; *see also* VAT common system
re-importation of goods, 129, 166
rebates, 128
recovery of unlawfully charged tax, 76–77
reduced rates of tax (VAT), 202–5
reductions of taxable amount (VAT), 128
refrigeration, 95
refund of tax
exports, imput tax paid on (Article 96), 77–78, 79
unlawfully charged tax, 76–77
regional goverment authorities
taxable persons, whether, 115–17
registration fees
pharmaceutical products, 47
reinsurance transactions
VAT exemption, 181–82
related companies
double taxation, elimination of, *see* Arbitration Convention

religious institutions
  supplies of staff by, 178
repairs, 96–97
reporting requirements (common VAT system), 208–10
  intra-Community transactions, 209–10
  periodical returns, 208–9
  yearly statements, 209
resale of goods, 219
residence, *see* fiscal residence
restaurant services, 204
returnable packaging costs, 129
reverse discrimination, 35, 49, 323
right of disposal, transfer of, 93–95
right of establishment, *see* freedom of establishment
rights *in rem*, 95
road fuels, *see* motor fuels
road tax, 72, 73, 225
  commercial vehicles, 17
  double taxation, 241, 242
  fuel tax and, 241
  harmonization, 18, 225, 241–44
  heavy goods vehicles, 6, 243, 244
  passenger vehicles, 18
  tolls, 241, 243, 244
road use charges, 241, 243, 244
roadworthiness tests on cars
  fees for, 47
royalty payments
  definition, 294
  parent and subsidiary companies, between
    legislation proposals, 293–95, 338
Ruding, Onno, 32, 296
Ruding Committee Report, 247, 250, 255, 296–99
  Commission's reaction, 298–99
rule of reason, 70, 326

safe custody services, 186
safes, hire of, 182
sales goods
  destination taxation, 3
  origin taxation, 3
sales taxes, 3, 47
savings deposits, 48
Schonewille, P. H. 266
schools, 177
  private tuition, 177–78
scientific services
  place of supply, 154
sea fishing undertakings
  import exemptions, 166
second-hand goods
  common VAT system, 129–30
    reduced rates of tax, 202, 203
    special rules, 219–22
    transitional provisions, 221–22
  double taxation, 219
  VAT legislation, 26, 29, 89, 220
secondary establishments, 160
securities, dealings in, 186
Segre, Claudio, 20
self-supplies, 106–8
services, 48
  definition, 99–100
  excise licence duties, 225
  freedom to provide, *see* free movement of services
  place of supply (common VAT system), 154–60
  private use of, 100–101, 104–6
  supply of
    common VAT system, *see* supplies of services; VAT common system
set-aside land, 241
share acquisitions, 113
share exchanges, 278, 279, 285; *see also* Merger Directive
share issue, 99–100
share transactions, 186
silver coins, 186
similar products, imports of
  tax treatment, 56, 57–65
simplification measures, 222–24
single capital market
  tax obstacles, 20
Single European Act, 7, 8, 27–28, 82
single European tax system, 10
single market, 2, 23, 25
  fiscal obstacles, 13, 14, 15
  goods, 35
  tax harmonization and, 27–32, 337–39
  White Paper (1985), 27–28, 226
slot machines, 189
small businesses, 12, 30
  common VAT system, 214–15
social considerations
  discriminatory taxation, 75
social security work
  VAT exemption, 177–78
solid fuels, 239–40
solidarity levy, 132
special schemes (VAT), 214–24
  flat-rate scheme for farmers, 215–17
  second-hand goods etc., 219–22
  simplification and anti-avoidance measures, 222–24
  small undertakings, 214–15
  travel agents, 217–19
spirits
  excise duties, 232–33, 235, 236
spiritual welfare, 178
sport

VAT exemption, 179–80
sporting activities
services connected with
place of supply, 154
staff, supply of
place of supply, 155
stamp duties, 3, 19, 20, 132
State aid, 7, 45–46
State authorities
taxable persons, whether, 115–17
State institutions
aircraft used by, 189
State monopolies of commercial character
discriminatory internal taxation and, 44–45
tobacco, 229
statutory levies, 125
stock exchange transactions
harmonization of taxes, 19
subsidiarity, principle of, 23, 33, 338
subsidies
concealed subsidisation of exports, 77–78
national industries, to, 7
VAT taxable amount
direct link criterion, 126–27
sugar and sweeteners, *see* excise duties
superficie, 96
supplies of goods (common VAT system), 92–93
consideration, *see* consideration
definition, 93–99
extensions, 96–97
domestic exemptions, *see* domestic exemptions
import exemptions, *see* import exemptions
intra-Community acquisitions, *see* intra-Community acquisitions
mixed or composite supplies, 97–99
persons responsible for payment of tax, 206
place of supply
intra-Community acquisitions, 135–53, *see also* VAT transitional arrangements
rates of tax, *see* VAT rates
self-supplies and cessation of trading, 106–8
tangible property, 95–96
taxable persons, 108–18
transfer of the right of disposal, 93–95
supplies of services (common VAT system), 92–93, 99–100
consideration, *see* consideration
cross-frontier services, 87, 88, 154–60
definition, 93, 99–100
exemptions, *see* domestic exemptions
mixed or composite supplies, 97–99
persons liable for payment of tax, 206
place of supply, 154–60
advertising services, 155–56
application of the rules, 157–58
concept of fixed establishment, 158–60
transitional arrangements, 156–57
private use of goods and services, 100–106
rates of tax, *see* VAT rates
self-supplies and cessation of trading, 106–8
taxable persons, 108–18
travel agents, 217–19
synthetic alcohol, 36, 74

tangible property, 93
definition, 95–96
exploitation of, 108
transfer of right to dispose of, 93
tax as policy instrument, 11–12
tax discrimination, *see* discriminatory taxation
tax evasion, 8, 24
tax-free allowances
harmonization, 18–19
tax frontiers, 2, 14, 135–36
abolition of, 2, 15, 16, 22
transitional arrangements, 29, 135–60, *see also* VAT transitional arrangements
White Paper (1985), 28, 87, 135, 226
tax harmonization, *see* harmonization of taxes
tax havens, 19, 24, 257
tax monopolies, 5
tax rates
turnover taxes, 79–81
VAT, *see* VAT common system
tax refunds, *see* refund of tax
tax residence, *see* fiscal residence
tax union system, 3
taxable amount (common VAT system), 119, 126
consideration, meaning of, 119–26
credit cards, 127
definition, 126
detailed provisions on particular items, 127–28
discounts, 128
exclusions, 128
foreign currency transactions, 129
imports, 129
incidental expenses, 127–28
reductions, 128
returnable packaging costs, treatment of, 129
second-hand goods, 129–30
subsidies, 126–27
transitional provisions, 128–29
valuation of deemed supplies, 127
taxable dealers, 220–21
taxable events (common VAT system), 90–91
taxable persons (common VAT system), 108–18
acquisition of goods as, 112
acts preparatory to trading, 112

taxable persons (*cont.*):
  associated companies, 118
  conflicting considerations, 110–11
  definition, 108
  economic activity, what constitutes, 108–11; *see also* economic activity
  fiscal groups, 117–18
  holding companies, 112–14
  independent activity, 114–15
  intra-Community acquisitions, 137, 140–41
  invoicing and accounting requirements, 207–8
  non-business activity, supplies made in course of, 111
  notaries and bailiffs, 108, 114–15
  occasional transactions, 108, 109
  persons liable for payment, 205–6
    obligations of, 207–12
  private hospitals, 109
  public authorities, 115–17
  reporting and payment requirements, 208–10
  VAT identification numbers, 207
taxation advice, 186
technical exemption, 185
telecommunications services
  supplied by public postal services
    VAT exemption, 175
television licences, 225
temporary imports
  import exemption, 164
Terra, B. 99
territoriality principle (VAT), 91–92
Tinbergen Committee, 13
tobacco duties
  approximation of taxes, 231
  harmonization of rates, 23, 228–31
  minimum total excise duty, 231
tolls on motorways etc., 241, 243, 244
trade organizations, 179
trade promotion services, 109–10
trade unions
  VAT exemption, 178–79
transactions, taxes on, 3
Transfer of Losses Directive, 297
transfer of the right of disposal
  VAT common system, 93–95
transfer of title, 93
  land and buildings, 95
transfer pricing disputes
  mutual agreement procedure, 27; *see also* Arbitration Convention
transfers of assets, 278, 284–85, 316; *see also* Merger Directive
transfers of securities
  taxation of, 6, 289–90
transitional arrangements
  common VAT system, *see* VAT transitional arrangements
transitional exemptions (VAT), 174, 189
transparency, 338
transport, 7
  expenses of, 127, 128
  harmonization of taxes, 17, 241–43; *see also* motor fuels; road tax
  intra-Community transport of goods
    transitional arrangements, 156–57
  new means of, *see* new means of transport
  place of supply of services, 154
travel agents, 189
  special VAT arrangements, 217–19
Treaty of Rome, *see* EC Treaty
Treaty on European Union, 8, 334
treaty-shopping, 257–58
triangular transactions, 152–53, 206
trustee services, 186
turnover taxes, 3, 47, *see also* VAT
  average rates (Article 97), 79–81
  border tax adjustments, 79–81
  'cascade' systems, 4, 14, 34, 79
    replacement by VAT common system, 81
  common calculation method, 81
  compatibility with VAT, 132–34
  competitive neutrality, 14, 15
  existing systems in Member States, 4, 13
  financial rationality, 14
  general requirements, 14–15
  harmonization, 2, 9, 13–14, 14, 17
    EC Treaty provisions, 6, 82–84
  prohibited taxes, 132, 133
types of taxation, 2–3
  pre-existing systems in Member States, 3–6

undertakers
  services supplied by, 189
United Kingdom, 5, 92, 204, 251
university education, 177
  private tuition, 177–78
unjust enrichment, 76–77
unlawfully charged tax
  recovery of, 76–77
unleaded petrol, 11, 240
use of products
  taxation on, 47
usufruct, 96

value added tax. *see* VAT
Van den Tempel, A.J., 21
Vanistendael, F., 272, 273
VAT, 1, 4, 5, 6, 11, 15
  common system, *see* VAT common system
  harmonization moves, *see* VAT harmonization
VAT Committee, 212–13, 214

VAT common system, 1, 2, 9, 17–18, 246
  abuse of exemptions, 172
  administration
    persons responsible for payment of tax, 205–6
  Advisory Committee, 212–13
  agriculture, 18, 215–17
  aim of, 99
  anti-avoidance measures, 172, 222–24
  approximation of rates of tax, 89
  basic principles, 85–86
  chargeability of tax, 199–200
  chargeable event, 199–200
  co-operation between tax authorities, 211–12
  Community directives, *see* VAT legislation
  compatibility of other taxes, 132–34
  consideration, 119–26; *see also* consideration
  consumer expenditure, tax on, 183
  cross-frontier services, 87, 88, 154–60
  deduction of input tax, 190–98
    apportionment, 194–95
    capital goods, 196–97
    exclusions, 194
    exports or intra-Community transactions, 191–92
    formalities, 197
    rules, 190
    taxable persons not established in the territory of the country, 192–93
    total and immediate deduction, 190
  definition, 85
  derogating measures, 214–24
  domestic exemptions. *see* domestic exemptions
  evasion, 172
  exemptions
    domestic, *see* domestic exemptions
      exports, 167–69
    imports, *see* import exemptions
    small undertakings, 214–15
  export exemptions, 167–69
  fiscal control, 38, 211–12
  flat-rate schemes
    farmers, 215–17
    small undertakings, 214–15
  harmonization of rates, 337
  identification numbers, 207
  illegal transactions, 130–32
  imports from non-member countries, 90–91, 161–62
    exemptions, 161–67; *see also* import exemptions
  intra-Community acquisitions
    transitional arrangements, *see* VAT transitional arrangements
  invoicing and accounting requirements, 207–8
  miscellaneous matters, 130–32
  persons responsible for payment of tax, 205–6
    obligations of, 207–12
  place of import, 161–62
  place of supply, *see also* place of supply
    intra-Community acquisitions of goods, 150–52
    services, 154–60
  private use of goods and services, 100–106
  rates of tax, 9, 200–205
    approximation, 89
    flat-rate schemes, 214–17
    gradual alignment, 29–30
    imports, 205
    intra-Community acquisitions, 205
    minimum standard rate, 30, 201, 202
    reduced rates, 30, 202–5
    supplies of goods or services, 205
    taxable transactions, 205
    transitional arrangements, 203–4
    zero rates, 30, 201, 204–5
  reporting and payment requirements, 208–10
  scope, 86–89
  second-hand goods etc., 26, 29, 89, 129–30, 219–22
  self-supplies and cessation of trading, 106–8
  simplification measures, 222–24
  small undertakings, 30, 214–15
  special schemes and derogating measures, 214–24
  supplies of goods, 92–99; *see also* supplies of goods
  supplies of services, 92–93, 99–100; *see also* supplies of services
  taxable amount, 126–30; *see also* taxable amount
  taxable events, 90–91
  taxable persons, 108–18; *see also* taxable persons
  territorial scope, 91–92
  theoretical model, 85
  trade in goods with non-Member countries
    imports, 161–67
  transitional arrangements, *see* VAT transitional arrangements
  travel agents, 217–19
VAT harmonization, 9, 22, 23, 25, 28–30
  Article 95 and, 37
  first steps, 17–18
  legislation, *see* VAT legislation
  Neumark Report, 16
  single market proposals, 28–29
VAT identification numbers, 207
VAT legislation
  codification, 337

VAT legislation (*cont.*):
  Community directives, 26, 30, 37, 85–89, 164
    First and Second Directives (1967), 9, 18, 85–86, 170
    Sixth Directive (1977), 9, 26, 86–87, 89, 108, 119, 126, 132, 135–36, 154, 155, 161, 162, 170, 190
  interpretation of, 89–90
VAT returns, 208–10
VAT transitional arrangements, 9, 29, 87–88, 90–91, 135–60, 337
  assembled and installed goods, 138
  chargeable event, 200
  consideration, 119–30; *see also* consideration
  cross-border shopping
    special arrangements to prevent, 88, 137–38
  definition of 'intra-Community acquisitions', 141
  deliveries of contract work, 145–46
  exempt acquisitions, 149–50
  exempt supplies, 147–49
  fiscal control, 138
  goods subject to excise duty, 138, 143–44
  new means of transport, 137–38, 144–45
  non-taxable acquisitions, 142–43
  non-taxable legal persons, 137–38, 139, 140–42
  non-taxation of acquisitions from certain suppliers, 141–42
  period of application, 88, 136
  person liable for payment of tax, 206
  place of supply, 150–52
    intra-Community transport of goods, 156–57
  private individuals and assimilated persons, 88, 137–38, 139–40
  purpose of, 136
  summary of arrangements, 136–38
  taxable amount, 128–29
  taxable event, 141
  taxable persons, trade between, 137
  transfer of goods to other Member States, 146–47
  triangular transactions, 152–53
vegetable oils, 241
vehicles, *see* motor vehicles
vertical integration, 14
vocational training, 177

war dead
  monuments commemorating, 189
warships, 189
water supply, 189
wealth tax, 3
  harmonization, 33
  pre-existing systems in Member States, 5
welfare, 111
  VAT exemption, 177–78
Werner, Pierre, 22
White Paper (1985), 27–28, 87, 135, 226, 227
wine
  harmonization of duties on, 23, 232, 233–34, 235, 236–37
witholding taxes, 9, 10, 19
  dividends, 10, 31, 253
  harmonization, 16, 17, 21, 23–24, 31
  interest and royalty payments, 10, 31, 293–95
  meaning of, 274
  relief from, 270–71, 274–75, 316; *see also* Parent-Subsidiary Directive
workers, free movement of, *see* free movement of workers
works of art, 29, 89
  reduced rates of VAT, 202, 203
  special VAT rules, 219–22
works of construction
  definition, 97
  handing over of, 96–97
Wouters, J. 325

yearly statements (VAT), 209

zero rates of tax (VAT), 201, 204–5

The manufacturer's authorised representative in the EU for product safety is Oxford University Press España S.A. of el Parque Empresarial San Fernando de Henares, Avenida de Castilla, 2 – 28830 Madrid (www.oup.es/en or product.safety@oup.com). OUP España S.A. also acts as importer into Spain of products made by the manufacturer.

www.ingramcontent.com/pod-product-compliance
Lightning Source LLC
LaVergne TN
LVHW011905200926
848484LV00002B/537
* 9 7 8 0 1 9 8 2 5 7 6 4 6 *